Sport Governance

Governance has become a hugely important issue within sport. Issues of corruption and 'bad governance' have become synonymous with some aspects of sport and closer scrutiny than ever before is being applied to ensure organisations are following international best practice in respect to how they are governed. As sport organisations are required to become more professional and to adopt a more transparent and accountable approach to their operations, it has become important for all students, researchers and professionals working in sport to understand what good governance is and how it should be achieved.

This book is the first to examine sport governance around the world. It offers a series of in-depth case studies of governance policy and practice in 15 countries and regions, including the USA, UK, China, Australia, Canada, South Africa, Latin America and the Middle East, as well as chapters covering governance by, and of, global sport organisations and international sport federations. With an introduction outlining the key contemporary themes in the study of sport governance, and a conclusion pointing at future directions for research and practice, this book is essential reading for any course on sport management, sport policy, sport development, sport administration or sport organisations, and for any manager or policy-maker working in sport and looking to improve their professional practice.

Ian O'Boyle is a lecturer in sport and recreation management within the School of Management, at University of South Australia. His major research interests focus on the governance of sport organisations and broader sport management topics.

Trish Bradbury is a senior lecturer in the School of Management at Massey University, New Zealand. Her major research interests concern a variety of aspects of sport management related to sport governance, event management, people management and strategic management in non-profit sport organisations.

Foundations of Sport Management

Series Editors:
David Hassan, University of Ulster at Jordanstown, UK
Allan Edwards, Griffith University, Australia

Foundations of Sport Management is a discipline-defining series of texts on core and cutting-edge topics in sport management. Featuring some of the best-known and most influential sport management scholars from around the world, each volume represents an authoritative, engaging and self-contained introduction to a key functional area or issue within contemporary sport management. Packed with useful features to aid teaching and learning, the series aims to bridge the gap between management theory and practice, and to encourage critical thinking and reflection among students, academics and practitioners.

Also available in this series:

Managing Sport Business
An introduction
David Hassan and Linda Trenberth

Managing Sport
Social and cultural perspectives
David Hassan and Jim Lusted

Managing High Performance Sport
Popi Sotiriadou and Veerle De Bosscher

**Routledge Handbook of Sport and
Corporate Social Responsibility**
*Kathy Babiak, Juan Luis Paramio-Salcines
and Geoff Walters*

Sport Governance
International case studies
Ian O'Boyle and Trish Bradbury

Sport Governance

International case studies

**Edited by Ian O'Boyle and
Trish Bradbury**

 Routledge
Taylor & Francis Group

LONDON AND NEW YORK

First published 2013
by Routledge
2 Park Square, Milton Park, Abingdon, Oxfordshire OX14 4RN

Simultaneously published in the USA and Canada
by Routledge
711 Third Avenue, New York, NY 10017

First issued in paperback 2014

Routledge is an imprint of the Taylor & Francis Group, an informa business

British Library Cataloguing in Publication Data
A catalogue record for this book is available from the British Library

Library of Congress Cataloging in Publication Data
A catalog record for this book has been requested

ISBN 978-0-415-82044-8 (hbk)
ISBN 978-0-415-85737-6 (pbk)
ISBN 978-0-203-40877-3 (ebk)

Typeset in Times
by HWA Text and Data Management, London

Contents

Figures

Tables

Contributors

Petri Bester is a lecturer in business management at the University of South Africa within the Department of Business Management. She is also involved in the Centre for Business Management. Her academic qualifications include an M.Com in business management conferred by the University of South Africa. Her research dissertation focused on the business environment of South African non-profit sport organisations. Her B.Hons (tourism management) was conferred by the University of Pretoria and the research project investigated the influence sport events have on destination branding. She is currently busy with her D.Com in business management at the University of South Africa. Her research focus is on the quality management of sport events brands.

Matthew T. Bowers, PhD, is a clinical assistant professor in the Department of Kinesiology and Health Education at the University of Texas at Austin. His published research examines the management of systems for athlete and coach development. Specifically, he investigates the potential supplemental impact that non-organised sport settings, such as pick-up sports and video games, may have on these development systems. Drawing from an interdisciplinary blend of quantitative, qualitative, and historical methodologies, his research focuses on leveraging this understanding of settings to influence the design and implementation of sport programmes and policies that promote both elite performance and mass participation throughout the lifespan. He also considers the development of creativity and innovation in and through sport at both the individual and organisational levels.

Trish Bradbury, PhD, is a senior lecturer in the School of Management at Massey University, Auckland. Trish's major research interests concern a variety of aspects of sport management related to event and people management, governance and athlete selection. She has published in journals such as *Sport, Business and Management: An International Journal*, the *International Journal of Sports Marketing and Sponsorship*, and the *Journal of Excellence*. She has extensive experience in coaching at the national and domestic levels and has held such roles as chef/assistant chef de mission at four World University Games and the 2000 Paralympic Games. She has been a board director for various national and regional sporting bodies and was a Foundation Board Member for the Sport Management Association of Australia and New Zealand (SMAANZ).

Gonzalo Bravo, PhD, is an associate professor of sport management at West Virginia University. His research interests include organisational behaviour as applied to sport organisations, the policy aspects of sport from a cross-cultural perspective, and sport management education. His work has been published in journals such as *Managing Leisure*, the *Journal of Sport Management*, the *International Journal of Sport Marketing and Sponsorship*, and the *International Journal of Sport Policy and Politics*. He is also the co-editor of the book *International Sport Management*. Gonzalo was instrumental in the creation of two Latin American academic organisations related to the study of sport: the Latin American Association for Socio-Cultural Studies in Sport (ALESDE), and the Latin American Association for Sport Management (ALGEDE).

Laurence Chalip, PhD, is Brightbill-Sapora Professor at the University of Illinois (Urbana-Champaign), where he serves as head of the Department of Recreation, Sport and Tourism. He earned his PhD in policy analysis from the University of Chicago. He has co-authored or co-edited three books, four monographs, over a dozen book chapters, and over one hundred peer reviewed articles. He was founding editor of *Sport Management Review*, and also served as editor for *Journal of Sport Management*. He serves on the editorial boards of eight other scholarly journals, and also consults widely to industry. He was a founding board member of the Sport Management Association of Australia and New Zealand, from which he won the Distinguished Service Award. He is a research fellow of the North American Society for Sport Management, from which he won the Earle F. Zeigler Award.

Mary Charalambous-Papamiltiades is the Coordinator of Sport Management Studies and a lecturer in sport management at the European University Cyprus. She also served as the President of the Cyprus Sport Management Association (2010–2012) and is a member of the European Sport Management Association. She has published in areas of sport governance and sport marketing and has participated in many international conferences. She is a graduate of the Sport Sciences Faculty of the Aristotle University of Thessaloniki, Greece and holds two postgraduate degrees, an MSc in sport and exercise science from Leeds Metropolitan University and an MBA in sport management from the University of Leicester. She submitted her PhD in March 2013 at Loughborough University.

George Costa is the Vice-Rector of Democritus University of Thrace (2010–2014) in Komotini, Greece. He works as a professor in the Department of Physical Education and Sport Science at Democritus University of Thrace. He was the head of the Master Studies Programme 'Exercise and Quality of Life' and also teaches at the graduate level in the School of Economics at the University of

Athens. He received his doctoral degree in recreation management and sport tourism from the University of Oregon in 1992. He has been a member of the European Association for Sport Management since 1993 and has been elected twice as a board member. From 2007 to 2011 he was the president of the Hellenic Association for Sport Management. Areas of interest include sport tourism, sport management and recreation management.

Paul Cummins, MSC, MBA, is currently finishing his PhD examining leadership in sport coaching at the University of Ulster School of Psychology. He lectures in performance psychology and has published articles in sport psychology journals. His research interests include leadership, athlete transitions, culture change and social identity, particularly as they apply within the sport coaching context. Within the applied sports setting, Paul is a qualified sport psychologist who has worked with Olympic-level athletes and top coaches in increasing their performance.

James M. Dorsey is a senior fellow at the S. Rajaratnam School of International Studies at Nanyng Technological University and co-director of the Institute of Fan Culture of the University of Würzburg. An award-winning former foreign correspondent for *The Wall Street Journal* and other major media, Mr. Dorsey is also a syndicated columnist and author of the acclaimed 'The Turbulent World of Middle East Soccer' blog. Mr. Dorsey looks at national, ethnic, religious, social and economic fault lines in the Middle East and North Africa. He is the author of the forthcoming book, *The Turbulent World of Middle East Soccer*.

Ryan Feeney, BEd, LLM, is a member of the Ulster GAA Senior Staff Team responsible to the provincial director (CEO) with executive lead responsibility for six areas of Ulster Council operations. Ryan is also the servicing officer for Ulster GAA Management Committee, Developments Committee and is also the lead officer for the following Committees: Community Committee, PR and Marketing Committee, Integration Committee and Club Planning, and Physical Development Committee. He is one of Ulster GAA's event controllers and a member of the Ulster GAA event team with the role of deputy event controller for major Ulster GAA fixtures.

Lesley Ferkins is associate professor in sport management at Unitec Institute of Technology, Auckland. Her area of specialisation is the governance of sport organisations, a primary focus of her teaching and research. Lesley has worked closely with boards of national and state sport organisations in New Zealand and Australia and has held the position of president of the Sport Management Association of Australia and New Zealand. Prior to joining Unitec, Lesley spent time at Deakin University in Melbourne and was postgraduate head within the School of Sport and Recreation at AUT University in Auckland. Lesley has presented at numerous conferences around the globe and is published in the world's top sport management journals (*Journal of Sport Management* and *Sport Management Review*).

Libor Flemr is an assistant professor in the Department of Pedagogy, Psychology and Didactics of P.E. and Sport, Faculty of Physical Education and Sport, Charles University in Prague (Czech Republic), where he received his PhD in 2009. He also teaches in the Department of Sport Management at the Charles University. He is interested in the education of young P.E. teachers and sport coaches, sport facilities, sport policy, and active lifestyles. His most widely known article is 'Spatial conditions for the support of active lifestyles in today's population', which he published in the *International Review for the Sociology of Sport.* He regularly publishes in two Czech leading kinanthropological journals: *Czech Kinanthropology* and *Studia Sportiva*. He is the author of a number of sport policies for Czech towns and regions.

John Forster has been associated with Griffith University, The University of the South Pacific, The University of Waikato, Canberra CAE, Queensland University of Technology, North-East London Polytechnic, Sydney University, McMaster University, Keele University, London University and The American University of Sharjah (UAE). Academic interests include global sport organisations, art economics and the Taiwanese construction industry, authoring and editing ten books in these areas. Non-academic interests include collecting contemporary Australian art and Arabic and Farsi calligraphy.

B. Christine Green is an associate professor and coordinator of the Sport Management Programme at the University of Texas. Her research examines the nexus of sport and development. She seeks to enhance effectiveness in the governance, administration, marketing, and policymaking for sport programmes and sport systems in ways that facilitate development at the individual, community and societal levels. She is a past editor of *Sport Management Review*, and currently serves as associate editor for the *Journal of Sport Management* and the *Journal of Sport & Tourism*. She is a research fellow for the North American Society for Sport Management.

Fan Hong is a professor in Chinese Studies and the head of the School of Asian Studies at the University College Cork, National University of Ireland. She is an academic editor of *The International Journal for the History of Sport.* Her research areas include historical and contemporary cultural values, beliefs and attitudes, with particular reference to women, education and emancipation in China and Asia; gender and politics in Asia; comparative studies in sport, politics, policies and organisations in China and other Asian countries.

Fuhua Huang is a PhD candidate in the School of Asian Studies, University College Cork. He received his BA degree in international business from Zhaoqing University and MA degree on sport studies from Soochow University. His main research interests focus on the professionalisation and commercialisation of sport and sport policy in China. He has recently published chapters and articles on glocalisation of sport in China and marketisation of Chinese sport.

Uma Jogulu is a senior lecturer at Monash University where her research focuses on equity, diversity and inclusion in the workplace. Uma's academic training in organisational studies, theory and human resource practice provided a strong foundation for pursuing theoretically rigorous and empirically grounded research. Her publications to date span areas of inequalities and governance in the context of career outcomes of women and men, workplace experiences of immigrants and minority groups, and aspirations and expectations for organisational leadership.

Trevor Meiklejohn is a lecturer in sport management and marketing at Unitec Institute of Technology, Auckland. Before embarking on an academic career, Trevor held positions in sport development, marketing and facility management for regional and national sporting organisations including North Harbour Rugby, the New Zealand Rugby Union and the Millennium Institute of Sport and Health. Trevor's research interests include sport governance, interorganisational relationships, sport sponsorship, and high performance sport.

Dino Numerato is a research fellow at University of West Bohemia in Pilsen, Department of Sociology (Czech Republic) and Bocconi University (Milan, Italy). He is also a guest lecturer in sociology of sport at Masaryk University (Brno, Czech Republic), where he received his PhD in sociology in 2006. From September 2013 he will be a research fellow at Loughborough University to carry out research into civic engagement of football fans. His research interests are in sociology of sport, sport governance and its transformation in the post-communist Czech Republic. He has also been working on the nexus between sport and the media and the relationship between sport and politics. He published articles in journals such as *Sociology,* the *International Review for the Sociology of Sport, Sport in Society,* the *International Journal of Sport Communication,* and the *International Journal of Sport Policy and Politics.*

Ian O'Boyle, PhD, is a lecturer in sport and recreation management within the School of Management, at University of South Australia. His research interests relate to the broader topic of sport governance and other associated disciplines within the field of sport management. He has previously been affiliated with University of Ulster in the UK and Massey University in New Zealand. He has most recently been involved in a number of research projects analysing issues such as performance management and governance within non-profit sport organisations and has been successful in obtaining numerous research grants to carry out this work.

Milena M. Parent, PhD, is an associate professor in the School of Human Kinetics, University of Ottawa and at the Norwegian School of Sport Sciences. She is a research fellow of the North American Society for Sport Management and Early Researcher Award holder of the Government of Ontario. She has published numerous articles in top management and sport management journals, as well as books, including being a co-author on *Managing*

Major Sports Events: Theory and Practice (with Sharon Smith-Swan) and *Understanding Sport Organizations: The Application of Organization Theory* (with Trevor Slack). Her research interests include organisation theory and strategic management, particularly as they apply to sport events. Particular topics of interest include stakeholder network management and coordination, governance, and knowledge management.

David Patterson has been a sport practitioner for over 20 years, including being Chief Executive Officer of Ringette Canada as well as Water Ski and Wakeboard Canada. In addition to working as a practitioner, Patterson is a PhD candidate at the University of Ottawa, studying power in the function and role of local sport organisations. His scholarly work has also included examinations of the roles of sport officials in sport development programming.

H. Thomas R. Persson is a researcher and part of the Sport Management Group at the Department of Leadership and Strategy at the University of Southern Denmark. He completed a PhD at the University of Warwick and the Centre for Research in Ethnic Relations (Coventry, UK) in 2006. Between 2006 and 2008 he was a Marie Curie Research Fellow in the research project 'Sport and Social Capital in Europe' at Universitá Bocconi (Milan, Italy). He holds a guest researcher position at Malmö University, where he worked as senior lecturer at the Department of Sport Sciences between 2009 and 2013. His research interest and publications cover sport governance, good governance, CSR, social capital, SGB governed recreational physical activity in the third age, social integration, and finally sport participation.

Shayne Quick's university career has spanned three decades and five countries. He is a past president of the Sport Management Association of Australia and New Zealand and co-author of Australia's first text in sport marketing. *Strategic Sport Marketing* which is now in its fourht edition and has been published in four languages, including Grcck. In 1999, while at University of Technology, Sydney (UTS), he established the Hellenic Master of Sports Management Programme in conjunction with the Greek General Secretariat of Sport and the Democritus University of Thrace. This initiated what has become an enduring relationship with the country of Greece and her people. A modern day 'philhellene' Professor Quick now calls Athens home for part of each year.

David Shilbury is the Foundation Chair in Sport Management and a former head of the School of Management and Marketing at Deakin University. He was the Foundation President of the Sport Management Association of Australia & New Zealand (SMAANZ) (1995-2001) and a member of the AFL Tribunal from 1992-2003. He was editor of *Sport Management Review* from 2002–2004 and is the senior associate editor of the *Journal of Sport Management*. Professor Shilbury has published over 60 refereed articles and is co-author of *Strategic Sport Marketing* and *Sport Management in Australia: An Organisational Overview*. He is a research fellow of the North American Society for Sport Management (NASSM), a winner of the Victorian Sports Federation's Eunice

Gill Award for Sport Management, the inaugural SMAANZ Distinguished Service award in 2009, and was the 2011 Earle F. Zeigler lecture recipient awarded by NASSM. Research interests include sport governance, strategy, and sport development.

Peter Smolianov, PhD, is an associate professor of sport management at Salem State University near Boston. Educated in Australia, Russia and USA, he went through the USSR system of athlete development and competed for Moscow Dynamo in modern pentathlon, Moscow University in swimming and fencing, and in the USA for Brigham Young University in fencing. He managed Australian athletes in preparation for the 2000 Sydney Olympic Games and provided business analysis and strategic planning as an internal and external consultant to corporations as well as governmental and sporting organisations. His output includes over 50 sport management-related publications and conference presentations in such editions as the *International Journal of Sport Management*, *Managing Leisure: An International Journal*, *Sport Marketing Quarterly*, *Sport Science Bulletin*, and at sport management conferences world-wide. His recent related publication was a chapter on international sport comparative models in another 2013 book by Routledge – *Managing High Performance Sport*.

Richard Tacon has been a lecturer in management at Birkbeck, University of London since 2012 and is currently completing doctoral research on the development of social capital within voluntary sport clubs. From 2006 to 2008 he worked as a researcher at the Sport and Recreation Alliance, the umbrella organisation for the governing and representative bodies of sport and recreation in the UK. Current research involves governance in sport and the wider non-profit sector in the UK and Europe. Beyond this, other areas of research interest are social capital, social networks, governance and, more broadly, organisational ethnography.

Geoff Walters is a lecturer in the Management Department at Birkbeck, University of London and a director of the Birkbeck Sport Business Centre. He graduated from Lancaster University Management School and the University of Manchester before completing a PhD at Birkbeck on corporate governance in the football industry and the relevance of stakeholder theory. He has published in the fields of corporate governance and corporate responsibility and is the co-editor of the *Routledge Handbook of Sport and Corporate Social Responsibility*. In 2010 he was awarded a grant through the Universities Research Grant Programme to undertake research on CSR in European football and more recently has been involved with the development of the Voluntary Code of Good Governance for the Sport and Recreation Sector, an initiative led by the Sport and Recreation Alliance in the UK.

Acknowledgements

We would like to thank all the contributors who have given up their time to write chapters for this text. All contributors cooperated fully with the timelines we had to adhere to and were extremely professional in their presentation of their chapters and making any additional edits that were asked of them. Together they have contributed to the most relevant and up-to-date sport governance text book available on the market. It has been an excellent experience to work with each contributor and our publishing colleagues at Routledge. Special thanks must go to Dr. David Hassan, who has given us the opportunity to edit this text as part of the wider *Foundations in Sport Management* series. Dr. Hassan's knowledge and experience of editing texts such as this has been invaluable throughout the course of the project. Our thanks also go to our partners and families whose constant support enable us to work in an environment that often demands many hours away from them.

Introduction

Ian O'Boyle and Trish Bradbury

Welcome to the first edition of this new book, *Sport Governance: International Case Studies*. In developing this text we were eager to produce a high-quality sport governance book that provides information to students and industry practitioners on the various topics related to sport governance through presentation of theory and analysis of relevant case studies. Our aims were also to analyse the key issues related to sport governance such as board composition, board structure, ethics in sport governance, leadership, volunteer–employee relationships, board roles, board independency, appraisal of board members and strategic development; and to analyse case studies on sport governance in countries throughout the world rather than a specific geographical location to understand the similarities and differences between governing sports in various nations and continents.

Governance has become a hugely important issue within sport. Issues of corruption and 'bad governance' have become synonymous with some aspects of sport and closer scrutiny than ever before is being applied to ensure sport organisations such as national governing bodies (NGBs) are following international best practice in respect to how they are governed. As sport organisations are required to become more professional and to adopt a more transparent and accountable approach to their operations, it has become important for all students, researchers and professionals working in sport to understand what good governance is and how it should be achieved.

There are a small number of other sport governance texts in the market in response to the rapidly increasing number of sport studies programmes in universities throughout the UK, USA, Australasia and the world at large, but there are no texts that analyse sport governance from a truly international perspective, as comprehensive or as well-authored as this current text. This book has attracted the contributions of leading sport studies scholars and professionals who are the most well known and most published in their respective fields in the UK, North America, Australia, New Zealand and indeed throughout the world. *Sport Governance: International Case Studies* brings together an abundance of knowledge and information for sport studies students and practitioners working in the field of sport governance and management.

As the first to examine sport governance around the world, this book offers a series of in-depth case studies of governance policy and practice in 15 countries and regions, including the USA, UK, China, Australia, Canada, South Africa, Latin America and the Middle East, as well as chapters covering governance by, and of, global sport organisations and international sport federations. With an opening chapter outlining the key contemporary themes and issues in the study of sport governance and a conclusion pointing at future directions for research and practice, this book is essential reading for any course on sport management, sport policy, sport development, sport administration or sport organisations, and for any manager or policy maker working in sport and looking to improve their professional practice.

There follows a brief overview of the chapters. The chapters within this text are a starting point for readers, and as editors we encourage you to advance your understanding of particular sport governance themes or topics by utilising the resources provided at the end of each chapter. We hope you enjoy expanding your knowledge of the sport governance area and as students and practitioners of sport, this book will, in some small way, help guide and develop sport on the global stage in the years to come.

1 Current issues within modern sport governance (Ian O'Boyle and Trish Bradbury)

This chapter introduces the core concepts, functions and current issues within sport governance, sets out a variety of definitions and discusses how governance plays such a crucial role in the operations of a sport organisation. It looks at the unique aspects of the sport industry that make it different from governance in other industries and also serves as an introduction to the remaining chapters in the book, highlighting the importance of the topics that are covered.

2 United States of America (B. Christine Green, Laurence Chalip and Matthew T. Bowers)

This chapter examines the coordination of challenges in governing a sport, and then illustrates that with a case concerning USA Football which is the national sport governing body for American football, operating under the International Federation of American Football (IFAF). The governance challenges in the United States are important, particularly given the poorly linked and poorly coordinated systems of school and nonschool sport, and the importance of the professional leagues in a few sports, which are also separate systems. As well, the centrality of sport outside the Olympic movement, especially American football, further complicates the matter.

3 Australia (David Shilbury)

This chapter contains a general overview of sport governance within organisations in Australia, with a specific focus on the challenges confronting federal models of governance. The chapter examines the major structural issues associated with a federal model of governance and the current changes occurring within Australian sport in response to these structural barriers. Trends influencing contemporary sport governance relevant to the Australian context are also explored. Cricket Australia is used as the case study to highlight the difficulties of change from traditional delegate/federated models of governance to other structural reforms.

4 Canada (Milena M. Parent and David Patterson)

This chapter analyses the Canadian sport system including examination of the evolution of its governance structure, highlighting key governance controls (e.g., laws, policies) that have shaped the Canadian sport system over the years, as well as jurisdictional issues (e.g., sport participation vs. elite sport jurisdictions) are examined. The changes to the sport system brought about by the hosting of the 2010 Vancouver Olympic Winter Games, such as the creation of the 'Own the Podium' programme and its impact on the Canadian sport system (comparing both winter and summer sports) are also discussed. Ringette Canada is used as a case study, which demonstrates the changes that have occurred in the Canadian sport system as well as the differences between the Olympic and non-Olympic sports within the country.

5 Russia (Peter Smolianov)

Russian sport governance has distinct features. Philosophical and organisational principles inherited from the Russian Empire and the Soviet Union guide the comprehensive governmental leadership; scientific, educational and medical support; and management by such objectives as maximising both mass fitness and elite performance. The Russian Modern Pentathlon Federation is used to exemplify the nation's governing practices and challenges.

6 South Africa (Petri Bester)

This chapter provides a brief overview of sport governance within a South African context. Concepts that are explored include the unique governance challenges within the African environment such as access to sport across all demographic groups, the development of an appropriate sport infrastructure, improvement of social cohesion and nation building, and improving the quality of life of all South Africans. Cycling South Africa is used as a case study to highlight the challenges and issues pertaining to sport governance within South Africa.

7 United Kingdom (Geoff Walters and Richard Tacon)

This chapter considers how the modernisation process has impacted upon the sport system within the UK. Specifically, it looks at the implications of modernisation on board involvement in strategy at the NGB level. The chapter is split into two main parts with the first providing background detail and analysis of the key issues and the second presenting an illustrative case study.

8 China (Fan Hong and Huang Fuhua)

This chapter analyses sport governance within China mainly from a historical perspective. Before the 1980s the Chinese sport governance system was a huge state-run enterprise. The Chinese government was responsible for funding and overseeing sport related affairs and operations under a centrally planned, hierarchical economic system. The sport governance system then gradually evolved under the free market system to become more self-sufficient. The State Sports Commission was restructured to become the State General Administration of Sport in 1998. Although the sport governance system has been reformed considerably in the last two decades, the government at all levels still has extensive control of sport operations in China.

9 Brazil (Gonzalo Bravo)

This chapter examines the evolution of sport policies in Brazil by looking at the role played by public and private structures. It also discusses the role of the federal constitution in shaping policies and the perceived importance of high performance sport in influencing these policies. Among the factors that have influenced priorities for funding and governance of sport in Brazil are: the constitution of 1988 and the subsequent laws enacted since then; the political context with the return to democracy; and the economic growth of the country during the last decade.

10 The Middle East (James M. Dorsey)

This chapter explores how autocratic regimes in the Middle East and North Africa prevent good governance by seeking to control soccer for political purposes. Boards of soccer associations are by and large populated by government appointees, often under the guise of elections that serve to satisfy nominal demands for transparency by the Fédération Internationale de Football Association (FIFA), or members of royal families.

11 Scandinavia (H. Thomas R. Persson)

This chapter introduces the reader to Scandinavian sport governance and the central issues facing sport governance in a Scandinavian context. It uses football governance in the three countries as a case study to discuss the development of good governance and social responsibility (or corporate social responsibility).

12 Greece (Shayne Quick and George Costa)

This chapter explores the major stages of governance in sport in Greece from 1974 until the present day. It examines sport governance from four perspectives. These are professional sport, youth sport, sport for all and the Olympic movement in Greece. Such perspectives are contextualised against a backdrop of changing political and cultural forces and illustrates how sport in Greece is inextricably linked to the prevailing government agenda. PAOK, a regional sport club with both professional and non-professional teams, is used as the case study to exemplify contemporary sport governance in Greece.

13 Ireland (Ryan Feeney, Ian O'Boyle and Paul Cummins)

This chapter reviews the changing role, structure and governance procedures of Ulster GAA – one of the provincial councils within the Gaelic Athletic Association in Ireland. This includes an overview of the entire GAA structure, focusing on the governance structure within the organisation. The chapter highlights the significant change the Ulster GAA has undertaken over the past decade and outlines its now significant links with government.

14 Cyprus (Mary Charalambous-Papamiltiades)

This chapter contains a general overview of the development of the sport sector in Cyprus. The chapter focuses on the role of the Cyprus Sport Organisation, which is the umbrella organisation under which all national federations and associations operate. Special emphasis is given to the sport governance problems that the sport system experiences, mainly due to the involvement of politics and the central role of volunteers in running sport. The Cyprus Sport Organisation is used as a case study highlighting sport governance issues that the sport sector is confronted with.

15 The Czech Republic (Dino Numerato and Libor Flemr)

This chapter contains a general overview of sport governance within organisations in the Czech Republic. The foremost umbrella/multisport associations, the relationship between them and a description of the ways in which they are interconnected to public authorities is presented. Major trends influencing contemporary sport governance and historical developments that are relevant in the Czech Republic context are also explored.

16 New Zealand (Lesley Ferkins, Uma Jogulu and Trevor Meiklejohn)

This chapter begins by introducing the sport governance landscape in New Zealand, establishing context for the ensuing discussion of national sport organisation (NSO) governance. Key historical influences on the way that sport is governed in New Zealand are identified, with an emphasis on the influence of sustained government involvement in sport. The issue of balancing competing roles within NSO boards is discussed, and the issue of gender diversity in relation to NSO boards in New Zealand is analysed.

17 Global sport organisations (John Forster)

This chapter examines the relationship between national sport governing bodies of sport and global ancillary sport organisations such as WADA (World Anti-Doping Agency) and ICAS (International Court of Arbitration for Sport). With the increased call for professionalism and transparency in all levels of sport, organisations such as these are beginning to play a larger role in the broader sporting landscape.

18 The future: trends and challenges in sport governance (Trish Bradbury and Ian O'Boyle)

This concluding chapter describes why the dominant discourse and approach to sport today is a business one. It compares and contrasts developments in sport governance throughout the world and identifies emerging trends that will have an impact on sport governance in the future. It also discusses the present and future challenges facing sport practitioners, managers and those involved in the governance of sport.

1 Current issues in modern sport governance

Ian O'Boyle and Trish Bradbury

Topics

- Sport governance defined
- The role of the board
- The size of the board
- Board independency
- Board conflict.

Objectives

- To understand current issues within modern sport governance
- To establish a link between board calibre and organisational performance
- To examine to board's role in evaluating CEO performance
- To demonstrate areas of potential conflict within sport governance
- To provide a best practice approach to current issues within modern sport governance.

Key terms

Stakeholders   Groups or individuals who have a vested interest in the operations and performance of a given sport organisation.

Board   A group of individuals charged with leading strategic development within a sport organisation and assuming overall accountability for the future direction of the organisation.

Parochialism   The protection of one's owns interests based on their association with a particular club or region affiliated with a sport organisation.

Accountability   The obligation of an individual or organisation to accept responsibility for their activities in creating a strong sustainable future for the organisation.

Competencies   The calibre of the board in terms of their knowledge and skills to be an effective board member.

Overview

Sport organisations (SOs) such as national governing bodies (NGBs) in modern society are faced with multiple performance challenges and pressures from various stakeholders such as the general public, players and athletes, coaches, media and the organisations' own members. Combined with these new and existing performance pressures, there is a call for SOs to be more transparent and accountable as ever growing levels of finances, garnered through evermore divergent streams, become a major issue within the sector. The contemporary SO must meet these challenges along with striving to produce elite athletes and coaches while recruiting and retaining a strong membership base. Governance is clearly an imperative aspect for SOs as it is concerned with the development of policy and strategic direction, which directly affects organisational performance (Ferkins, Shilbury & McDonald, 2005; Hoye, 2006; Hoye & Auld, 2001).

Sport governance

If an organisation adopts suitable systems of governance, this can facilitate a level of high performance throughout the organisation's various roles and responsibilities. A lack of a proper structure of governance can ultimately result in shortcomings within the organisation through poor strategic planning, policy making and poor decision making. Aside from these internal issues that can arise from 'bad' governance, external consequences such as withdrawal of funding, sponsorship, membership and possible intervention from external entities such as government may arise (Hoye, 2006; Mason, Thibault & Misener, 2006).

A single definition of sport governance is yet to be established, suggesting that the issue of governance within any organisation is a multi-faceted concern. It has previously been defined as 'the exercise of power and authority in sport organisations, including policy making, to determine organisational mission, membership, eligibility, and regulatory power, within the organisation's appropriate local, national, or international scope' (Hums & Maclean, 2004, p.5). In contrast, sport governance has also been described as 'the structure and process used by an organisation to develop its strategic goals and direction, monitor its performance against these goals and ensure that its board acts in the best interests of the members' (Hoye & Cuskelly, 2007, p.9). Within these definitions some core themes present themselves: direction, power, regulation and control.

Within this textbook, governance will be defined in a number of different ways including: the provision of a clear *direction* that aligns with the mission and vision for the organisation; the delegation of *power* is critical in order for each area of the organisation to operate and achieve results at the desired level; the issue of *regulation* in terms of sport governance is required to establish clear rules, guidelines and procedures for members and governed entities to adhere to; and the concept of *control*, like direction, is to ensure that any decisions and activities undertaken by the board are strictly aligned with the overall objectives and best interests of the organisation. In relation to regulation and control, a good system of governance should incorporate the power to impose penalties on individuals or groups who are not meeting compliance responsibilities (Ferkins *et al.*, 2005; Hoye & Cuskelly, 2007; Hums & Maclean, 2004; Slack & Parent, 2006).

Using this definition of governance in sport, it is clear that the role of the board is to act in the best interest of the SO and its stakeholders and therefore, it is argued that the manner in which these activities are conducted should be scrutinised regularly to ensure best practice (Hoye & Cuskelly, 2007). Moreover, key to any successful system of governance lies in the composition, roles, activities and decision making of the board. Board members must have appropriate previous experience and knowledge of how these unique entities operate, combined with expertise to address the various performance pressures and challenges that they face. It will be evident that a system of 'good' governance (Hassan, 2010) is in operation within an organisation that has been effective in making real progress towards the organisation's various objectives and overall vision, and is providing a valuable service to its membership. In order to fully understand how the board impacts the issue of governance in a SO, it is essential to conduct an analysis of previous research within this area.

The board

SOs are central to the development of participation in sport and fostering the development of sport in general within their jurisdiction. These entities not only foster increases in participation, but are also responsible for coaching development, staging events and competitions, volunteer training and other important aspects of sport management and development. Government agencies, both sport and non-sport, are beginning to fully realise the importance of having effective structures and systems of governance in place within these entities (Hoye & Doherty, 2011). Furthermore, the negative impacts that 'bad' governance practices can have on these organisations has been documented by a number of agencies (Australian Sports Commission, 2005; SPARC, 2004, 2006; UK Sport, 2004). As noted above, Hoye and Cuskelly (2007) have suggested that the board is a central feature of the governance system and structure that operates within these organisations. The calibre of board members in terms of their knowledge of both sport and traditional business acumen that is required to govern such an organisation is clearly an important factor is facilitating board effectiveness and therefore organisational success (Papadimitriou & Taylor, 2000; Papadimitriou, 2007). This has been further highlighted by Bayle and Robinson (2007) who state 'the system of governance, most notably the permanence and position of the main executives, are one of the keys to a [national governing body's] NGB's success' (p.258). Supporting Bayle and Robinson's (2007) study, Herman and Renz (2008) noted that research has demonstrated that board performance is directly related to organisational performance.

Although it is widely claimed throughout various studies in the literature (Bayle & Robinson, 2007; Papadimitriou & Taylor, 2000) that board performance is related to organisational performance, there are only a limited number of empirical studies that have been conducted to confirm this hypothesis. Hoye and Auld's (2001) research applied a specific board performance scale, the Self-Assessment for Non-Profit Governing Boards Scale (SANGBS), which had previously been developed by Slesinger (1991). In their research, by applying the SANGBS scale, they were able to empirically measure a SO's board performance by distinguishing between ineffective and effective boards. This scale has also been used in later studies by Hoye and Cuskelly (2003, 2004) and Hoye (2004, 2006).

Other studies have analysed issues that are directly associated with the performance of the board in SOs. These studies largely focus on the internal workings of the board in relation to the extent of authority between the board and the CEO (Hoye & Cuskelly, 2003), the relationship between staff members and chairpersons of the board (Hoye & Cuskelly, 2003), the relationship between board chairpersons, board members and staff (Hoye, 2004, 2006) and issues of board cohesion (Doherty & Carron, 2003). Central to one of the major themes to be discussed within this text, in exploring the composition (calibre) of the board and recruitment of board members Hoye and Cuskelly (2004, p. 95) state:

> Board members who do not possess appropriate skills, who are unsure of their role due to the absence of individual role descriptions, or have not been adequately orientated to an organisation, may find it difficult to contribute optimally to the board and thereby impact negatively on board [and organisational] performance.

As noted above, there is consensus in the research that board performance is directly related to organisational performance and in addition to this, Hoye and Doherty (2011) argue that 'expectations of board performance are tied to how well a board undertakes its role' (p.274). Furthermore, Bayle and Robinson (2007) and Papadimitriou (2007) suggest that how effective the board is in performing its role is related to organisational performance and success. Given the profound impact that the role of the board can have on overall organisational performance, it is also necessary to examine this imperative area of SO governance.

The role of the board

Academics and some government sport agencies have attempted to develop governance guidelines in order to help SOs implement effective systems to improve their governance capacity. The majority of these guidelines focus on defining and providing clarification of the role of the board within these organisations. For instance, Walters, Tacon and Trenberth (2011) suggest SO 'boards consider their most important roles to be financial, strategic and legal' (p.14). The Australian Sports Commission (ASC) (2005) describes the role of the board in terms of having a legal, strategic, financial and moral function. In addition to this, the ASC suggests the board has the responsibility of recruiting the CEO, conducting analysis of organisational and financial risks and being accountable to stakeholders through periodic reporting. SPARC (2006) provides a more vague definition of the role of the board advocating that it involves advancing and protecting 'the long-term interests of the organisation as a whole, which it holds in trust' (p.19). UK Sport (2004) also provides four fundamental roles of SO boards: ' (1) to set the organisation's strategic aims; (2) to provide the leadership to put those aims into effect; (3) to supervise the management of the entity; and (4) to report to members on their stewardship' (p.6).

Agencies such as the Australian Sports Commission, Sport NZ (formally SPARC) and UK Sport have shown leadership and realised the need to define the role of the board within sport organisations in order to implement effective governance structures and systems.

Board members have a variety of roles within the organisation in which they govern. However, little research has been conducted providing empirical evidence of these roles (Inglis, 1997; Shilbury, 2001). Of the research that has been conducted relating to roles of board members in SOs, four different factors can be identified. According to Inglis (1997) these are:

1   Mission – ethics within the organisation, not deviating from agreed direction, developing policy which relates to the overall vision;
2   Planning – strategic planning, risk management, financing, staffing, compliance with relevant legislation;
3   CEO – recruitment and retention, assessing performance, establishing joint leadership;
4   Public image – establishing ties with the community, sourcing funding and sponsorship, ensuring relationship with the general public is positive.

Perhaps a significant point worth noting in relation to Inglis' (1997) research is that the perceived performance of the board varies greatly between members of the board and employees within the subject organisations; and major discrepancies in board roles and performance are also noted between male and female members. Inglis (1997) concludes that 'understanding additional explanations for varying perceptions of the roles by gender should be a focus for further research' (p.174).

The size of the board

The size of the board within SOs is an area of research that few studies have addressed even though this may potentially be an integral issue in determining board and organisational effectiveness. For the purposes of this textbook, a large board is described as having more than 10 members. Conversely, a smaller board is described as having less than 10 members. Miller-Millsesn (2003) suggests the size of the board should be large enough to ensure that the CEO or managers within the organisation do not possess complete control of decision making and strategic direction within the organisation. In addition, Chaganti, Mahajon, and Sharma (1985) claimed that a larger board size reduces the control function of the CEO over the board and provides greater depth of leadership. Furthermore, it has been argued that the size of the board should be large enough to attract various valuable resources required by the organisation in addition to availing of the experience, knowledge and skills that are available through the establishment of larger boards (Goodstein, Gautam, & Boeker, 1994). 'The greater the need for effective external linkage, the larger the board should be' (Pfeffer & Saloncik, 1978, p.172). If a SO is largely concerned with satisfying external individuals and entities, the board size should be large enough in order to facilitate this through creating a diverse range of knowledge and expertise (Abzug, 1996; Luoma & Goodstein, 1999). A notable study carried out by Zahra and Pearce (1989) used empirical evidence to claim that financially viable for-profit organisations had larger boards (between 10 and 15 members) in comparison with organisations that were less profitable.

Although there appears to be evidence that suggests a large board provides greater benefit to a SO, not all researchers agree over this issue. Herman (1981) and Goodstein *et al.* (1994) claim that large boards can be ineffective in a number of areas mainly because constructive meetings and efficient decision-making becomes less likely. This scenario arises due to board fragmentation, contention, and factions within the board resulting in delays in the decision-making process. The cohesiveness and participation of large boards may also be negatively affected, further impacting on the board's effectiveness. Moreover, it is suggested that communication issues may be a significant factor within large boards and a failure to keep all board members informed of important information within the organisation may affect the contributions of various board members (Dalton, Daily, Johnson & Ellstrand, 1999; Forbes & Milliken, 1999; Goodstein *et al.*, 1994). In direct contrast to studies that show large boards increase organisational performance, Jenson (1993) claims smaller boards are the mechanisms which can help an organisation perform at the optimum level. Empirical studies have also been conducted which suggest that greater financial performance can be achieved through the implementation of a smaller board (Daily, Certo & Dalton, 1999; Yermack, 1996).

From the studies listed above, it can be easily determined that research findings concerning the relationship between board size and effectiveness are mostly inconsistent. However, some valuable information can be extracted from these studies. Most research would suggest that boards within non-profit organisations such as many SOs are large with as many as 30 members (Callen, Klein & Tinkelmon, 2003; Cornforth & Simpson, 2003) in some cases. It can be assumed that this large board size is a direct result of the SO's need to attract valuable and diverse resources, experience and knowledge into the organisation. Studies have also been conducted attempting to establish a relationship between board size and board performance within the non-profit sector. Again, the evidence to support either side of this argument is inconclusive. Research has suggested that there is a positive correlation between a large board and donations to the non-profit organisation, and on the contrary, a number of studies have shown that there is no notable relationship between board size and organisational performance (Bradshaw, Murray & Wolpin, 1992).

Although there is still much debate surrounding the issue of best practice in terms of board size, a general consensus within the body of literature available would suggest that large boards are currently necessary within SOs due to their dependency on attracting donations, funding, experience and knowledge to the organisation (Yeh & Taylor, 2008). However, for-profit organisations with a professional board of directors can rely on a smaller board membership by adopting a suitable recruitment and retention strategy in order to ensure the composition of the board is directly aligned to the specific needs of the organisation. Therefore, given the need for SOs to 'professionalise', an emerging trend is that SOs should adopt a small professional board of directors to ensure that board composition directly aligns with performance challenges for the organisation in terms of having the correct mix of knowledge and expertise, and as a result the need for larger boards and the negatives associated with their size can be removed.

The independence of the board

Within this textbook, board independence refers to two types of scenarios within a governance system. First, board independence refers to the situation where the CEO of an organisation is classed as a board member and has equal voting rights as other board members. As one of the major roles of the board is to monitor the performance of the CEO, this is clearly not a healthy governance structure as it undermines the board's ability to carry out this function. Second, an independent board also refers to the establishment of a board that does not contain representatives who are current members of the organisation, such as those from affiliated regional associations. Parochialism has been identified as a major issue that impacts upon the performance of many sport boards and the selection of independent board members in now seen to be best practice in organisational sport management (Walters *et al.*, 2011). Furthermore, the selection of an independent board should be carried out following a national open recruitment campaign to ensure the best possible candidates can be selected to lead the organisation.

Research suggests that if the board is composed of individuals who have been former employees or even individuals who have a vested interest within the organisation, then the CEO/management's performance is less likely to be monitored on a continuous basis, and an independent board is far more likely to scrutinise CEO/management performance at an adequate level (Dalton *et al.*, 1999). Another benefit from selecting board members from the external environment is that they may bring an understanding and 'voice' to stakeholders of the organisation who may have not been heard previously (Yeh & Taylor, 2008). Furthermore, with the adoption of an independent board, it can be ensured that appropriate knowledge and expertise is present within the board in order to deliver on strategic imperatives; a situation which cannot be guaranteed with the election of a dependent board.

In contrast to the body of literature which is divided relating to board size, there is a clear consensus that board independence is positively related to board effectiveness (Dalton *et al.*, 1999). According to Jenson (1993) a completely independent board may be an unrealistic ideal, as the CEO and senior managers are routinely required to sit on the board due to their intimate knowledge of the organisation and their inclusion can aid the board in the decision-making process. Aside from this sometimes necessary exception, as stated previously, the emerging trend is that a SO should strive to implement an independent professional board of suitable external directors. Although there has been little research conducted analysing the relationship between board independence and organisational performance in SOs, within the traditional business environment it has been proven to be effective. Dalton *et al.* (1999) and Zahra and Pearce (1989) found there to be a positive relationship between board independence and financial performance in particular. Likewise, following the implementation of an independent board within New Zealand Cricket after the Hood Report (1995), the financial position of the organisation strengthened greatly.

Board conflict

In the absence of a clearly laid out and articulated role description, members of boards or committees can occasionally feel it is necessary to become involved in the daily operations of the organisation in order to exercise their control and supervision function. This practice inevitably leads to conflict with management and other employees whose role within the organisation is to carry out those very tasks (Kilmister, 2006). Adding to this, it is almost always outside of the board's remit to become involved with operational plans being executed within the organisation. The board's role in planning is at the strategic level and it is important for a SO to differentiate between strategic and operational plans. The operational plans within an organisation are the responsibility of the CEO and staff. When a board or committee wrongfully become involved in operational planning within an organisation they are often stepping outside of their area of competence and become involved in problematic issues that are not their responsibility. This practice becomes even more problematic as it draws the board away from their strategic planning responsibilities (Garratt, 1996). It is also likely within this situation that the board will anger and demotivate specialist staff employed for their operational expertise. Furthermore, when the board within a SO empowers itself to establish operational plans instead of allowing management to do so, it denies itself the opportunity to hold employees accountable for the role that they are employed to carry out (Kilmister, 2006).

It is a relatively recent practice for boards within SOs to establish clearly defined boundaries between their governance role and the role of management. While it is common practice and a relative necessity for CEOs to have a detailed job description outlining the reporting line to the board, the board itself can often fail to clarify the nature of their own roles and responsibilities (Kilmister, 2006). Examples of this occur when there is confusion over the CEO's role in the organisation in relation to finance, setting salary levels for staff or in relation to the power of the board in making operational decisions within the organisation. Unless boundaries and specific role descriptions are set in place, conflicts will inevitably arise relating to such issues. When boundaries have been drawn up, it is important for board members to remove themselves from operational functions and allow the CEO to carry out his/her responsibilities. Intrusion and interference across agreed boundaries can result in a loss of trust and the potential for diminished performance.

Furthermore, new members to boards within SOs can be poorly informed of what their role is in relation to the organisation and 'regrettably, most new board members just drift with the tides' (Chait, Holland & Taylor, 1996, p.1). Due to the fact that very few boards within SOs have role descriptions or terms of reference little attention is often paid to the introduction of new members into the board's affairs (Walters *et al.*, 2011). In addition, in terms of individual performance management, it is a rare occurrence for a board to establish a budget for its own development requirements. Training for board members takes place 'on the job' which can result in wasted potential contribution from the new board member and does not allow for constructive criticism of current practices or exploration of new methods to conduct board responsibilities.

A further problem that exists within sport governance is the potential for the board and its members to focus on the past or near future within the organisation instead of conducting its role of creating an achievable strategic vision for the SO. While monitoring the financial and non-financial performance of the organisation is an important role of the board, it is not the exclusive component. The board will inevitably be required to expend some time and energy analysing these issues, but it must not lose focus of its true value to the organisation, which lies in its collective creativity and wisdom to ensure the long term vision of the organisation is being strategically aligned with the ever changing external environment.

Summary

'Good' governance (Hassan, 2010) is not something that can be easily achieved, much like the development and maintenance of the management-governance relationship which exists within SOs. By definition, managers within SOs are usually goal-driven, focused and often practical. They are expected to be highly motivated to make an example to everyday staff within the organisation. In contrast, good governors should be thinkers. They are required to focus on the long term aspects of the organisation in relation to outcomes, values, vision and 'high level strategic direction rather than operational strategies and goals' (Kilmister, 2006, p.173). Good governors should establish a clear relationship with the CEO and make them accountable for their performance in that role. Boards that operate effectively within SOs add value to the organisation that is greater than what the CEO or general staff can contribute. Good boards must make a difference through valued contributions to the life of the organisation that is shown in the delivery of superior outcomes to those stakeholders on whose behalf the board exists.

The statutory requirements, corporate and non-profit governance codes and guides to principles and standards, including those specific to sports governance stipulate how sports organisations should determine their governance structures, systems and processes and what sort of behavioural standards are expected of those in charge of fulfilling the governance role.

(Hoye & Cuskelly, 2007, p.178)

In addition to these codes and guides, SOs are also subject to a number of other performance pressures from agencies and organisations to develop and adapt their own codes of behaviour with a goal of improving governance standards. With such a diverse range of pressures and accountability being placed on SOs, the need for adequate governance structures and systems to be in place is now a necessity in order for core competencies to be implemented most effectively.

The board must play a vital role in ensuring a SO is effective in delivering benefits and contributing to the overall sustainability and success of the organisation. As one of the core competencies of the board lies in effective decision-making, it is clear that the impact the board can have on a SO is substantial. From previous research relating to the roles, composition, size and independence of the board it is possible to gain a greater understanding and perhaps develop a best practice structure of governance to be implemented within this unique sector.

Review questions

1   Discuss the major roles of the board within a sport organisation identifying boundaries where the roles of management take over.
2   Much debate exists surrounding the ideal size of the board within the governance structure of a sport organisation. Identify some of the benefits and challenges associated with large and small boards within sport organisations.
3   The adoption of independent boards within sport organisations is becoming popular within many nations. Provide reasoning and justification for this trend and critically analyse the potential value that they may add to a sport organisation.

Further reading

Groeneveld, M. M., Houlihan, B., & Ohl, F. (2011). *Social capital and sport governance in Europe*. New York: Routledge.
Hoye, R., & Cuskelly, G. (2007). *Sport governance*. Sydney: Elsevier.
Hums, M. & Maclean, J. (2008). *Governance and policy in sport organisations*. London: Holcomb Hathaway Publishers.
King, N. (2009). *Sport policy and governance: Local perspectives*. London: Butterworth-Heinemann.

Websites

Sport NZ: http://www.sportnz.org.nz/en-nz/our-partners/Developing-Capabilities/Governance-Templates/
The Irish Sport Council: http://www.irishsportscouncil.ie/Governing_Bodies/NGB_Support_Kit/2_Governance/
UK Sport: http://www.uksport.gov.uk/pages/governance/

References

Abzug, R. (1996). The evolution of trusteeship in the United States: A roundup of findings from six cities. *Non-profit Management & Leadership*, 7, 101–11.

Australian Sports Commission (2005). *Governing sport: The role of the board, a good practice guide to sporting organisations*. Canberra: Australian Sports Commission.

Bayle, E, & Robinson, L. (2007). A framework for understanding the performance of national governing bodies of sport. *European Sport Management Quarterly*, 7, 240–68.

Bradshaw, P., Murray, V., & Wolpin, J. (1992). Do non-profit boards make a difference? An exploration of the relationship among board structure, process and effectiveness. *Non-profit and Voluntary Sector Quarterly*, 21(3), 227–49.

Callen, J. L., Klein, A., & Tinkelmon, D. (2003). Board composition, committees, and organizational efficiency: The case of non-profits. *Non-profit and Voluntary Sector Quarterly*, 32(4), 493–520.

Chaganti, R. S., Mahajon, V., & Sharma, S. (1985). Corporate board size, composition, and corporate failures in retailing industry. *Journal of Management Studies*, 22(4), 400–17.

Chait, R., Holland, T. & Taylor, B. (1996). *Improving the performance of governing boards*. Westport, CT: Oryx Press.

Cornforth, C., & Simpson, C. (2003). The changing face of charity governance: The impact of organizational size. In C. Cornforth (Ed.), *The Governance of Public and Non-profit Organizations*. New York: Routledge.

Daily, C. M., Certo, S. T., & Dalton, D. R. (1999). A decade of corporate women: Some progress in the boardroom, none in the executive suite. *Strategic Management Journal*, 20(1), 93–100.

Dalton, D. R., Daily, C. M., Johnson, J. L., & Ellstrand, A. E. (1999). Number of directors and financial performance: A meta-analysis. *Academy of Management Journal*, 42(6), 674–86.

Doherty, A., & Carron, A.V. (2003). Cohesion in volunteer sport executive committees. *Journal of Sport Management*, 17, 116–41.

Ferkins, L., Shilbury, D., & McDonald, G. (2005). The role of the board in building strategic capability: Toward an integrated model of sport governance research. *Sport Management Review*, 8(3), 195–225.

Forbes, D. P, & Milliken, F. J. (1999). Cognition and corporate governance: Understanding boards of directors as strategic decision-making groups. *Academy of Management Review*, 24(3), 489–505.

Garratt, B. (1996). *The fish rots from the head*. London: Harper Collins Business.

Goodstein, J., Gautam, K., & Boeker, W. (1994). The effects of board size and diversity on strategic change. *Strategic Management Journal*, 15, 241–50.

Hassan, D. (2010). Governance and the Gaelic Athletic Association: Time to move beyond the amateur ideal? *Soccer & Society*, 11(4), 414–27.

Herman, E. S. (1981). *Corporate control, corporate power*. New York: Cambridge University Press.

Herman, R.D., & Renz, D.O. (2008). Advancing non-profit organizational effectiveness research and theory. *Nonprofit Management and Leadership*, 18, 399–415.

Hood, J. (1995). *The Hood report: A path to superior performance*. Christchurch: New Zealand Cricket.

Hoye, R. (2004). Leader-member exchanges and board performance of voluntary sport organizations. *Non-profit Management & Leadership*, 15(1), 55–70.

Hoye, R. (2006). Leadership within voluntary sport organization boards. *Nonprofit Management & Leadership*, 16(3), 297–313.

Hoye, R., & Auld, C. (2001). Measuring board performance in non-profit sport organizations. *Australian Journal of Volunteering*, 6(2), 109–16.

Hoye, R. & Cuskelly, G. (2003). Board-executive relationships within voluntary sport organisations. *Sport Management Review*, 6(1), 53–73.

Hoye, R. & Cuskelly, G. (2004). Board member selection, orientation and evaluation: Implications for board performance in member-benefit voluntary sport organisations. *Third Sector Review*, 10(1), 77–100.

Hoye, R., & Cuskelly, G. (2007). *Sport governance*. Oxford: Elsevier Butterworth-Heinemann.

Hoye, R. & Doherty, A. (2011). Nonprofit sport board performance: A review and directions for future research. *Journal of Sport Management*, 25(3), 272–85.

Hums, M. A., & MacLean, J. C. (2004). *Governance and policy in sport organisations*. Scottsdale, AZ: Holcomb Hathaway.

Inglis, S. (1997). Roles of the board in amateur sport organizations. *Journal of Sport Management*, 11, 160–76.

Jenson, M. C. (1993). The modern Industrial Revolution, exit, and the failure of internal control systems. *Journal of Finance*, 48(3), 831–80.

Kilmister, T. (2006). Governance. In S. Leberman, C. Collins, & L. Trenberth (eds), *Sport business management in New Zealand* (pp. 147–75). Wellington: Cengage Learning.

Luoma, P, & Goodstein, J. (1999). Stakeholders and corporate boards: Institutional influences on board composition and structure. *Academy of Management Journal*, 42(5), 553–63.

Mason, D. S., Thibault, L., & Misener, L. (2006). An Agency Theory perspective on corruption in sport: The case of the International Olympic Committee. *Journal of Sport Management*, 20, 52–73.

Miller-Millsesn, J. L. (2003). Understanding the behavior of non-profit boards of directors: A theory based approach. *Non-profit and Voluntary Sector Quarterly*, 32(4), 521–47.

Papadimitriou, D. (2007). Conceptualizing effectiveness in a non-profit organizational environment: An exploratory study. *International Journal of Public Sector Management*, 20, 572–87.

Papadimitriou, D., & Taylor, P. (2000). Organisational effectiveness of Hellenic national sports organisations: A multiple constituency approach. *Sport Management Review*, 3, 23–46.

Pfeffer, J., & Saloncik, G. R. (1978). *The external control of organizations: A resource dependence perspective*. New York: Harper & Row.

Shilbury, D. (2001). Examining board member roles, functions and influence: A study of Victorian sporting organisations. *International Journal of Sport Management*, 2, 253–81.

Slack, T., & Parent, M. M. (2006). *Understanding sport organizations: The application of organization theory*. Champaign, IL: Human Kinetics.

Slesinger, L.H. (1991). *Self-assessment for non-profit governing boards*. Washington, DC: National Centre for Nonprofit Boards.

SPARC (2004). *Nine steps to effective governance: Building high performing organisations*. Wellington: SPARC.

SPARC (2006). *Nine steps to effective governance: Building high performing organisations* (2nd edn). Wellington: SPARC.

UK Sport (2004). *Good governance guide for national governing bodies.* London: UK Sport.

Walters, G., Tacon, R. & Trenberth, L. (2011). *The role of the board in UK national governing bodies of sport.* Birkbeck Sport Business Centre Research Paper Series. London: Birkbeck University.

Yeh, C. & Taylor, T.L. (2008). Issues of governance in sport organisations: A question of board size, structure and roles. *World Leisure Journal*, 50(1), 33–45.

Yermack, D. (1996). Higher market valuation of companies with a small board of directors. *Journal of Financial Economics*, 40(2), 185–211.

Zahra, S. A., & Pearce, J. A. (1989). Boards of directors and corporate financial performance: A review and integrative model. *Journal of Management*, 15(2), 291–344.

2 United States of America

B. Christine Green, Laurence Chalip and Matthew T. Bowers

Topics

- Unique nature of American sport governance
- U.S. sport governance policies
- Governance structures and authority
- Lack of coordinated governance
- Governance without authority: USA Football.

Objectives

- To illustrate the distinctiveness of American sport governance
- To present the complexity of an uncoordinated system of sport governance
- To describe the effect of federalism on sport governance in the United States
- To discuss the importance of partnerships in the absence of formal integrated governance structures
- To demonstrate the potential for governance without formal authority.

Key terms

Federalism   A system of government in which authority is constitutionally divided to ensure shared governance between the federal and state governments. American federalism results in power distributed to the states and even local governments.

Amateurism   A system by which athletes are expected to play for little to no remuneration. Instead, they are expected to play for the love of the game.

Amateur Sports Act (PL95-606)   U.S. law granting authority over the governance of Olympic sports to the United States Olympic Committee (USOC) through the national governing bodies (NGBs) for each sport. The Amateur Sports Act was formulated with the explicit purpose of keeping government out of sport governance.

Stakeholder   An individual, group or organisation that has a stake in the organisation's actions and its outcomes. A stakeholder can be positively or negatively affected by the actions of an organisation.

Flag football   A modified version of football in which players wear a belt with 2–3 tear away flag strips. Instead of tackling the player to end the play, defenders must pull a flag to stop the player. It is a less expensive, safer version of the game of football played by all ages and genders.

Overview

This chapter describes sport governance in the United States. Unlike most nations, the United States has no federated or coordinated system of sport governance. Instead, sport governing bodies function as parallel systems, often with a deep disconnect between elite sport and mass participation sport. A combination of a federalist model of government and an avowedly free-market economy has resulted in a plethora of sport organisations claiming governance over the same sport. The coordination of this array of governing bodies represents a deep challenge to the development of American athletes and teams. Methods of asserting governance without formal authority are illustrated in a case study of American (gridiron) football.

The successes of American athletes in some high-profile sports at the Olympic Games, particularly the Summer Olympic Games, have been the envy of many countries seeking to attain a similar level of success. Others have admired the profitable professional leagues, particularly baseball, gridiron football, and basketball. Those who are outside the system often assume that the high Summer Olympic medal tally and the profitable professional leagues are enabled by a systematic and carefully rationalised system of sport governance. In fact, at the national level, the United States has long eschewed any formal system of sport governance, preferring instead to rely on market forces and institutions established outside government. Successes in sport might more readily be attributed to American wealth, which was estimated at over US$15 trillion in 2011, or almost a quarter of the world's wealth (International Monetary Fund, 2012). In other words, American sporting wealth and success might be attributed no less to American affluence than to its systems of sport governance.

Distilled to its essential premises, sport in the United States lacks systematic national level governance because of the country's history of both an avowedly capitalistic, market-driven politico-economic philosophy and a cultural resistance to any type of government 'imposition' on free markets. The tenets of American free market capitalism pervade even the sporting landscape, as stakeholders at virtually all levels (often, even policymakers) subscribe to the American ethos that individual actors operating within the free market will render optimal outcomes. Therefore, government intervention would represent an affront to the core beliefs of the stakeholders. These philosophical incompatibilities, in turn, render a sport governance system that avoids policy driven solutions and, when forced to develop policy, often undermines its legitimacy by failing to provide within the policy any mechanisms for implementation or enforcement. In fact, the structure of governance within the U.S. sport 'system', a term which itself only marginally applies in the American context, is organised in a way that shares little in common with sport in the rest of the developed world (Chalip, Johnson & Stachura, 1996).

At the federal level, there are only three policies that govern sport or aspects therein (Bowers, Chalip & Green, 2011a). Moreover, two of these three policies only address sport indirectly. The most well-known federal policy, and the most openly debated, is Title IX of the Education Amendments of 1972 (PL 92-318). The second federal policy is the Americans with Disabilities Act, which was initially signed into law in 1990 (PL 101-336), and amended in 2008 (PL 110-325). Neither of these pieces of legislation was explicitly designed to redress issues related to sport, but their provisions prohibit discrimination in settings where sport may occur. The former prohibits discrimination in educational activities and programmes by any institution that receives federal funds, while the latter prohibits discrimination on the basis of disability in employment, government, public accommodations, commercial facilities, transportation, and telecommunications.

The other federal policy having to do with sport participation does, on the other hand, directly address sport governance in the United States, although it has proven ineffectual. The Amateur Sports Act, initially signed into law in 1978 (PL 95-606) and amended in 1996 through inclusion in the Omnibus Consolidated and Emergency Supplemental Appropriations Act (PL 105-227), officially grants authority over the governance of Olympic sports to the United States Olympic Committee (USOC) through the national governing bodies (NGBs) for each sport. The Amateur Sports Act was formulated with the explicit purpose of keeping government out of sport governance. It vests the USOC and its NGBs with the power 'to coordinate and develop amateur sport in the United States, to encourage the development of sport facilities, and to encourage and provide assistance to sport for women, the handicapped, and ethnic minorities' (Bowers, Chalip & Green, 2011a, p.257). The objective of keeping government out of sport also rendered the act's critical failing. The only requirement provided to assist with enforcement is that the USOC must provide a report to congress each year regarding its activities. No congressional committees or federal agencies are assigned even to read the report, so the USOC and its NGBs are effectively free from government oversight. Having no oversight, in turn, enables the very lack of coordination that the legislation was designed to redress, rendering a sport governance system in which the elite sport focus of the USOC and its NGBs often undermines – or even counteracts – efforts to develop mass sport participation at the grassroots levels, even though the act requires that of the USOC and its NGBs (Bowers, Chalip & Green, 2011b).

American courts have also chosen to keep sport free from government oversight. In the second decade of the twentieth century, Major League Baseball (MLB) was sued under American antitrust laws on the grounds that the MLB conspired to prevent competing leagues from operating. The appellate court ruled that baseball was not the kind of commerce that American antitrust laws were intended to regulate. The Supreme Court subsequently supported that ruling, with the result that professional sport leagues in the United States, the MLB in particular, are not subject to the same kinds of antitrust oversight to which all other private businesses in the United States arc subjected (Duquette, 1999).

Although American policymakers have chosen not to develop national-level government-run sport governance or regulation, government has involved itself with sport provision at local and regional levels, which has necessitated some involvement in governance at those levels. The American system of government relies on a federalist model (Bellia, 2011; Robertson, 2012). Accordingly wherever possible, responsibility for policymaking and policy implementation falls to the lowest possible level of government. Since the federal government takes no responsibility for sport, each of the 50 states (and the territories) is free to formulate and manage sport policies. Since states largely choose not to do so, sport is left to local and county governments. The result is that a few sports (usually baseball, basketball, swimming, athletics, and gridiron football) are managed and governed through publicly funded schools and universities. These sports and some others are also managed and governed by parks and recreation systems that are run at city or county level. The National Recreation and Park Association (NRPA) provides a national level organisation to lobby for local parks and recreation, as well as to provide training and certification for local level administrators. However, neither training nor certification is required, so the organisation has scant governance authority.

Some states stage multisport competitions every year or few years. Those competitions are managed separately by each state, although there is a National Congress of State Games (NCSG) that provides advice and information. It does not govern state games, however.

The lack of government management of sport beyond mostly local or regional levels created a void in sport governance. That void has been an opportunity for entrepreneurs who own professional sport franchises and who run the leagues in which those compete. They are free to run their teams and their leagues as they see fit (within the confines mandated by American business law). Consequently, each professional league has its own rules and systems for governance.

Entrepreneurs have also found opportunities at local and regional levels, as many sport clubs and leagues are run as private businesses, operating under their own rules for eligibility and competitions. Churches have also banded together to form their own leagues for participants, while private non-profit organisations like the YMCA, Police Athletic Leagues, and Jewish Community Centres also form teams and leagues in some sports. While some private and church teams and leagues operate independently, others affiliate to local leagues run by parks and recreation departments. Other sport clubs choose to affiliate directly to their national governing body, which is the national federation that reports to the international federation for its sport, and also to the United States Olympic Committee, which is run by its NGBs. On the other hand, many choose not to affiliate to their NGB, but choose instead to affiliate to the Amateur Athletic Union, which provides an alternative system of national governance for programmes affiliated to it.

The void in American sport governance has also created a need for private coordinating bodies to establish rules for competition and sometimes to lobby government (largely to keep its hands off sport). Consequently, university and college systems of governance have emerged, yielding three separate systems: the National Collegiate Athletic Association (NCAA), which governs sport for the vast majority of universities and colleges offering four-year undergraduate degrees; the National Association of Intercollegiate Athletics (NAIA), which governs sport for approximately 350 small universities and colleges offering four-year undergraduate degrees; and the National Junior College Athletic Association (NJCAA), which governs sport for community colleges offering two-year undergraduate education. Similarly, high schools band together to form leagues, which they then govern, while their national body, the National Federation of State High School Associations (NFHS), provides a venue for discussions and lobbying efforts nationally. The NCAA, NAIA, NJCAA, and NFHS are considered voluntary associations, so schools can form their own leagues without affiliating to a national body, although this has become rare.

At the same time, parallel systems of sport competition are run on university campuses by campus recreation services, which enable intramural sport leagues as well as club sports that may compete against other universities. However, sport run by campus recreation operates separately from and is typically independent of the athletics programmes run by the NCAA affiliated athletics department. Indeed, the coordinating body for campus recreation services is not the NCAA, but is the National Intramural-Recreational Sports Association (NIRSA), although campus recreation programmes are comparatively self-contained, so NIRSA has less governance authority over its members than the NCAA, NAIA, or NJCAA have over theirs.

Athletes whose circumstances require special consideration have their own associations, such as Armed Forces Sports for athletes in the military, and organisations that manage sport for the disabled. These are affiliated with the USOC, largely to have a voice in policymaking having to do with Olympic and Paralympic athletes. However, these organisations are separate from the USOC.

Meanwhile, there are other organisations that support sport development, although they typically play merely advisory roles in sport governance. These include coaches' associations, the National Association of Sports Commissions (NASC), American College of Sports Medicine (ACSM), the National Strength and Conditioning Association (NSCA), etc. The President's Council on Physical Fitness, Sports and Nutrition is intended to promote physical activity, including sport, nationally, but it has had meagre budgets and no governance authority whatsoever. The National Sporting Goods Association (NSGA) provides statistical and trade support to sporting organisations to the degree that so doing supports its membership, which seeks to sell sporting goods.

The result, as shown in Figure 2.1, is an alphabet soup of organisations claiming some sport governance authority. There is no single system of sport governance in the United States. Rather, there are a number of parallel but separate systems, some of which are loosely connected through personal contacts or because they occasionally have shared interests that bring them together. At other times they compete for the loyalty of athletes and coaches.

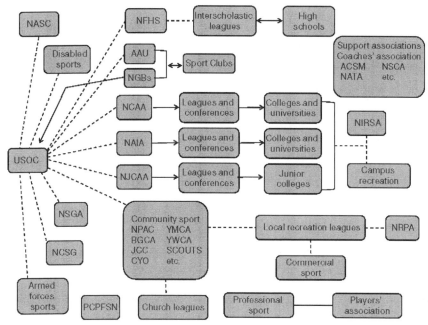

Figure 2.1 Array of sport governing authorities

Non-Americans who mistake effectiveness for efficiency in the performance of U.S. athletes on the international stage can take solace in the fact that many Americans themselves rarely have much understanding of the structure and governance of American sport. Indeed, Americans who work in sport take the parallel and loosely connected systems of American sport for granted, and consequently neither understand nor value integrated systems for sport governance, as those are outside their experience (Sparvero, Chalip & Green, 2008). American sport managers typically understand only a very narrow sliver within the particular realm in which they work. Further, Americans grow up exposed to a mass media filtered version of American sport that often simplifies and mythologises sport in a manner designed to buttress the hegemonic spectator sport ethos in the United States (Koppett, 1994). This often leads to misunderstandings and misperceptions when American sport leaders communicate with sport leaders from other countries. It has also led to a great deal of misleading scholarly work. As Bowers, Chalip, and Green (2011a, p. 254) lament,

> those who seek to learn about American sport by interviewing sports executives or through content analysis of American media actually learn only about isolated corners of American sport, or about the popular mythologies that masquerade as fact throughout American sport.

To better understand the United States, either as model or analogue, it is instructive to explore the disconnect that the development system in the United

States fosters with respect to elite spectator sport and mass participant sport – which, in countries with centralised, coordinated sport governance structures, is likely to be known simply as 'sport' – a telling distinction.

Consequences of an uncoordinated governance system

The core challenges for American sport governance derive from American sport's lack of coordination. There is no definable pathway to excellence for athletes. There are often starkly different rules for eligibility and even for competition between systems, which can be confusing for athletes, coaches, and spectators. These matters lead to particular concerns for sport development, as the lack of coordination requires harmonisation across systems that are often incompatible.

Spectator sports predominate the national consciousness in the United States, and the reasons for this cultural fascination are both universal and particular to the U.S. context. On the one hand, spectator sports are a culturally valued form of mass entertainment that is believed to unite people in a manner not dissimilar to other forms of entertainment like music, cinema, or theatre. When tracing the roots of the country's obsession with spectator sports, however, there are factors specific to the United States that drive the emphasis on engaging with sport through spectator channels as opposed to participation channels, particularly as individuals age.

Significantly, the sport development model for America's most popular sports is predicated on the delivery of elite youth sport through the school systems. Compared with much of the world, where membership-based sport clubs organised within national sport federations form the dominant structure to participate in sport, the American sport delivery system is more heterogenic, and at the youth level often integrated with the locally administered school system. Under the influence of developmental theory and a growing capitalist economy in the middle of the twentieth century, policymakers in the U.S. saw competitive sport as an important character building experience in childhood (Bowers & Hunt, 2011). With the advent of organised youth sport during the mid-twentieth century, public, private, and commercial sponsors founded organised youth programmes. Consequently, the sport systems for school-age young people are deeply intertwined with the education system and have become an important part of American high schools and colleges. The U.S. is the only nation in the world where it is taken for granted that high schools and universities sponsor and fund highly expensive interschool varsity sport programmes (Coakley, 2002). Millions of students participate in athletics programmes operated by high schools and colleges and, currently, the NCAA is the largest national governing body for university sport in the world.

While the role of the school systems as the primary providers in the sport delivery equation may seem to relate more directly to participant sport, there are flow-on consequences for spectator sport. As a result of the fact that sport development is tied into the education system, university sport offers the opportunity to earn college scholarships based on athletic excellence. Moreover, the university sport setting provides an attractive pathway for individuals pursuing a professional career as an athlete. The nature of the elite development pathways in the United States, therefore, renders a system in which both academic and athletic achievement are tied to the pursuit of attending college on an athletic scholarship. Hence, much of the focus of youth sport participation naturally turns to positioning the youth athlete to perform at such a level so as to earn a college scholarship, which may position him/her to be in line for professional opportunities following college. This development system creates a motivational climate that shifts the value of sport participation from process-based development to results-based outcomes. As a direct result of this shift from process to outcome, the values that become fostered in youth sport at even very young ages are ones that have traditionally been associated with adult models of work – competitiveness, achievement, etc. – as opposed to child-centred models of play.

In the United States, this philosophical splintering of play from work has manifested itself at the governance level through an increase in the marginalisation of leisure for sport providers. The notion that sport is perceived to function primarily as a forum for competition and achievement implies that play and leisure are somehow incompatible with modern sport, or at least less legitimate activities. This narrowly perceived function of offering the opportunity to compete and achieve has, in turn, yielded a limited scope of activities that are brought under the rubric of sport. Moreover, the narrow scope of sport activities has generated a number of temporal and contextual boundary conditions on the activities that merit participation. As a result of these legitimations and boundary conditions for sport, the childhood pursuit of excellence does not easily transfer to an adulthood characterised by recreational play driven by the social and health benefits of sport. Instead, the pursuit of excellence through active participation in childhood converts to a (vicarious) pursuit of excellence through fanship and consumption in adulthood, evidenced by the apparent diminishment in motivation to participate beyond the school system.

With respect to participant sport, the trends have been quite startling over the past few decades. As a natural result of the sport governance and sport development models discussed in the preceding paragraphs, participant sport, although popular, has been relegated as a leisure pursuit in favour of more passive, spectator-based consumption. What this means, however, is not that the people of the United States are abstaining from participating in physical activity; in fact, participation in fitness related physical activity has increased dramatically. This shift toward individual, fitness-oriented pursuits has occurred at the expense of participation in team sports throughout the lifespan. This trade-off, while being potentially problematic for sport organisations and national health trends, is not unexpected given the values associated with sport participation. Consequently, the drop-off in participation rates for individual and team sport as adults leave the school system is dramatic (Physical Activity Council, 2012).

The sport system's fragmentation enables each part to shed overall responsibility for recruitment, retention, and development of athletes. The challenges sport faces to govern itself in what is ostensibly an unencumbered, free-market system are exacerbated by the fact that USOC and NGB policies prioritise funding to develop a few elite athletes (Bowers, Chalip & Green, 2011b; Sparvero, Chalip & Green, 2008). Consequently, the USOC and its NGBs are, for the most part, failing to carry out the very development requirements with which they are charged by the Amateur Sports Act. Yet, the lack of any enforcement mechanism in the legislation renders no ready solution, as the USOC and its NGBs have not been equipped with the resources to manage or govern sport effectively, and must operate in a system of parallel and sometimes competing governance systems.

These challenges extend to NGBs operating outside the USOC, including those that govern some of America's most popular sports. American (gridiron) football provides a particularly instructive example of the tribulations that are a consequence of governing a sport in the chaotic American system. The challenges faced by its NGB, USA Football, are described below.

Case study: Coordinating the entrenched: the case of USA Football

USA Football is a relatively new national governing body in the United States. It was established in 2002 as an independent, non-profit organisation. Its initial funding came through the National Football League (NFL) Youth Football Fund endowed by the NFL and the NFL Players Association (NFLPA), who remain active partners with USA Football. The sport of American football is firmly entrenched in American sport culture, and there are numerous organisations with a long history of governance within the sport. USA Football is clearly the last entrant in an already crowded governance arena. Because USA Football is only a recent player in the governance of the sport, the coordination issues faced by many NGBs in the United States are even more problematic for the new NGB. To understand the challenges facing USA Football, we must first understand the governance of the sport more broadly.

Elite football

Football is one of the most popular sports for school-age boys in the United States. It also enjoys immense popularity as a spectator sport. A 2009 ESPN poll of favourite spectator sports listed NFL (pro) football as first, NCAA (college) football third, football (unspecified) eighth, and high school football ninth in popularity (Sports Business Daily, 2009). The elite, entertainment sport programmes are all tackle football, with the main organisations forming a very loosely linked elite sport system. NFL players are drafted from the college ranks, and college players are recruited from the high school ranks. However, there is no investment and little coordination among these governing bodies. In fact, they play under three different sets of rules and structures. Each of these organisations has its own internal governance structure as well as a different vision and mission for the governance of the sport.

Professional football

The NFL is a private, for-profit enterprise. The mission of the NFL is 'To present the National Football League and its teams at a level that attracts the broadest audience and makes NFL football the best sports entertainment in the world' (NFL, 2012). The league is headed by a Commissioner (much like a CEO), who reports to the Executive Committee. The Executive Committee has representation from each of the 32 NFL teams. League policies are made on the basis of a three-quarters majority of team owners. All but one of the teams is owned by an individual, corporation, or an LLC owned by individuals.

College football

The non-profit National Collegiate Athletics Association (NCAA) is the main governing body for college football, which offers membership to schools and conferences in three separate divisions. The most competitively elite division is Division I, which for football is further divided into the Football Bowl Subdivision (FBS) with 120 member institutions, and the 122 member Football Championship Subdivision (FCS). The FBS programs have post-season opportunities outside of the NCAA structure and the highest financial aid allocations to players. Division II schools offer some athletically related financial aid, and Division III offers no athletically related financial aid to its participants. According to the NCAA, 'each division creates its own rules governing personnel, amateurism, recruiting, eligibility, benefits, financial aid, and playing and practice seasons – consistent with the overall governing principles of the Association' (NCAA, 2012). All three divisions share the same mission, 'to be an integral part of higher education and to focus on the development of our student-athletes' (About the NCAA, 2012).

The NCAA is led by the President, and supported by a Chief Operating Officer (COO) and Vice Presidents assigned by functional area. The NCAA President reports to the Executive Committee, a board responsible for association-wide policy and budget oversight. A presidential group leads each of the three divisions: the Division I Board of Directors, the Division II Presidents Council and the Division III Presidents Council. An extensive committee structure functions with representatives from member institutions including athletics department personnel, faculty representatives, and student athletes. These committees make recommendations to the leadership groups in each division. In addition to conducting 89 national championships in 23 sports, the NCAA focuses its efforts on eligibility and rules enforcement in an attempt to maintain a level playing field.

The NCAA is by far the largest and most influential governing body for college football with over 1000 member institutions. Two other governing bodies work in parallel to the NCAA. The National Association of Intercollegiate Athletics (NAIA) has slightly fewer than 300 member institutions and provides 23 national championships in 13 sports. Athletic scholarships are available to NAIA athletes. Similarly, the National Junior College Athletics Association (NJCAA) provides athletic opportunities to teams from two-year junior colleges. Like the

NCAA and the NAIA, the NJCAA monitors eligibility, enforces rules, provides championships, and sets policies for its conferences and 525 member institutions.

High school football

The sport of tackle football is the most popular high school sport for boys, with nearly 1.1 million participants (NFSH, 2012). Due to the federalist system of American government, high school football programmes are governed first and foremost by their local school district. Typically, the school districts within a state also affiliate to a state athletics league. For example, high schools in Austin, Texas are part of the Austin Independent Schools District (AISD). The AISD as well as the other school districts in the state, compete within the University Interscholastic League (UIL). The UIL administers regional and state championships in 14 sports. It creates regional alignments, administers and enforces rules and eligibility requirements, trains coaches and game officials, and sets policies regarding all aspects of the game and competitions. The UIL is the largest inter-school organisation of its kind in the world. It is one example of a governance structure for high school football, but each state has its own organisation with its own mission and priorities. Most, but not all, of these state organisations are affiliated with the National Federation of State High School Associations (NFSH). Although the NFSH has no direct governance over high school football (or any other sport), it provides a standardised rulebook, keeps records and statistics, as well as providing extensive training for coaches and officials. Despite the NFSH's efforts at standardisation, there is not even common agreement about the number of players on the field at any one time (see Table 2.1). While the most common version is 11 v 11 tackle football, there are also 6 v 6, 8 v 8, and 9 v 9 versions of the game played in some states.

Although there are clearly differences in the mission, goals, and implementation of elite tackle football programmes in the U.S., the sport is universally developed through the schools. Players supplement their skills through participation in camps and clinics offered by university football programmes, private, and not-for-profit organisations, including USA Football. The pathway to the NFL runs clearly through the high schools and universities. The picture gets murkier at the developmental levels of the game.

Table 2.1 Participation rates for high school football 2011–2012

Sport	Boys	Girls	Total
Tackle football			
11-player	1,095,993	1,604	1,097,597
6-player	4,427	1	4,428
8-player	16,326	200	16,526
9-player	4,998	0	4,998
Flag football	251	6,260	6,511
	1,121,995	8,065	1,130,060

Youth and recreational football

More than three million youth aged 7–14 play organised tackle football in leagues across the United States (USA Football, 2010). Nearly all of these leagues are governed and administered at the community sport level. There are a few national-level organisations responsible for youth football, most notably Pop Warner Little Scholars (established in 1929) and American Youth Football (established in 1996), but even these organisations are thought to control only about 15 per cent of the youth football programmes across the country. The rest are governed by local community organisations. Each organisation determines its own eligibility requirements, sets its own rules, sanctions play, and trains its own coaches and officials. Some determine eligibility by weight, some by age, and some by age and weight combined. Some organisations have regulations concerning minimum playing time requirements; others do not.

But tackle football programmes are not the only game in town. Flag and touch football programmes are offered by local, state, and national sport organisations of all kinds.

The variety of flag football programmes is even more diverse than that of tackle programmes. Flag football programmes vary in terms of the number of players (i.e., 9 v 9, 8 v 8, 7 v 7), the amount of contact allowed (no contact, full blocking allowed, no downfield blocking), and who is eligible as a receiver (all players eligible, linemen ineligible). Unlike tackle football, it is common to find co-ed flag football teams. The rules and policies change from programme to programme. At the youth level, flag football is considered an appropriate introduction to the game and a way to develop skills and understand strategies with less risk of injury than the tackle version of the game. However, once a player enters high school, flag football is perceived by many to be a lesser version of the game. Still, it is a popular sport for university students and adults of all ages.

Youth flag football programmes are offered by local youth sport organisations and recreation departments. Numerous local and regional bodies have adopted NFL flag for their youth programmes. NFL flag is an increasingly popular version of the game, serving young people from 5–17 years of age. However, most leagues fail to attract high-school-age players. Instead, these leagues serve as development leagues for young boys. Most of them go on to transition to tackle programmes as they get older. The youngest leagues are often co-ed. As a result, girls have been picking up the sport and now seek out opportunities to keep playing. The NFL has responded by championing girls' flag football programmes in junior high and high schools. Although the number of programmes is still small, it is growing. In fact, the state of Florida now hosts state high school championships in girls' flag football.

Colleges and universities offer intramural flag football leagues to students via campus recreation services. These are indirectly governed by the National Intramural-Recreational Sport Association (NIRSA). NIRSA produces rules, monitors eligibility, provides training materials for football officials, and sanctions regional and national flag football competitions. Outside of colleges and universities, flag football has become a popular recreational sport for adults. It is a common offering by parks and recreation departments, sport and social clubs, and has developed a number of parallel governing bodies for the sport. The U.S. Flag and Touch League sanctions leagues, tournaments, and national championships. The United States Flag Football Association also sanctions leagues, tournaments, and national championships. Yet they play under dramatically different rules and offer parallel and competing national championship opportunities.

The need for coordination

Traditionally, the purpose of national governing bodies is to develop the sport. This encompasses the dual task of developing participation in the sport while also enhancing the competitive excellence of its players and teams. In practice, this usually results in an emphasis, both financially and programmatically, on the elite side of the sport. NGBs usually support a national team programme, select and manage teams for international competitions, and run national championships. USA Football, due to its late entry into the sport and its close relationship to the NFL and NFLPA, has positioned itself to serve the development side of the sport and has developed an extensive group of loosely affiliated partners (see Figure 2.2). Like most NGBs, it selects and supports national teams, but its main focus is on youth. This is clearly reflected in the mission statement: 'USA Football, the sport's national governing body, leads the game's development, inspires participation and ensures a positive experience for all youth and amateur players' (USA Football, 2012a). They go further, explaining that USA Football 'Creates innovative educational resources for commissioners, coaches, players, parents and game officials; authors unified rules, standards and best practices; conducts research relative to youth and amateur football; and fields national teams for international competition' (USA Football, 2012a).

The NFL and NCAA are powerful stakeholders in elite-level football. In point of fact, the pathway from college to professional football is the clearest and most coordinated part of the development system. Consequently, there is little need for development assistance from USA Football at this level. Why, then, would the NFL invest in USA Football?

USA Football explains its partnership with the NFL and NFLPA this way: 'this partnership allows the NFL, its 32 teams and the NFLPA to focus on fan development while utilising USA Football's expertise in developing youth football players and coaches' (USA Football, 2012b). Yet this is only a partial picture. In an address at Georgetown University in 2004, then Commissioner Paul Tagliabue discussed challenges facing the sustained development of the NFL: (1) the need to maintain the public's respect for those involved in the game; (2) loss of traditional geographic sources of playing talent related to the loss of blue-collar jobs that necessitates making the game more attractive to young people; (3) an increase in women's sports that has created a more crowded sport marketplace; and (4) globalisation and the need to expand uniquely national sports to the global community (Tagliabue, 2004). USA Football is part of the NFL's strategies to overcome each of these challenges.

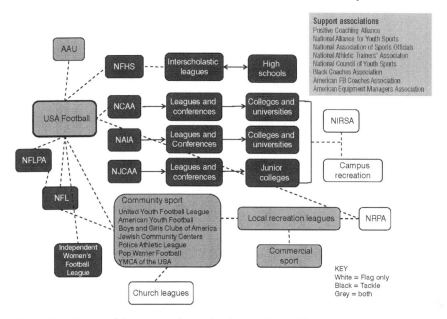

Figure 2.2 Sectors of the game and associated governing bodies

As the official youth development partner of the NFL, USA Football provides the NFL with a positive image in the communities. The emphasis on youth development and education, along with their status as the national governing body brings with it a level of respect and legitimacy that can transfer to their NFL partner. Making the game fun and 'inspiring participation' are key elements of the mission of USA Football. Unlike many other football organisations, USA Football works to develop the women's game as well as the men's. They are highly involved with NFL Flag's push to get girls' flag football into the schools as a varsity sport, and have even funded a study examining ways to promote girls' participation in the sport. Along with the national team programmes, USA Football provides significant support to the women's game. These three elements are all designed to support players. At the same time, they create positive perceptions and an affinity for football that can build fanship for the NFL and its teams domestically. The fourth challenge, globalisation, is not traditionally the purview of an NGB but football has been a uniquely American sport. The diffusion of the sport has often followed the U.S. military to other countries, yet there was no international governance of the sport until 1998. USA Football has been instrumental in the development of American football internationally, and currently shares its educational materials with the International Federation of American Football (IFAF) members via the IFAF website. It hosts the annual International Bowl, which pits the U-19 US National Team against a world all-star team, and has hosted development camps and the U-19 World Championship. In short, USA Football is doing its part to develop interest, participation, and fanship in the sport worldwide.

International participation, national teams, and women's participation have been a natural platform for USA Football to assert itself into the governance landscape. These areas were not well served by existing football organisations. The youth market, on the other hand, has thrived without any real governance. The intense fragmentation of youth football development is the biggest challenge to a coordinated development system for football in the United States. Football has been played in American communities for many decades. Some of the football organisations have been in place for decades as well. Yet USA Football has just a brief ten-year history as a national governing body. Like many American NGBs it has low brand awareness and competes with the more firmly entrenched organisations governing school and professional football. In short, many players (and their parents) either aren't aware of USA Football or don't understand its relevance. Without institutional legitimacy or formal linkages to existing youth football organisations, USA Football has had to create and communicate its value to these organisations.

They have done that in two ways: (1) providing practical assistance to leagues, which opens a line of communication and establishes a positive relationship, and (2) establishing themselves as the premier organisation for football knowledge, including coaching, officiating, injury prevention, player development, and football related scientific research.

In this way, USA Football has been able to develop relationships with community football programmes across the country. They assist them with player safety, background checks, insurance, league websites, even fundraising. With the help of the NFL, they have been able to distribute equipment to leagues as well. These are attractive elements to community league commissioners. As leagues affiliate with USA Football, they are required to educate their coaches through the coaching education programme. Coach education and training materials provided to all USA Football members communicate and socialise administrators, coaches and players into the core values of USA Football. Most notably, this enables them to diffuse the Player Progression Development Model – the beginnings of a more coordinated system of development governed by USA Football.

In summary, USA Football has established itself as a valued and relevant governing body for youth football development in the United States in a very short time period. While there is still fragmentation in programme delivery, USA Football is increasingly seen as the established provider of science based expertise in player and league development. Partnerships with numerous established football providers, most notably the NFL and NFLPA, have facilitated the emergence of USA Football as an accepted national governing body for the development side of the sport. There is still work to do to develop its presence on the elite side of the sport.

Summary

American sport governance is characterised by a laissez-faire or hands-off philosophy in which the government does nothing to assert itself into the governance of sport. Consequently, sport governance is a function of numerous parallel systems, each claiming governance over part of their sport (or sports). This system creates chaos for an athlete trying to move through a development pathway to become an elite athlete, and results in serious coordination issues among the self-proclaimed sport governing bodies. Loosely formed partnerships, often based on personal relationships, are a key coordination strategy. Newer governing bodies, like USA Football, are working toward creation of a more coordinated system by standardising rules and disseminating best practice based on scientific research. However, many governing bodies are in competition with one another for resources, including athletes. Thus far, they have little incentive to coordinate.

Review questions

1   What is the key legislation affecting American sport governance? Discuss the passage of this act in relationship to American federalism.
2   Choose a sport. Using Figure 2.1 or 2.2, identify the pathway to excellence. How many pathways could get you to the same place? Why?
3   What are the strengths and weaknesses of a loosely coordinated governance system?

Further reading

Ganz, H.L., & Kesler, J.L. (2001). *Understanding business and legal aspects of the sports industry*. New York: Practicing Law Institute.
Gerston, L.N. (2007). *American federalism: A concise introduction*. Armonk, NY: M.E. Sharpe.
Overman, S.J. (2011). *The Protestant ethic and the spirit of sport: How Calvinism and capitalism shaped America's games*. Macon, GA: Mercer University Press.
Smith, R.A. (2011). *Pay for play: A history of big-time college athletic reform*. Urbana, IL: University of Illinois Press.

Websites

National Governing Body for Youth Football Development: www.USAFootball.com
National Collegiate Athletics Association: www.ncaa.org
NFL Flag Football: www.nflflag.com
Official website for the oldest youth football program in America: www.popwarner.com

References

Bellia, A.J. (2011). *Federalism*. Austin, TX: Wolters Kluwer Law & Business.
Bowers, M.T., & Hunt, T.M. (2011). The President's Council on Physical Fitness and the systematization of children's play in America. *International Journal of the History of Sport*, 28, 1496–511.
Bowers, M.T., Chalip, L., & Green, B.C. (2011a). Sport participation under laissez-faire policy: The case of the United States. In M. Nicholson, R. Hoye, & B. Houlihan (eds),

Participation in sport: International policy perspectives (pp.254–67). Abingdon: Routledge.

Bowers, M.T., Chalip, L., & Green, B.C. (2011b). Beyond the façade: Youth sport development in the United States and the illusion of synergy. In B. Houlihan and M. Green (eds), *Routledge handbook of sports development* (pp.173–83). Abingdon: Routledge.

Chalip, L., Johnson, A., & Stachura, L. (1996). *National sports policies: An international handbook.* Westport, CT: Greenwood Press.

Coakley, J.J. (2002). Using sport to control deviance and violence among youths: Let's be critical and cautious. In M. Gantz, M.A. Messner, & S.J. Ball-Rokeach (eds), *Paradoxes of youth and sport* (pp.13–30). Albany, NY: State University of New York Press.

Duquette, J.J. (1999). *Regulating the national pastime: Baseball and antitrust.* Westport, CT: Praeger.

International Monetary Fund. (2012). World economic outlook database. Available online at http://www.imf.org/external/pubs/ft/weo/2012/02/weodata/download.aspx

Koppett, L. (1994). *Sports illusion, sports reality.* Urbana, IL: University of Illinois Press.

NCAA (2012). About the NCAA. Available online at http://www.ncaa.org/wps/wcm/connect/public/ncaa/about+the+ncaa

NFL (2012). Values. Available online at http://www.nfl.com/careers/values

NFSH (2012). 2011–12 high school athletics participation survey. Available online at http://www.nfhs.org/content.aspx?id=3282

Physical Activity Council (2012). *Participation report.* Available online at http://www.physicalactivitycouncil.com/PDFs/2012PacReport.pdf.

Robertson, D.B. (2012). *Federalism and the making of America.* New York: Routledge.

Sparvero, E., Chalip, L., & Green, B.C. (2008). The United States. In B. Houlihan & M. Green (eds), *Comparative elite sport development.* Oxford: Butterworth-Heinemann.

Sports Business Daily (2009). ESPN Sports poll: Pro football remains most popular spectator sport. *Sports Business Daily*, 15(213) , July 24. Available online at http://www.sportsbusinessdaily.com/Daily/Issues/2009/07/Issue-213/The-Back-Of-The-Book/ESPN-Sports-Poll-Pro-Football-Remains-Most-Popular-Spectator-Sport.aspx

Tagliabue, P. (2004). *The business of football.* Executive Policy Seminar Series. Washington, DC: Georgetown University. Available online at http://faculty.msb.edu/prog/cmrc/seminars/TagliabueAddress.pdf.

USA Football (2010). *Partnership opportunities.* Available online at http://www2.usafootball.com/pdfs/USA_Football_Sponsorship.pdf

USA Football (2012a). *Partnership opportunities.* Available online at http://www2.usafootball.com/pdfs/USA_Football_Sponsorship.pdf.

USA Football (2012b). About USA Football. Available online at http://usafootball.com/about?context=about

3   Australia

David Shilbury

Topics

- Federation and Australia's political system
- Australia's traditional sports structure
- Federal model of governance
- Delegate system of governance
- Professionalisation of sport
- Hybrid model of governance
- Collaborative governance theory.

Objectives

- To introduce Australia's federal form of government
- To establish a link between Australia's federal form of government and sport governance systems and structures
- To demonstrate the role and impact of the delegate system of governance in Australian sport organisations
- To demonstrate the link between the professionalisation of sport and sport governance
- To examine alternative governance models
- To introduce collaborative governance theory and its importance in a federal governance structure.

Key terms

Federation   The creation of Australia on 1 January, 1901, as an independent nation via the Commonwealth of Australia Act passed by the British Parliament.

Federal system of governance   Powers are divided between a national governing body and separate state associations.

Delegate system   Nominated delegates by a state association or club to a decision-making body, such as a national sport organisation, to represent the views of the state association.

Board of directors   Appointed or elected officials charged with steering an organisation to achieve its charter.

Independent board of directors   Directors elected without affiliation to any other state or regional sport organisation, and therefore not elected to represent any specific constituent group.

Hybrid model of governance   Board of directors with a mix of delegates appointed by state associations and independently elected directors.

Collaborative governance theory   A form of collective decision-making based on consensus seeking and negotiation and well suited to federal governance structures.

Institutional theory   Focused on the social structures of an organisation and how they have been embedded within an organisation and how those social structures influence social behaviour.

Resource dependence theory   Organisations are recognised as open systems and are reliant on other organisations for resources and must, therefore, learn to adapt to maintain resource acquisition for survival.

Stakeholder theory   Organisations need to take account of the range of organisations and individuals affected by the work of an organisation.

Inter-organisational relationship theory   Forming of partnerships and relationships, collaboration and coordination between organisations.

Network theory   Complex web of interrelationships between stakeholders, each with varying power.

Overview

This chapter contains a general overview of sport governance in Australia with a specific focus on the challenges confronting federal models of governance. The chapter will examine the major structural issues associated with a federal model of governance, and the current changes occurring within Australian sport in response to these structural barriers. Trends influencing contemporary sport governance relevant to the Australian context are also explored. Cricket Australia is used as a case study to highlight the difficulties of change from traditional delegate/federated models of governance to other structural forms.

Background

Australia, as a nation, collectively comes alive on 26 December every year as it celebrates two of its great sporting traditions. Following traditional Christmas Day celebrations with family and friends, Australians turn their attention to the Boxing Day public holiday where sport assumes prominence. Two great sporting events commence on Boxing Day: the Sydney to Hobart yacht race and Test Match Cricket at the Melbourne Cricket Ground (MCG). Both sports, in varying ways, illustrate what defines Australia during the summer months. The beach- and water-based activities generally, together with cricket, assume an iconic role in the fabric of an Australian summer and both signal the arrival of the summer holiday season. Cricket, in particular, captures Australian heritage through the Boxing Day 'Ashes' Test Match at the MCG. An Ashes Test Match is played between arch cricket rivals England and Australia. It involves five full days of intense cricket with both countries seeking to assert dominance over the other. One slip in concentration during any one of the three two-hour sessions during each day of the match can see the other country gain the upper hand. Ultimately, bragging rights go to the winner, as has traditionally been the case in all matters relating to sporting contests between England and Australia.

The reasons for this rivalry can be traced back to Australia's origins: 'in May 1787, 11 British ships, known as the First Fleet, set sail from Portsmouth, England, for New South Wales. Ostensibly, the 1500 people aboard, including 759 convicts, were sent to establish a penal settlement' (Deane, 2011, p.39). This penal settlement was the genesis from which the Commonwealth of Australia was created. On 1 January 1901, some 114 years after the First Fleet set out from Portsmouth, the British Parliament passed the Commonwealth of Australia Act, which recognised six colonies and allowed each to govern in their own right. Although federation of these colonies meant that Australia became an independent nation, it did so as part of a constitutional monarchy with the king or queen of England as head of state. To this day, some commentators note the need for Australia as a nation, and Australians generally, to prove themselves of worth to England. No better example of this rivalry can be found than at the MCG on a Boxing Day morning where England is scheduled to commence a test match against Australia.

The original six colonies remain in place, although they are now referred to as states, and include New South Wales, Victoria, South Australia, Tasmania, Queensland and Western Australia. Together with two recognised territories, the Northern Territory and the Australian Capital Territory (home of Australia's capital city – Canberra), these regions form the structural backbone of the constitution and division of power throughout Australia. The birth of the Commonwealth of Australia on 1 January, 1901, is typically referred to as 'federation' because a federal system of governance was created. Under this system, powers are divided between the states and the commonwealth government. For example, defence, taxation and foreign affairs are commonwealth government responsibilities; police, education, public transport and hospitals were enshrined as powers belonging to each state. Consequently, Australia is governed with a curious mix of common law applicable across the nation, yet distinctive and differing law from state to state. Ambiguities also occur from time to time in determining what is, or is not, a federal or state government responsibility. This being the case, from a sport governance perspective, it is no wonder that Australian sporting organisations confront exactly the same dilemma in determining the responsibilities of national governing bodies in relation to its constituted state governing bodies.

This background to Australia's political system is important because sport has been governed in Australia as a mirror image of the federal system. That is, sport has grown from the bottom up and, as it has done so, it has 'grown' the arms of sport governance over many years. Figure 3.1 illustrates the traditional sport system in Australia. Typically, the organisation of sport grew from the community. Essentially, a group of people within a local area shared a common desire to play a specific sport. In due course, this desire transforms into organised structures, in

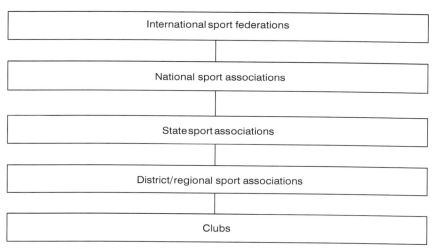

Figure 3.1 Traditional sport structure

that there must be other teams to play against, a fixture needs to be arranged to organise some form of competition, and there must be agreement on the rules of competition. On top of this is the need for facilities, approval to use the facilities, recording of results, and so the list of administrative tasks grows. Eventually, clubs in a local region wish to identify their best players and compete against other regions, and then the best in the state are selected to play against other states culminating in Australia wanting to identify its best talent and compete against other countries, as is the case in test cricket against England. As each level evolved, as shown in Figure 3.1, administrative and governance arrangements were required.

Figure 3.1 also provides direction on how Australia's infamous delegate system of governance evolved. As groups of willing administrators became involved in the organisation of sporting contests, decisions were required on a raft of matters relating to playing conditions, cost of entry, equipment, facilities and rules, to name but a few. As a region or association was created, typically, it was established by sending one or two delegates to a meeting to consider all these and other matters. The same applied as state associations were formed. Delegates were nominated from the level below to represent the local associations or the constituent clubs.

Finally, the same delegate system was enshrined as national sport organisations were formed to represent the national interests of the sport, and significantly coordinate the elite participation of athletes in national teams. The case study in the second half of this chapter deals specifically with cricket, and describes how the Australian Board of Control was established in 1905. The Board of Control was composed of its member associations, all of which, like the states in Australia, were established as separate legal entities. The founding member states were New South Wales, Victoria and South Australia, and, as founding members, each association was entitled to three delegates representing it as part of the board of directors of what we now know as Cricket Australia. Subsequent to the formation of the Board of Control in 1905 by the three foundation member associations, Queensland and Western Australia joined the Board of Control and were allowed two delegates each, with Tasmania, the most recent affiliate granted one delegate. These 14 delegates compose the board of directors and, as such, govern cricket in Australia.

Typically, delegates nominated by member associations are actively involved in cricket matters in their respective states. A single delegate, therefore, will be a board member of Cricket Australia, a board member of the state association, and quite possibly a board member of their local cricket club affiliated with the state association. This is formally known as the delegate system of governance, and has been the cornerstone of sport governance in Australia.

Combined with the previously described federal system of governance, sport governance in Australia has been described as cumbersome, and replete with self-interest. Control has also been a source of great concern. Remembering that the system was built from the community up, control has always resided with the level below in terms of decision-making and governance. For example, a national sport organisation wishing to change its constitution, or make simple decisions about policy across the sport, requires the issues to be debated at national level and sent back to the member associations for further debate before instructing delegates how to vote. Typically, this debate ebbs and flows between national and state boards for some time before an outcome is achieved. When an outcome is likely, or the debate over, often the instruction on how to vote on behalf of a state association is based on how the decision would affect a respective state rather than what is in the best interests of the sport. Consequently, an entrenched cycle has emerged.

The delegate system does, however, represent a form of 'pure' democracy in which constituents are involved in the debate and decision-making processes. Moreover, the sport system in Australia has traditionally been driven by volunteers, and the nature of the delegate system was suited to volunteers becoming involved in sporting organisations as part of their leisure time. This pattern of governance, and volunteer involvement dominated Australian sport during the nineteenth century and the greater part of the twentieth century. By the 1980s, Australian sport commenced a metamorphosis that continues today, largely as the result of the commercialisation, professionalisation and bureaucratisation of the sector.

Contemporary sport governance

Volunteer involvement in the administration of sport has been vital and it was this involvement that sustained sport until the 1980s. By the 1980s, pressure was building in response to increasing commercial interests. In other words, television broadcasting, and the money to be garnered from granting the rights to broadcast sports such as cricket, the Australian Football League (AFL), tennis, golf, rugby league and motor sports, injected new demands into a system that was largely reliant on the goodwill of volunteers. These commercial imperatives were further driven by the players, who, in the 1970s and 1980s, began to demand greater compensation for their efforts.

The fabric of Australian sport was turned on its head in 1977 when Kerry Packer, a media magnate, enticed Australia's leading cricketers to join a breakaway 'rebel' competition to form World Series Cricket. As a result, cricket warfare erupted, with the Australian Cricket Board (ACB) having to fight to protect its right to be the sole custodian for cricket in Australia. Players from around the world joined World Series Cricket so that an Australian team could play against the best the world had to offer in a series of Super Tests and, significantly, in one-day cricket matches that would ultimately redefine the economics of the sport. Packer was able to entice the players away from the established cricket competitions because players were unhappy with their remuneration as the demands on them to play and train increased. In essence, the forces of professionalisation began to sweep across the sporting landscape in the late 1970s and 1980s. Packer's dispute with the ACB related to broadcast rights, with the ACB committed to renewing the Australian Broadcasting Corporation's long-standing contract to televise cricket, despite Packer's Nine Network offering more money. Eventually, in May 1979, Packer through his Nine Network, gained the exclusive rights to broadcast international cricket throughout Australia. The Packer revolution had a huge effect on the sport's administrative arrangements and the economics of sport management generally.

Although it was the cricket revolution that changed the commercial dynamics of contemporary sport in Australia, it was the Victorian Football League (VFL) that reacted first by changing the governance arrangements of its Victorian competition. In the mid-1980s, the VFL was a local suburban competition with 12 teams. It was also the premier football league in the country with the ability to entice footballers from other states of Australia to play in the VFL. Player payments and the opportunity to compete against the best provided the main reasons for relocation. But, by the mid-1980s, with player payments ballooning relative to the income generated, and overall club costs rising, the VFL recognised that its clubs were struggling financially. Until 1984, VFL governance was also based on a delegate system, where one delegate from each of the 12 clubs composed the board of the VFL. This structure, as previously described, vested power with the clubs rather than the governing body. Consequently, when the VFL began to recognise the signs of an ailing competition, it was somewhat powerless to do anything because the power resided with the clubs. This is in direct contrast to the situation in a reasonably large corporation, whose board could quite quickly direct changes to strategy to militate against changing circumstances.

This nexus was broken in 1985 when the VFL released a report entitled *Establishing the Basis for Future Success*, which was the blueprint for restoring the fortunes of football in Victoria and, as has been seen, throughout Australia (Victorian Football League, 1985). This report was the catalyst for the expansion of the VFL competition beyond Victoria, with the South Melbourne Football Club having relocated to Sydney in 1983, followed by new clubs from outside Victoria joining the competition in 1987, 1991, 1997, 2011 and 2012. Although a downturn in the financial fortunes of the clubs and, in turn, the governing body was the primary reason for the report, the need to change the governance and decision-making structures associated with the VFL was the paramount reason. Without the power to control the destiny of the sport in an increasingly commercialised environment, coupled with spiralling player payments, and the demands on footballers to professionalise, the VFL had little chance of positioning the sport to capitalise on its popularity.

The VFL report recommended the adoption of an independent commission which, in the context of sport governance in Australia, was a radical change. The appointment of independent commissioners meant that the board governing the VFL was composed of people who had no direct involvement with the constituent clubs, or state associations. In other words, they were to represent the best interest of the sport, rather than be bound by a duty to represent any one club or state association. This allowed the commissioners to focus on the major roles of a board of directors, which include monitoring overall performance of the organisation, ensuring conformance to legal and fiduciary matters, determining policy, and overseeing the operations of the sport through the CEO. From this point forward, the VFL, which was renamed the Australian Football League (AFL) (and also became the national sport organisation) in 1990, was to become the benchmark in sport governance terms. Very few sports have been able to make the change from the delegate system of governance, with those elected to board positions reluctant to vote themselves out of office. The most viable means national governing bodies have been able to use to extract themselves from the confines of a delegate system, has been via a hybrid model of sport governance.

Hybrid model of sport governance

In 1990, Basketball Australia was one of the first sports to adopt a hybrid model of governance. The hybrid model is largely a 'halfway house' between a delegate system of governance and a fully independent board. The term 'halfway house' is used because, over time, it is likely that sports using a hybrid model will slowly gravitate to a fully independent board, where the constituents have the right to elect board members, but the directors are not representing any member association or club, and are not involved as a director of those associations or clubs.

In a hybrid model, approximately half of the board members are either nominated as delegates by constituent members or elected by the member associations. The remaining positions on the board are filled by independent directors. Those directors may be elected by member associations or clubs, or specifically invited to fill vacancies as independent directors. The advantage of the second method of appointment is that a board can evaluate the range of skills and knowledge currently available to it through its elected members, and seek to add the skills and knowledge it may be missing. This option is less viable where the independent directors are elected by the constituents.

Many variations of the hybrid model exist, but the main principle of this approach is to combine member association representatives with non-member-affiliated directors for the purposes of achieving more independent and 'whole of sport' decision-making. Some hybrid models are composed of delegates, nominated by member associations, who remain representatives of the member association; others remove the alignment between delegate and member association. Bowls Australia (BA), for example, has recently updated its constitution and the composition of its board of directors. The BA board is composed of up to nine directors, of which six are elected by the members which, in this case, are the state associations. Note that the number six equals the number of states in Australia, in other words the member associations. The elected directors are not able to hold a position as an employee of BA or a member state, nor hold a position as a director of a member state. In addition to the elected directors, 'the board may themselves appoint up to three other directors because of their special business acumen and/ or technical skills' (Bowls Australia, 2012, p.29).

This form of hybrid model is closer to a genuinely independent model because the six elected directors are not delegates of the member states, and are specifically not able to hold director positions with a state member association. Entrenched state positions should, therefore, not influence the six elected directors in their decision making and governance role with BA. Given their experiences in bowls in their respective states, these directors should have working knowledge of the bowls community which allows them to bring a variety of views and perspectives to the board when charting the course for bowls in Australia. Regardless of the benefits of the hybrid model, in terms of the composition of the BA Board, the stumbling block in this model remains the federal structure where the member states are legal entities in their own right with their own board of directors. It does not always follow that the strategic direction of a member association is consistent with the strategic direction mapped out by the national sport organisation. This has obvious implications for governance and a 'whole of sport' approach. As long as a federal model exists, there is a need to think about how collaborative forms of governance can help overcome the inherent weaknesses of the federal model.

Collaborative governance theory

In a search for theoretical perspectives that shed light on the federated nature of sport governance, stakeholder theory (Hung, 1998; Oliver, 1990), institutional theory (Hoye & Cuskelly, 2007), resource dependence theory (Ferkins & Shilbury, 2010; Pfeffer & Salancik, 1978), inter-organisational relationships (Dickson, Arnold & Chalip, 2005), and network theory (Henry & Lee, 2004; Kooiman, 1993) have emerged as important theories through which sport governance can be investigated. Network theory and the construct of inter-organisational relationships are considered particularly insightful for examining federal governance structures. In relation to structure, Lynn, Heinrich, and Hill (2000) contend that governance 'generally refers to the means for achieving direction, control, and coordination of wholly or partially autonomous individuals or organisations on behalf of interests to which they jointly contribute' (p.255).

This definition is particularly relevant to sport governance in Australia, with sport organisations such as Bowls Australia, Netball Australia, Swimming

Australia and others all grappling with the challenge of providing direction and coordinating wholly or partially autonomous organisations, in the form of state associations. In reality, this complex network of structures, which extends to local associations and regions linked with each sport, requires a more collaborative approach to governance. According to Ansell and Gash (2008), collaborative governance is a governing arrangement between organisations where agencies engage in a 'collective decision-making process that is formal, consensus-orientated, and deliberative and that aims to make or implement public policy or manage public programs or assets' (p.544).

How this works is succinctly summarised by Henry and Lee (2004, p. 29) when highlighting the implications of systemic governance structures.

> First, it is clear that in such a context, a significant policy change can only be achieved by negotiation and/or trade-off between various parties in the network. Second, governing bodies of sport in such contexts no longer govern, or wholly control, their sport, or at least if they do, they do so by virtue of their ability to negotiate outcomes rather than dictating those outcomes to passive recipients of their message. Third, this has implications not only for the organisations but also for the skills required of the people who work within them. The skills are much more those of negotiation and mutual adjustment than of rational, ordered planning and control.

The exceptions to the above description provided by Henry and Lee are those national sport organisations that generate substantial revenues through their sport's operations. The AFL is perhaps the best example of this in Australia. Through its management of the AFL competition, sufficient revenues are generated from broadcast rights, sponsorship and ticket sales to ensure the players are well paid, the spectators watch games in first-class facilities, and that there is enough money available to promote the sport through well-crafted sport development plans. In other words, the AFL, in governance terms, needs to be less concerned with collaborative arrangements because they distribute the resources that the states require to fulfil their charters and that are aligned with an overall strategic direction for the sport. In this example, the resource distribution approach has led to a steady dismantling of the federal structure, with AFL New South Wales, AFL Queensland and, significantly AFL Victoria, all now state offices of the AFL rather than being granted, or retaining status, as a legally incorporated state association.

The majority of sport organisations in Australia, however, have not arrived at this point in terms of their governance structures. Therefore, collaborative governance theory remains important as a means to better understanding how sport organisations in a federal structure can fulfil their governance role. Notwithstanding the implementation of a hybrid model, or a genuine independent board for that matter, a network of state associations may still prevail, requiring deft skill to coordinate wholly or partially autonomous organisations on behalf of interests to which they jointly contribute.

Case study: Good governance at Cricket Australia

> Cricket has lost a generation in Australia and the Big Bash League (BBL) –
> replacing the Twenty20 Big Bash – is the answer says Cricket Australia's
> (CA) general manager of cricket marketing services, Mike McKenna.
> 'Cricket has traditionally always been Australia's favourite sport but, with a
> change in society and people having more entertainment options, we found it
> wasn't connecting as well with new generations as it had in the past'.
>
> (Ridley, 2011, p.24)

The BBL made its debut in December 2011, following the announcement of
the new concept in October 2010. The BBL consists of eight teams with 28 regular
season matches played in the summer holiday season commencing just prior to
Christmas and concluding in late January. Owned, controlled and managed by CA,
this was not always going to be the case, with CA seriously considering private
investment in each of its franchises. The projected level of investment fell short
of total control, with CA mooting a 49 per cent ceiling on private ownership to
ensure control remained with CA and the state associations. According to Ridley
(2011), offers of US$15 million each from Indian backers for stakes in the Sydney
Thunderbirds and Melbourne Renegades were nowhere near CA's valuation of
US$50 million for a 49 per cent stake in each franchise.

Ultimately, the BBL was established not only to reconnect with a new generation
of Australians, but as another viable product capable of generating substantial
revenues for a sport steeped in history and the traditions associated with the long
forms of the game. As McKenna stated, 'We are not hampered by the baggage
of the last 100 years of evolution. We've got a chance to start again, which is
pretty rare in the world of sport' (Ridley, 2011, p.25). One can only wonder what
the foundation delegates to the newly formed Board of Control in 1905 would
make of the directions cricket has taken in the twenty-first century to position the
sport in a rapidly changing Australian society – a society heavily influenced by
social media and instant gratification through shorter, impact-oriented recreation
and leisure options. The prospect of private ownership would likely see the
nine foundation delegates turn in their graves. To this day, CA is governed by
14 directors, each nominated by their respective state associations. As indicated
earlier in this chapter, New South Wales, Victoria and South Australia, as the
foundation member associations, are each represented by three delegates, with
Western Australia and Queensland two delegates, and Tasmania one delegate.

Cricket, after all, is a sport owned by no one, yet metaphorically owned by all
Australians. For all of its 100-plus years, the sport has been governed by volunteers
committed to maintaining cricket as the country's preeminent summer sport and,
of course, ensuring it continued to foster talent capable of beating England in the
biennial battle for the Ashes. Yet, here was CA, itself still governed by a group
of 14 delegates nominated by the states, seriously considering 'selling off' some
of its new properties in the form of part-private investment in BBL franchises.
Private ownership, or part-private ownership, brings with it forms of corporate style
governance not normally associated with the governance of cricket in Australia.

This paradox was further compounded by the review of cricket governance in 2011. Undertaken by corporate doctors, David Crawford and Colin Carter, at the invitation of CA, their remit was to:

> Review the governance structure of Australian cricket which essentially means the role and composition of the Board, and its relationship with the various State cricket organisations. The intention of this review was to ensure Australian cricket, and in particular Cricket Australia and its constituent State members, have a governance structure to create an environment for correct and efficient decision-making so that Australian cricket maximises its ability to administer the game of cricket in the best interest of all its stakeholders (p. 35).

Specifically, the terms of reference were to review:

1 The Memorandum of Association and the Constitution and By-Laws of Cricket Australia to ensure Australian cricket has a decision-making process and lines of authority/decision-making to enable Australian cricket to obtain the maximum benefit to cricket and all its stakeholders.
2 The composition of the Cricket Australia Board and the process of election of members of the Board so that the Board can act in the best interest of Australian cricket whilst at all times being conscious of the need to protect the interest of the members of Cricket Australia (i.e., the State Associations) and other relevant stakeholders
3 The roles and responsibilities of Cricket Australia, its Board, CEO and Management and the role and responsibilities of the member States in Australian cricket.

> (Crawford and Carter, 2011, p.35)

The purpose of the review, as had been the case in the AFL and other sports, was to find a mechanism to rid cricket of its traditional delegate system of governance. If successful, this would be part of a solution to identify and apply best-practice governance in Australia's iconic summer sport. This solution would, of course, only be a part solution as it was unlikely that such a review could change the federal structures associated with cricket. That proved to be the case.

In reviewing the main thrust of meetings with stakeholders and observing that an independent, skills-based board is the future for CA, the report noted:

> In many of our meetings, it was often described as the 'AFL Model', but this is a misunderstanding. Twenty years ago the AFL simply adopted what is now seen as the best governance model which is the same design as that of BHP Billiton and a not-for-profit like Mission Australia. These boards are designed, as far as possible, to remove 'conflicts of interest' and attract relevant skills. Among our professional sports, this is also the structure now adopted by the Football Federation of Australia.

> (Crawford and Carter, 2011, p.6)

There is little debate about the extent to which the AFL Commission represented best practice but, unlike BHP Billiton and Mission Australia, the AFL is still composed of some member states that remain separate legal entities, as is the case in all six states in cricket. At board level, the independent commission approach adopted by the AFL is widely regarded as best practice. When describing what this best practice looks like, Crawford and Carter (2011, p. 7) stated:

> The Board's main role is to agree on strategy and appoint and oversee highly competent management on behalf of the owners. The owners appoint the Board as their representatives and are able to dismiss the Board, if necessary. A good board will be comprised of Directors who understand their primary duty is to act on behalf of all owners and not sectional interests. A good board will be of a workable size and its members will be chosen for their complementary skills, experience and their capacity to contribute. A good Board understands that its role is different to that of management. The Board's delegation to management will be clear and those major decisions that are retained by the Board will also be clear. Similarly, the Board's accountability to the owners will be understood, and those few matters that must be referred to the owners for approval will be clearly defined.

In summarising findings from the review, Crawford and Carter (2011, p. 7) found:

- Current governance structures fall well short of best practice
- The Board is far too large to be effective
- The Board is widely perceived to have conflicts of interest
- Process for appointing Directors does not take adequate account of Board skill needs
- There is a lack of clarity around the respective roles of CA Board, the States, and management
- Board and management roles overlap leading to confused accountability
- Decision-making roles of management, the Board and the States lack clarity which leads to indecision and conflict and the constant need for re-opening of issues.

In the seven points above, the review summarised the pitfalls of the delegate and federal forms of governance. But the question still remained: what to recommend so that the goal of striving for best practice governance was achievable and acceptable to CA and the member states. The following 10 points summarise the recommended changes. Some of these are considered further in reflecting on how the cricket community responded.

1   Clarity around the states' roles as owners (shareholders)
2   A smaller Board
3   Removal of conflicts of interest
4   A skills-based Board

5 Reconsideration of voting rights
6 Clarity of Board role relative to management
7 A partnership with management
8 The Chairman's role
9 Other attributes of a high performing Board
10 A workable financial model.

(Crawford and Carter, 2011, p.8)

The size and composition of the new board was the central element of the ten-point plan for change. A smaller board, and how a director is appointed to the board, deal directly with, for example, board size, conflict of interest and a skills based board. Fundamentally, the member associations as the 'owners' are to be responsible for the appointment of directors, but not to nominate directors as delegates of the association. A nominating committee would be formed comprised of four persons, two state presidents plus the chairman of CA and one other CA director.

The review ultimately recommended a board of nine non-executive directors plus the executive director who also has full voting rights. The directors are to be appointed via the nominations process described above, and as Crawford and Carter noted, 'it would be possible to require that, of the nine candidates, one is resident in each of the six States. This would be a better system than the current one, but it is not our preferred option' (p.15). The politics of the federal model are clearly reflected in this statement. What the review team preferred is for all nine directors to be appointed on merit and a balance of skills rather than imposing restrictions relating to geographic representation. However, the likelihood of this approach being accepted by member states is reflected in the need to make the statement. Interestingly, Lalor (2012), in his summary of outcomes, 'took it as read' that at least one director would have to come from each of the six states.

Following the release of the review in late 2011, newspaper headlines such as: 'Reforms go by the Board' (Conn, 2011), 'States to reject AFL-style cricket reform' (Lalor, 2012), 'States hold key to change – Cricket – the Reforms' (Saltau, 2012), indicated the possible resistance to change from within the cricket community. By mid-2012 no change had resulted and, following the June Board meeting, CA released the following statement.

Cricket Australia has moved a step closer to a new governance structure following today's Board of Directors' meeting in Melbourne
Following the meeting, CA Chairman Wally Edwards said that after receiving and reviewing the consolidated feedback from CA Members on the proposed governance changes, the Board resolved to implement a three-year transition to a new Board structure.

'Fundamentally, everything is proceeding as planned. Today we resolved that a special meeting for Members will be called for 17 August where the relevant recommendations will be put to that meeting,' Mr Edwards said. 'We're confident we'll get a constitutional majority of acceptance'.

A special meeting on 17 August will now ask Members to vote on this resolution that would lead initially to a Board consisting of six State Association–appointed Directors plus three independent Directors. If State Associations choose not to nominate a Director during this period, the nomination will be made by Cricket Australia.

On or before the 2014 Cricket Australia Annual General Meeting, Members will then decide the structure of the Board post-2015, with focus on assessing the effectiveness of the new structure and the recommendations contained in the Governance Review conducted by David Crawford and Colin Carter.

Today's resolution is a continuation of the process that started earlier this year after the review tabled by governance specialists Crawford and Carter recommended Cricket Australia consider a range of changes including moving to a smaller, independent Board.

Cricket Australia (2012, 15 June)

This statement further illustrates the difficulty of change, and the resistance of the current board to effectively vote themselves out of office. It also highlights the reluctance of the state associations to forego control of the sport nationally. Agreement to move to a smaller board is the only recognisable change to emerge from the 15 June meeting. The delegate structure will remain, with six state-association-appointed directors, thereby ignoring, in the short term, key issues pertaining to conflict of interest and the need for a skills-based board. However, the introduction of the three independent directors is consistent with the recommendations, although there is no comment on how these three directors are to be appointed. What potentially remains after the 17 August annual general meeting, if there is agreement, is a hybrid board structure. That it will take until 2015 to determine whether there is merit to the recommendations proposed in the review is further evidence of resistance and reluctance to embrace best practice governance as it is prescribed by Crawford and Carter.

Lalor (2012) illustrates the depth of the challenge to convince cricket administrators of the need for change and best practice sport governance. Bob Merriman, a former chairman of CA and long-time cricket administrator in Victoria, was firm in his convictions about the need for change when he argued:

> that the AFL shift to an independent commission might have been appropriate for a Victorian competition looking to nationalise itself, but pointed out that the federal model cricket used was the right one. 'We are already a national game', Merriman said. Merriman claimed that 'conflict of interest' issues had been eradicated at the board level for some time and that there had been a wide range of people with many skills at board level. Merriman believes that while the AFL clubs voted to give up their control of the game, cricket bodies would be less likely to.
>
> (Crawford and Carter, 2011, p.8)

Cricket's position as a sport with genuine national importance and a rich history and strong traditions can also be a disadvantage. The likelihood of 'cricket bodies' giving up their control as Merriman opines, further reinforces the entrenched views ingrained in both a delegate and federal form of governance. The contrast between the old and the new is brought into sharp focus when comparing the establishment of the BBL and the reasons for its existence, and views in relation to best practice governance.

Summary

This chapter introduced the federal form of governance, describing how it has formed the backbone for the governance of sport organisations in Australia. The federal model was examined in conjunction with the delegate system of governance and its impact on decision-making. This chapter has also highlighted the pressures for changes to traditional sport governance models in Australia, largely due to the professionalisation and commercialisation of sport. Hybrid models of governance were discussed, as was collaborative governance theory, as it was acknowledged that a change from a delegate system of directors to independent directors did not necessarily change federal structures. The need to negotiate, seek consensus and work collaboratively in a federal structure was highlighted as critical to good sport governance. Finally, the case study which explored pressures on Cricket Australia to reform its governance structures, provided a current example of how the delegate system works within a federal model, and why change was deemed necessary.

Review questions

1 Describe how Australia's political system has influenced sport governance in Australia.
2 Find examples of another country where the political system has influenced sport governance models in a different way to that found in Australia.
3 List the advantages and disadvantages of the delegate system of governance.
4 List the advantages and disadvantages of the federal model of governance.
5 List the reasons why Cricket Australia governance systems and structures require reform. Do you agree or disagree with the need for reform?
6 How would collaborative governance theory assist Cricket Australia, or any national sport organisation, with good governance practices? Provide examples to support your case.

Further reading

Cricket Australia (2012). New CA board a step closer. Available at http://www.cricket.com. au/news-list/2012/6/15/governance

Ferkins, L., Shilbury, D., & McDonald, G. (2005). The role of the board in building strategic capability: Towards an integrated model of sport governance research. *Sport Management Review*, 8, 195–225.

Ferkins, L., Shilbury, D., & McDonald, G. (2009). Board involvement in strategy: Advancing the governance of sport organizations. *Journal of Sport Management*, 23, 245–77.

Henry, I., & Lee, P. C. (2004). Governance and ethics in sport. In J. Beech & S. Chadwick (eds), *The Business of Sport Management* (pp.25–41). Harlow, Essex: Pearson Education.

Hoye, R., & Cuskelly, G. (2007). *Sport governance.* Sydney: Elsevier.

Shilbury, D., & Kellett, P. (2011). *Sport management in Australia: An organisational overview* 4th edn. Sydney: Allen & Unwin.

Websites

Australian Sports Commission: Sport Governance Principles http://www.ausport.gov.au/__data/assets/file/0010/485857/ASC_Governance_Principles.pdf

Crawford, D. A., & Carter, C. B.: http://www.cricket.com.au/pv_obj_cache/pv_obj_id_19039AB9E5AE9CC63F3691FEDED93D80B4865B00/filename/CA-Governance-Review-Part-1.ashx

De Zwart, F. B., & Gilligan, G. The relationship between good governance and sustainability in Australian sport http://www.clta.edu.au/professional/papers/conference2007/2007FBdZGG_RBGGSAS.pdf

Harris, B. ARU to announce corporate governance review http://www.theaustralian.com.au/sport/rugby-union/aru-to-announce-corporate-governance-review/story-e6frg7o6-1226336588367

Schwab, B. Sports governance. A hot topic players are passionate about. http://sportbizinsider.com.au/news/category/financial-and-governance/brendan-schwab-sports-governance-a-hot-topic-players-feel-passionately-about/

References

Ansell, C., & Gash, A. (2008). Collaborative governance in theory and practice. *Journal of Public Administration Research and Theory*, 18, 543–571.

Bowls Australia (2102). *Constitution.* Melbourne: Bowls Australia.

Conn, M. (2011). Reforms go by the Board. *Herald Sun*, 9 December, p.123.

Crawford, D. A., & Carter, C. B. (2011). *A good governance structure for Australian cricket.* Melbourne: Cricket Australia.

Cricket Australia (2012). *Cricket Australia has moved a step closer to a new governance structure following today's Board of Directors' meeting in Melbourne.* Available online at http://www.cricket.com.au/Global%20Items/news/2012/6/15/governance

Deane, J. (2011). The origins and history of Australian sport. In D. Shilbury & P. Kellett (eds), *Sport management in Australia: An organisational overview* 4th edn (pp. 36–58). Crows Nest, NSW: Allen & Unwin.

Dickson, G., Arnold, T., & Chalip, L. (2005). League expansion and interorganisational power. *Sport Management Review*, 8, 145–65.

Ferkins, L., & Shilbury, D. (2010). Developing board strategic capability in sport organisations: The national–regional governing relationship. *Sport Management Review*, 13, 235–54.

Henry, I., & Lee, P. C. (2004). Governance and ethics in sport. In J. Beech & S. Chadwick (eds), *The Business of sport management* (pp. 25–41). Harlow, Essex: Pearson Education.

Hoye, R., & Cuskelly, G. (2007). *Sport governance.* Sydney: Elsevier.

Hung, H. (1998). A typology of theories of the roles of governing boards. *Corporate Governance*, 6(2), 101–11.

Kooiman, J. (1993). Social-political governance: Introduction. In J. Kooiman, (ed.). *Modern governance* (pp.1–6). London: Sage.

Lalor, P. (2012). States to reject AFL-style cricket reform. *The Australian*, 31 January, p. 40.

Lynn, L. E., Heinrich, C. J., & Hill, C. J. (2000). Studying governance and public management: Challenges and prospects. *Journal of Public Administration Research and Theory*, 10, 223–61.

Oliver, C. (1990). Determinants of interorganizational relationships: Integration and future directions. *Academy of Management Review*, 15, 241–65.

Pfeffer, J., & Salancik, G. (1978). *The external control of organizations: A resource dependence perspective.* New York: Harper and Row.

Ridley, R. (2011). Let's have another bash. *SportBusiness International*, 174(12), 24–5.

Saltua, C. (2012). States hold key to change – CRICKET– The REFORMS. *Sydney Morning Herald*, 28 February, p. 19.

Victorian Football League (1985). *Establishing the basis for future success: Report presented by the VFL Commission to the VFL clubs.* Melbourne: Victorian Football League.

4   Canada

Milena M. Parent and David Patterson

Topics

- Canadian sport system
- Elite sport
- Historical evolution
- Jurisdictional issues
- Participatory sport.

Objectives

- To provide an overview of the historical evolution of the Canadian sport system
- To critically analyse the Canadian sport system
- To present challenges facing the current Canadian sport system
- To present strategies the Canadian sport system is using to mitigate challenges
- To present a case of a non-Olympic sport and its place in the Canadian sport system.

Key terms

Canadian sport system   The network of individual, group and organisational actors that can be found at the local, provincial, national, and international levels involved in or associated with participatory and/or elite sport in Canada.

Elite sport   Sport in which participants are actively striving to compete in world championship, Olympic or top professional levels.

Divisionalised form   An organisational type outlined by Mintzberg (1979) wherein a parent organisation oversees several distinct organisational sub-units.

Participatory sport   Sport in which participation is its own reward and not an instrument towards another goal such as a championship; also known as mass (sport) participation.

Policy   The sum of decisions, actions and non-actions taken by an organisational entity or government in relation to a subject or outcome that it is capable of implementing (cf., Houlihan, 1997).

Overview

The governance of sport in a federation as geographically diverse as Canada is certain to be convoluted. Canada's sport governance system includes a complex network of sport organisations such as community clubs/schools, provincial (regional) programmes, national programmes, international events, and other supporting organisations (apparel, sponsors, media, etc.). Each sport has its own network, which competes with other sports and other sectors of society for resources (e.g., athletes, money, and legitimacy). Sport also finds itself in the middle of provincial–federal jurisdictional struggles and has suffered from a lack of a clear direction in the past. Despite these challenges, the Canadian sport system has experienced recent successes.

This chapter will critically analyse the Canadian sport system's governance by first providing a brief overview of its historical evolution. This is followed by a critical analysis of the current governance structure and key challenges, as well as a discussion of strategies used to mitigate the system's challenges. The Ringette Canada case study illustrates changes that have occurred in the Canadian sport system and differences between Olympic and non-Olympic sport in the country.

A brief history of the Canadian sport system

The system known today as the Canadian sport system was formalised in 1961 with the passing of Bill C-131, the Fitness and Amateur Sport Act. For the first time, sport was supported by the federal government and sports were encouraged to formalise themselves into organisations, most of which would be created as kitchen-table organisations, which are organisations led by a volunteer or very small group of volunteers essentially from their kitchen tables (see Mintzberg, 1979). This set the stage for a move from a sport system geared to participatory sport/recreation/leisure towards a sport system focused on elite athletes and performance. This was in part due to the fact that sport was officially a provincial responsibility, not a federal one. For the federal government to get involved in sport, it needed an angle that had a 'national' focus or impact. Focusing on a Canadian team, on elite athletes helping to build national unity and pride, was perceived as a way to not infringe (too much) on provincial jurisdiction. A second key development was the creation of the Canada Games in 1967. The Canadian federal government was looking for a *raison d'être*, something that was concrete for the Canadian sport system. The Canada Games allowed for:

- the development of sport in each province, inter-province competition, and building towards elite competition;
- the promotion of sport and athletes through television (i.e., putting a face on up and coming athletes for the general public);
- a multisport competition environment as practice for developing athletes;
- infrastructure development.

In 1969, a task force on sport was organised by Prime Minister Pierre Elliot Trudeau. Nancy Greene was on the task force (she had won gold and silver medals at the Winter Olympic Games the previous year and was known as the 'queen of winter sport'). The task force put forth recommendations for the Canadian sport system, including:

- the creation of a national sport centre in Ottawa (the James Naismith building, now defunct) – to help sport organisations move away from kitchen-table structures;
- the creation of the Coaching Association of Canada (CAC);
- the creation of a sport medicine organisation;
- the separation of Hockey Canada (international hockey in which professionals were eligible to participate) and the Canadian Amateur Hockey Association (local development and amateur international events).[1]

Next, Game Plan '76 and the introduction of the Quadrennial Planning Programme (QPP) in 1984 led to sport organisations increasing their levels of specialisation, standardisation, formalisation and centralisation (Slack & Parent, 2006) if they wanted funding from the federal government. The focus on elite athletes was solidified with the introduction of the Sport Funding and Accountability Framework (SFAF) in 1995, which linked funding with athlete performance levels (Sport Canada, 2011). Meanwhile, Ben Johnson's eviction from the 1988 Seoul Olympic Games due to testing positive for drugs (a likely result of the emphasis placed on elite athlete performance) and the subsequent Dubin Inquiry led to at least part of the sport system focusing on anti-doping and ethics in sport.

Next, the 1998 Mills Report actually began as an exploration of professional sport subsidisation but resulted in a review of the whole Canadian sport system as it became clear during the process that Canadians would not accept public subsidies for professional sports teams, despite the reverence given to ice hockey, and its associated sports organisations like the National Hockey League by Canadians (see Whitson, Harvey & Lavoie, 2000). Among the multitude of recommendations some were realistic such as the creation of a secretary of state (for amateur sport) and accepted by the federal government, while others were not realistic or were vague or superficial such as the acknowledged importance of coaches not being afforded appropriate space in the report to develop such an implication properly. The recommendations often lacked linkages with, or implications on, other elements of the system (such as needing a pool of mass participants from which to draw the elite athletes) to truly be able to implement them in any effective way.

Thus, until recently, the Canadian sport system had suffered from a lack of a clear, unified direction. Its participatory sport–elite sport pendulum has swung back and forth, and even has tried to do both at the same time, with the federal government aiming for the elite athletes in a bid for national unity and identity, and the local and provincial governments focusing on the other end of the spectrum, resulting in frictions between government levels and resources being stretched thinly. An attempt to unify the Canadian sport system came with the introduction of the first Canadian Sport Policy (CSP) (Government of Canada, 2002) and its four pillars of enhanced excellence, participation, interaction, and capacity (described later in this chapter). With this national policy, the federal government claimed a stake in both the elite (enhanced excellence) and participatory (enhanced participation) sport arenas. Still, with the advent of the Vancouver Olympic Winter Games 'Own the Podium' (OTP) programme, initially only for winter athletes but extended to summer athletes in 2006 and described later in this chapter, Bill C-47: The Olympic and Paralympic Marks Act (Government of Canada, 2007) and the revision of the federal hosting policy (Sport Canada, 2008), the federal government still seems to place greater emphasis on the elite level. In 2012, Sport Canada is set to unveil the second CSP; the direction it takes and the implications for the Canadian sport system have yet to be confirmed. Table 4.1 illustrates the evolution of the Canadian sport system.

An analysis of the current Canadian sport system

Sport can be inherently confounding to rational analysis (CCES, 1993) with arbitrary lines, distances, and times throughout. The Canadian sport system can be equally confounding to a managerial analysis given the structure that both mimics and bypasses the structure of Canadian governmental institutions. In this section, the structure of Canadian sport organisations is examined and a comparison to Mintzberg's (1980) five ideal type of organisational configurations is undertaken. In short, the structures of Canadian sport organisations defy easy categorisation (Kikulis, Slack, Hinings & Zimmermann, 1989; Kikulis, Slack & Hinings, 1995b). Mintzberg (1980) developed five organisational configurations, or 'ideal types'. For the purpose of explaining the Canadian sport system, focus is on the divisionalised form as it cosmetically reflects Canadian sport. This section will conclude by contrasting the realities of Canadian sport with the ideal type.

According to Mintzberg (1980), divisionalised forms are organisations that are broken into component sub-units based on specialisation, market segment or geography. These organisations tend to confer considerable autonomy upon the divisions to work within their speciality while leaving coordination and performance standards to the strategic apex, or central authority. Divisionalised forms are often found in governmental organisations, and Canadian sport organisations reflect this state-like configuration as well.

Generally speaking, Canadian sport is organised in a manner that reflects the basic structure of the Canadian government with a national organisation, provincial organisations, and local organisations each taking on a segment of the continuum of tasks associated with the organisation of sporting activity. National sports organisations (NSOs) tend to focus on the high-performance elements of sport and specifically on the preparation and development of athletes for participation in world championships and the Olympic Games. Coordinating with the federal government, NSOs also work with nationally focused support organisations such as the Canadian Olympic Committee (COC) and the Canadian Paralympic Committee (CPC).

Table 4.1 A brief historical overview of the Canadian sport system's development

Date	Occurrence	Comment
1961	Bill C-131, the Fitness and Amateur Sport Act is passed	First time sport is supported by the federal government. Kitchen-table sport organisations are created.
1967	Canada Games	First edition of a national sport event that would prove to become an important part of many athletes' development calendar.
1969	Task Force Report on Sport	First task force on sport. Many recommendations suggested and implemented over the following years such as having the federal government assist (kitchen-table) sport organisations in administrative and human resource costs for those desiring it.
1970	1976 Olympic Games awarded to Montreal	
1971	Game Plan '76	The Canadian Olympic Association (now Canadian Olympic Committee or COC), federal government, and national sport organisations (NSOs) try to work together yet 'fight' for ownership or independence of the sport system. A plan that saw the creation of federal government financial assistance for elite athletes, which ultimately increased the government's control over the sport system.
1976	Montreal 1976 summer Olympic Games Canada's first Minister of Sport, Iona Campagnola	No gold medals won by Canadians on home soil. Due to increased security costs (following Munich 1972) and considerable construction costs, the Games' financial overruns plagued taxpayers (mainly smokers) for 30 years. Canada named its first 'leader' of the Canadian sport system, 15 years after its formalisation at the federal level. These activities increased the visibility of sport at the federal level.
1978	Commonwealth Games in Edmonton	Canada: top country.
1981	Abby Hoffman at Sport Canada Best Ever '88 Programme is created for elite athletes 1988 Winter Olympic Games awarded to Calgary	Abby Hoffman becomes the first woman director of Sport Canada. She institutes the Best Ever Programme for elite athletes in light of the upcoming 1988 Calgary Olympic Winter Games. The programme was extended to summer athletes in 1984.
1983	Universiade Games in Edmonton	

Date	*Occurrence*	*Comment*
1984	Quadrennial Planning Programme (QPP)	The mandatory QPP process included planning and consulting guidelines to be implemented by all NSOs as a condition for federal funding.
1988	1988 Calgary Olympic Winter Games 1988 Seoul Summer Olympic Games – Ben Johnson caught doping	Canada earns the dubious honour of having hosted the Olympics twice and not winning a gold medal on home soil. Canada is embarrassed by Canadian sprinter Ben Johnson having been caught for doping.
1988-1990	Dubin Inquiry	Inquiry into the doping problem following Johnson's eviction from the 1988 Olympics. Conclusions included a 'conspiracy of silence' between athletes, coaches and physicians.
1992	Task Force: Sport the Way Ahead	Put a value on the Canadian sport system in economic terms. Many recommendations ignored.
1994	Core Sport Report Commonwealth Games in Victoria	The Core Sport Report categorised sport and funding
1995	Sport Funding Accountability Framework (SFAF) developed	Focused on elite athlete achievements as a determinant of NSO funding.
1998	Mills Report	Initiated to examine the state of professional sport which was then extended to the whole sport system.
2002	Canadian Sport Policy (CSP)	First national sport policy document since 1961.
2003	Vancouver wins the right to host the 2010 Olympic Winter Games	
2005	'Own the Podium' programme (OTP) created	Funding to help Canadian athletes at the 2010 Winter Olympic Games and then extended to Summer Olympic athletes in 2006.
2007	Bill C-47: The Olympic and Paralympic Marks Act	Federal bill protecting the marks (words and logos) associated with the 2010 Winter Olympic Games passed.
2008	Federal Hosting Policy revised	
2012	Second CSP created	

Canada is divided into ten provinces and three territories. Sport is also divided similarly with provincial sport organisations (PSOs) in most provinces and territories for most sports. These organisations are closely connected to their respective provincial governments and are largely charged with both high performance and core development mandates.

Finally, local sport organisations are largely responsible for the recruitment and retention of athletes at the local club or team level. While there is some responsibility for elite and high performance programming, the developmental aspect of sport is the emphasis at the local level.

At these three levels, one sees a coordinating strategic apex (NSO) and divisions (PSO) and sub-divisions (local clubs) that execute an overall strategy but have considerable freedom to act in a manner of their own choosing. The commonalities with Mintzberg's divisionalised form are clear at this level, as the sport system appears to be rationally and clearly delineated. However, the overlap with Mintzberg breaks down from this point on.

A central conceit of Mintzberg's divisionalised form is that the divisions are parts of the organisational whole and that the authority flows from the strategic apex as the component parts struggle to be given greater levels of authority from the centralised power base. Any such success can lead to further decentralisation and:

> As a result, they exert a pull to Balkanize the structure, to split it into market-based units which can control their own decisions, coordination being restricted to the standardization of outputs.
>
> (Mintzberg, 1980, p.329)

The struggle for control over the resources of the national organisation is not simply a case of divisions with the PSOs wrestling control away from the NSO. In Canada, the PSOs, more often than not, own the NSO and thus can use authority rather than persuasion or politics to gain and assert power.

The structure of NSOs in Canada generally dictates that the NSO only has a handful of voting members. These members are the PSOs, and their numbers are restricted to the amount of provinces, concentrating authority over NSO operations to a select few stakeholders. Unlike the organisation of the Canadian state, wherein the federal and provincial governments are nominally sovereign equals, the NSOs derive their existence from the PSOs. Mintzberg's view of the divisionalised form warns against Balkanisation even in a conventional organisation where the divisions are owned by the parent organisation. Balkanisation is nearly assured when the divisions are co-owners of the parent.

Balkanisation of the sport system is the central governance challenge in Canada. To be sure, as in the United States where the states are often regarded as 'laboratories of democracy', a fragmented sport system can allow for a spectrum of approaches and practices from which the best may emerge. Canadians are leaders in the development of coaching professional development, the principles of 'long-term athlete development' (Balyi, Cardinal, Higgs, Norris & Way, 2005), and were atop the gold medals table at the 2010 Olympic Winter Games. There is much to trumpet in Canadian sport.

While there are successes, the fragmentation has exerted a considerable drag on the effectiveness of Canadian sport. The inefficiency that goes with the core structure of amateur sport noted above creates rivalry within sport and sport communities that divert resources away from the core mission of delivering sport to Canadians. Canadians have long realised, for instance, that the usage of municipal ice arenas is inefficient, with the ice time being oversubscribed on weeknights and weekends while it sits unused during weekdays. A fix to this problem would require that several sport organisations (ice hockey, ringette, figure skating, speed skating, broomball and lacrosse) work together at the national level to create a multiple user strategy. This strategy would then have to be adopted by 13 or more provincial organisations (per sport) and up to 500 local associations. A significant change to ice usage would require the adoption by up to 1000 independent organisations, not including the municipalities that own most arena facilities. With so many organisations (and stakeholders within each organisation) asserting a role, negotiating the decision-making environment can be sclerotic and slow – long after broad agreement on both the problem and the preferred solution.

Canadian sport system strategies: policies and programmes

The preceding section has laid out the configuration challenges faced by Canadian sport. While the organisational structures can provide some creative freedom, they can also create paralysis through an over-abundance of authorities. The following section will outline some of the mitigating strategies employed by Canadian sport, namely a national sport policy and the OTP.

With numerous overlapping jurisdictions and lines of authority, policy has been used as a tool to demarcate who does what in Canadian sport. The CSP (Government of Canada, 2002) was an attempt to create four core priorities (or pillars) for sport in Canada, as delineated lines of jurisdiction for execution. The CSP outlined a vision for Canadian sport and four pillars for action by the stakeholders in the sport system. Each has contributed to further aligning the actions of sport organisations, but none of them have succeeded to the degree expressed in the policy document (Sutcliffe, 2010).

The policy puts forth a vision of, 'a dynamic and leading-edge sport environment that enables all Canadians to experience and enjoy involvement in sport to the extent of their abilities and interests and, for increasing numbers, to perform consistently and successfully at the highest competitive levels (Sutcliffe, 2010, p. 4). This vision statement is certainly laudable, but is sufficiently vague as to be robbed of any specific meaning. Given the amorphous nature of the goals, it is not necessarily surprising that the areas around high performance sport were the most successful, 'participants noted that setting targets has had a positive effect on the changes needed in the sport system to achieve the targets' (Sutcliffe, 2010, p.15). Certainly, a student of sport management is aware of the importance of specificity in goal-setting (cf., Slack & Parent, 2006) and will thus not be surprised to see that

Figure 4.1 Vancouver 2010 Olympic flame during the closing ceremonies (credit: Milena M. Parent)

the CSP has coincided with a highly successful period for Canada on the world sporting stage.

The 'excellence' pillar of the CSP envisioned that, 'the pool of talented athletes has expanded and Canadian athletes and teams are systematically achieving world-class results at the highest levels of international competition through fair and ethical means' (Government of Canada, 2002, p.4). Canada set a record for gold medals won by a home nation at the 2010 Winter Olympic Games, providing ample evidence of the success of this goal. A key development in the path towards podium success was the creation of a non-governmental organisation, the OTP.

OTP was created as a cooperative effort among winter sports to ensure that Canada could be atop the total medals table at the Winter Olympic Games. OTP was intended to streamline high-performance funding and to ensure the effectiveness of high performance programmes. The concept of a high performance sport organisation at arm's length from government was not new in sport, with Australia and Germany having already tread this ground in the past. But for Canada, this was a major departure from a sport system that had previously generally emphasised participation over high performance and had twice set a record as the only nation to host an Olympic Games without winning a gold medal.

The increased funding that OTP generated also impacted the organisational structure within Canadian sport. The newly formed positions of 'High Performance Director' became commonplace at the NSO level, and several NSOs added considerable staffing in support of their high-performance programmes (Davis, 2008). Borrowing once more from Mintzberg's configurations, OTP moved NSOs away from the divisionalised form to something more akin to a 'professionalised bureaucracy' wherein highly trained personnel did largely self-directed work based on their considerable training and qualifications.

In order to have high-performance athletes, they must have first been participants (see Sotiriadou, Shilbury & Quick, 2008) in the sport – another key pillar of the CSP. The 'participation' pillar has had the least progress of the four (Sutcliffe, 2010). In fact, overall sport participation in Canada has been on a steady decline (Statistics Canada, 2008). The continued diminishment of sport participation is part of a larger trend, but has not been slowed through a specific inter-governmental effort resulting from the CSP. The lack of specific goals, as noted above, can be attributed as a potential reason for slow progress. Goals are not the end of the story though – jurisdictional overlaps and gaps between the myriad of organisational players also present a very real challenge.

The challenge of coordination between organisations was addressed in the CSP under the pillar 'enhanced interaction'. The pillar acknowledged that the atomised elements of the Canadian sport system needed to coordinate actions in order to generate stronger outcomes, 'the components of the sport system are more connected and coordinated as a result of the committed collaboration and communication amongst the stakeholders" (Government of Canada, 2002 p.14).

The coordination among stakeholders brings about another theoretical perspective, stakeholder theory (Freeman, 1984). Freeman defined a stakeholder as, 'any group or individual who can affect or is affected by the achievement of the organization's objectives' (p. 46). Stakeholder theory has been used frequently in the attempt to explicate elements of the Canadian sport system (Parent & Harvey, 2009; Parent & Séguin, 2007; Parent, Olver & Séguin, 2009; Thibault & Harvey, 1997) and certainly applies to the mishmash of jurisdictions that mark the Canadian sport system.

Canadian governments have used legal and policy frameworks to divide the responsibilities, and in participation these divisions are most hazy. The federal government and its provincial counterparts have tried a National Recreation Statement (Sport and Fitness Ministers, 1987) outlining that the provincial governments would take primary responsibility for recreational sport, the statement on High-Performance Athlete Development that applied primary responsibility to the federal government (Federal–Provincial Sport Ministers, 1985). Despite these agreements, the CSP was needed to provide a forum for a consensus on the goals of the Canadian sport system. As Freeman posited, any policy framework that did not include the perspectives of multiple stakeholders would likely fall short of its goals. In this case, the fact that the provincial departments of education, health, and sport are rarely housed in the same ministry has created a gap in sport initiation programmes in that the school and health systems are not meaningful participants in the sport system. Only recently, non-governmental organisations in the system have tried to work with the school systems independently of government sport ministries (Norris, 2010) with mixed results. Without involvement of all stakeholders in the policy development process, successful interaction within the community has been elusive.

The fourth pillar of the CSP was 'increased capacity'. It is difficult to untangle capacity from the other pillars, as the capacity of the system both contributes to and is reliant upon the other three pillars. Despite these murky waters, Canadian sport organisations have increased their capacity to act (willingly or reluctantly), starting in the early 1980s (Slack & Hinings, 1992) and progressing further at both the provincial and federal levels (Kikulis, Slack, Hinings & Zimmermann, 1989; Kikulis, Slack & Hinings, 1995a, 1995b). The ability of the organisations to act has progressed significantly, allowing sport organisations to take a greater lead in their own future (independent of government) and to form, in some cases, large organisations that have broken the mould of previous volunteer-led organisations (cf., Stevens, 2006).

Still, the funding emphasis of the Canadian sport system has been on elite-level sport (read Olympic sport). This is not surprising since having one's sport at the Olympics means more visibility, which means more sponsors, which means more financial support, which in turn should mean more success – and the cycle continues. However, the challenges faced by the Canadian sport system are perhaps even more evident for non-Olympic sports, as the case study will demonstrate. But what about Gretzky?

The reader can be forgiven for having expected to read a great deal in this chapter about the National Hockey League (NHL) and other professional sports in Canada. Certainly, the NHL is central to professional sport in Canada and is one of the central organising elements of the system in general. The relative separation between professional leagues and the 'sport system' is germane to this chapter and will be covered briefly in this section.

Several professional leagues operate within Canada. Some of these leagues are at least partially under the purview of the NSO for that sport, such as the Canadian Hockey League (affiliated with Hockey Canada), the National Rugby League (operated by Rugby Canada), and the National Track League (owned by Athletics Canada). However, the most prominent of these are not formally affiliated with their respective amateur sport colleagues.

The lack of formal affiliation can be attributed to historical precedent and perhaps to the multinational nature of North American leagues (where these leagues often straddle the United States–Canada border). This leads to a situation where the Toronto Blue Jays work with Baseball Canada, but are not formally affiliated or in any way beholden to the NSO. (The reverse is also true.) Generally the 'two solitudes' of professional and community/Olympic sport is a symbiotic relationship with professional leagues providing funding, exposure, and context for athlete development in their respective sports, and the community levels providing a steady stream of athletes for the leagues. The marriage becomes rocky at times, with the impetus for conflict coming from ongoing development of athletes (cf., TSN.ca, 2011).

A chapter of this length does not allow for a full exposition of the role professional sport plays in Canada. Certainly in the case of the NHL and the

Canadian Football League (CFL), Canadian culture plays a role. In the case of Major League Soccer (MLS) and Major League Baseball (MLB), economic and sport development issues are front and centre. In all cases, professional sport can be a strong institutional force at all levels of Canadian sport, leading to an ethic of creating scaled-down professional leagues in age-group sport, rather than developmentally appropriate programs (Balyi *et al.*, 2005). It is certainly fair to summarise that professional sport is an important subset of the Canadian sport system, but one that exists largely outside the core 'playground to podium' continuum.

Case: Ringette Canada – a true Canadian (non-Olympic) sport

The Canadian sport experience can be effectively described through the lens of a particular sport. This case study on ringette will give insight into the entirety of the Canadian sport system. Ringette is used to explain the processes and connections that make the Canadian sport system function, and to point out the inequities and inefficiencies that still mark Canadian sport.

Ringette is a uniquely Canadian sport. Played widely in only Canada and Finland, the sport was invented in 1963 by municipal recreation manager Sam Jacks. Jacks, the Director of Recreation in the City of North Bay (Ontario, Canada), worked with other recreation directors in the region to create a sport that would provide an on-ice alternative to ice hockey, specifically aimed at girls and women. Since the foundation of the sport, it has grown to include nearly 30,000 athletes across Canada.

The sport grew quickly through the 1970s and into the 1980s as girls and women flocked to arenas for the chance to play on the ice. As women's ice hockey became more established, and eventually was added to the Olympic programme, this growth slowed and then reversed as national registration fell in ringette. Since the early 2000s, registration in ringette has grown steadily and shown no correlation between its registration and that of women's ice hockey.

The core unit: the team

Ringette is a team sport, played in teams of 12–18 athletes against another team. As a result, the core functional unit in ringette is the single team. The following section will use a single team to outline the sport system, by outlining what interactions and elements are required for that team to play a single game. These include the infrastructure to form a team, a coach, two referees, a venue and another team. Each of these elements is significantly connected to the entire Canadian sport system.

Forming a team

Generally speaking, team formation is more substantial than randomly selecting a group of athletes. In ringette, teams are formed by local ringette associations.

These associations are not-for-profit organisations that function in a geographically bound region, municipality, or neighbourhood. Led almost entirely by volunteers, these associations take registrations, form teams, train coaches and officials, and assign teams to particular times for practices and games. The local association will often have ringette teams in most, if not all, age categories that range from U9 up to 35+. Of note, ringette associations are single sport clubs.

Local associations do not own their competition or training venues. The ice arenas used by ringette associations are owned by municipal governments, private operators, educational institutions, community associations or other sport associations. Likely due in part to the high cost of construction, ice arenas are most often owned and operated by municipal governments and ice rental fees on an hourly basis are usually charged. This fee is often lower for non-profits that service youth. The rental model for venues allows local associations to focus on the development of their sport and their athletes, but does reduce control over a vital resource for these clubs. The third-party ownership structure also opens up another competitive front as ringette clubs compete with ice hockey, figure skating, speed skating, broomball, and other user groups for finite usage time at these training and competition facilities.

Coaching

Ringette teams must be led by a coach; coaches are not generally professionals, but volunteers who are trained to provide basic skills and maintain a safe training environment for their players. Quite often, the coaches of ringette teams have daughters that play on the teams they coach.

Coach training is standardised through the NSO, Ringette Canada, in partnership with the CAC. The model for coach training mandates that the content of coach education programmes are developed at the national level while it is delivered at the local level. Through this programme, ringette coaches are trained at standards that vary with the level of athlete they intend to coach. Coaches can be certified at any one of three levels, each designed to give the coach the knowledge they need to work with athletes at a particular age or skill level.

Officiating

Ringette games are usually overseen by two on-ice and up to five off-ice officials. Referees (on-ice officials) are trained by local and provincial level trainers, using content of a national certification programme developed entirely by the NSO. The officials are commonly paid a stipend for officiating games, but are rarely paid enough to treat their career as anything more than a hobby. Off-ice officials, such as clock operators, scorekeepers and shot clock operators, are rarely trained in any formal way and are rarely paid a stipend. Most are volunteers who have an interest in the sport, and training is either informal or not present at all.

Providing context: leagues and championships

While teams at the community level are often able to find opposing teams from within their own local association, some teams must play against teams from other associations. The process of scheduling league games most often falls to informal networks among volunteers, but can also fall to groups of local associations or to PSOs.

The single game for the team is usually played in the context of a season. Depending on the age category for the team involved, at the end of the season there may be a local, regional, provincial or national championship tournament. End of season competitions are overseen by various organisations, with the provincial and national championships overseen by PSOs and the NSO respectively.

Ringette within Canadian sport

The paragraphs above, dealing with only one team playing only one game illustrate that the Canadian sport system is a complicated clutch of competing and overlapping jurisdictions and priorities. Volunteers at the local level must work closely with local and provincial governments, regional associations, provincial governing bodies, and national governing bodies. Complicating matters further is that, in ringette, professional coaches are effectively not present in the system and professional administrators exist only at the provincial level and higher. Thus, volunteers are left doing considerable work, relying on vastly different levels of professional preparation they may have had before taking on the volunteer role.

The European model of multisport clubs is largely not present in Canadian sport, and almost entirely non-existent in ringette. So, the challenges that exist for local ringette associations are largely copied by other sports and the entire pattern is repeated in each municipality across the country. While volunteers are almost solely responsible at the local level, the professionalisation of the Canadian sport system is not complete at any level. PSOs and NSOs often have professional and technical staff, but are still led by volunteer boards of directors, so volunteers still hold significant sway in the organisations.

Ringette at the national level

Now moving on to the status of ringette in the broader Canadian sport system, it becomes immediately clear that there is a system of preference among sports, namely a preference for those that are on the Olympic programme at the cost of those that are not. This system both helps and harms in the case of ringette and its national governing body, Ringette Canada.

The government of Canada, through Sport Canada, funds Ringette Canada with over 30 per cent of its annual revenues. The 30 per cent funding is part of an overall set of revenue streams that includes membership fees (30 per cent), educational resource sales (20 per cent) sponsorship (10 per cent) and funds (10 per cent) generated by programmes (such as national team identification camps) and events (such as national championships). Sponsorship remains a relatively low revenue source as attaining funding from sponsors in a marketplace preoccupied by professional and Olympic sport is nearly prohibitively difficult.

Ringette and owning a podium

Ringette is not widely practised throughout the world and lacks the resources of a major international federation to support its international growth. The lack of an international game in ringette is a disqualifier for high-performance funding for national team programmes. Strictly from the perspective of funding regulations, ringette does not field a national team, but only a team that wears Canadian colours. In terms of direct impacts, this means that athletes on national teams in ringette often must pay thousands of dollars in team fees once they have been selected to represent their country. This is in contrast to athletes in other sports who have access to professional leagues and funding through the federal government's Athlete Assistance Programme that pays a stipend to athletes selected to national team programmes.

The high-performance funding for ringette stands in stark contrast to other sports, often with much smaller participation levels, that receive funding based on their ability to generate medals at the Olympic and Paralympic Games. For instance, ringette, with 30,000 athletes participating in Canada, receives no funding, while diving, with only a fraction of the participation base, receives over CAD2 million for its high-performance programmes (Sport Canada, 2012). Without a spot on the Olympic programme, ringette suffers as do its athletes.

Conversely, ringette benefits from its status as a Canadian Heritage sport. Ringette Canada is afforded special funding from the federal government under this programme. The funding is based on ringette's history of having been invented in, and largely played in, Canada. While this is of considerable benefit to ringette, it is of little help to high-performance athletes as the funding is designated for recruitment of new athletes to the sport.

Ownership and Ringette organisations

In ringette, authority is delegated upward from the membership. Individual members are owners of local associations, local associations own regional associations, who own PSOs, who own the NSO. That the national body derives its authority from the membership through this chain of authority is often counterintuitive.

At a glance, the structure of ringette bears a strong resemblance to a franchise–franchisee corporation or a divisionalised form. From the outside, it appears that the national authority sets the rules of the game, the policies to be followed, and then organisations responsible for ever smaller geographic divisions are responsible for the execution thereof. What makes such a view all the more compelling is that on a day to day basis, this view is accurate. The role of the national body is skewed towards rule-making and the role of local associations skews to execution.

This view of the ownership model breaks down in times of change or upheaval, such as after a disappointing national team performance or in the face of funding cuts. It is in these times in ringette when it is clear that the authority to make rules is conferred upon the national body only with the express and revocable permission of its provincial members.

Other stakeholders can certainly influence ringette organisations through funding, partnerships, and specifically through access to a facility that is expensive to both build and maintain. Decisions by the news media to cover, or often, not to cover non-Olympic sport such as ringette, certainly limits the sport in terms of sponsorship and the ability to attract new athletes. The influence of these stakeholders gives them incremental power over ringette organisations, but not ownership. Through an ownership structure, authority rests within the members of the organisation.

Ownership: benefits and costs

Conferring ownership of the national association demands responsiveness and a connection to local associations. The leaders of the national body must be in tune with their members or they will be replaced. In ringette, an ongoing emphasis on coach education for introductory level coaches is largely a response to the need for this training expressed at the local level, for instance.

Internal ownership leads to an internal focus by the organisation, sometimes at the expense of external opportunity. Having nearly 90 per cent of the ringette players in the world, Ringette Canada will ultimately need to lead international growth efforts but that effort is not immediately valuable to its members, resulting in a long-term project being deferred to make room on agendas for the immediate. The authority structure of Ringette Canada predicts such an outcome.

Ringette and Canadian sport

In many ways, ringette is typical of Canadian sport, and no more so than in terms of its structural properties. The ongoing balancing act between the competing demands of external stakeholders such as government funders and internal stakeholders who deliver few resources, but hold ultimate authority enables and disables Ringette Canada.

With over 30,000 members spread out over the second largest nation in the world, a systemic focus on the local is likely necessary as it could very well be forgotten among the myriad of other challenges. The focus on the local, however, limits the scope of the organisation and its ability to coordinate nationally, to compete internationally, and to help grow the sport internationally.

Summary

In Canada, there are three jurisdictions involved in the Canadian sport system: the federal level with Sport Canada, the NSOs and other national sport bodies, the

Figure 4.2 Ashley Peters of Canada shoots on Anna Vanhatalo (Finland) in the gold medal game of the 2007 World Ringette Championships (credit: Ringette Canada/F. Scott Grant Photography)

provincial level with the PSOs, and the local level with community clubs/teams and schools. Until recently, the Canadian sport system has suffered from a lack of a clear, unified direction. Its participatory sport–elite sport pendulum has swung back and forth, and even has tried to do both at the same time. The Canadian sport system was formalised in 1961; but it took until 2002 for it to be provided with a seemingly unified direction through the first CSP.

Taken as a whole, the Canadian sport system could be akin to what Mintzberg (1980) called the divisionalised form. However, it is the local sport organisations that usually own the PSOs, who in turn own the NSOs, not the other way around. This structure has led to the Balkanisation of the sport system, arguably the central governance challenge in Canada. While there are successes, such as those stemming from the 2010 Winter Olympic Games and the OTP, the system's fragmentation has exerted a considerable drag on the effectiveness of the Canadian sport system. The inefficiency surrounding the core structure of amateur sport has resulted in rivalries within sports and sport communities that divert resources away from the core mission of delivering sport to Canadians. Policies and programs such as the CSP and OTP are seen as strategies to mitigate the system's challenges. The challenges faced by Canadian sport organisations are perhaps most evident in Canadian non-Olympic sports such as ringette. The ongoing balancing act of such largely participation-based sports between the competing demands of external stakeholders (e.g., government funders) and internal stakeholders who deliver few resources, but hold ultimate authority, enables and disables such sports. The focus on local action and on participatory sport only serves to limit the scope of such sports organisations and their ability to coordinate nationally, to compete internationally, and to help grow the sport internationally.

Review questions

1 Provide the dates and explain three key moments in the Canadian sport system's history.
2 Describe a key challenge faced by the Canadian sport system.
3 Explain the importance of the Canadian Sport Policy and Own the Podium for the Canadian sport system.

Further reading

Green, M. & Houlihan, B. (2005). *Elite sport development: Policy learning and political priorities*. New York: Taylor & Francis.
Harvey, J. & Cantelon, H. (eds) (1988). *Not just a game: Essays in Canadian sport sociology*. Ottawa: University of Ottawa Press.
Kidd, B. (1996). *The struggle for Canadian sport*. Toronto: University of Toronto Press.
Macintosh, D. & Whitson, D. (1990). *The game planners: Transforming Canada's sport system*. Kingston, Canada: McGill-Queen's University Press.

Websites

The Canadian Encyclopaedia – Amateur Sports Organisations: http://www.the canadianencyclopedia.com/articles/amateur-sports-organization
Own the Podium: http://ownthepodium.org/
Sport Canada: http://www.pch.gc.ca/eng/1268160670172

Note

1 This cleavage has since been reversed with the subsequent merger of the two organisations (Stevens, 2006).

References

Balyi, I., Cardinal, C., Higgs, C., Norris, S. & Way, R. (2005). *Long-term athlete development – Canadian Sport for Life*. Available online at http://www.ltad.ca/Groups/LTAD%20Downloads/English/LTAD_Resource_Paper.pdf
CCES (1993). *Ethical rationale for promoting drug-free sport*. Ottawa: Canadian Centre for Ethics in Sport. Available online at http://www.cces.ca/pdfs/CCES-PAPER-EthicalRationale-E.pdf
Davis, P. (2008). Coaching with a 'pit crew'. *Coaches Plan/Plan Du Coach*, 15(1), 15–19.
Federal–Provincial Sport Ministers (1985). *High performance athlete development in Canada: A delineation of responsibilities of the federal and provincial territorial governments*. Ottawa; Canada: Federal–Provincial Sport Ministers.
Freeman, R. (1984). *Strategic management: A stakeholder approach*. Boston: Pitman.

Government of Canada (2002). *Canadian sport policy*. Canada: Government of Canada. Available online at http://www.pch.gc.ca/progs/sc/pol/pcs-csp/2003/polsport_e.pdf

Government of Canada (2007). *Olympic and Paralympic Marks Act.* Available online at http://laws-lois.justice.gc.ca/eng/acts/O-9.2/FullText.html

Houlihan, B. (1997). *Sport, policy and politics: A comparative analysis*. New York: Routledge.

Kikulis, L. M., Slack, T. & Hinings, B. (1995a). Does decision making make a difference? Patterns of change within Canadian national sport organizations. *Journal of Sport Management*, 9(3), 273–99.

Kikulis, L. M., Slack, T. & Hinings, C. R. (1995b). Sector-specific patterns of organizational design change. *Journal of Management Studies*, 32(1), 67–100.

Kikulis, L. M., Slack, T., Hinings, B. & Zimmermann, A. (1989). A structural taxonomy of amateur sport organizations. *Journal of Sport Management*, 3(2), 129–50.

Mintzberg, H. (1979). *The structuring of organizations*. Englewood Cliffs, NJ: Prentice Hall.

Mintzberg, H. (1980). Structure in 5's: A synthesis of the research on organization design. *Management Science*, 26(3), 322–41.

Norris, S. R. (2010). Long-term athlete development Canada: Attempting system change and multi-agency cooperation. *Current Sports Medicine Reports (American College of Sports Medicine)*, 9(6), 379–82.

Parent, M. & Harvey, J. (2009). Towards a management model for sport and physical activity community-based partnerships. *European Sport Management Quarterly*, 9(1), 23–45.

Parent, M. M. & Séguin, B. (2007). Factors that led to the drowning of a world championship organizing committee: A stakeholder approach. *European Sport Management Quarterly*, 7(2), 187–212.

Parent, M. M., Olver, D. & Séguin, B. (2009). Understanding leadership in major sporting events: The case of the 2005 World Aquatics Championships. *Sport Management Review*, 12(3), 167–84.

Slack, T. & Hinings, B. (1992). Understanding change in national sport organizations: An integration of theoretical perspectives. *Journal of Sport Management*, 6(2), 114–32.

Slack, T. & Parent, M. M. (2006). *Understanding sport organizations: The application of organization theory* (2nd edn). Champaign, IL. Human Kinetics.

Sotiriadou, K., Shilbury, D. & Quick, S. (2008). The attraction, retention/transition, and nurturing process of sport development: Some Australian evidence. *Journal of Sport Management*, 22(3), 247–72.

Sport and Fitness Ministers (1987). *National recreation statement, Quebec*. Ottawa: Fitness Canada.

Sport Canada (2008). *Federal policy for hosting international sport events*. Available online at http://www.pch.gc.ca/pgm/sc/pol/acc/2008/accueil-host_2008-eng.pdf

Sport Canada (2011). *Sport funding and accountability framework*. Available online at http://www.pch.gc.ca/pgm/sc/pgm/cfrs/index-eng.cfm

Sport Canada (2012). *Sport Canada contributions report*. Available online at http://www.pch.gc.ca/pgm/sc/cntrbtn/2011-12/index-eng.cfm

Statistics Canada (2008). *Sport participation in Canada*. No. 81-595-MIE2008060. Ottawa: Minister of Industry.

Stevens, J. (2006). The Canadian Hockey Association merger and the emergence of the amateur sport enterprise. *Journal of Sport Management*, 20(1), 74–101.

Sutcliffe, J. (2010). *Interprovincial Sport and Recreation Council: Evaluation of the Canadian sport policy*. Ottawa: Sport Information Resource Centre.

Thibault, L. & Harvey, J. (1997). Fostering interorganizational linkages in the Canadian sport delivery system. *Journal of Sport Management*, 11(1), 45–68.

TSN.ca (2011). *Hockey Canada's Nicholson urges NHL to raise draft age.* Available online at http://www.tsn.ca/nhl/story/?id=378351

Whitson, D., Harvey, J. & Lavoie, M. (2000). The Mills Report, the Manley subsidy proposals, and the business of major-league sport. *Canadian Public Administration*, 43(2), 127–56.

5   Russia

Peter Smolianov

Topics

- Philosophy, organisation and financing of Russian sport
- Role of government and military, political and business leaders
- Science-based and participant-oriented development of sport including the system of education, training, certification, facilities and competitions
- Fight against corruption and doping.

Objectives

- To outline the philosophy, organisation and financing of sport for maximising mass participation and elite performance
- To explain the role of government and military as well as political and business leaders
- To describe education, ranks, rewards and careers of participants, coaches and referees as well as competition and preparation systems
- To depict the structure of sport societies, sport schools, sport colleges and sport universities, as well as regional and national training centres
- To discuss the challenges of developing and enforcing policies, rules and regulations particularly aimed at fighting corruption and doping.

Key terms

Physical culture   Part of culture which embraces values, norms and knowledge pertained to the development of physical and related intellectual capacities and perfect movement abilities, ensuring healthy lifestyle and social adaptations.

Sport societies   Multisport clubs developing all aspects of sport within certain organisations or nationwide industries.

GTO (Gotov k Trudu i Oborone or Ready for Labour and Defence)   Fitness programme involving gender-specific tests for all to progress through six age-appropriate levels.

Uniform sport classification   Seven mass and three elite sport-specific athlete ranks based on the results achieved in designated competitions.

Sport reserve preparation A long-term process of sport-specific education and training uniting various organisations with the goal of raising athletes with a potential to get qualified for international competitions.

Overview

The philosophical and organisational principles inherited by present-day Russia from the Tsarist Empire and the former Soviet Union continue to guide the comprehensive governmental leadership, scientific, educational and medical support aimed at maximising mass fitness and elite sport performance. The governing mechanisms providing lifelong paths in sport from grassroots to professional careers and ensuring expertise of all involved with sport include uniform education, ranks and rewards of participants, coaches and referees as well as a pyramid structure of sport clubs, sport schools, sport colleges and sport universities, and a unified plan of amateur and professional competitions and preparation programmes. Sport governing organisations in this highly centralised, integrated and increasingly democratic system carry difficult responsibilities for fair spending of state money, ethical achievement of ambitious goals, enforcement of rules and control over doping and corruption. The Russian Modern Pentathlon Federation exemplifies the nation's sport governance practices and challenges.

Issues related to governance in Russian sport

The republics of the former USSR, led by Russia, overpowered global sport competitions during the period 1952–1992 winning in 13 out of 18 and being second in five Olympic appearances by the total medal count. Following the dissolution of the Soviet Union in 1991 they continue to succeed as independent states, still dominating the Olympic podium if counted together. Decades before the former USSR started to succeed on the Olympic stage, the nation's devotion to physical culture had allowed for the Tsarist and later the Soviet authorities to integrate fitness objectives into public policies across various socioeconomic sectors. In the nineteenth century sport had been developed in the Russian Empire under the State Departments of Education, Health and Defence. Regional Military Sport Commissions were concerned with mass fitness, and the army sport teams had been paid to participate in national and international competitions since 1912.

With the fall of the Russian monarchy in 1917 and the onset of the era of socialism, sport has become a religion supporting nation's health, defence, productivity, multinational integration, and social and industrial advancement. In the 1920s, the Soviet government established the National Physical Culture Department with regional and local branches, and scientists and coaches were commissioned to construct uniform mechanisms for all to participate in recreation and sport. In order that sport facilities, programmes and professional instruction were available at no or minimal costs at childcare, schools, universities, places of work, community centres and through national networks of multisport societies and clubs, the USSR government had been allocating increasing amounts of money which reached \$US2.2 billion annually in the 1970s compared to \$US680 million in the 2009 Russian federal sport budget, which was increased to \$US1.8 billion in 2011, \$US1.7 billion in 2012, \$US1.6 billion in 2013, and \$US1.3 billion in 2014 on the way to the 2014 Winter Olympics and Paralympics in Russia.

The way sport has been developed and governed in Russia was influenced by frequent wars the nation suffered, making preparation for military fitness permanent. Professional sport had started and is being developed now largely within the army, including commercial and relatively independent soccer, ice hockey and basketball as well as all other Olympic sports. Out of 88 medals won by the Russian team at the 2000 Sydney Olympics, 63 came from the military. Centralisation, rational organisation, competent personnel, and effective systems of training, education and competitions as well as creative application of best global practices spread from the army to the whole Russian sport system (Pochinkin, 2006).

Mass fitness and participation in over 100 types of sport in this holistic system is integrated today with preparation of athletes for international competitions led by the government and state sport authorities who put national goals above interests of particular organisations. Coaches run this sport system as they are employed by the state and rewarded according to achievements of participants. According to the USSR's ideology of preventative medicine and atheism, Russian coaches assume the role of holistic physicians as well as spiritual leaders, being well-educated in biomedical and pedagogical sciences. Coaches receive constant help from medical doctors and scientists in order to nurture participants through a long-term development process, directing each participant to the sport appropriate for the individual's health conditions and opening more opportunities for the talented to progress. The two leading national sport societies providing favourable conditions for all from first steps to high performance in 45 sports through their branches across the former USSR and present-day Russia have been the army-governed CSKA established in 1911 and Dinamo which was established in 1923 by the police and security forces. The public had been also involved in the governance and development of sport through less medal-oriented voluntary multisport societies created in the 1930s at places of study, work and service. These civilian sport societies in the former USSR were governed mostly by trade unions, and complemented Dinamo's and CSKA's colossal investments into sport. Trade unions devoted up to 20 per cent of their budgets or \$US1.5 billion to sport in 1987.

Out of 99 sport societies of the former Soviet Union, 6 were national, 15 belonged to Republican industries, 15 to rural farm networks of the republics, and the rest to regional and local organisations. Participants and fans of the current 15 All-Russia sport societies still express their geographical, professional and political belonging through strong and exciting competition among such local teams as Spartak (trade unions from different industries) and Lokomotiv (railways), Dinamo (police) and CSKA (army).

Mass fitness had been a priority and an integral part of the Soviet strategy aimed at a comprehensive high-quality education and healthy development of each individual in the vast country of 293 million people representing 15 Republics and over 100 ethnic groups with their own languages. Competitive sport participation by one-third of the population contributed to peaceful socioeconomic progress by means of balancing the stress from intense work for the benefits of industrialisation with rich sports, arts and cultural recreation. However, freedoms had been constrained in the USSR before Mikhail Gorbachev came to head the country in 1985. In an attempt to introduce democracy the government liberated the country's political and economic systems by setting the republics free in 1991 and privatising public assets, which, regretfully, resulted in a shift of wealth to elite, a decline in the living standards for the majority, and led to wars among the newly independent republics with 100,000 killed or wounded and over 3 million displaced from their homes.

Preoccupied with market economy reforms during Boris Yeltsin's presidency in 1991–1999, the government was largely concerned with making sport profitable. As a result Russian sport lost much of its state funding, which caused deterioration in the mass participation and in the number of qualified coaches, managers and sport scientists. Russia was left with about half of the Soviet Union's sport facilities and human resources, though retained the world's leading sport research institutes in Moscow and St. Petersburg. Russian youth were found to be 20 per cent less fit in the 1990s than in the 1970s, and its elite performance deteriorated. Russia was third in the total medal count at the Summer Olympic Games in 1996, second in 2000 and 2004, and third in 2008 and 2012. In the Winter Olympics Russia was third in 1994 and 1998, sixth in 2002, fifth in 2006 and sixth in 2010.

In the twenty-first century the Russian government started to restore political and economic stability, and the quality of life increased as a result of higher investments in education, healthcare and sport. Russia was second in the medal tallies at the 2010 Youth Olympic Games and at the 2011 Summer World University Games. The Russian Paralympic team moved from eleventh place in the 2004 Summer Paralympic Games to eighth in 2008, while in the Winter Paralympics Russian athletes moved from fifth in 1994 and 1998, and fourth in 2002 to be first in 2006 and 2010.

Under President Putin's leadership, mass fitness and international sport success started to regain their importance from the year 2000. Sport development has been particularly emphasised since 2007 when the Russian city of Sochi won the bid to host the 2014 Winter Olympics. In 2008 the Ministry for Sport, Tourism and Youth Policy of the Russian Federation was re-established with a higher status and broader responsibilities employing 220 administrative staff in the head office and a total of 310,974 coaches and other sport specialists across the country. The ministry issues new laws and revives old laws pertaining to sport across all socioeconomic spheres. Regulations for local authorities increasingly specify support of sport programmes. The 1968 National Construction Code required developers to provide sport centres within 20 minutes by transport, and basic fitness grounds within seven minutes by foot from every house. The Sport Ministry has committed to reach the following goals by 2020:

- have 40 per cent of the overall population, 20 per cent of disabled individuals, and 80 per cent of students participating in sport
- attract everyone to exercise 3–4 times or 6–12 hours a week
- ensure that 45 per cent of all organisations have sport clubs
- employ 360,000 qualified public coaches and other sport professionals
- win the right to host the 2013 University Games and the 2014 Olympics
- place within the top three in all future Olympics and Paralympics by total medal count

(Ministry for Sport, 2012)

Besides the goal of winning first place in the Sochi Olympic Games in 2014, President Putin stated that the number of people who regularly go to gyms and stadia in Russia had to be increased from 25 million in 2011 to over 42 million by 2015, and in the longer term to reach 70 per cent of the population or over 100 million.

While sport in the USSR and post-Soviet Russia has been in the hands of physical culture experts driven by the results-oriented state funding, the involvement of political leaders with sport has a long history. Tsar Peter the Great introduced physical education as a school and college discipline at the beginning of the eighteenth century. The last Russian Tsar, Nicholas II, made the state responsible for the management of mass physical culture and organisation of the national Olympics in 1913. Sport has been a way of life for the present-day leaders of Russia. President Yeltsin enjoyed many sports and was a keen volleyball and tennis player. His fanship helped Russia to become one of the top tennis nations.

President Putin was a judo champion of his home city of St. Petersburg. He co-authored a book in 2004 which publicised the Russian contribution to the development of judo and connected Putin's leading roles in sport and in politics. Putin's increasing popularity during his eight years as president and then four years as prime minister, which helped him to become president again in 2012, can be attributed, *inter alia*, to his personal devotion to a wide variety of sporting activities (e.g., skiing, ice hockey, fishing, horse and motorcycle riding), and also to his governance principle that the level of sport development defines the nation's level of health and overall advancement. In 2011 the then Prime Minister Putin played badminton with President Medvedev promoting the game in a video placed on the internet. Medvedev who competed for his university in rowing and weightlifting, works out twice a day doing weights, yoga, jogging and swimming.

Putin's policy of supporting sport was consistent across healthcare and education where wages doubled between 2006 and 2010. His speech at the IOC session in 2007 and the plan to provide a $US12 billion of state support appeared to be an important part of the successful Russian bid for hosting the 2014 Winter Olympic Games. Putin's governance also helped Russia to be chosen as the host of the 2013 Summer University Games, the 2017 FIFA Confederations Cup, the 2018 FIFA World Cup, the 2013 World Championships in Athletics, the 2015 World Aquatics Championships, the Russian Grand Prix from 2014 and the 2016 World Ice Hockey Championships.

The Presidential Office executives lead the Council of Winter Olympic Sports Association and the Russian Volleyball Federation. In 2012 the Vice Prime Minister of Russia Alexandr Zhukov, an elite chess player and a midfielder of the Russian Parliament football team, was responsible for state funding of public health, education, housing, physical culture and sport, being also the President of the Russian Olympic Committee (ROC) and the Chess Federation. The support of sport at the parliamentary and governmental levels is strong in Russia also due to the fact that many successful athletes are attracted to politics. A high level of athlete education in Russia is one of the reasons why many of them operate successfully at the top national level. At least five Olympic champions were elected to the Russian Parliament with at least two holding doctoral degrees.

The importance of sport for personal and social development was preached to all those who grew up in the USSR. This notion is spreading across the globe together with the growing role of Russian business people in sport governance. The prominent Russian businessman and 2012 presidential candidate Mikhail Prokhorov bought the NBA New Jersey Nets for $US200 million in 2009 and financed half of the team's $800 million new arena, making him the first person from overseas to acquire such a deep stake in a major American sport team. He bought the Moscow CSKA basketball team on the verge of collapse in 1997 and within seven years turned it into one of the best in Europe, thanks to his background as a basketball player. His two-hour daily exercises also include soccer, volleyball, and martial arts, as well as alpine and jet skiing. He is a board member of the Russian National Multi-Sport Society, President of the Russian Biathlon Union and an Ambassador for Peace and Sport, an international organisation committed to serving peace in the world through sport. Another Russian businessman Alisher Usmanov in 2012 co-owned England's Arsenal Football Club, sponsored the Moscow Dinamo Football Club and invested into fencing worldwide being the President of the International Fencing Federation. The influence of Russian capital in international sport governance has been also increasing through ownership of such properties as England's Chelsea and Portsmouth football clubs.

During the Soviet times, the government had provided all necessary resources to sport and demanded top medal counts in return. After the neglect of sport during the transition to free market economy in the 1990s, the resources are now returning back to sport though slower than dictated by the nation's sport aspirations. After the 2010 Vancouver Olympic Games where Russia placed eleventh (a top three in the medal standings was the target), the ROC chief and a deputy sport minister had to resign. The growing democracy was manifested by the fact that the Skiing Federation president also resigned after 14 skiers openly blamed the federation leadership for doing little to develop the sport.

Striving for sport excellence, Russian sport scientists and managers study best global practices and try to implement them. The Russian Sport Minister, who was a USSR and National Hockey League star and won the Stanley Cup as a player and a coach, wrote a book in 2005 analysing the best methods of sport development around the world, which still helps the Sport Ministry and its regional and municipal branches to govern comprehensive sport development in the following organisations and institutions:

- National Olympic and Paralympic Committees, sport-specific federations/ associations/unions and multisport societies and their regional, municipal and local branches and commercial professional teams
- federal and regional training centres and other sport facilities
- sport schools, clubs and physical culture centres at childcare, schools, colleges and universities
- sport educational and research institutes
- sport product manufacturers
- mass media.

Under direct presidential supervision a Council for Development of Physical Culture and High Performance Sport and for Preparation to the 2012 Olympic and 2014 Paralympic Games was established. The Russian Government also provides a direct guidance for sport societies particularly those fostered within public service organisations.

All sport-related organisations and activities are guided by the 2007 Federal Law on Physical Culture and Sport based on the following principles:

- free access to sport for physical, intellectual and moral development of everyone, and consecutive connection in physical education across ages
- unified nationwide legislation, combining top-down state and bottom-up organisational regulations in compliance with international agreements
- state guarantees of sport-related rights to citizens, prohibition of discrimination and violence, assistance to persons with disabilities and other groups requiring special social protection and provision of safety of participants and spectators
- interaction between federal and local governments in the field of sport, between sport authorities and federations, and development of all types and components of sport as social and educational voluntary activity.

The above-mentioned law serves as a guide for the Sport Ministry's governance of amateur and professional sport, which it exerts based on advice from medical, biological and pedagogical scientists it employs. The Central Research Institute for Physical Culture (most known as VNIIFK) was established in 1933 to conduct research into all aspects of sport and coordinate it at similar regional institutes and sport universities. Russian sport scientists have developed policies for guiding and regulating a lifelong progression of all involved in sport. Before competing in a particular sport, the participants are supposed to achieve certain results within the GTO programme involving running, long and high jumping, pull-ups, push-ups, crawling, rope/pole/tree climbing, grenade/ball throwing, and skiing or swimming, and also to demonstrate theoretical and practical knowledge of health, physical culture, sport and defence. GTO was first introduced in 1931 and after a number of revisions and scientific tests by 1985 it comprised 21 gender-specific tests at six age levels from 7 to 60 years old. GTO was instructed and awarded through sport organisations as well as at places of study, work and service, making it free and available for all and mandatory for youth. After the USSR dissolution in 1991, GTO was not practised in most of the former Soviet Republics but was revived in Russia in 2003.

After passing the GTO tests, participants are to progress through sport-specific stages of the Unified Sports Classification, namely, three junior, three senior, and four master ranks. Each rank requires specific results against such criteria as seconds or metres as well as victories in competitions of a certain level. The classification system is revamped in each four-year Olympic cycle through an immense amount of research work and consultation. The above concept started to develop for figure skating in the Tsarist Russia at the end of the nineteenth century and it became the key regulatory instrument for Soviet sport success. Russian sport scientists extended the Soviet system of ranks from 60 sports in 1980 to 143 in 2011. This ranking system is designed to guide long-term athlete development, to monitor performance and to ensure a proper distribution of public resources between regions, organisations, sports and different levels of performance within each sport. The Sport Ministry registered a total of 18,738,855 people or 19 per cent of Russia's population as organised participants in the sports the ministry coordinated in 2012.

The state sport officials regulate most aspects of athlete development according to scientists' advice. The guidelines for coaches include such criteria as the minimum starting ages for each sport (e.g., seven for swimming and 13 for weightlifting) and uniform training and educational curricula. Russian sport authorities provide control over the quality of genetic tests which are based on the analysis of blood and hair, accompanied by recommendations from sport scientists regarding the right sport for particular individuals, specialisation within a given sport and optimal training and lifestyle programmes. The Sport Ministry also ensures regular visits of coaches to schools in order to identify and invite sport-predisposed children to sport clubs. Since the early 1970s, groups of scientists in pedagogy, medicine, psychology, physiology, biomechanics, biochemistry and engineering have been consulting to the national teams for improved athlete performance and health. In 2012 the Russian Sport Ministry supported the summer Olympic sports with 41 scientific groups, the winter sports with 15 groups, and Paralympic and other special needs sport activities with 26 groups, and it also coordinated 98 sport conferences in 2011.

To ensure a continuation of athletes' careers, the Sport Ministry governs the sport personnel education, certification and rewards. Coaches must compete in and study the sport they plan to coach. They must pass fitness tests in addition to academic exams, enter sport universities for five-year programmes and progress upon graduation through five certification stages. The uniform curriculum for physical and sport-specific coaching education is sustained by sport and pedagogical universities across Russia. Educational, methodological, medical and scientific support for Russian coaches creates conditions for guided professional progression in 117 kinds of sport governed by the Sport Ministry in partnership with sport federations. Developed and regulated by the ministry are also the requirements for certification of referees in 128 sports through four–five stages, including seminars, theoretical exams and practical experience.

Thanks to the emphasis on education and science, Soviet and Russian sport has been mostly governed by specialists holding degrees equivalent to or higher than masters' and who are knowledgeable in physical education and coaching, and pedagogical and biomedical sciences. In the 1970s to 1980s, eight national team coaches defended their doctoral dissertations. The current Sport Minister and three of his six deputies have PhD equivalents. The ROC president is a graduate of Moscow and Harvard universities. Comprehensive education helps Russian sport policy-makers cooperate effectively with researchers and base their practices on scientific principles.

Soviet sport authorities had been directing the mass national Spartakiads since 1928, which comprise more types of sport than the Olympic Games. By 1975 one third of the population participated in Spartakiads. Post-Soviet Russia revitalised Spartakiads in 2002, making them annual events integrated with school competitions. The 2011 Youth Spartakiad had four tiers of competition: first at individual educational institutions, then at the municipal and regional levels, culminating in the national finals. Olympic preparation starts five years ahead of each Games. The athlete preparation plans integrate medal objectives, training programmes, and competition calendars. In the 1970s, the Soviet annual sport calendar included up to 300 different competitions. In 2011 the Russian Sport Ministry coordinated a total of 10,000 competitions and training camps in 132 sports.

The Sport Ministry rules and subsidises sport facilities and programmes at 164,213 organisations of all types from workplaces and recreation centres to the athlete development pyramid at:

- 4,074 children's sport schools
- 781 Olympic reserve schools
- 135 high performance schools
- 40 Olympic reserve colleges and 13 sport universities
- 25 regional Olympic training centres.

Similar to the Sport Ministry, ROC (2012) is being financed by the state and it also operates under the Physical Culture and Sport Law, primarily supporting federations in:

- high performance
- sport science and medicine
- Olympic education
- international relations
- marketing.

ROC's important task is the search for new financial sources to complement the State budget. ROC counts on the rich individuals to provide medal winners of the 2012 Olympic Games between $US500,000 and $US1 million through the Federations alone, before any endorsement money. The Head of the Summer Sports Association has $US30 billion, so if he gives every winner $1million, it's not very much for him (Johnson, 2012). In preparation to the 2008 Olympics, the government helped to deploy billionaires to participate in the effort. The country's 10 richest businessmen, in addition to aiding other sport projects, donated $US12 million to the Fund for the Support of Olympians (Schwartz, 2008). Russian corporations increasingly finance sport, devoting over $1 billion to the 2014 Sochi Olympics. The Russian gas and oil company Gazprom was reported to choose not to sign sponsorship contracts but simply donate US$130 million to the country's Olympic teams to help them prepare for the 2012 London and 2014 Sochi Olympic Games (RT, 2010).

The Sportloto lottery has been providing support to sport since 1970, but following the post-Soviet privatisations, industry is struggling to fulfil its obligations to sport, and has been witnessing bankruptcies and fraud. After the Sport Ministry sued the lottery for $US67 million in 2011, a full jurisdiction over Sportloto was given to the largest state-controlled commercial bank. Under growing competition with the gambling businesses, Sportloto and the Ministry of Finance are now working together on stricter regulations limiting the use of the term 'lottery' and on a reduction in licensed operators.

The problematic areas of sport governance in Russia appear to be not significantly different from those in the rest of the world. However, gender equality is less of an issue there as compared to many other countries because Soviet women were granted equal rights in the 1920s and since then they have made a decisive contribution to the country's sport success. During the 1980s 'sport for all' retained precedence over elite sport and opportunities for women and disabled persons were increased (Riordan, 1989).

More concerning issues for Russian sport-governing organisations are doping and corruption. The decade following the dissolution of the USSR in 1991 brought new political and economic freedoms, accompanied by commercialisation and criminalisation of sport. Possible reasons for threats, assaults and even killings of athletes, coaches and sport administrators during this time lie in the fact that criminals were eager to grab the money made in sport and to launder the stolen money. This painful process of introducing a free economy in Russia had been mostly completed by the end of the century, but corruption still remains a problem. In 1996 a law was introduced imposing severe punishment for bribery among participants, coaches, referees, managers and organisers of sporting events. Offences, such as influencing the outcome of a game, would incur a fine of 500 minimum salaries and up to six months in prison (Pochinkin, 2006).

In July 2008, President Medvedev introduced more severe sanctions against corruption, such as dismissal of state and municipal officials involved in minor corruption and making it obligatory for officials to report cases of corruption. In 2010–2011 the public oversight of government's budgets and sociological research related to corruption control were endorsed, and fines for giving or taking bribes were raised to up to 100 times the amount of the bribe. As part of the increased national anti-corruption efforts, any legal claims against the Sport Ministry are now publicised on its website together with 28 documents detailing how corruption is being fought including the current legislation, strategies, and reports on completed measures. Particular attention is given to ensuring the Ministry's transparency by informing all personnel about regulations and reporting of violations. In light of match-fixing scandals that have been rocking the European soccer leagues, the Russian Football Association proposed a new law in 2012 aimed at the severe prosecution of anyone involved in fixing the outcome of a match. Russia also plays an active role in the IOC's anti-corruption campaign to combat the international illegal gambling industry which is believed to be worth tens of billions of American dollars annually.

Liberated post-Soviet Russia has been struggling to prevent sport doping disqualifications. One week before the 2008 Olympics, seven Russian female medal contenders were suspended for tampering with their urine samples. The timing of the accusation allowed almost no time for appeal, indicating weak Russian representation in the international sport governing bodies. Russian performance at the 2010 Winter Olympic Games was also influenced by drug scandals when seven skiers were disqualified mostly for using the banned EPO drug in 2009–2010. Test results are now openly analysed on the internet site of the Russian Anti-doping Agency RUSADA (2012). Out of a total of 14,500 athlete dope tests taken in 2009, 81 were positive, and out of 15,000 tests made in 2010, 88 were positive. The IOC President expressed a deep concern about the number of positive dope tests in Russia to the country's president and sport minister. Subsequent Sport Ministry's measures included stricter penalties for doping violations and closer cooperation with event organisers, regional sport authorities and federations, and active involvement with international organisations such as the 16-country Anti-Doping Working Group within the European Council, as well as the introduction of new courses aimed at prevention of doping at schools and universities, and anti-doping television programmes.

The key peculiarities of Russian sport governance, particularly the philosophy of holistic human development, the leading roles of the government, state, the military and science as well as comprehensive education and instructions for lifelong participation and professional progression in sport, are further illustrated with reference to the Russian modern pentathlon.

Case study: The Russian Modern Pentathlon Federation (RMPF)

When the Greek philosopher Aristotle admired the pentathlon for endowing both strength and speed, thereby producing most beautiful athletes in the ancient Olympics, the sport tested military skills of the time such as discus, javelin, long jump, running and wrestling. The founder of the modern Olympics, Baron Pierre de Coubertin, included the modern pentathlon into the 1912 Olympic programme believing that pistol shooting, epée fencing, swimming, show-jumping and cross-country running produced an ideal complete athlete and soldier. The women's contest was first introduced at the 2000 Olympics. Modern pentathlon can be viewed as a true representation of the entire Olympic movement. The five Olympic rings are reflected in participation from all five continents and in pentathlon's five events.

From 1956 onwards, Soviet and then Russian pentathletes have won medals at all the Olympics they have attended, and at the 2000, 2004 and 2008 Games, the medals were gold. This success is based on a massive foundation comprising 96 state-employed coaches training 5,000 athletes of which 1,250 are females and 15 are disabled individuals. The sport manifests Russia's philosophy of a holistic human development and preparation of youth for military service. The strategic partnership role is played here by an RMPF advisory council member, who is also member of parliament and a board member of the Dinamo Sport Society. By supporting pentathlon across the nation, Dinamo and CSKA contribute considerably to preparing youth for army service and nurturing high performers for leading military positions.

Present-day Russia has inherited the Soviet tradition of keeping pentathlon affordable to participants in all the 15 republics of the former USSR. Despite the high costs for the state and sponsoring organisations, pentathlon had been successfully developing across the country from Lithuania and Ukraine in the west to Georgia in the south and Kazakhstan in the east in accordance with the uniform guidelines and resources. As a result, all these regions delivered strong mass participation and top-class international competitors. The rivalry for state funding among sponsoring organisations stimulated strong competition both between and within the sport societies. Nowadays the local growth of modern pentathlon across Russia is being stimulated through such global events as those depicted in the picture below.

There are currently 18 regional RMPF training centres integrating facilities with coaching, medical and general education support for the athletes, particularly through sport schools, colleges and universities funded jointly by local and federal sport authorities. The pentathlon coaches employed by these centres strive to follow the USSR tradition of working in teams, recruiting participants in at least three age categories, and taking athletes through all-year training and education. This allows coaches to successfully implement the long-term plans recommended by sport scientists and required by head coaches and the RMPF Board.

The holistic participant-focused and science-supported governance of Russian sport is clearly reflected in the RMPF Board composition. Most of the 18 members are former high-performance pentathletes holding master's equivalents in pentathlon coaching with emphasis on biomedical and pedagogical sciences. The majority of board members are full-time pentathlon employees:

- seven head coaches: one chief, two senior, two junior and two reserve
- three 'physician coaches', the post which requires a unique qualification established in the USSR in 1961 combining fundamental medical and sport science with sport-specific coaching education
- managers of pentathlon training centres which integrate daily year-round training in all five disciplines, lodging and boarding, as well as medical support and other services.

The top board members connect RMPF with strategic partners. The RMPF president is also an advisor to the head of Russia's presidential administration and a board member in several national corporations. The RMPF's first vice president is also a regional deputy governor. They both are vice presidents of Union International de Pentathlon Moderne (UIPM), pentathlon's global governing body. UIPM has awarded Russia the right to host the World Championships in 2016, the event is critically important in preparation of pentathletes for the 2016 Olympic Games. Spectators will be able to watch all five pentathlon events from one seat at the World Championships in Russia, a facility rarely available around the world. The role played by the UIPM vice presidents from Russia was also important in the bid to host the 2016 World Championships.

The RMPF is successful largely because its board and athletes form a single cohesive team from different generations. Similar to the pattern of other competitions, Russian pentathletes were nurtured to victory at the 2011 European Championships by key board members present at the event, including:

- RMPF president and two vice presidents
- Two training centre managers
- RMPF coaching council chairman
- RMPF women's head coach
- RMPF men's head coach.

Most of these board members were Olympic and World Champions and passionate pentathlon experts. Most of these board members were Olympic and World Champions and passionate pentathlon experts. The family-like relationships between participants and officials as well as the humanistic and mass participation principles of Russian sport lead to effective but sometimes inefficient achievement of the desired goals.

The RMPF president devoted the year of 2012 to improving conformity and issued an 'Order of Raising Responsibility and Discipline' stressing that coaches may lose their jobs and athletes their support for non-compliance with deadlines for reports and other duties. The order focused on the systematic progress of athletes, coaches and referees, demanding that:

- detailed yearly plans for each athlete must be timely submitted by coaches to the RMPF
- camp coaches must timely report to the RMPF about the health of participants and conditions provided by the training centre
- a mobile set of equipment must be acquired by the RMPF in order to organise competitions at locations without specialised pentathlon facilities
- pentathlon events must be integrated into the Sport Ministry's plan for over 100 sports
- after competitions have been planned for the following year, the Coaching Council chairman in consultation with head coaches must submit the annual plan of training seminars for coaches to the president

- progression of referees through their certification stages and international refereeing must be provided through education of regional representatives, creation of referee teams and seminars during competitions
- The RMPF and regional federations must utilise new income sources to provide cash and non-monetary compensation of referees.

The focus on athlete care is also evident through the requirements stated in the interregional and national competition regulations jointly administered by the RMPF and the Sport Ministry as part of 70 pentathlon competitions and camps integrated into the 2012 all-Russia event calendar. The requirements admitted are as follows:

- minimum age of 18 years for participation in individual full pentathlon events, while younger participants must be offered less challenging events which feature fewer disciplines
- medical checks as part of comprehensive long-term athlete monitoring
- competitors' mandatory insurance that may be covered by local authorities and sporting organisations
- on-site ambulance and medical personnel provided by local authorities
- doping control in accordance with international standards and IOC.

The RMPF defines relations between athletes and sport organisations and conditions of changing coaches and sport organisations in accordance with:

- the country's labour legislation
- respect for athletes' freedoms and organisations' investments in athletes
- rules of resolving disputes in court through the Sports Arbitration Chamber.

The RMPF requires that its Judiciary Board which governs all arbitration matters must comprise the RMPF umpires who:

- devote a minimum of 30 days each year to the board's activities
- have sport-related education and knowledge of pentathlon governance
- have experience in organising competitions.

RMPF stipulates its Coaching Council's monthly duties focusing on maximising athlete's performance and requires that the following personnel be elected to the council:

- head coaches
- personal coaches of top athletes from different age categories
- team physicians
- leaders of the scientific group assigned by the Sport Ministry to provide methodological and medico-biological support.

In this country's nurturing, comprehensively regulated and extremely competitive pentathlon environment, scandals involving the Russian and Soviet pentathletes have been relatively rare but dramatic. One of the leading athletes was disqualified from the 1976 Olympics for using an epée with a built-in mechanism which could fake a victory. Though he confirmed his supremacy by winning eight of his nine bouts with a replacement weapon, he was stripped of his military and sport ranks and removed from the sport permanently. Another unprecedented incident was a 30-month long doping-caused disqualification of 12 pentathletes including five from the USSR at the 1986 World Championships. The RMPF currently requires the national team candidates to provide their whereabouts throughout the year for random testing. There were no violations found with 73 tests in 2009 and 30 tests in 2010, but one violation punished by a three-month ban happened in 2011 (RUSADA, 2012).

When leaders of military, government and commercial organisations pursue mutual interests with sport authorities, as it is the case with pentathlon in Russia, the support for the sport can be sufficient for the world's top performance in different economic and political conditions. Military-style governance and scientific advice can be effective in keeping sport focused on systematic mass and elite development and in keeping cheating and doping under control, particularly in Russia, where more than tough laws are needed to compensate for somewhat loose compliance.

Summary

Russian sport governance is based on the Soviet philosophy of a holistic science guided development of each individual and on a highly integrated system of physical culture and sport led by federal authorities. It is hard to emulate the intrinsic passion, original research, dedication and rigour with which sport was delivered in the USSR. Present-day Russia has inherited and advanced the following practices which appear useful for successful sport governance across the world:

- coaches entrusted to prevent mass illnesses (with support from biomedical education and healthy participation guidelines) and to achieve high performance (with support from multidisciplinary scientific groups and sport specific physicians)
- uniform guidelines for integrated mass and elite participation in more than 100 sports, regulating:
  - talent identification and long-term athlete development
  - education and certification of athletes, coaches and referees
  - integrated plans of competitions and camps
  - training centres providing complete year round nurturing of athletes in multiple sports
- governing boards comprising the sport's experts from different generations and sport leaders who also occupy influential government and business positions and combine responsibilities for financing sport, education and health as part of national social wellbeing policy.

Review questions

1   What mechanisms ensure lifelong participation and career progression in the Russian sport system?
2   Which sport governance features has present-day Russia inherited from the former USSR?
3   Which governing methods have helped Russian pentathletes to succeed?

Further reading

Kuznetsova, Z., Kaline, I., & Kaline, G. (2002). Russia: Traditions, political interventions and the educational system as foundations of sport for all. In L. P. DaCosta & A. Miragaya (eds). *World experiences and trends of sport for all*. Oxford: Meyer & Meyer Sport.

Riordan, J. (1980). *Sport in Soviet society: Development of sport and physical education in Russia and the USSR*. Cambridge: Cambridge University Press.

Smolianov, P. & Zakus, D. H. (2008). Exploring high performance management in Olympic sport with reference to practices in the former USSR and Russia. *The International Journal of Sport Management*, 9, 206–32.

To, W.W.H., Smolianov, P. & Semotiuk, D.M. (2012). Comparative high performance sport models. In P. Sotiriadou & V. De Bosscher (eds). *Managing high performance sport*. London: Routledge

Websites

Russian Olympic Committee: http://www.roc.ru
Russian Government: http://government.ru/en/
VNIIFK: http://www.vniifk.ru

References

Johnson, S. (2012). *Russian Olympic Committee promises huge financial rewards for winning Olympic gold*. Available online at http://ca.sports.yahoo.com/olympics/news?slug=ycn-10877957

Ministry for Sport, Tourism and Youth Policy of the Russian Federation. (2012). Available online at http://sport.minstm.gov.ru

Pochinkin, A.V. (2006). *Formation and development of professional commercial sport in Russia*. Moscow: Soviet Sport.

Riordan, J. (1989). Soviet sport and Perestroika. *Journal of Comparative Physical Education and Sport*, 6(2), 7–18.

ROC (2012). Russian Olympic Committee. Available online at http://www.roc.ru

RT (2010). Gazprom to spend $130m on Russian Olympians. Available online at http://rt.com/sport/gazprom-russian-olympic-sponsorship/

RUSADA (2012). Russian Anti-doping Agency. Available online at http://www.rusada.ru

Schwartz, M. (2008). A major tuneup for a sports machine. *The New York Times*. Retrieved from: http://www.nytimes.com/2008/07/29/sports/olympics/29russia.html?th&emc=th

6 South Africa

Petri Bester

Topics

- Definition of sport governance
- The legacy of sport governance within South Africa
- The new road to success: the sport road map
- Sport governance structure
- Addressing the challenges.

Objectives

- To accurately define sport governance
- To explain the different tasks of sport governance
- To understand the effect a country's heritage has on its sport governance structure
- To explore the unique challenges developing countries face when it comes to sport governance
- To grasp the practical application of theory by referring to a case study.

Key terms

Sport governance   The structure and processes put in place by the government that allow national sports bodies to develop strategic goals and direction, monitor their performances against these goals and ensure their respective boards act in the best interest of all citizens.

Accessibility   The provision and facilitation of appropriate resources that enable the increase of participants in sport with the emphasis on the disadvantaged and marginalised groups (including women, children, youth, the elderly, persons with a disability and people living in rural areas).

Equality   The full and equal enjoyment of all rights and freedoms, including participation and access to sport and sport infrastructure.

Corporatism   A political situation where power is exercised through larger organisations such as businesses and trade unions, which work together under the direction of the state.

Nation building   Refers to the process of constructing or structuring a national identity using the power of the state. This process aims at the unification of the people or peoples within the state so that it remains politically stable and viable in the long run. Sport has been a strong medium for this process.

Overview

This chapter will provide a brief overview of sport governance within a South African context. Attention will first be given to the definition of sport governance within the South African context, after which the history of sport governance is briefly discussed. The governance structure of South African sport is preceded by the new approach to successful sport organisations and the development of a democratic sport system. The last section of this chapter will explore concepts regarding the unique governance challenges within the African environment such as access to sport across all demographic groups, developing appropriate sport infrastructure, improvement of social cohesion and nation building and improving the quality of life of all South Africans. Cycling South Africa will be used as a case study to highlight the challenges and issues pertaining to sport governance within South Africa.

Sport governance in South Africa

Sport governance within South Africa is in all likelihood very different compared to sport governance systems across the globe. This is predominantly due to the historical developments within the country, the essence of which is quoted here by Cheryl Roberts:

> Our officials (and sportspersons) who gave so much to the development and organisation of non-racial sport (South Africans, black and white) who were involved in sport (and recreation) from way back in the 1950s are still involved in sport today, giving their time to sport (and recreation) and still loving sport. Post-apartheid South Africa has gone on to record international sports victories and sports prowess of our sports has surfaced with the eradication of apartheid. Elite and professional sports stars abound in all sports and South Africa derives much joy and pride from international sport. And through all of this, our stars from behind the bars are still involved in sport, still organising and loving sport, but never forgetting where we came from and what got us where we are today.
>
> (Mbalula, 2011a)

And this is the epiphany of sport governance within South Africa, knowing where it has come from allows sport organisations and officials to effectively and efficiently manage the present situation within sport governance in South Africa. Sport governance within the South African environment can therefore be seen as the structure and processes put in place by the government which allow national sport bodies to develop strategic goals and direction, monitor their performances against these goals and ensure that their respective boards act in the best interest of all South Africans. It is evident that the legacy left behind should first be explored before the current structure can be discussed.

The legacy of sport governance within South Africa

The Republic of South Africa is well known for its turbulent past, rife with racial and social discrimination. This discrimination has stretched across all aspects of government, including sport governance. Since the inception of the democratic rule in 1994, however, the South African government has been involved in a vigorous process of transformation. This process has included a new democratic constitution, the transformation of the state machinery and changes to virtually all of the South African policies that had been in existence during the previous regime. The result of these dramatic changes has cumulated into the emergence of a democratic society, based largely on the principles of non-racialism, non-sexism and democracy. During this transformation, sport has played a crucial role in breaking down racial barriers and has been a powerful tool for progress and development within the South African democracy (Mbalula, 2011a).

Although the governance of sport has seen major changes during the past few decades, it is evident that strategies, frameworks and plans require improvement so as to be utilised for the benefit of the whole population. At the forefront of strategy development lays the sluggish transformation of sport policies, with resistance to change within South African sporting circles at an all-time high. Another major area of concern for sport governance within South Africa is the broadening of access to sport and recreation facilities to all and responsibility for building and constructing such facilities. The revival of school sport and the promotion of physical education are crucial when considering the extent of societal problems youth is experiencing.

In 1996, the late Minister of Sport and Recreation released a White Paper on Sport and Recreation, which formed the basis of sport governance within the democracy of South Africa. The paper was the first of its kind for South African sport, but 14 years later, at the end of 2000, the continued poor performance of the athletes led to the government appointment of a Ministerial Task Team (MTT). The main task of team was to investigate the challenges South African athletes faced concerning high-performance and elite sport. Recommendations were to be given, which was approved in 2003 by the cabinet. These recommendations ultimately led to the amalgamation of the then separate sport bodies into a fully fledged and holistic Department of Sport and Recreation (DSR) (which later became Sport and Recreation South Africa – SRSA). The South African Sports Confederation and Olympic Committee (SASCOC) were then also established.

A major concern during this period was the lack of resources allocated to the department and to sport in general. This was mainly due to a deficiency in knowledge of the individuals responsible for decision making, sport's role in society and its potential as an instrument of transformation. The situation was even more dismal for the recreational dimension of the department as even less resources were allocated to this section. It was decided that sport was to be included as one of the beneficiaries of the planned national lottery. The theme of this period then became 'getting the nation to play' and SRSA set the first sport governance guidelines (Mbalula, 2011a):

- To increase the levels of participation in sport and recreation activities
- To raise sport's profile in the face of conflicting priorities
- To maximise the probability of success in major events
- To place sport in the forefront of efforts to reduce the levels of crime.

The basis of the first Sports White Paper was seated in a conscious effort, firm commitment and close collaboration between government, non-governmental organisations (NGOs), the private sector and the South African society in general. Each stakeholder's role in laying the foundation for a culture of sport and recreation within South Africa was strongly emphasised. Despite the emphasised focus on non-governmental stakeholders' role in the transformation of sport, the SRSA took full responsibility for the policy, provision and delivery of sport and recreation. The realisation that there existed substantial imbalances between advantaged urban communities and disadvantaged rural communities, a lack of strategic vision and policy for the development of sport and recreation and the expectation that the SRSA would cater for the needs of the entire population with a budget that previously only served 20 per cent of the population, proved to be key challenges that needed to be addressed in order for the white paper to be successful.

A general illiteracy existed in the country regarding the role sport could play in the transformation of the country, as said by the Commonwealth Heads of Government Working Group in Harare (Department of Sport and Recreation, 1997):

It is time that the integral role which sport [plays] in the process of nation-building is fully recognised. Sport is an investment. It is firstly an investment in the health, vitality and productivity of one's people. It is secondly an investment in their future. The social benefits include an overall improvement in the quality of life and physical, mental and moral well-being of a population. Furthermore, the successful athletes serve as role models for the youth of the country, as achievers, as unofficial ambassadors, and as individuals committed to equality and fairness in competition. Because of its visibility, sport can play an enormous part in addressing gender inequalities and discrimination against the disabled and minorities.

For South Africans, sport's most important role during this period in the country's history, was that of fostering national unity. The white paper reiterated that the impact of sport and recreation reached well beyond the confines of participation.

The white paper was updated after a strenuous process and finalised in 2011, together with the road map which outlined priority areas for sport and recreation discourse in the country. The project kicked off with collaboration between SRSA and SASCOC, committing themselves to conversing with the people of South Africa. The collaboration strived to ensure that, through a consultative process, the entire nation was involved in a national and robust debate on transformation, resulting in a national sport plan that culminated in a conceptual and recreational plan for the country. The strategic imperative was to launch a rolling, interactive and progressive process that, in 2012, is strongly seated in mass-based and people-centred developmental and transformative discourse that will continue to evolve from a grassroots level. This innovative vision then led to a new era in sport governance with the inception of the Road Map to Optimal Performance and Functional Excellence.

The new road to success: the sport road map

From this context, sport governance and sport policies are largely based on the foundations of 'sport for all' where cooperation between capital, labour, and civil society as the basis for corporatism, and represents an important measure for the developmental state as to the integration and unity of the nation. Despite the strong emphasis on capital, sport governance should, to a certain extent, strive to locate desire and passion within the South African community so that interpersonal concerns are addressed rather than profit and false solidarity. The SRSA aims to accomplish these goals with the Road Map to Optimal Performance and Functional Excellence which contains five strategic priorities namely (Mbalula, 2011b):

- transformation
- school sport
- institutional mechanisms
- mass mobilisation
- recreation.

The above-mentioned elements are considered to be the critical success factors which aim to provide a new paradigm, guiding and directing the new thinking and vision of the Department of Sport and Recreation. The new paradigm will affect the department in its entire functionality as well as the five-year strategic horizon of sport governance. This is then further disaggregated into annual operational frameworks in the short, medium and long term. In essence, this means that the South African sport system will be predicated on this new vision as stipulated in the road map. It is envisaged that the road map will be an integrated and wholesale strategy to reposition the department and prompt functional efficiencies and accelerate service delivery. The main objective of the road map is to act as the catalyst for the transformation of sport governance within the department and the sport sector as a whole, into an agile, athletic and responsive institutional architecture.

Currently the country is experiencing large-scale sport activism, with expansions in the participation in sport at all levels. Sport has become a seminal activity in the social pursuit of cultivating a healthy nation, specifically through encouraging healthy bodies and healthy minds of all South Africans. Greater prominence and impact, both national and international, was achieved primarily through the public nature of sport and more efficient and effective broadcasting efforts by SRSA. By taking cognisance of both the past and present of sport governance in South Africa, the structure can now be discussed in detail.

Sport governance structure

From the above discussion it is clear that the SRSA, its affiliates and sport governance within South Africa has experienced many and diverse changes during the past few decades of transformation. Needless to say, so has the sport governance structure that was put in place by the previous government. The governance of sport and recreation within South Africa can be best described by using an organogram.

Parliament, particularly through the Minister and the Standing Committee on Sport and Recreation, is principally responsible for defining government policy, legislation and budget allocations. The SRSA, within the above context, then focuses on the following issues on a national level:

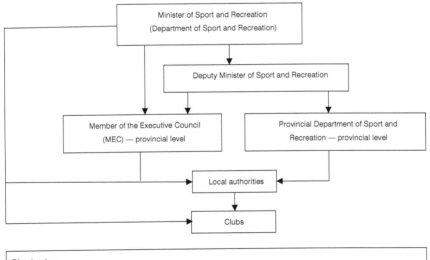

Figure 6.1 Sport governance organogram

- The promotion of sport and recreation policy and its implementation through several affiliates e.g. the National Sports Council (NSC), SASCOC and the national federations (NFs).
- The recreation policy, with the principal agent being the South African National Recreation Council (SANREC).
- Funding of the above agencies.
- The researching, auditing and upgrading of facilities for national and international events.

South Africa is divided into nine provinces (Gauteng, Mpumalanga, Kwa-Zulu Natal, Northern Cape, Eastern Cape, Western Cape, North-West and the Free State), which is then managed at provincial level by the Member of the Executive Council (MEC) and the provincial department of sport and recreation. They are charged with the following responsibilities:

- Policy development, within the context of the national sport and recreation policy, with the principal agents being provincial federations and national governing bodies.
- Implementation of recreation policy, via the provincial recreation councils.
- Funding of the above agencies.
- Creating facilities as established by local authorities, for national and provincial events.

The local authorities then have the following roles within the context of national and provincial sport governance:

- Policy development at local level.
- Implementation of recreation policy.
- Funding of its principal agencies such as sports clubs and individuals.
- Creating facilities for local and provincial usage.

Within the sport governance organogram, several individuals are responsible for operational duties that need to be performed. Certainly the most crucial of these role players are the ministry and the SRSA whose main task is to develop the policy framework within which the governance of sport in South Africa is managed. They are tasked with making sport accessible to all South Africans and to provide the needed infrastructure to reach these goals. In addition, it is their duty to ensure the existence of programmes that develop the human resource potential in sport. Without the SRSA, the coordination of the involvement of the various departments of the national government would be chaotic and congruency with the national sport and recreation policy would be insufficient. The SRSA is also responsible for providing the mechanism for unlocking crucial resources, so that the budget provided for sport and recreation by outside parties such as the National Lottery, sponsors and overseas funding, can be extended.

It is the SRSA that enters into international agreements for the purpose of sharing technology, skills transfer and the development of sport and recreation for its agencies, provincial governments and local authorities. Whenever conflict arises that lead agencies are not able to resolve, it is expected that the SRSA will intervene in the interest of sport and recreation, as well as the public. As previously mentioned, sport reaches beyond its own portfolio and the SRSA is responsible for coordinating input provided to other departments such as the Department of Education and the physical education curriculum at school and tertiary levels. Lastly, the SRSA is also responsible for the provision of incentives for excellence in sport and recreation.

The governance structure makes provision for a portfolio committee on sport and recreation. It is this committee's responsibility to further the cause of sport and recreation at a political level. By achieving this, the committee strives to monitor the governance of sport and recreation in terms of the national government policy, advance the cause of sport and recreation in parliament, debate and suggest enabling legislation and advice on international trends in sport and recreation.

The MEC and provincial SRSA are one step closer to the actual delivery of sport and recreation to the community, than their national counterparts. For this reason they are responsible for ensuring the accessibility of sport to all people within the province they serve. This ties in closely with the provision of infrastructure and facilities required for sport as well as the maintenance thereof. As mentioned it is the MEC that is responsible for ensuring the development of sport talent by creating and ensuring the existence of relevant programmes as well as the development of a policy framework for the governance of provincial sport and recreation. It is crucial that provincial policies tie in with the national policy as set by the SRSA.

The fourth key role player in South African sport governance is the local authority. These role players are in direct contact with the sites of delivery and have the primary function to develop a policy framework for the governance of sport at a local level that takes both national and provincial policies into account. In collaboration with the MEC, local authorities are responsible for ensuring accessibility of sport and recreation facilities to all people and to create infrastructure that enables them to do so. Local authorities are an important link in this value chain and play a crucial role in the development of human resources as well as the implementation of international agreements set in place by the SRSA.

Within the sport governance structure, several additional agencies exist that each play an important role in sport in South Africa (National Department of Sport and Recreation, 1998):

- The National Sport Council (NSC) who is responsible for the participation and development of sport mandate, with specific focus on talent identification, capacity building, to fast-track delivery and act as a lead agent for provincial sport bodies.
- SASCOC, which ensures the participation of South African athletes at the Olympic Games as well as the execution of its high-performance sport mandate.

- The South African Commonwealth Games Association (SACGA) that coordinates the participation of South African athletes in the Commonwealth Games. This is an independent committee elected by its own national federations and is affiliated to the Commonwealth Games Federations (CGF).
- National ferations (NFs) which are responsible for the implementation of government policy on sport and recreation at national, provincial and local levels. Their core business is to act as the principal delivery agent for their respective sport disciplines. This is mainly achieved through equitable access to its sport, talent-identification programmes, the establishment of a volunteer corps and increased participation rates. National federations are also expected to make representations on behalf of their sports to the SRSA and to proactively promote their sports so as to ensure maximum participation. They are responsible for ensuring that their provincial affiliates conform to accepted provincial boundaries, as set per national government policy.
- Provincial federations have a similar role and responsibilities to that of national federations. The most important distinction between the two lies in their respective areas of jurisdiction.
- School/junior/youth sport which is managed by the United School Sport Association of South Africa (USSASA). USSASA's functions include, amongst others, the implementation of government policy on school sport, talent identification, maximising participation, coordinating intra- and inter-school competition, and coaching and developmental programmes.
- Clubs are the basic unit of sport and provision of sport. Clubs' functions include the implementation of policy on sport at group or individual level, to increase participation through proactive recruitment programmes, being the primary vehicle for the identification, development and nurturing of talent and the provision of a unique social support structure.
- The corporate sector is crucial for the unlocking of resources the government does not possess. SRSA is constantly exploring new avenues in which they can attract corporate sponsors to underfunded sport disciplines.

The structure above has been developed by combining past organisations and present transformation. This should enable the SRSA to manage and address the unique challenges they face.

Addressing the challenges

The discussion above highlighted South Africa's past, and the impact it has had on the development of sport strategies and sport governance. Although much has been done to rectify the grievances left by South Africa's legacy, it is evident that there are unique challenges still to be addressed by proper and appropriate sport governance. The last part of this chapter will discuss these challenges (Department of Sport and Recreation SA, 2011).

The maximisation of access

A crucial task and challenge for SRSA is to maximise the access to sport and sporting facilities. The main focus here should be to develop sport governance that will allow for an increase in the number of participants in sport and recreation, with strong emphasis on previously disadvantaged and marginalised groups. This includes women, children, youth, the elderly, persons with a disability and people residing in rural areas. The responsibility here lies in the provision and facilitation of appropriate resources to enable the desired levels of access and participation in sport.

Development of sport resources

To develop sport, it is crucial that sport governance should make allowance for the early identification and nurturing of talent on the entire spectrum of participation that ranges from local to national level. To manage the development of sport resources, proper governance should also be in place for the development of sport support personnel. The appropriate infrastructure and organisational structures should be provided for so as to support such development. SRSA should also explore and utilise development opportunities available in the local, continental and international arenas.

Social cohesion and nation building

As mentioned, sport was used as a catalyst for nation building during the turbulent transformation period. Sport should once again be used as a medium to enhance social interaction and to further understanding and cooperation between the different cultural groups of South Africa. Sport governance should be developed that allows sport to contribute to social inclusion and the combating of anti-social behaviour. In addition, such governance should utilise sport as a medium that contributes to national unity and the fostering of a South African identity by promoting a common sense of belonging.

Quality of life

Sport governance should emphasise the benefit of sport to a country's citizens in terms of the mental and physical development through participation in sport and the contributions this can make towards the improvement of quality of life. Research has shown that participants in sport and recreation generally have a higher quality of life than those that do not participate. This is especially crucial in developing countries such as South Africa. For example, the Qhubeka Bike Project, in conjunction with MTN and Team Qhubeka (a professional cycling team), aims to provide children from rural areas with bicycles. This provides transportation to and from school, reducing travelling time, allowing children significantly more time to do homework and play. Children are awarded bicycles in return for doing work in their community and environment, teaching valuable life lessons. In addition, the project strives to improve the quality of life of adults by transferring skills such as bicycle maintenance and mechanics to individuals. Micro-financing is provided by assisting people in building spare parts supply and bike transporter businesses (Qhubeka, 2012).

Now that the legacy of sport governance has been discussed, along with the new road map, the governance structure and the specific challenges to sport governance in South Africa, the aspects can be applied by looking at the governing body for cycling in South Africa, CyclingSA.

Case study: Cycling South Africa

Cycling South Africa (CyclingSA) was established on the 31 December 2004 to replace a defunct South African Cycling Federation, which had been in operation since 1882. It was established as a voluntary, non-profit organisation and is one of the UCI's (Union Cycliste Internationale) 173 member federations. CyclingSA is affiliated to the South African controlling body of sport, the South African Sports Confederation and Olympic Committee (SASCOC). It was initially established to control cycling, including all of its various disciplines, within South Africa and is responsible for the following (CyclingSA, 2010):

- Competitive road racing and time trials
- Recreational road cycling (with focus on the 'Cycling for All' as determined by the UCI)
- Track cycling
- Competitive off-road cycling – cross-country, mountain biking and downhill mountain biking
- Recreational off-road cycling
- BMX cycling
- Commuting
- Touring.

CyclingSA was established as the sovereign governing body of the sport and set the following objectives when its manifesto was drawn up in 2004 (CyclingSA 2010):

- Recognition as the controlling body for cycling within the Republic of South Africa.
- Affiliation with the world controlling body of cycling, namely the UCI.
- To ensure the affiliation of domestic and regional cycling bodies and associations of whatever kind with CyclingSA.
- To remain vested in the sole right to select individuals and teams to represent the Republic of South Africa internally.
- To control cycling events throughout South Africa in accordance with the rules and regulations of the UCI and CyclingSA.

The organisation is managed with limited control and the main focus has been on the basic administration principles which included the number of registered cyclists, running the national championships across the different tiers, helping to prepare and select teams and individuals to compete in respective world cycling championships or world events which include, amongst others, the Olympic Games.

In 2008, CyclingSA simplified their aims and objectives into two pillars that formed the main support and focus of all cycling in South Africa. During the year of 2008, mass participation in cycling events such as the Cape Argus Cycle Tour and the Momentum 94.7 Cycle Challenge were at an all-time high and the official calendar boasted over a 1,000 events, which has since been reduced to 800 events (Till, 2008). The UCI Junior Worlds 2008 and the UCI Mountain Bike and BMX World Cups 2009 were all hosted in South Africa. However, with mass participation, increased safety issues has become the main area of concern and an obstacle of growth. A joint initiative with ThinkBike was initiated to create increased awareness of cyclists' presence on South African roads. To further increase the safety of cyclists, CyclingSA must however attempt to change the attitudes of South Africans towards cyclists. This will prove to be far more difficult than anticipated as attitude is much more tangible than awareness (Till, 2008).

Cycling is ranked under the top 15 sporting codes in South Africa and has had a year-on-year growth of 7 per cent (2009–2010). There are approximately 526,900 adult and junior cyclists in South Africa of which approximately 22 per cent (4 per cent are serious participants and 18 per cent are club participants) are registered members of CyclingSA (BMI, 2009). Of these, 86 per cent of cyclists fall within the LSM7–10[1] band and the majority are male. In 2009, only 61,000 black cyclists were recorded compared to 330,000 white cyclists. This is generally attributed to it being pegged as an elitist sport. Even though it is a sport dominated by males, cycling is ranked as the sixth most popular participation sport amongst female adults. It is however interesting to note that cycling had 1,176,000 black spectators compared to 916,000 white spectators in 2009. Additionally, black spectators preferred local events (74 per cent) to international events (59 per cent) which is a positive indication towards support for South African sport. Despite improving statistics, one of the major challenges in terms of sport governance for CyclingSA remains to increase participation in the sport and provide access for all South Africans. The prevalent discipline for members to engage in is road cycling, followed by mountain biking.

As a sporting organisation, CyclingSA receives funding from memberships and the organisation has, to generate additional funding, entered into an agreement with the National Lottery. Any surplus funds are to be utilised towards the accomplishment of its mission and vision and not to make a profit (CyclingSA, 2010).

When it was initially established, CyclingSA appointed a congress whose primary function was to set the sport governance policy and a board of trustees whose responsibility was to carry out the policies set by said congress. It also consisted of several commissions which carried the responsibility for each

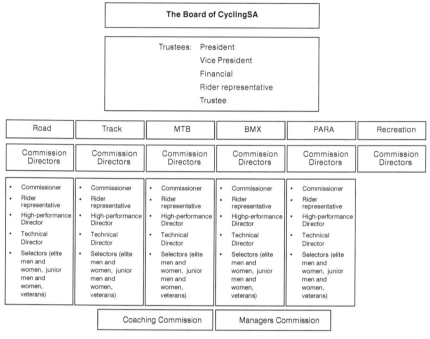

Figure 6.2 The Board of CyclingSA

separate discipline and the administration of these disciplines nationwide. Each commission was and still is accountable to the board (CyclingSA, 2010). Apart from the president, a vice president and financial president were also elected. Since the initial appointments, a coaching commission was added as well as a managers' commission and a transformation commission. An accountant, with a direct link to the financial trustee and a licensing officer were also added to the structure of the organisation. All directors, irrespective of their commissions, serve on the board of CyclingSA in addition to the commission they manage. Commisioners only serve on the specific commission that they are assigned to. The board of CyclingSA's structure is shown in Figure 6.2.

In addition to the board and the different commissions, CyclingSA also have 14 affiliates within South Africa. During 2011, SASCOC recommended that these be reduced to nine so as to represent the nine provinces. The reduction in affiliates would also result in CyclingSA adhering to the new management format as set by SASCOC. The original 14 affiliates are listed below (CyclingSA, 2010):

- Boland Cycling
- Central Gauteng Cycling
- Eastern Province Cycling Association
- Pedal Power Association
- Western Province Cycling Association

- Southern Gauteng Cycling
- Southern Cape Cycling Association
- Northern Cape
- North West Cycling
- Mpumalanga Cycling Union
- Kwa-Zulu Natal Cycling Union
- Free State Cycling

The Border Cycling Association was removed from the affiliate list and Free State South and North were combined to form Free State Cycling.

CyclingSA prepares an annual business plan that is consistent with the mission, vision and objectives of the organisation and defines the structure, roles and responsibilities (Till, 2008):

- Internal changes have presented staff with myriad operational challenges.
- Bringing prudent financial controls and confidence into CyclingSA.
- Position assets to realise maximum commercial benefits.

In 2010, in conjunction with the appointment of a new CEO, fundamental changes were made to the management of the organisation which required a unified and binding vision by all key CyclingSA stakeholders. The '2020 Vision' encompassed the organisation's overall strategic objectives and, as in line with sport governance set by the national body, was done through a rigorous consultation process. The new vision statement for the organisation contained core strategic elements that catered for both elite and 'Cycling for All' stakeholders. One of the important focus areas was that of transformation and development where cycling should be made more accessible to all groups of people. This ties in closely with the UCI concept of 'Cycling for All' as well as the road map set by government. Not only will this allow the sport to grow significantly, but also promote female cyclists and increase the pool of South African cyclists at national and international events (Till, 2008).

The four pillars of the new '2020 Vision' are closely linked with the South African sport governance guidelines as found in the new road map and are centred on world-class performance, financial stability, rider-centric service and social responsibility. The objectives set within the realm of the four pillars are to be achieved by enhancing the organisation's strengths, growing and sustaining a successful and effective high performance programme, and establishing financial sustainability. Through this, CyclingSA is aiming to gain widespread respect for being a professionally administered business with an entrepreneurial spirit (CyclingSA, 2010). Additional objectives included: developing a comprehensive strategic plan that guides CyclingSA through to 2020, aligning all financial resources under one banner and accounting system, growing illicit/illegal market appeal and participation in events and securing one million registered cyclists in South Africa by 2020.

Being primarily a volunteer organisation results in management consisting of mostly elected volunteers (Till, 2008). CyclingSA experienced problems with accountability and it became evident that most office-bearers only did their duties when they had spare time available. The ideal situation, as identified by CyclingSA, would be to have paid staff members that are based in a central location (Till, 2008).

CyclingSA and SASCOC are currently working very closely together to eradicate any claims of fraud and unethical behaviour that has surfaced in recent allegations against the organisation and its board members. During the latter part of 2011, SASCOC met with the board of CyclingSA to determine whether or not a series of emails, alluding to widespread fraud within the organisation, were fraudulent. A three-hour meeting, chaired by the chair of Transformation, Ethics and Dispute Commission of SASCOC, was held to determine whether or not the allegations were unfounded and were non-factual with the sole purpose to bring the organisation into disrepute.

CyclingSA's president assured SASCOC and the media of sound governance of the organisation, pointing out that all financial statements are published publicly, as per regulations, and can be scrutinised at any given point in time. Ongoing emails and social media communication caused by these allegations were only served to damage CyclingSA's already frail reputation, despite continuous reassurance that all financials were managed according to strict guidelines and that allegations were not authentic and inaccurate. Each of the 17 allegations against the organisation was discussed and explained. During this process SASCOC also took the opportunity discuss CyclingSA's constitution and realigned this with the approved SASCOC format. The new format, which is being implemented across South Africa, will allow for the uniform management of all sporting codes. One of the critical elements within the new format is the exclusion of unsanctioned associations within the structure of CyclingSA. Emphasis was also placed on the transformation of the board so as to represent the South African demographic profile.

The allegations against CyclingSA financial malpractices were found to be unsubstantiated and unacceptable. The relevant affiliate was instructed to take necessary action to avoid bringing the organisation into disrepute in future. The transformation charter was redrafted to allow for the following:

- The 14 historical affiliates will be reduced to nine so as to represent the nine provinces.
- No individual will be permitted involvement in areas outside of their responsibility.
- CyclingSA is to take the lead in dealing decisively in similar situations.
- Transformation is imperative and requires continued special focus.
- Development should occur across the entire South Africa.
- CyclingSA must continue to present audited financials.

From the above discussion it is evident that CyclingSA is striving to attain and conform to the guidelines and policy set in place for sport governance by SRSA. The board composition, with the majority of members remaining volunteers, and the board structure is in the process of being transformed so as to reflect the changes made to sport organisation's structures by SASCOC. The board's role is still however clear and remains to control cycling, in all its varied disciplines, despite changing and fluent objectives. Strategic development remains high on the list of management issues, especially in the pursuit of CyclingSA's '2020 Vision'. Ethical issues, such as the recent allegations of financial fraud, need to be dealt with the utmost scrutiny to ensure that all organisations, including CyclingSA, adhere to the strict sport governance guidelines set in this regard.

Summary

Sport governance within South Africa is characterised largely by the legacy left from the previous government and the attempts since then to address the challenges created by the country's past. The SRSA, the national government department responsible for sport within South Africa, solution came in the founding of the Road Map to Optimal Performance and Functional Excellence. This document addresses five strategic priorities including transformation, the development and promotion of school sport, improving institutional mechanisms, mass mobilisation by creating access for all and a refocused emphasis on recreation and funding. The focus of sport governance within South Africa then clearly lies in the maximisation of access to sport, the development of sport resources, social cohesion and nation building and the improvement of quality of life for all South Africans. Sport organisations and federations such as CyclingSA are expected to function within these parameters to realise the objectives set by SRSA.

Review questions

1 Explain in your own words how SRSA and the new road map accomplished the tasks of sport governance.
2 Look at the organogram of sport governance within South Africa. Do you think this is an effective system? If you were part of portfolio committee, what changes would you suggest?
3 If you were the Minister of Sport, how would you address the challenges South African sport is facing?

Note

1 LSM stands for Living Standard Measure, a universal measurement of the living standards or quality of a country's residents. It is primarily used as a segmentation tool where the basis for segmentation is living standards. LSM groups 7–10 are generally higher income groups with greater literacy skills.

Further reading

Hoye, R., & Cuskelly, G. (2006). *Sport governance*. Oxford: Elsevier Butterworth-Heinemann.
Kluka, D.A.; Schilling, G. & Stier, W.F. (2005). *Aspects of sport governance*. Berlin: Meyer and Meyer Sport.

Louw, A. M. (2010). *Sports law in South Africa*. Alphen aan den Rijn, Netherlands: Kluwer Law International.

Sawyer, T.H., Bodey, K.J. & Judge, L.W. (2008). *Sport governance and policy development: An ethical approach to managing sport in the 21st century*. Champaign, IL: Sagamore Publishing.

Websites

Sport and Recreation South Africa: http://www.srsa.gov.za/
Cycling South Africa: http://www.cyclingsa.com/
Play the game.org: http://www.playthegame.org/

References

BMI (2009). *The status of cycling in South Africa 2009*.

CyclingSA (2010). Statistics compiled from the official CSA website. Available online at http://cms.cyclingsa.com/

Department of Sport and Recreation (1997). Getting the nation to play. White Paper: Sport and Recreation South Africa. Pretoria: Government Printer.

Department of Sport and Recreation South Africa (2011). Mission and Values. Available online at http://www.srsa.gov.za/pebble.asp?relid=30

Hoye, R., & Cuskelly, G. (2006). *Sport governance*. Oxford: Elsevier Butterworth-Heinemann.

Mbalula, F.A. (2011a) Opening address of the Minister of Sport and Recreation, Natonal Sport and Recreation Indaba, 21 November. Available online at http://www.srsa. gov.za/MediaLib/Home/DocumentLibrary/Opening%20Address%20of%20the%20 Minister%20of%20Sport%20and%20Recreation%20-%20(21%20Nov%202011).doc

Mbalula, F.A. (2011b). The SRSA/Provinces Strategic Planning Workshop, 10 January. Available online at: http://www.google.com/url?sa=t&rct=j&q=&esrc=s&frm=1&s ource=web&cd=2&cad=rja&ved=0CDsQFjAB&url=http%3A%2F%2Fwww.srsa. gov.za%2FMediaLib%2FHome%2FDocumentLibrary%2FSRSA-Provinces%252 0strategic%2520planning%2520workshop%2520-%2520Misty%2520Hills%2520-%252010-12%2520Jan%25202011.doc&ei=PEM4UZmiMuPQ0QXa0ID4CA &usg=AFQjCNGWXrr-flpieUcRzGIqXCqjFZ_2sw&sig2=a0gQo6XD4jo3_FC8jYdFOg&bvm=bv.43287494,d.d2k

National Department of Sport and Recreation (1998). National Department of Sport and Recreation White Paper. Available online at http://www.info.gov.za/whitepapers/1998/sports.htm

Qhubeka (2012) Bike Project. Available online at http://www.qhubeka.org/ qhubeka/PROJECTS+.html

Till, G. (2008). *CSA Annual Report*.

7 United Kingdom

Geoff Walters and Richard Tacon

Topics

- Modernisation
- Non-profit governance
- Board involvement in strategy
- Strategy formulation
- Strategy evaluation.

Objectives

- To critically analyse modernisation and its key drivers in the context of UK public policy
- To identify the sport-specific factors that underpin the modernisation agenda in sport in the UK
- To analyse the impact of modernisation on key sport organisations in the UK
- To explain the importance of board involvement in strategy
- To examine the impact of modernisation on a specific non-profit sport organisation in the UK.

Key terms

Modernisation   The process of continuing organisational development towards greater effectiveness, efficiency and independence.

Non-departmental public body   A body which has a role in the processes of national government, but is not a government department or part of one.

National governing body of sport   Typically a self-appointed organisation that governs a sport through the common consent of that sport.

Sport governance   The structures and processes used by a sport organisation to develop its strategic goals and direction, monitor performance and ensure that its board acts in the best interests of its members.

Board strategic involvement   The involvement of the board of an organisation in formulating new strategic decisions and evaluating prior strategic decisions.

Overview

This chapter considers how the modernisation process has impacted upon the sport system within the UK. Specifically, it looks at the implications of modernisation on board involvement in strategy at national governing bodies of sport (NGBs). The chapter is split into two main parts, the first providing background detail and analysis of the key issues, the second presenting an illustrative case study. The first part of the chapter is itself divided into five sections. The first sets out the structure of the sport sector in the UK. The second discusses the historical development of the modernisation agenda in the UK and identifies four sport-specific factors that underpin the implementation of modernisation in sport. The third section examines the impact of modernisation on Sport England and UK Sport, key sport agencies in the UK, while the fourth considers how the same process has impacted on NGBs. The final section looks specifically at modernisation and board involvement in strategy. The second part of this chapter presents a case study of an NGB in the UK. It draws on the analysis in the first part of the chapter to consider closely the implications of modernisation on the board's involvement in strategy.

Sport governance in the United Kingdom

The sport sector in the UK

The sport sector in the UK is complex. Many organisations, both governmental and non-governmental, are involved in the development and implementation of sport policy and this creates a crowded and sometimes confusing policy space. Any attempt to set out diagrammatically all the relevant organisations, their various responsibilities, the network of inter-dependencies and the funding arrangements for sport in the UK is likely to appear over complicated and, moreover, is likely to become outdated quite quickly. Nevertheless, it is important to try to set the scene, so Figure 7.1 provides a rough picture of the sport sector in the UK in 2012.

The Department for Culture, Media and Sport sets sport policy for England and the devolved administrations in Scotland, Wales and Northern Ireland set sport policy in their countries. Other government departments, such as (in England) the Department for Communities and Local Government, the Department of Health, and the Department for Environment, Food and Rural Affairs, play a role in the broader policy context around sport, for example by determining funding levels for local authorities, setting policy around physical activity and establishing access to land and water. The bulk of the funding for sport in the UK comes from the National Lottery set up in 1994 and from central government (although a significant proportion of this is actually channelled through local government). The majority of this government and lottery funding goes to the key non-departmental public bodies, UK Sport and the home country sport councils (Sport England, Sport Scotland, Sport Wales and Sport Northern Ireland), that are responsible for delivering government policy on sport. The rest

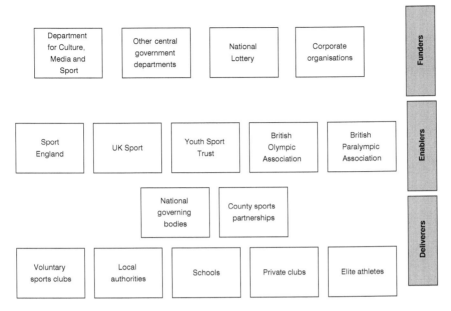

Figure 7.1 The sport system in the UK

of this section sets out, in very basic terms, the roles of UK Sport, Sport England and national governing bodies of sport, as they are the main subjects of this chapter. Readers interested in more detailed analysis of these organisations, or the other organisations in Figure 7.1, are advised to consult the many excellent reviews of sport policy and structure in the UK that already exist (e.g. Houlihan & White, 2002; Bergsgard *et al.*, 2007; Hylton & Bramham, 2008; Bloyce & Smith, 2010).

UK Sport manages investment in high-performance sport. It invests around £100 million of public money every year, distributing funds to national governing bodies of sport, so they can implement their Olympic and Paralympic plans, coordinating the bidding and staging of major international sporting events and working with partner organisations in international development. Sport England (and each of the other home country sport councils) manages investment in community sport and in certain areas of school sport. Its main role is to distribute public funds to national governing bodies of sport (around £450 million between 2013 and 2017) to implement their plans for increasing and maintaining sport participation, improving sport club structures and systems, coaching, volunteering and so on. It also invests in sport facilities, in other areas of community sport and in competitive school sport. National governing bodies, a number of which were founded in the nineteenth century, are responsible for setting rules for their individual sports. Most require either clubs or individuals to affiliate in order to take part in the competitive structures they oversee. Many have specific programmes for increasing participation and improving performance in their sports and receive funding from the sport councils to carry them out.

The modernisation agenda in the UK

Following the Labour Government's success at the 1997 General Election, a commitment was made to the modernisation of public policy-making, a process that had significant effects on local government as well as on other aspects of public services such as health, welfare, and environmental planning (Brooks, 2000; Houlihan & Green, 2009). Critics have argued that modernisation is a 'suitably vacuous concept' (Midwinter, 2001, p. 313) that is poorly defined and lacking in consensus on what it actually means (Powell, 2008). However, Falconer (2005, p.82) has argued that modernisation can be seen as associated with three main themes, namely: including improving the quality of public services by focusing on performance standards; improving the responsiveness of public services by considering the end user rather than delivery providers; and a belief in the value of public–private partnerships and joined up government to deliver services. These themes are reflected in the move towards improving efficiency and delivering 'best value', underpinned by a belief in managerialism, accountability, and performance assessment (Midwinter, 2001).

At the same time, it was argued that modernisation reforms would place greater autonomy and empowerment with providers of local services. In the context of local government, this claim has been questioned, with the concern that modernisation simply leads to local government implementing national government policies (Brooks, 2000), accompanied by the increasing audit and regulatory oversight in order to sanction those that fail to meet central targets (Lusted & O'Gorman, 2010). This signifies that a key aspect of modernisation has been a reduction in levels of individual trust, replaced by a belief in systems in which audit and performance management are critical (Houlihan & Green, 2009).

As such, Midwinter (2001) and, more recently, Houlihan and Green (2009), argue that modernisation reflects the (previous) Labour government's attempts to strengthen their ability to set the strategic direction of policy from the centre and that notions of autonomy are contradictory. This is termed by Rose, cited in Houlihan & Green (2009, p.680) as 'government at a distance' in the sense that government does not directly impose its authority upon public-sector organisations, but institutional pressures on organisations to 'modernise' still exist. Such pressures can be meaningfully understood within the context of institutional theory which holds that pressures within the environment lead organisations to conform to the norms and expectations in order to achieve legitimacy and acceptance (DiMaggio & Powell, 1983). So, for example, the drive towards increasing professionalism, as evidenced through a focus on performance management, audit and assessment, is a key institutional pressure faced by many public-sector organisations.

The desire to improve performance standards, improve responsiveness to meet end-user needs and implement public–private partnerships (Falconer, 2005) were central to the modernisation of sport in the UK during the period in which the Labour Government was in power. These three themes were accompanied by four sport-specific factors that further supported the implementation of modernisation in sport. First, the sport industry had, following the introduction of the National

Lottery in 1994, begun to receive increased public funding. As a result, there was the expectation that the performance of sport organisations (however measured) would improve. Improving governance was one aspect of performance and there was a need to demonstrate this: an example of the need for accountability to justify the increase in funding. Second, and linked to the aforementioned increase in funding, sport was seen by the Labour Government as a way to address broader policy objectives relating to social exclusion, obesity and health, education, antisocial behaviour, and youth crime. This demonstrates how sport was seen in an instrumental manner as a way to meet the needs of end users often through the development of public–private partnerships. These two factors related directly to government funding and policy. The third factor was that many sports in the UK were undergoing significant commercial growth and this had resulted in the need for sport's administrative structures to move from amateurism to professionalism (Henry & Lee, 2004). At the same time, there had been instances of poor management and failures in organisational governance, particularly amongst NGBs. These two final factors, although not directly linked to government, evidently fall within the remit of modernisation as they led to calls for improved performance standards.

Modernisation, Sport England and UK Sport

These sport-specific factors, combined with the general themes of modernisation, created a powerful case for the need to change the way that sport organisations are structured and governed. This was certainly the case for Sport England and UK Sport. Policy documents produced by the Department for Culture, Media and Sport (DCMS) in 2000, *A Sporting Future for All,* and in 2002, *Game Plan,* emphasised the need to ensure clarity of the roles of Sport England and UK Sport and to ensure that each had clear objectives to measure performance (Houlihan & Green, 2009). This was a clear example of the application of managerialism, accountability, and performance assessment within the context of sport.

These documents emphasised that government had come to see sport as a critical mechanism through which to address key policy objectives. As such, it was important that both UK Sport and Sport England were able to demonstrate that they were 'fit for purpose' (Houlihan & Green, 2009). What this meant in reality was that both organisations were subject to numerous structural reforms as part of the modernisation process, the point of which was to demonstrate that they were more efficient and modern organisations. For example, Houlihan and Green (2009, p. 688) outline the different ways in which the modernisation agenda had an impact on Sport England. These included: the creation of a Modernisation Project Board to oversee structural and strategic changes; the rationalisation of staff; the recruitment of senior staff with business experience; a renewed focus on ensuring clarity of strategy; and the adoption of performance management and key performance indicators. In 2003, UK Sport also underwent an internal review that resulted in similar changes including organisational restructuring, reducing staff numbers, and a new strategic focus, although these changes were not as extensive as those at Sport England (Houlihan & Green, 2009).

Although these reforms have been bound up in the discourse of increasing autonomy and empowerment, Houlihan and Green (2009) argue that a paradox exists in that the modernisation agenda focuses attention on a narrow series of objectives. For Sport England this has meant increasing participation in sport and for UK Sport the objective is to excel, that is achieve medals, at Olympic Games and world championships. Although this provides a clear strategic focus, it reflects the government's attempts to strengthen their ability to set the strategic direction of policy from the centre, to attach funding requirements to these narrowly defined objectives and, ultimately, to increase accountability.

Modernisation and national governing bodies of sport

While both Sport England and UK Sport have faced pressures to reform, they in turn have been responsible for promoting modernisation to NGBs in the UK that receive public funding. Modernisation in this context has been perceived as a way to improve the governance and management of NGBs. Indeed, it has been defined as 'the process of continuing development of a Governing Body towards greater effectiveness, efficiency and independence' (UK Sport, 2003, p. 1). This was clearly in response to a series of NGB failures. For example, in 1997 the governing body for athletics, the British Athletics Federation, was dissolved due to poor financial management, to be replaced by UK Athletics. However, Sam (2009, p. 505) has argued that the modernisation of NGBs is underpinned by three additional key reasons: first, it will enable their ability to increase participation and elite performance; second, NGBs will be better able to attract commercial sponsorship and reduce the reliance on government funding; and third, it will allow for the building of social capital of national and regional sport organisations.

The impact of modernisation on NGBs was first evidenced in *A Sporting Future for All*, within which there were some key recommendations relating to the governance of NGBs. The government stated that NGBs would receive increased control over the allocation of public funding, but they had to become more accountable by modernising administration structures and practices, and implementing robust management, planning and monitoring of all activities (DCMS, 2000). NGB modernisation was further advocated in *Game Plan* (DCMS, 2002), where it was clearly reiterated that government investment should be used to drive modernisation and that NGBs should have clear performance indicators that could be used as the basis on which to determine funding. To support the modernisation process, the government announced in 2001 that it would provide £7 million in funding, managed through UK Sport, as part of a NGB Modernisation Programme (DCMS, 2002). The objective of the modernisation programme was to 'help NGBs to improve their organization, the skills of their staff and volunteers, and the standards of their policies and procedures' (UK Sport, 2004, p. 1).

Between 2001 and 2005, UK Sport invested £5 million of government funding into 114 NGB projects across the UK as part of the modernisation programme (Houlihan & Green, 2009, p.693). In 2003, a high-level review of the modernisation programme, *Investing in Change,* was undertaken with two key objectives: to identify the optimum models for NGB performance and to develop change management action plans to guide NGB performance (UK Sport, 2003). *Investing in Change* made it clear that modernisation was an ongoing process in which NGBs would be provided with support to improve their administrative structures to increase efficiency and effectiveness. It was argued that this would help to increase participation, develop talent and deliver elite success (UK Sport, 2004).

In 2005, Sport England, with input from UK Sport, developed the Funded Partner Assurance Programme, the self-assurance process. This is an annual requirement that each funded NGB has to undertake to ensure that they are fit to receive public funds. Key criteria include financial management, human resource management, risk management and organisational policy. Further developments took place in 2007 when UK Sport launched 'Mission 2012', which focuses on the performance of Olympic sport NGBs in three areas in the build-up towards the London 2012 Olympic Games: athlete success and development; performance system and structures; and governance and leadership. The aim of 'Mission 2012' is to continually monitor NGB performance in relation to the three areas and to evaluate standards based on a traffic light system. Those NGBs that are given a red rating face the potential withdrawal of funding or UK Sport intervention. The focus on governance and leadership requires that NGBs have in place appropriate structures. This can be clearly seen as a continuation of the NGB modernisation programme.

Modernisation and board involvement in strategy

One key aspect of modernisation is board involvement in strategy. *Investing in Change* identified a long-term strategic plan and strategic-review procedures as two key elements necessary to improve the governance of NGBs (UK Sport, 2003). Academic research has also started to examine board involvement in strategy within sport organisations. For example, recent studies by Ferkins, Shilbury and McDonald (2005; 2009) looked at how boards of national sport organisations might enhance their strategic capability. Overall, however, research in this area remains underdeveloped. Hoye and Cuskelly (2007), in their wide-ranging review of international sport governance literature, conclude that while various sets of guidelines on board involvement in strategy have been developed, there is a need for more empirical research that probes how it actually works in practice. This conclusion still applies to the UK context.

In 2004, the Institute of Chartered Secretaries and Administrators produced a guide of governance for NGBs, in collaboration with UK Sport. Leadership was one of the key functions of the board. This incorporated setting the strategic aims, developing the long-term plans and providing leadership to implement them. Moreover, the Funded Partner Assurance Programme, described above, sets out minimum standards that must be met in relation to a number of areas relating to corporate governance including strategic planning. In relation to strategy, there are five key aspects that NGBs have to demonstrate (Dutton, 2009):

- a long-term strategic plan is in place for the whole organisation which outlines the key long-term objectives of the organisation and the strategies which are being implemented to achieve these goals;
- the strategic plan has been reviewed and approved by the board;
- an annual business/operational plan is in place which outlines the tasks to be undertaken to contribute to the achievement of strategic objectives;
- key performance indicators are in place to monitor the achievement of strategic plan and business/operational plan objectives;
- responsible committees, employers and volunteers reported to the board on the achievement of objectives and key performance indicators.

It is clear then that involvement in strategy is considered to be one of the roles that the board of an NGB should fulfil. This mirrors the broader governance literature, in which board involvement in strategy is considered as a way to focus board activities; to align board, CEO and others' interests; to improve board member commitment; to improve the quality of decision-making; and, ultimately, to improve organisational effectiveness (Fishel, 2003; Nadler, 2004).

It has been acknowledged, in some places, that board involvement in strategy may be different in non-profit organisations than in for-profit organisations (Stone, Bigelow, & Crittenden, 1999; Parker, 2007). Nevertheless, the modernisation agenda places importance on values associated with the commercial sector and the emphasis on board involvement in strategy is indicative of the institutional pressures that NGB boards face. Indeed, similar pressures have been felt across the non-profit sector. Many non-profit organisations face pressures from external funders and involvement in strategy development is often one of their key requirements (Stone *et al.*, 1999; Stone & Ostrower, 2007). However, Judge and Zeithaml (1992a) warn that imitation may not be appropriate and highlight the necessity of analysing non-profit organisations within their institutional context.

These various developments constitute a basic historical account of the implementation of modernisation within the context of NGBs in the UK. The self-assurance process and 'Mission 2012' are key mechanisms through which the government has been able to push through changes within NGBs to promote a decreasing reliance on government grants – a move from parochial governing boards towards more formal governance and management (Sam, 2009). There is a clear parallel with the broader process of modernisation and how it has operated within both Sport England and UK Sport, in that NGBs are only given more responsibility if they are able to meet the funding criteria (Houlihan & Green, 2009). This is one way in which NGBs are constrained by the need to conform to a set of strictly defined and measurable criteria in order to justify public spending and demonstrate accountability.

In relation to strategy, two interrelated issues arise from this. First, although NGBs exist in complex stakeholder environments, the modernisation agenda has meant that many NGBs are first and foremost accountable to their key funding bodies – government (via funding from the sports councils) and, for a select few, commercial sponsors. This, it has been argued, constrains the ability of NGBs to balance multiple stakeholder demands (Sam, 2009). Second, the pressure to meet certain targets and comply with key performance indicators in order to receive public funds may reinforce the compliance role of the board and de-emphasise its strategic role (Cornforth & Edwards, 1999). Within this context, the development of strategy and strategic review processes can become a tick-box approach to justify funding, rather than a detailed process in which board members actively engage. In the context of sport, it has been argued that an increasing focus on conformance has created uncertainty around the board's role in strategy and a lack of understanding around the boundaries of strategic involvement (Ferkins & Shilbury, 2012).

Such issues, and the various developments discussed above, suggest that modernisation, while often perceived as a progressive force for good, can also have negative consequences. Indeed, Sam (2009, p. 500) has argued that the modernisation of NGBs results in 'tradeoffs, conundrums and consequences that cannot be easily "undone" or reconciled'. Any analysis of modernisation in sport, therefore, needs to recognise the potential for both positive and negative outcomes.

Case study: Board involvement in strategy

This second part of the chapter presents a case study of a national governing body of sport in the UK, looking specifically at the implications of modernisation on the board's involvement in strategy. This case study is part of a research project that was undertaken throughout 2012 looking at board processes. Data was collected through non-participant observation (of board and committee meetings), semi-structured interviews with board members, executive staff and committee members, and documentary analysis of board minutes, board manuals, and so on. For reasons of confidentiality the identity of the NGB has been anonymised.

Case study background

The NGB involved in this research has an annual turnover of just less than £1million. It is therefore a relatively small organisation, particularly in comparison with NGBs of professional sports in the UK such as football, rugby or cricket. It is also a unique NGB within the context of the sport sector in the UK in that it oversees the development of two separate but very similar sports. These two sports each have their own governing body meaning that the NGB in this study has a very specific remit, which is to act as the development agency for the two sports. Therefore this NGB has an explicit focus on increasing levels of participation, skill and achievement across the two sports at both junior and adult levels.

The NGB is one of the 46 NGBs in the UK that is funded through Sport England. The majority of its income is derived from this source. In recent years it has been successful in funding applications and income has risen. For the four-year period from April 2009 to March 2013 a total of £2.7 million was awarded to the NGB based on their whole sport plan. The whole sport plan is the document produced for Sport England to determine funding levels. It sets outs the achievements of the sport over the previous funding period and is used to set out the strategic aims of the organisation. The funding award for the 2009–2013 period was an increase on the amount of income received from Sport England for the previous funding period.

The NGB is a company limited by guarantee, governed by a board consisting of 13 members. The board is composed of the chair, four independent directors, and three representative directors from both governing bodies in the sports for which the NGB acts as the development agency. In addition the two joint chief executive officers were voted on as full members of the board in 2012. (Previously they attended board meetings but were non-voting members). The appointment of independent directors can be seen within the broader context of modernisation in the sport sector where there have been calls for appropriate business skills on the board of NGBs, reflecting the inclination towards commercially driven, business values. Indeed, the reasoning at the NGB was that independent directors bring additional expertise and knowledge to the board to help govern the NGB. There are also three standing committees of the board (Development and Strategy, Governance, and Finance) on which board members sit as well as executive members of staff and additional individuals that bring outside expertise to these committees. There are nine full-time members of staff based in the head office with a further six regional development managers. Throughout 2011 the two sports in which the NGB is responsible for experienced an increase in participation levels and satisfaction levels amongst participants and the NGB itself received a positive audit from Sport England.

Board involvement in strategy

Trying to identify board involvement in strategy is a complex task. For example, Edwards and Cornforth (2003, p.78) noted the 'fuzziness of the boundary between operational detail and strategic focus'. More fundamentally, there is a lack of consensus, both in the academic literature and in practice, over what constitutes board strategic involvement. Having said that, previous conceptual and empirical studies do provide some guidance. One well-known study is Judge and Zeithaml's (1992b) examination of board involvement in strategic decision-making. The authors defined board involvement in strategy as 'the overall level of participation of board members in making non-routine, organization-wide resource allocation decisions that affect the long-term performance of an organization' (1992b, p. 771). More specifically, they considered that board involvement in strategy included two dimensions: the formation of new strategic decisions and the evaluation of prior strategic decisions. This understanding of board strategic involvement provides a useful framework of analysis for the case study.

In 2011, as part of a wider survey of governance in NGBs in the UK (Walters, Tacon & Trenberth, 2011), replicated elements of Judge and Zeithaml's study. NGBs were asked to describe their board's level of strategic involvement by selecting one from a series of statements, replicated from the original study. In its response, the case study organisation suggested that the following two statements (corresponding to the two dimensions discussed above) most accurately described their level of board strategic involvement:

The board usually helps to form strategic decisions with top management within and between board meetings.

The board usually determines the timing and criteria of evaluation and it often requests additional information after receiving the progress report from top management.

For general reference, these responses were at the upper end of the scale on both dimensions, suggesting a high level of board strategic involvement. (For further reference, including the full list of statements, please see Judge and Zeithaml, 1992b). Of course, these are just individual, snapshot responses; the case study allowed much fuller exploration of relevant governance processes.

The board of the case-study organisation was indeed highly involved in strategic decision-making. There was clear recognition that one of the key roles of the board was to debate and decide issues of strategic importance. This was demonstrated in several ways. For example, the organisation was in the final stages of developing its whole sport plan (WSP) funding proposal for Sport England. This, therefore, was seen as a, perhaps the, key element of organisational strategy; and the board, and especially the Development and Strategy Committee, was regularly involved in discussions with management concerning the WSP. Over the observation period, however, board involvement in strategy was perhaps most clearly exemplified in a series of discussions around the vision and mission of the organisation. In an early discussion at one board meeting, one of the independent directors said, quite stridently, 'I think we *should* decide vision, mission and so on here. That's our fundamental responsibility as a board'. The other board members agreed. Indeed, over the next three months, the board debated, consulted on, and ultimately decided, the vision and mission of the organisation.

The process went as follows. After the initial discussion at the board meeting, all board members were invited to submit their ideas and reflections concerning what the organisation's vision and mission should be. One of the joint chief executives and one of the independent board members met between board meetings to work up different proposals. At the next board meeting (there were six per year), the chair, in discussion with the joint chief executives, had specifically allocated two-thirds of the meeting time to discussions of strategy. The joint chief executive presented to the board two alternative visions and missions, based on the board members' ideas and reflections. The slides were entitled 'For the board to consider', setting out clearly the board's key role in strategic decision-making. This presentation was followed by an open, constructive and wide-ranging discussion. This discussion covered key questions and themes, including the following: (i) for whom were the vision and mission intended, i.e. should they be considered internal (predominantly *for* the organisation) or external (a statement to relevant stakeholders about what the organisation stood for)?; (ii) the links and or/contradictions between different aspects of the organisation's overall strategy, i.e. increasing participation vs. developing member clubs vs. improving elite performance, etc.; (iii) the organisation's priorities in these various areas; (iv) the different ways in which the words in the vision and mission might be interpreted by members, potential participants, funders and so on (as well as by the board members themselves).

After this lengthy discussion, the chair said, 'I think we need to start drawing this together. I'm sensing (a pause and a look around the table) a broad consensus around Mission Idea 1 – with tweaking round the bullet points'. There was indeed a broad consensus on this and on one of the vision ideas too. During the discussion, however, several of the board members expressed a desire that the staff be consulted before they reached a final decision. This happened – again between board meetings – and, at the next board meeting, the board signed off on the new vision and mission. This particular process, just one extended example, illustrated the board's involvement in formulating new strategic decisions, one dimension of board strategic involvement identified above.

The second dimension, the evaluation of prior strategic decisions, was also apparent at board level in the case-study organisation. Again, this was exemplified in several ways, but perhaps the clearest illustration was the regular discussion (it was a standing item on the board meeting agenda) of the organisation's 'balanced scorecard'. The previous four-year strategy, encapsulated in the whole sport plan (2009–2013), included a series of specific targets around participation, number of junior and adult teams and so on, linked to the funding received from Sport England. This previous strategy was the result of a series of strategic decisions taken by the board and management, but, in order to monitor and evaluate these prior strategic decisions, the organisation developed a balanced scorecard, which contained information about the four-year targets, interim targets and so on. These were coded with a red, amber and green traffic light system. This mirrored the self-assurance process, employed by Sport England and UK Sport, described above.

At each board meeting, the board members would evaluate progress against the targets and ask detailed questions of the chief executives on various issues. The following excerpts from one board meeting give a flavour of the discussions.

One of the chief executives presents the figures from the latest Active People Survey, which tracks participation in various sports in England. These are used to measure progress against the organisation's participation targets. The latest figures are below the interim target for adult participation on the balanced scorecard. This leads to a discussion between several board members and the chief executive around whether this is a blip, or a longer-term trend.

There is recognition from board members, especially two of the independents, that Sport England place great emphasis on the figures. 'It's the *only* measure!' one says.

There is a broader debate about how exactly the board ought to respond to areas of concern. One of the independent board members says, 'I'm looking at the ambers and reds and saying, "is this the direction we want to be travelling in"'?

The chair says, 'For me it's the "so what?" question. What are we actually doing in response to the ambers and reds?'

Later in the discussion, one of the independent board members says, 'I like the balanced scorecard. It's big, chunky figures'. (He mentions this again later.) This leads to a discussion around precisely what information it ought to contain, i.e. how much detail.

The chair says, 'We don't want to over engineer it [i.e. make it too confusing a document]'.

There seems to be recognition among all the board members of the importance of maintaining a distinction between operational detail and the higher level, strategic thinking that is appropriate at board level. One of the board members says, somewhat jokingly, 'I'm not worried about bean counting. That's management's role'.

These are only some brief snapshots of an ongoing process, but they illustrate the way in which the board of the organisation continued to scrutinise previous strategic decisions. This is an important dimension of board involvement in strategy, as conceptualised in governance research (Judge & Zeithaml, 1992a). Moreover, research has found that boards are more likely to formulate new strategic decisions (in the way discussed above) than evaluate prior strategic decisions. Indeed, this is the case with NGBs in the UK, as measured by the survey of governance discussed earlier in the chapter (see Walters *et al.* (2011) for a more detailed breakdown of the results).

The case-study organisation, therefore, can be seen as an example of a UK-based NGB that has a high level (certainly higher than average) of board strategic involvement. Forthcoming research, including analysis of the survey results and of the in-depth case study, will reveal more about the general picture of governance within NGBs and the interplay of ongoing governance processes. In the next section, we return to the theme of modernisation and examine how the key aspects and drivers of modernisation, discussed in the first part of the chapter, have affected governance processes within the case-study organisation.

Modernisation and the impact on the board

There are two key implications of modernisation on NGB strategy. The first is that many NGBs increasingly feel accountable to their main funding bodies. This was evident for the case-study organisation, as the four-year strategy for the previous whole sport plan (2009–2013) was linked to the funding (and strategy) of Sport England, while the development of the balanced scorecard reflected the objectives/targets of Sport England. It was also clearly evident in discussions around the whole sport plan for 2013–2017. For example, in one board meeting, the objectives of Sport England were explicitly discussed and concern was raised about the prospect of Sport England not supporting the strategy of the NGB. Moreover, in another board meeting in which the main objective was to define the mission and vision of the NGB, there was discussion about whether the key themes of the proposed mission would be recognised by Sport England.

The focus on Sport England objectives demonstrates an entirely rational and understandable approach. The fact is that this NGB is heavily dependent upon Sport England funding and therefore is it clear that they feel the need to align the objectives of the NGB with those of Sport England (who, in turn, are aligning their objectives with those set by central government). However, for large NGBs in the UK that are less dependent on government funding, the need to align with Sport England is perhaps not as pressing an issue as it is for those NGBs (and third-sector organisations more generally) that are heavily dependent on a single funding source. What it means is that lines of accountability, a key theme of modernisation, move upwards towards Sport England. This demonstrates that it is important for the board to be able to balance multiple stakeholder demands and not to lose sight of the needs of other key stakeholders such as members that participate in the sport. It also shows that despite the notion of autonomy and empowerment associated with modernisation, NGBs face strong institutional pressures to conform to Sport England targets – in effect central government targets – and the board may feel that they lose a certain degree of independence in determining the strategic direction of the organisation. This was an issue that was discussed at a board meeting; should the organisation develop strategy in accordance with what the board felt was best for the two sports or to align with Sport England targets? However, these two approaches are not necessarily incompatible.

The second implication linked to strategy is that the strategic role of the board may suffer at the expense of the compliance role. Indeed, if the strategy is designed to meet the needs of Sport England and the self-assurance process then there is concern that the development of strategy can simply become a tick-box approach to justify funding. This concern is potentially exacerbated by the recommendations contained within various documents such as *Investing in Change* (UK Sport, 2003) that are prescriptive in nature and do not provide guidance on dealing with the complexities that exist surrounding the process of developing board strategy. In this sense, strategy development may be perceived as something that NGBs need to demonstrate that they *do*, rather than a detailed process in which board members actively engage. At the NGB in this case study this was not the case. The section above noted the detailed process by which the board engaged in strategy development and although there was a concern for aligning with Sport England targets, there was never a sense that this was simply a 'box-ticking' exercise.

Summary

This chapter has shown the importance of understanding the issue of governance from a broad perspective that takes into account trends in public policy. More specifically, it has shown how strategic decisions taken by boards of NGBs are affected by government policy. In the UK this has been evident through the modernisation agenda that has had an impact on the sport sector. This chapter has shown how modernisation has impacted on NGBs and more specifically on the involvement of the board in strategy. The key issue is that the impact of public policy will depend on the nature of the governing body and, in particular, the degree of dependence on government for funding. The case study has demonstrated that for an NGB with a high dependence on government funding there is concern about ensuring that strategy is aligned with the objectives of Sport England. However, the fundamental issue is that despite the institutional pressures, a well-governed board with appropriate people in place is essential to the process of governance of an NGB.

Review questions

1   What reasons underpin the application of the modernisation agenda in sport within the UK?
2   In what ways has modernisation had an impact on the way in which boards of NGBs develop their strategy?
3   To what extent has modernisation given boards of NGBs in the UK more autonomy?

Further reading

Bloyce, D. & Smith, A. (2010). *Sport policy and development: An introduction*, London: Routledge
Houlihan, B. & Green, M. (2009). Modernization and sport: The reform of Sport England and UK Sport, *Public Administration*, 87(3): 678–98
Hoye, R. & Cuskelly, G. (2007). *Sport governance*, Oxford: Elsevier.

Websites

Sport England: http://www.sportengland.org/
UK Sport: http://www.uksport.gov.uk/
Department of Culture, Media and Sport: http://www.culture.gov.uk/sport/index.aspx

References

Bergsgard et al. (2007). *Sport policy: A comparative analysis of stability and change*, Oxford: Butterworth-Heinemann.
Bloyce, D. & Smith, A. (2010). *Sport policy and development: An introduction*, London: Routledge.

Brooks, J. (2000). Labour's modernization of local government. *Public Administration,* 78(3) 593–612.

Cornforth, C.J. & Edwards, C. (1999). Board roles in the strategic management of public service of non-profit organizations: Theory and practice. *Corporate Governance,* 7, 346–362.

Department for Culture, Media and Sport (2000). *A sporting future for all,* London: DCMS.

Department for Culture, Media and Sport (2002). *Game plan: A strategy for delivering Government's sport and physical activity objective.* London: DCMS.

DiMaggio, P. & Powell, W. (1983). The iron cage revisited: Institutional isomorphism and collective rationality in organizational fields. *American Sociological Review,* 48, 147–60.

Dutton, T. (2009). *Report of the inquiry into the World Class Payments Bureau: Schedule two.* London: Sport England.

Edwards, C. & Cornforth, C. (2003) What influences the strategic contribution of boards? In Cornforth, C. (ed.) *The Governance of Public and Non-profit Organisations: What Do Boards Do?* London: Routledge.

Falconer, P. (2005). New labour and the modernisation of public services. *Public Policy and Administration,* 20, 81–5.

Ferkins, L. & Shilbury, D (2012). Good boards are strategic: What does that mean for sport governance? *Journal of Sport Management,* 26, 67–80.

Ferkins, L., Shilbury, D. & McDonald, G. (2005). The role of the board in building strategic capability: Towards an integrated model of sport governance research. *Sport Management Review,* 8, 195–225.

Ferkins, L., Shilbury, D. & McDonald, G. (2009). Board involvement in strategy: Advancing the governance of sport organizations. *Journal of Sport Management,* 23, 245–77.

Fishel, D. (2003). *The book of the board: Effective governance for non-profit organisations,* Sydney: Federation Press.

Henry, I. & Lee, P.C. (2004). Governance and ethics in sport. In J. Beech and S. Chadwick (eds). *The business of sport management,* London: Prentice Hall.

Houlihan, B. & Green, M. (2009). Modernization and sport: The reform of Sport England and UK Sport, *Public Administration,* 87(3) 678–98

Houlihan, B. & White, A. (2002). *The politics of sports development.* London: Routledge.

Hoye, R. & Cuskelly, G. (2007). *Sport governance,* Oxford: Elsevier.

Hylton, K. & Bramham, P. (2008). *Sports development: Policy, process and practice.* London, Routledge

Judge, W.Q. & Zeithaml, C.P. (1992a). An empirical comparison between the board's strategic role in nonprofit hospitals and in for-profit industrial firms. *Health Services Research,* 27(1) 47–64.

Judge, W.Q. & Zeithaml, C.P. (1992b). Institutional and strategic choice perspectives on board involvement in the strategic decision process. *Academy of Management Journal,* 35 (4) 766–94.

Lusted, J. & O'Gorman, J. (2010). The impact of New Labour's modernisation agenda on the English grass-roots football workforce, *Managing Leisure,* 15, 140–54.

Midwinter, A. (2001). New Labour and the modernisation of British local government: A critique, *Financial Accountability and Management,* 17(4) 311–20.

Nadler, D.A. (2004). What's the board's role in strategy development?: Engaging the board in corporate strategy, *Strategy & Leadership,* 32(5) 25–34.

Parker, L.D. (2007). Boardroom strategizing in professional associations: Processual and institutional perspectives. *Journal of Management Studies,* 44(8) 1454–80.

Powell, M. (2008). Introduction: Modernising the welfare state. In M. Powell (ed.). *Modernising the welfare state: The Blair legacy* (3rd edn). Bristol: Policy Press.

Rose, N. (1999). *Powers of freedom: Reframing political thought.* Cambridge: Cambridge University Press.

Sam, M.P. (2009). The public management of sport: Wicked problems, challenges and dilemmas. *Public Management Review*, 11(4) 499–514.

Stone, M. & Ostrower, F. (2007). Acting in the public interest? Another look at research on nonprofit governance. *Nonprofit and Voluntary Sector Quarterly*, 36(3) 416–38.

Stone, M., Bigelow, B. & Crittenden, W. (1999). Research on strategic management in nonprofit organizations: Synthesis, analysis, and future directions. *Administration & Society,* 31 (3) 378–423.

UK Sport (2003). '*Investing in change' – High level review of the modernisation programme for governing bodies of sport*, London: Deloitte and Touche.

UK Sport (2004). *Good governance: A guide for national governing bodies of sport*, London: Institute of Chartered Secretaries and Administrators.

Walters, G., Tacon, R., & Trenberth, L. (2011). *The role of the board in UK national governing bodies of sport*. London: Birkbeck Sport Business Centre.

8 China

Fan Hong and Fuhua Huang

Topics

- Government and governance of sport in China and the study of the governance of Chinese basketball
- Chinese sport and political ideology
- China's sport system in transition
- Commercialisation of sport
- The role of government in sport governance in China
- Governance in professional sport in China and a case study of Chinese basketball.

Objectives

- To examine the impact of politics and national interest on Chinese sport governance
- To demonstrate the centralised 'top-down' governance structure of Chinese sport and the transformation of sport government and governance from the 1990s to the present
- To analyse the role of the Chinese government and private sectors, such as professional sports clubs, the governance of sport and the characteristics of Chinese sport government and governance during the transition period: the challenges, the progress and problems.

Key terms

Communist sport   Chinese sport, particularly in the Mao era, proved extremely valuable as a political and diplomatic resource, enabling the Chinese Communists both to oppose Western imperialists and to make approaches to the same Western imperialists through a medium that benefited from its 'apolitical' image, strengthening relations between socialist allies and deserving credit for helping the People's Republic of China reconstruct and transform both its internal and external image.

Reform and Opening-Up Policy   An alteration in China's economic system introduced at the end of the Cultural Revolution in the late 1970s and early

1980s. It opened the door for foreign investment and Western countries and began an era of substantial reformation of Chinese economy and society. From the 1980s to the present China has undergone a dramatic transition from socialist planned economy to capitalist market economy.

Sport reformation   The reformation of Chinese sport began in the 1980s. It includes two major parts: mass sport and elite sport. For mass sport the importance of public involvement in governing China's mass sport has been recognised. The change of structure of governance of mass sport gradually happens in urban areas accompanied with the urbanisation process. For elite sport the power struggle happens between the traditional government-controlled management system and the emerging privately owned sport club management system. It called for the transformation of the Chinese elite sport governance structure and for giving power to non-governmental sport federations.

Ju-guo-ti-zhi   A Chinese term which refers to the whole country support for the elite sport system, a concept approved by Chinese government at the highest political level, meaning that central and local governments should use their power to channel adequate financial and human resources throughout the country to support elite sport in order to win glory for the nation.

Olympic strategy   The strategy adopted by the Chinese government and Chinese Sports Ministry to ensure that Chinese athletes would win gold medals and that China would become a sports super-power at the Olympic Games.

Overview

This chapter will focus on the analysis of the characteristics of Chinese sport governance. It will map out the formation of the centralised 'top-down' governance model in Chinese sport from 1949 when the People's Republic of China was established, to the end of the 1970s when the Cultural Revolution finished. It will examine the transformation of the governing structure from the 1980s to the present, during which China undertook an open-door policy and economic reformation. The structure became a mix of government-oriented organisations and public involvement. The Chinese Basketball Association and its professional league will be used as a case study to illustrate the new models of governance and challenges during this transition in Chinese sport.

Introduction

Sport governance, within a universal perspective, has been broadly categorised into two models, corporate and non-profit. The former deals with the governance of profit-seeking companies or corporations that focus on protecting and enhancing shareholder value. In contrast, the latter is concerned with the governance of voluntary organisations that seek to provide a community service, promote a charitable cause, raise funds or facilitate the involvement of individuals in a variety of activities (Hoye & Cuskelly, 2007).

In terms of conceptualising 'sport governance', Henry and Lee offered three interrelated definitions: 1) *systemic governance*, which is concerned with the competition, cooperation and mutual adjustment between organisations in such systems; 2) *good organisational governance*, refers to the accepted norms or values for the just means of allocation of resources, and profits or losses (financial or other) and for the conduct of processes involved in the management and direction of organisations in the sports business; and 3) *political governance*, which relates to the processes by which governments or governing bodies seek to steer the sports system to achieve desired outcomes by moral pressure, use of financial or other incentives, or by licensing, regulation and control to influence other parties to act in ways consistent with desired outcomes (Henry & Lee, 2004).

In China, the governmental framework is an umbrella which comprises the central sport governing authority at the top, down towards the provincial and municipal sport governing bodies. It is the dominant power in China's sport governance. Therefore, rather than categorising sport organisations into non-profit and corporate in a straightforward way, China's sport organisations, to some extent, are mainly subject to the interest of the state.

Red sport and the centralised sport system 1949–1976

The ambition of Communist China to use sport to implement political ideology began as early as its establishment in 1949. The All-China Sport and Physical Education Congress took place on 26 and 27 October immediately after the establishment of the new republic. Zhu De (1886–1976), the Commander-in-Chief of the People's Liberation Army and Vice Chairman of the central government, indicated the role that sport ought to play in the future:

> Sport is a significant component of education and health. The central government must give it its place in building socialism … and it should serve the people, the national defence and the purpose of health. Chinese people including students, peasants, workers, citizens and soldiers should all participate in physical exercise and sport activities of all kinds.
>
> (Zhu, 1949)

Another major agenda item of the conference was to set up the Preparatory Committee for the All-China Sports Federation (PCACSF). Feng Wenbin (1911–1997), secretary of the Communist Youth League (CYL), was elected as the first director of the PCACSF. He announced three tasks for the PCACSF at his inauguration, one of which was to establish a sport organisation throughout the whole country (Feng, 1950).

In 1952, the PCACSF formally changed its name to the All-China Sports Federation (ACSF). It was a semi-governmental organisation which functioned under the leadership of the central government and the Chinese Communist Party (CCP). It followed Rule 48 of the 'Common Program of the Chinese People's Political Consultative Conference', and helped the government to organise and promote physical education and sport. The objective was to improve people's health and serve the national defence and the building of the state (All-China Sports Federation, 1952).

Zhu De was elected as the honorary president for the ACSF. Soon after its establishment, Feng Wenbin, the general secretary of the ACSF, wrote to the International Olympic Committee (IOC) and International Sport Federations to inform them that the ACSF was the organisation to represent China in international sport affairs (Fu, 2007). In 1954, the ACSF was recognised by the IOC. In the same year, the Central National Defence Sport Club was set up and operated under the ACSF. This semi-governmental system played a significant role in Chinese mass sport and military sport in the early 1950s with 30,505 local sport associations being established throughout the country and membership reaching 915,150 by 1956.

However, China's political dispute with Taiwan and the Soviet Union's victory over Western Europe and the USA at the 1952 Helsinki Olympic Games demonstrated that the ACSF was inadequate to meet the central government's political needs to utilise sport as a valuable tool to restore the nation's prestige in international politics. After the Helsinki Olympics, Rong Gaotang (1902–2006), the head of the Chinese Olympic delegation, visited the Soviet Union and learned about its centralised sport system and reported to the CCP Central Committee in April 1952.

At the same time, Ma Xulun (1885–1970), the Minister of Education submitted a similar report to the Government Administration Council in September. The two reports came up with the same proposal. They argued that the ACSF was merely a semi-governmental organisation which did not have enough power to lead sport and physical education in China. In order to further promote sport in China and to win recognition on the international sport stage, an influential sport organisation with authority, like the Ministry of Sport in the Soviet Union, was essential. They proposed that the central government should establish a national governing body for sport under the Administration Council of the Central Government and that it should appoint Marshal He Long (1896–1969) to be the leader (Li & Zhou, 2002).

The proposal was approved by the central government. In November 1952, the State Physical Culture and Sports Commission (SPCSC) was formally established following the Soviet Union model. It was a government ministry with the same status as other ministries such as Education, Finance and Commerce, all directly under the leadership of the State Council. At the same time, local sport commissions were established successively at provincial, municipal and county levels throughout China. These sport commissions were under the supervision of the SPCSC in terms of sport policy making and implementation, but under direct leadership from local government in terms of human resource, budgeting and general operation. Thus, a top-down governmental system took shape. It soon took over the ACSF system as the dominant power in governing Chinese sport.

Mass sport developed rapidly in the late 1950s, particularly under the Great Leap Forward and the implementation of the 'Ten-Year Guideline for Sports Development' in 1956 issued by the SPCSC. It aimed to promote mass and competitive sport simultaneously and to reach world levels within a decade. The major target was to have four million people achieve the standard of the Labour and Defence System (LDS; a nationwide assessing system of athletic performance which was adapted from the former Soviet Union), and to cultivate eight million active athletes and five thousand elite athletes in ten years' time (SPCSC, 1958). By mid-1958, inspired by the booming campaign in agriculture and heavy industry, the SPCSC believed that 'the goal of surpassing the capitalist West has stimulated the development of sport ... the old Guidelines could no longer suit the current situation and will reduce people's enthusiasm' (Fu, 2007). Therefore, the SPCSC revised the Guidelines in September 1958 and required '150–200 million people to achieve the standard of the LDS, and aimed to cultivate 50–70 million active athletes and 10–15 thousand elite athletes' (Fu, 2007). The revised 'Ten-Year Guideline for Sport Development' was approved by the CCP Central Committee in September 1958.

In 1960, the Party changed its slogan to 'readjustment, consolidation, filling out and raising standards'. In 1961, the SPCSC revised its policy to produce elite sport stars (Policy Research Center, 1982). The government determined to use the best of its limited resources to provide special and intensive training for potential young athletes so that they could compete on the international sporting stage. Under this policy, a centralised sport system which aimed to produce a few elite sport stars took shape. In 1963, the SPCSC also issued the 'Regulations for Outstanding Athletes and Teams' in an effort to improve the system. Under the instruction of the ministry, a search for talented young athletes took place in every province (Policy Research Center, 1982). Meanwhile 10 key sports were selected from the previous 43. They were: athletics, badminton, gymnastics, swimming, football, basketball, table tennis, shooting, weightlifting and skiing (Policy Research Center, 1982). It was a key turning point in Chinese sport ideology, changing from 'two legs walking' (elite and mass sport) to 'one leg walking' (only elite), as the Chinese saying goes.

However, the Chinese sport governance system went on a roller-coaster ride during the Cultural Revolution (1966–1976). This was a political movement initiated by Chinese Communist leader Mao Zedong. He believed he was losing control and that his enemies had changed the colour of the Party from Red (Communism) to Black (Capitalism and Revisionism). His aim for the Cultural Revolution was to regain and consolidate his power and to prevent China changing its colour (Hong, 1999). In matters of sport, the confrontation and turbulence ultimately focused on the relationship between elite sport and mass sport. The former was regarded as the representative of bourgeois and capitalist ideology and the latter as communist and proletarian. Mass sport survived and maintained steady development.

As a result, the SPCSC, which regarded elitism in sport as a promising solution for building China's international image within a shortest time in the planned economy system, broke down. The Revolutionary Communist Central Committee, the State Council and the Central Military Commission (which took over the top governing chair from the SPCSC) jointly issued a Military Order on 12 May 1968 to disband the SPCSC, including the Central National Defence Sport Club, and the provincial and local sport commissions.

He Long, the Sports Minister, was accused of neglecting mass sport and of supporting revisionist and capitalist sport policy. He was condemned, jailed and died in prison in 1975. PLA officers and soldiers were sent to replace sport administrators. More than 1,000 sport administrators from the SPCSC were sent to a May Seventh Cadres School in Shanxi province to be 're-educated' by doing physical labour. Administrators and coaches of provincial and local sport commissions were sent to the countryside to be 're-educated' as well.

The whole elite sport training system in China was dismantled. Sport schools were closed down. Provincial and local sport teams were dismissed. National squads stopped participating in international competitions. Sports facilities were destroyed by the Red Guards and revolutionary rebels. Sports stadia became venues for denunciation meetings. Top athletes, outstanding coaches, and sports scientists and scholars were condemned as counter revolutionaries, capitalist roaders and rightists and suffered mentally and physically. Some of the athletes died in the violent revolutionary storm. For example, three famous world-class table tennis players, Rong Guotuan, Fu Qifang, Jiang Yongning, committed suicide in 1969 as they could not endure the torture anymore.

The situation began to change after the 'Ping-Pong Diplomacy' which developed for political and diplomatic reasons when China felt threatened by the Soviet Union and sought the United States as a new ally. Sport was used to open the channel of communication with the Western powers. In February 1973, the SPCSC was restored its power to govern Chinese sport under the State Council. Provincial and municipal sport commissions were rebuilt accordingly to implement the central government and the SPCSC's political strategy and sport policy.

The reformation of sports government and governance in China (1977–1992)

Mao's death in 1976 brought the end of the Cultural Revolution. The Third Plenary Session of the 11th Central Committee was held in September 1978 and marked a new era for China. The Maoist 'class struggle oriented' political policy was replaced by economic reform and the 'open-door' policy. It was hoped that, through economic reform and communication with advanced countries in the West, China would catch up with the West and again be a modernised and strong country. Sport administration in Chinese sport also underwent institutional transformation in the new era, highlighting the importance of public involvement in governing China's mass sport. Meanwhile, government leadership was retained in elite sport. According to the 'Decisions about the Reform of Sports System (Draft)' issued by the SPCSC in 1986, the proposed structure of China's sport governance was that mass sport should be promoted by all kinds of public organisations in different sectors with support from sport commissions; but that elite sport should continue to be managed by the state but in cooperation with some public organisations. The purpose of this strategy was to transform the state-centralised sport governance model to a mix of state-centralised and public-involvement – a new model (SPCSC, 1986).

There was mediocre progress in mass sport due to the lack of public interest but, in contrast, reform in elite sport began. The SPCSC held a national sport conference in 1980 and officially established its strategy for the future development of sport. Wang Meng, then Sports Minister, stated on the one hand that China was still a poor country and was restricted in the amount of money it could invest on sport. On the other hand, elite sport was an effective way to boost China's new image on the international stage. Therefore, the solution was to bring elite sport into the existing planned economy and administrative system, which could assist in the distribution of the limited resources of the whole nation to medal-winning sports (Wang, 1982). It was hoped that international success of Chinese athletes would, in return, bring pride and hope to the nation, which were badly needed in the new era of transformation (Rong, 1987).

In response, in 1982 the SPCSC started to reallocate its governance power within the committee to carry out this strategy. Previously, three major departments had worked under the SPCSC, respectively on general management of athletes, military sports and ball games (both team sport and individual sports). However, in 1982, this structure was reorganised into six departments and they were named the Competition Sport Department One to Six. Each of them was responsible for certain sport events.

The purpose of this was to cover all the Olympic sports and to centralise all resources for victory on international competitions. It was a successful strategy which brought an immediate victory at the 1984 Los Angeles Olympic Games. China won 15 gold medals and was placed fourth in the Olympic medal table after its absence of 32 years from the Olympics. Although success in Los Angeles was partly attributed to the absence of the Soviet Union and the Democratic Republic of Germany, it nevertheless excited many in China from government officials to ordinary citizens. 'Develop elite sport and make China a superpower in the world' became both a slogan and a dream for the Chinese people.

The Chinese government captured the competitive spirit and inspiration of the Olympic victory to the Chinese people. As a result, the Society of Strategic Research for the Development of Physical Education and Sport produced the 'Olympic Strategy' for the Sports Ministry in 1985. This strategy clearly stated that 'elite sport is the priority'. It aimed to use the nation's limited sport resources to develop elite sport to ensure that China would become a leading sport power by the end of the twentieth century. The strategy was the blueprint for Chinese sport in the 1980s and 1990s while the target was primarily the Olympics.

Wu Shaozu, the Minister of Sport from 1990 to 2000, claimed that 'The highest aim of Chinese sport is success in the Olympic Games. We must concentrate our resources on it. To raise the flag at the Olympics is our major responsibility' (Wu, 1999). To achieve this goal the government must channel the best of limited resources to potential gold medallists in order to provide special and intensive training. Chinese athletes benefited from both the 'whole country support elite for the sport system' and the 'Olympic strategy' and achieved very satisfactory results.

To sum up, between the 1950s and the 1980s the national governmental body, the State Physical Culture and Sports Commission (SPCSC), was responsible for the formulation and implementation of sport policy; administration of national sport programmes and organisations; training elite athletes; and organising national and international competitions. The model of the Chinese sport administrative system reflected the political and diplomatic strategies and wider social system in China. Both the Party and state administration were organised in a vast hierarchy with power flowing down from the top.

Commercialisation: merging into a market economy (1993– the present)

The turning point from purely politicisation to commercialisation of sport came in 1992 when a major reform policy was initiated by Deng Xiaoping (1904– 1997). On his South Patrol in February 1992, Deng urged the central and local governments to speed up economic reform at all levels in Chinese society. In response, the SPCSC held a conference in Zhongshan, Guangdong province in November 1992 to discuss how to speed up Chinese sport reformation. At the conference, Wu Shaozu, Minister of Sport, pointed out that the major objective of sport reformation was to further transform the sport system, which was still based on a planned economy, to a new system, which would be based on the market economy. Sport should stand on its own feet.

Based on the principles coming out of the Zhongshan Conference, the SPCSC issued 'The Proposal of Moving Ahead of Sport Reformation' on May 24, 1993. It officially announced a market-oriented reform policy. In this policy document, the SPCSC, for the first time, publicly advocated the commercialisation of sport and the promotion of the sport industry. Wu Shaozu claimed,

> Chinese sports system must reform without delay. The strategy of the reform is to commercialise sport and to integrate sport into people's daily life. This includes people paying for sports and exercise; privately sponsored sport; the club system and promotion of sports commercial market.
>
> (Hong, 2009: 362)

After the official approval of the establishment of the socialist market economy system at the Third Plenary Session of the 14th Central Committee later in the same year, the SPCSC set the framework of the future development of Chinese sport, issuing three decrees in June 1995: the Olympic Strategy, the National Fitness-for-All Programme, and the Development of Sports Industry and Commerce Outline. These decrees were designed to be integrated, and were expected to support each other and to form a new model of sport policy and practice in China.

The implementation of the three decrees simultaneously legitimised the involvement of the public who would exert power in the form of non-governmental federations, and indicated that the role government played in the Chinese sport system should be transferred to leveraging, rather than commanding or direct

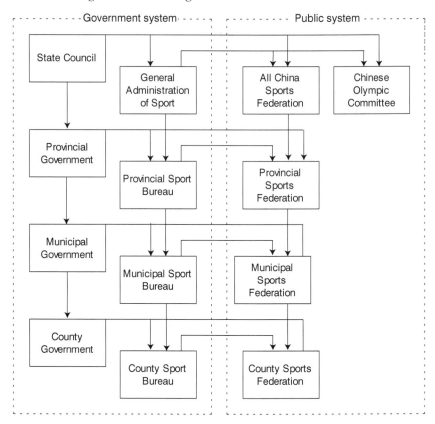

Figure 8.1 Governance structure of Chinese sport

control. Therefore, the SPCSC changed its name to the General Administration of Sport of China (GASC) in 1998. With the change of the name, a new governance structure of Chinese sport under the reformation towards market economy was introduced (see Figure 8.1). At the same time, 14 sport management centres were set up to work with 41 national sports federations in order to manage 56 sports outside the GASC.

However, as is depicted in the chart, non-governmental sport federations did not yet preside over sport bureaus. There was a slow transformation of power and the true power in governing Chinese sport effectively was old wine in a new bottle. Nevertheless there was a tendency and trend away from government direct control of sport. This reflected the globalising trends in sport in which market actors play an active role. In the Chinese context, the shift was gradually taking place but with 'a Chinese character'. The operation of this unique model of sport governance in China will be examined with a study on the Chinese Basketball Association and its professional league.

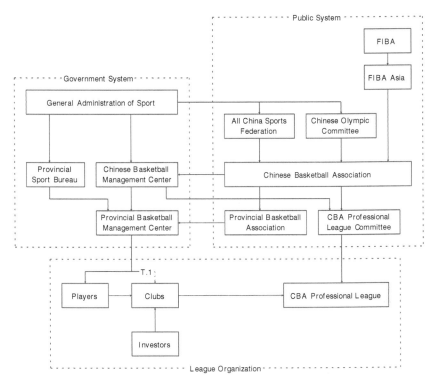

Figure 8.2 Governance structure of Chinese basketball

Case study: The governance of Chinese basketball

The Chinese Basketball Association (CBA) was established under the leadership of the ACSF in June 1956. Although the CBA had claimed jurisdiction over all Chinese basketball activities from late 1950s, it was not until the late 1970s that the CBA was endowed with power in managing Chinese basketball when in 1978 it was granted an official charter. The CBA was finally recognised by the International Basketball Federation (FIBA) while Taiwan's membership was successfully exempted.

According to the current structure, the CBA is defined as: a nationwide non-governmental sport organisation with independent juridical qualification; as a non-profit association comprising a hierarchical system of provincial, autonomous regional and municipality basketball associations or corresponding sport departments of the People's Liberation Army; a member of the ACSF; an Olympic organisation recognised by the China Olympic Committee; and the only legitimate Chinese organisation qualified to participate in the International Basketball Federation and the Asian Basketball Confederation (see Figure 8.2).

The national committee is the premier seat of power of the CBA, and is constituted with a standing committee and a group of representatives (normally heads) from lower basketball associations e.g. provincial basketball associations. In practical operation, the representatives' voice is very weak except for the right of presenting a proposal during the national committee meeting convened every four years. Routine affairs are undertaken by the standing committee, which is constituted with a group of governmental officials: including a president who is a head of the GASC; vice presidents who are heads of provincial sport bureaus; the head of the Chinese Basketball Management Centre (CBMC); a general secretary who is also the head of the CBMC; and vice secretaries who are directors of the CBMC departments.

The Chinese Basketball Management Centre (CBMC)

The Chinese Basketball Management Centre, the deputy secretary office for the CBA, was established on 24 November 1997 as a unit subordinate to the GASC. Therefore, the heads of the CBMC are appointed by the GASC. The CBMC is composed of seven departments (see Figure 8.3).

The National Teams Management Department is responsible for building and managing men's and women's national basketball teams of all levels. This is the CBA's foremost role and includes organising, instructing and supervising training, international match schedules, selection of coaches, and providing backroom services and ethics education for the national teams. The four most influential international basketball events are the basketball competitions in the Olympic Games, Asian Games, the World Basketball Championship with FIBA and the Asian Basketball Championship with the Asian FIBA. The CBA also organises the Intercontinental Stankovic Cup and some other friendly matches inviting or visiting other countries every summer. For example, the men's national team played 37 games in the summer of 2007.

The Training and Research Department is responsible for enhancing the performance of Chinese elite basketball; instructing and managing nationwide basketball clubs; scientific research on basketball movement; and assessment and registration of athletes and coaches.

The Competitions Department is responsible for scheduling all nationwide basketball competitions, including the National Basketball League (a secondary league), WCBA, women's Yiji (secondary) league, other national and international basketball tournaments and matches in major sport events and development of referees.

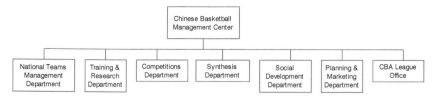

Figure 8.3 Administration structure of the Chinese Basketball Management Centre (CBMC)

The Synthesis Department plays a supporting role and deals with issues of regulations across the centre, foreign affairs, publicity and media, financing, party affairs, censorship and audit, personnel, labour union, property and security.

The Social Development Department is responsible for building basketball reserve squads; organising youth training camps and managing mass participation; and registration and management of lower basketball associations.

The Planning and Marketing Department is responsible for planning and developing the Chinese basketball industry; marketing basketball competitions relating to the national teams and professional leagues; and managing the properties of the Chinese Basketball Association Professional League (CBAPL).

The Professional League Office is responsible for all affairs of the CBAPL.

The Chinese Basketball Association Professional League (CBAPL)

The CBAPL is a general name adopted in this chapter to indicate the premier men's professional basketball league organised by the Chinese Basketball Association. The name in earlier seasons has varied with different corporate sponsors.

In the early 1990s, there was a Chinese mania for the National Basketball Association (NBA), the American professional basketball league. This was enabled by satellite media, transnational corporations and the force of globalisation. Chinese basketball was in an embarrassing position: on one hand, as basketball was not a 'medal sport' under the Olympic Strategy this meant that the state was cutting back its funding for basketball; on the other hand, the Chinese had been keen on this sport for more than a century since Lyon brought the game to China through the Tianjin YMCA in 1896 (Gao, 1989). Soccer had broken the ice in responding to the state's sport policy of self-sufficiency and the CBA initiated a new era of professionalising Chinese basketball in 1994.

The primary approach of the CBA was to reformat the former premier national competition, the Top-Eight Tournament, into a professional basketball league. As Michael Danielson stated, the formation of teams into leagues is significant to the business of professional team sports. Leagues become the primary market for the collective product; they structure games into seasons, play-offs, and championships. Customers prefer organised games among teams competing for pennants, division titles, or a place in post season play (Danielson, 2001).

There are two types of ownership structure for governance in professional sport leagues – joint ventures and single entities (Noll, 2003). Most leagues in the world are organised on a joint-venture model. Noll argued that in the joint-venture formation, member clubs are independently owned and managed and collectively create the league as a joint venture for coordinating their league activities. A commissioner or president is the chief operating officer, while club owners constitute the board of directors. The chief executive may have considerable authority in the league's rules and policies, but true power is in the hands of club owners. Typically, the chief executive serves at the pleasure of a majority of the teams, and can be removed without cause if a majority so desire. As a result, the league chief executive can exercise considerable authority in disciplining the bad behaviour of an individual owner or player, but is not likely to survive in office if a decision is made that harms most teams (Noll, 2003).

Noll further defined the 'single-entity' leagues as having true power centralised in the league office. In these leagues, teams are not independent organisations, but are operating divisions of the league. These leagues also have a chief executive and a board of directors, with the latter being the major investors in the league. In its pure form, team operators in a single-entity league serve at the pleasure of the league, and can be removed by either the chief executive or the board, depending on the league's rules. Thus, team operators are roughly equivalent to general managers, not owners as in joint-venture leagues (Noll, 2003). The most important distinction between joint-venture and single-entity leagues is the degree to which they centralise decisions on resource allocation and league membership.

In this sense, the CBAPL is a typical single-entity league and this can be seen in the operation of the league where there are three major actors: the league, the clubs and the players.

The Chinese Basketball Association Professional League Committee (CBAPLC)

In the early seasons, the CBAPL was organised by the Athletic Sports Department in the SPCSC. The power passed to the CBMC in 1997. With the implementation of the North Star Plan, the CBAPLC was set up in 2005 (see Figure 8.2) and is comprised of:

- Representatives from each club (usually the chairman or the CEO), experts in law, economics, or finance relating to the basketball industry from the public, and directors of the CBMC departments;
- A vice president, usually also a president of the CBA and vice director of the CBMC;
- A president, usually also a president of CBA and director of the CBMC.

All the members convene twice per annum, i.e. before and after a season. Routine affairs are undertaken by a standing committee, which comprise the president, vice president and representatives from the CBMC.

The Professional League Office under the CBMC is the CBAPLC's secretariat, the director of which is usually nominated the general secretary. According to the Chinese Basketball Association Professional League Committee Charter, ownership of the CBAPL's properties is possessed by the CBA; clubs are permitted to align with the league only when the clubs fulfil all terms required by the committee.

Taking the board composition of the CBA, CBMC and CBAPLC into account, it is clear that the CBMC is the true and dominant power in governing Chinese basketball. It should also be noted that the CBMC is under pressure to meet the AGSC's interest. Such a 'Chinese characteristic' personnel formation is also evident in broader public sectors, named 'one personnel, two boards'. In other words, the CBA and CBAPLC are still under control of the Chinese government in spite of its embrace of non-governmental principles in the charters.

The clubs

The government's power monopoly exists not only in the leagues, but also in the clubs (see Figure 8.2). The CBAPL was developed on the basis of the Top-Eight Tournament of the national basketball competition, and the first season saw eight army basketball teams participating in a 'professional' league. The reason for this was that the army teams in the mid-1990s were better able to provide for sport talent than their counterparts, the provincial commissions. As professional sport clubs emerged in the new market economy, army sport lagged behind and provincial teams (normally co-built with corporate investors) became dominant in elite basketball. By the end of the 1990s, Bayi Rockets was the only army team remaining in the premier league.

Currently, ownership of clubs in the CBAPL can be categorised into three types: 1) corporate and government joint-owned; 2) corporate owned; and 3) individually owned. For example in the 2010–11 season, out of the 17 clubs, 6 were of the first type; 10 of the second type; and one was of the third type.

Government/public joint-venture basketball clubs are, to some extent, resource efficient for both stakeholders. On one hand, the provincial sport bureaus are able to preserve their basketball teams without concern about finance. The corporate investors, on the other hand, require facilities to train and build the teams and squads, and stadiums or arenas to hold the games. However, the alignment of corporate investor and provincial sport bureaus has led to the power allocation becoming unbalanced. The power really lies with the government partner who controls the facilities and it is not unusual to see a corporate investor withdraw partnership. Shandong Gold Club, for example, has changed its corporate partner five times since it joined the league.

Even when some clubs are owned purely by corporate investors or individuals, those clubs are still unable to manage all their affairs without government participation. This is particularly relevant in contracting players and will be further discussed in the following section. Moreover, if the corporation is state-owned, the club will tend to be directly dependent on local government. Even privately-owned companies are still dependent on local government. A key reason for this is that no CBAPL club so far has been able to balance its books without grants and subsidies from local governments or sport bureaus. Therefore, dependence on local governments or subsidiary sport bureaus has greatly weakened the clubs' power in their dialogues with the league.

The players

Players of CBAPL clubs are the weakest actors and they are in the lowest position of the hierarchy of Chinese basketball (see Figure 8.2). The training and selection system of Chinese elite basketball players is the decisive factor that restricts players' individual rights. The selection system has undergone great transformation over the past decades (see Figure 8.2). Chinese elite basketball players are selected and trained in three systems: the sports school system, the educational system and the public system. The sports school system was formed in the 1950s which was

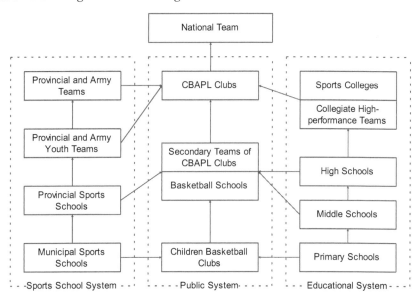

Figure 8.4 Selection and training system of Chinese elite basketball

adapted from the former Soviet Union model. Under this system young players are trained full-time in state-supported sport schools. Athletes with potential are promoted through a pyramid system from municipal-level sport schools to provincial-level or army teams and the best are selected for the national team. The educational system means that secondary school students can be recruited directly by professional clubs or college sports teams. However, few professional players have come directly from schools due to the lack of facilities and professional coaches. The public system (non-governmental), particularly youth teams of professional clubs, has evolved to develop young basketball talents. Over the past decade, the CBAPL clubs have all scrambled for young potential players to build their reserve teams. Another tendency is the emergence of the specialised basketball schools with the CBA's cooperation (Figure 8.4).

The players' personnel affiliation is the main cause for their weakness in China's basketball system. Undoubtedly, players selected and trained in the sports school system are affiliated to their supporters – the sport bureaus. But according to the CBA charter, all players participating in any national basketball competitions, including the CBAPL or its youth league, must be registered in local (provincial) basketball associations. These associations are governed by local sport bureaus (similar to the relationship between GASC and CBA). This means that when a player in a youth team is available to transfer to the public system, basketball school or CBAPL club, he is still required to register with another provincial sport bureau. This also applies where a player in a youth club or basketball school wishes to sign a contract with another club. A conclusion can be drawn here that any CBAPL player is under control of a local sport bureau rather than the club who is paying the salary. He is not a free agent as he would commonly be elsewhere in

Table 8.1 Synopsis of key actors in Chinese professional basketball

	Government power	*Public power*
Chinese Basketball Association	Very strong: All leaders on the board are government officials; the head office (CBMC) is a department of a wing of central government.	Very weak: Only a few non-government representatives are on the board; they are not authorised to vote on major decisions.
CBA Professional League Committee	Strong: All leaders on the board are simultaneously the leaders of the CBMC.	Weak: Representatives from the clubs are not authorised to vote on major decisions.
Club ownership	Strong: Some sport bureaus directly hold ownership of the clubs; while most clubs still rely financially on local government.	Medium: Corporate investors' voice is getting stronger.
Players	Very strong: The players must be registered with local basketball associations, which are controlled by local sport bureaus.	Very weak: In the lowest position with no labour organisations to support their rights.

the world. Worse still, a labour union to protect CBAPL players' right has never formed, unlike many other professional sport leagues, where labour unions are set up to protect players' rights and liaise with the league.

Summary

Table 8.1 shows a synopsis of the key actors in Chinese professional basketball and of the allocation of power between them.

Conclusion

The Chinese government's determination to promote global presence and achieve first place on the international sports table has resulted in the centralisation of sport governance power in order to channel elite athletes to world competitions since 1949. Although reformation in sport has been undertaken to mix government's power and public investment since the early 1980s and the determination was made to promote the sport industry since the early 1990s, public power has to give way to government's interest under the 'Olympic Strategy'. The decisive governance power of Chinese sport is still in the government's hand. The 2008 Olympics in Beijing proved that this has been effective in making China a world sport superpower. However, this power centralised system leads to the government having a monopolistic position in dealing with the emerging public investment and it is an obstacle for China's sport reformation and commercialisation. It will be hard for China's market-oriented sport industry to develop unless the government switches its role from steering to leveraging.

Review questions

1   Analyse the relationship between political ideology and sport in China.
2   Examine the advantages and disadvantages of the centralised 'top-down' governance structure of Chinese sport.
3   Demonstrate the newly emerging government and governance structure in Chinese basketball.

Further reading

Henry, I. & Lee, P. C. (2004). Governance and ethics in sport, in Beech, J., & Chadwick, S. (2004). *The Business of Sport Management*. London: Pearson Education, pp.25–41.
Hong, F., & Xiaozheng, X. (2002). Communist China: Sport, politics and diplomacy. *The International Journal of the History of Sport*, 19(23), 31–42
Noll, R. G. (2003). The organisation of sports leagues. *Oxford Review of Economic Policy,* 19(4): 530–51.
Wei, F., Hong, F. & Zhouxiang, L. (2010). Chinese state sports policy: Pre- and post-Beijing 2008. *The International Journal of the History of Sport*, 27(14–15), 2380–402.

Websites

Role of government in sport in China: http://www.humankinetics.com/excerpts/excerpts/sport-in-china-heavily-influenced-by-government
General administration of sport of China: http://www.sport.gov.cn/# (in Chinese)
Chinese Basketball Association: http://www.cba.gov.cn/

References

All-China Sports Federation (1952). General Statutes of the All-China Sports Federation. Available online at http://www.sport.org.cn/zt/09tyjz/speech/2009-05-21/248878.html
Danielson, M. N. (2001). *Home Team: Professional Sports and the American Metropolis.* Princeton, NJ: Princeton UP.
Feng, W. (1950). Discussions on People's Sport. *New Sports,* 3(1): 5–6.
Fu, Y. (ed.) (2007). *The history of sport in China. Vol. 5, 1949–1979.* Beijing: People's Sport Press.
Gao, W. (1989). The development history of Chinese basketball. *Journal of Xi'an Physical Education University,* 7(2): 2–9.
Henry, I. & Lee, P. C. (2004). *The Business of Sport Management.* London: Pearson Education.
Hong, F. (1999) Not all bad! Communism, society and sport in the great proletarian Cultural Revolution: A revisionist perspective. *The International Journal for the History of Sport,* 16(3): 47–71.

Hong, F. (2009).The change of Chinese government's sports policy: A historical review. Paper presented at the 2009 International Conference/Workshop at University College Cork, Ireland, March.

Hoye, R. & Cuskelly, G. (2007). *Sport governance*. Oxford: Elsevier.

Li, L. & Zhou, M. (2002) *The son of sport—Rong Gaotang*. Beijing: Xinhua Press.

Noll, R. G. (2003). The organisation of sports leagues. *Oxford Review of Economic Policy,* 19(4): 530–51.

Policy Research Centre of the Sports Ministry (1982). *Policy documents for sport (1949—1981)*. Beijing: People's Sport Press.

Rong, G. (1987). *The history of contemporary Chinese sport*. Beijing: China Social Science Press.

SPCSC (1958). The Ten Year Guidelines for Sports Development.

SPCSC (1986). Decisions about the Reform of Sports System (draft), in Hao, Q. (2006) *The History of Chinese Sport*. Beijing: People's Sport Press, pp.92

Tan, H. (ed) (2005). *History of sport*, Beijing: Higher Education Press.

Wang, M. (1982). *The Report to the 1980 National Sports Conference, Sports Policy Documents (1949–1981)*, Beijing: People's Sport Press.

Wu, S. (1999). *The history of sport of the PRC*. Beijing: China Books Press.

Zhu, D. (1949) Speech on the All-China Sport and Physical Education Congress, *New Sports*, 1, 1.

9 Brazil

Gonzalo Bravo

Topics

- The role of government and the enactment of public policies to organise and fund sport
- The constitutional rank given to sport in Brazil
- The perceived importance of high-performance sport and its influence over public policies and funding
- Business management practices and their role in shaping effective governance in sport organisations.

Objectives

- To explain the evolution of organised sport in Brazil and its impact over the governance of sport organisations
- To discuss governmental role and the struggle to achieve consensus for a national sport policy in Brazil
- To discuss how different sport laws, enacted since 1940, have influenced the Brazilian sport system
- To explain the role of sport leaders in shaping the governance of sport organisations
- To examine the organisational features of the Brazilian Volleyball Confederation and the reasons behind its success
- To examine the alignment of sport polices' goals with sport policies' interventions of public and private sport governing bodies.

Key terms

Mass sport Form of sport participation that is practiced on a voluntary basis. It contributes to promote social integration, health promotion and care for the environment.

Educational sport Form of sport participation that primarily takes place in school settings. It contributes to the overall individual's wellbeing by promoting civic values. This type of sport discourages early selectivity based on skills and excessive competitiveness among its participants.

High-performance sport Form of sport participation that is practiced in compliance to national and international rules. Its participation aims at reaching the highest level of performance. It is categorised as professional and non-professional.

Sport confederation A national governing body that groups a number of state federations. In Brazil, there is only one sport confederation for each sport.

Law Agnelo–Piva Federal law that assigns two per cent of the lottery to fund Olympic and Paralympic programmes.

Overview

The chapter examines the evolution of sport policies in Brazil by looking at the role played by public and private structures in the process and struggle to achieve national sport policies. It also discusses the role of the federal constitution in shaping these policies and the perceived importance of high-performance sport in influencing them. Among the factors that have influenced priorities for funding and governance of sport in Brazil are: the Constitution of 1988 and the subsequent laws enacted since then, the political context with the return to democracy, and the economic growth of the country during the last decade.

The Brazilian Volleyball Confederation (Confederação Brasileira do Voleibol – CBV) serves as a case study to illustrate the growth and success of a national governing body (NGB) in the current setting of sport policies in Brazil that, for years, had minimal impact. To understand the context in which the CBV operates, a description of the main issues related to the governance of sport in Brazil is also presented.

Sport governance in Brazil and the Brazilian Volleyball Confederation

Brazil, in terms of size and population, is not only the largest country in Latin America, but is also the largest economy too. In 2011, Brazil's gross domestic product (GDP) ranked sixth in the world (World Bank, 2012). Nevertheless, while some indicators related to human development like education, index of inequality, and life expectancy, still fall behind when compared to other developed nations, the last decade had seen Brazil, along with China, India and Russia, as a part of the new bloc of emerging economies of the world (Zakaria, 2009).

Across the Latin American region, Brazil's status and leadership is not only seen in terms of its economic power, but also in terms of its politics, culture and sport. Due to its geographical location, Brazilian national sport governing bodies fall under the jurisdiction of South American governance agencies like CONMEBOL in football, CONSUDATLE in track and field, and ODESUR or PASO for major regional competitions.

Considering the historical success achieved by Brazilian athletes, the entire Brazilian sport system represents a model to follow for most countries across

Latin America. Over the years, Brazilian athletes have reached world-class success which few other Latin American athletes and teams have achieved. For example, since the second half of the twentieth century, the men's national football team has dominated not only in South America, but also throughout the world. Brazilian athletes have also reached world and Olympic success in men's and women's volleyball, sailing, swimming, formula one, track and field, and judo. Overall, these athletes have obtained 108 medals at the summer Olympic Games, thus ranking them second in Latin America after Cuba.

Complementing the success of Brazilian sports has been the significant growth of the sport industry over the past three decades. DaCosta (2006a) estimated that in the early 2000s there were 85 million sport participants, of which 700,000 were categorised as very active. The sport market in Brazil represents the fifth largest market in the world with an estimated size of US$10.4 billion annually (DeMelo, Neto & Feitosa, 2006). Today, the gross domestic product for the industry is estimated at 1.7 per cent of Brazil's GDP, but during the late 1990s it grew 5.4 times more than the country's GDP (Kasznar & Graça, 2002). These statistics reflect not only the trend of sport participation and sport consumption, but also the product of government involvement and the sport policies created over the last decades. The impact of sport on Brazilian society, the size of the sport market, and the performance achieved by Brazilian athletes in world and Olympic competitions are three main factors that have influenced the current state in which sport is organised and governed in Brazil.

The next section discusses government involvement and the influence of sport policies. It follows a discussion of the Brazilian Olympic Committee (BOC) and a description of the role played by its leaders in forging some of the successes in today's sport.

Issues related to the governance of sport in Brazil

Modern sport in Brazil has its roots from the mid-nineteenth century as swimming, rowing, and fencing became common in military schools. During this time, a few public initiatives took place to promote the value of physical education in schools. However, it is the arrival of immigrants and the further establishment of sport clubs what would create the momentum for the future growth of sport in Brazil. Gymnastics clubs came to flourish in the southern part of the country (Tesche & Rambo, 2001). A few years later, rowing clubs emerged in Rio de Janeiro and football clubs spread all over, but mostly in the southern region (Melo, 2006). This trend of club expansion not only influenced how modern sport evolved, but it also set the need to organise, fund and legislate sport policies. The establishment of sport clubs were much more than the foundation block of the entire sport system. These clubs had a vast impact on the Brazilian culture, as immigrants and their descendants from Germany, Italy and Japan founded a large number of them. Consequently, many sport clubs served not only as a venue to exercise or play, but also to reinforce the customs and identity of these different ethnic groups (DaCosta, 2006b).

By the 1970s, sport associations had grown significantly in number and expanded throughout the country. A high concentration of these grew in the southern, more industrial and prosperous states. It is estimated that during the 2000s, there were more than 10,000 organised sport and recreation clubs in the country. Estimates also suggest that these clubs have contributed to create 100,000 jobs (DaCosta, 2006b). Therefore, as in many other countries, sport clubs in Brazil become the fundamental, and perhaps the most critical, organisational unit in which governance exerts its influence. It is at the club level where sport is practised and where rules and policies clearly reflect its effect.

The first legislation related to sport dates back to 1941 when President Getulio Vargas passed Law 3199. This law established the basis for organising the sport system in Brazil. An outcome of this legislation was the creation of the National Sport Council (Conselho Nacional do Desporto) which became the institution that ruled sport for the next five decades. Bueno (2008) noted that Brazilian leaders decided to legislate and intervene in the sport sector because there was a need to control an important area of social life that was poorly, or not regulated, at all. In addition, Law 3199 of 1941 recognised the hierarchical model of governance employed by Olympic organisations in which at the bottom lay sport clubs and at the top the Brazilian Olympic Committee (BOC). Although an Olympic structure has existed in Brazil since 1913, this Law provided governmental legitimacy and full recognition to the BOC. Furthermore, it implicitly recognised the importance of high performance sport within the Brazilian sport system.

Scholars who have examined the evolution of sport policies in Brazil agree that the intervention of government in sport has been a positive step aimed at better organising and fostering this area. Nevertheless, they noted that during the first 35 years since the enactment of Law 3199, governmental intervention provided minimal flexibility for sport organisations to manage and control their own destiny. Instead, this intervention was seen as obstructive and bureaucratic (Tubino, 2001). Government not only inhibited growth but also failed to satisfy the need of most sport organisations. As a result, during this period, the overall level of participation, growth and performance of most national governing bodies significantly suffered. The exception to this trend was football. Since the mid-1920s, the interest and popularity of football showed consistent growth among Brazilians of all spheres of life, particularly during the 1950s to 1970s when the men's national team won the FIFA World Cup three times. It was not until the mid-1970s that a new law was passed, and while mostly overlooked, the significance of Law 6251/1975 was that for the first time it called for the need to address a national sport policy. However, it was not until the late 1980s that significant changes occurred. In 1985, the Ministry of Education created a commission with the task to reformulate existing sport policies. This commission delivered 80 specific recommendations of what government and sport organisations should do in order to strengthen the sport system in the country. The most significant outcome of these recommendations was that in 1988 sport achieved constitutional status (Tubino, 2001). Furthermore, Article 217 of the Federal Constitution of 1988, included the following clause:

It established the autonomy of sport organisations; it established priorities of public funding related to sport; and established a clear distinction for the governance between professional and non-professional sport organisations.

(Constituição da República Federativa do Brasil, 1988, p.35)

Because the passage of the Federal Constitution of 1988 the National Sport Council disbanded in the early 1990s, thus, ending five decades of bureaucratic, and perhaps ineffective, control over sport. During the next two decades, the way sport was organised and governed began to shift.

Although the Federal Constitution of 1988 stated that government must promote opportunities to participate in organised and unorganised sport with the priority to allocate public resources for educational sport, most bills and policies discussed throughout the 1990s and 2000s focused on matters related to professional football and funding for high-performance sport. Perhaps the most contingent issues were those that affected football. It seemed natural that football took most of the attention, particularly considering the impact football historically has had in Brazil. Most of the discussions related to sport policies prior to the Federal Constitution of 1988 emphasised the need to make sport more democratic and accessible to people (Tubino, 2001). Nevertheless, while governmental policies in the early 1990s focused on establishing a coherent structure for the Brazilian sport system, some of the most visible and contentious issues involved matters related to professional football.

During the short presidency of Fernando Collor (1990–1992), the newly appointed secretary of sport was a well-known football player from the 1970s, Arthur Antunes Coimbra, better known as Zico, and during the two terms of President Fernando Henrique Cardoso (1994–2004), his first Minister of Sport was also a former football player, Edson Arantes do Nascimento or Pele. Both, Zico and Pele worked on bills that would become laws bearing their names.

In 1993, Law 8672, or Zico Law, brought important reforms to the way sport was organised. However, the most ambitious part of this bill, which looked to transform the structure and organisation of professional football, did not pass. The bill aimed to transform professional football clubs into private enterprises and remove the transfer fees of players. Club presidents, who opposed many of the clauses of this bill, fiercely lobbied for its removal. In spite of this unsuccessful attempt, the Zico Law provided a new structure for governance and established principles and guidelines for the functioning of sport organisations. It also provided a more precise definition of the different categories and types of sport (Presidência da República, 1993).

Five years later in 1998, Law 9651, known as Pele Law, was passed. This law included many of the aspects related to football that were crafted but never approved in the Zico Law. The Pele Law also included a reorganisation of the Brazilian sport system with the replacement of SEDES (Secretary for Sport) by INDESP (National Institute for the Development of Sport), and the CSD (Higher Council of Sports) for the CDDD (Council for the Development of Sport) (Bueno, 2008). The most controversial aspect of the Pele Law was the end of the transfer fees for football players. Consequently, in 2000 several amendments were introduced to this law. Some of the most relevant involved establishing more specific terms in regard to players' contracts, particularly after a player ended a contract with a club (Aidar, Bueno de Almeida & Miralla, 2004).

During the 2000s, more laws were passed. Among these were Law 10264/2001 known as Agnelo–Piva; Law 10671/2003 or Statute of the Fan (estatuto do torcedor); Law 16672/2003 or Club Moralising Law (lei de moralização dos clubes); Law 10891/2004 or Athlete Subsidy Law; and Law 11438/2006 known as Incentive Fiscal Law (Queiroz, 2006). Two of these laws were directly related to football (Laws 16671 and 16672), two were aimed to provide funding for high-performance sport (Laws 10264 and 10891), and the Incentive Fiscal Law aimed to attract resources for any of the three categories of sport as stated in the Zico Law of 1993.

The Agnelo–Piva Law assigns two per cent of the federal lottery to fund Olympics and Paralympic programmes hosted by the Brazilian Olympic Committee. Of the total amount, 85 per cent goes to support national governing bodies (NGBs) that are part of the Olympic programme. The remaining 15 per cent goes to NGBs that are part of the Paralympic programme. For the Olympic programme, funds are distributed with a performance criterion. Thus, the BOC categorised all NGBs into four groups based on the most recent level of sporting success. This mean athletes and teams from NGBs that have achieved medals or won championships at the (a) Olympic level; (b) Pan-American level; (c) South American level; or (d), those that have not achieved any major title, yet but have the potential to do so. In 2009, NGBs grouped at the Olympic level obtained 4.2 per cent (e.g., basketball) to 6.2 per cent (e.g., track and field, swimming, judo, sailing and volleyball) of the total amount transferred to all NGBs. Those grouped at the Pan-American level received 3 per cent (e.g., triathlon) to 4.5 per cent (e.g., equestrianism); and those grouped at the South American or lower level received 1.5 per cent (e.g., skiing) to 2.5 per cent (e.g., taekwondo) (Almeida & Marchi Júnior, 2011).

The Athlete Subsidy Law provides a yearly stipend to support the athlete's career. Amounts are categorised based on the athlete's level of performance ranging from junior, national, and international. Priorities are given to athletes that are part of the Olympic and Paralympic programmes (Presidência da República, 2004). The Incentive Fiscal Law provides 1–6 per cent tax deduction for organisations and individuals that invest in programmes related to mass sport, educational sport or high-performance sport (Presidência da República, 2006).

In terms of laws that affected professional football, the Statute of the Fan aimed to raise the standards at sporting events by treating fans as consumers. This law looked to influence not only safety at stadiums, but also the entire service provided during sporting events. In a study conducted in six states, Mezzadri *et al.* (2011) noted that 61 per cent of fans attending football matches during 2006 and 2007 showed minimal or no knowledge at all on the existence of this law. They also found that most fans feel safe at the stadiums. They concluded that while this law had a positive effect in raising the safety standards of sporting events, it failed to reach its main purpose, as fans could not exercise their scrutiny role as consumers due to lack of knowledge they have on this law. Finally, the Moralising Club Law imposes administrative responsibilities on professional football clubs and establishes penalties for club directors in cases of mismanagement.

When discussing the role of sport in Brazilian society, politicians, scholars, and sport leaders have repeatedly struggled to reach balance, and provide fair treatment, for the different categories of sport. According to the Federal Constitution of 1988, sport constitutes a right for every Brazilian citizen. Moreover, Law 8672 from 2003 (Zico Law) establishes three categories of sport: mass sport, educational sport, and high-performance sport.

A number of factors have influenced the priorities for funding and governing sport in Brazil. First, the legal context for sport as established in the Constitution of 1988 and the subsequent laws enacted since then. Second, the new political scenario that emerged during the 1980s. Finally, the economic growth the country has shown during the last decade has also influenced the priorities to fund and govern sport. Although in the last two decades, several public programmes were implemented to attend to the need of these three categories of sport. High-performance sport has received, and continues to receive, the highest attention and funding not only from the Ministry of Sport but also from several public offices as well (Almeida & Marchi Júnior, 2010; Bastos, 2011; Bueno, 2008).

While obtaining greater autonomy for sport organisations should have resulted in less financial dependency from government, Almeida and Marchi Júnior (2010) noted that over the past decade most NGBs remain heavily dependent on public funding. Moreover, in spite of the constitutional mandate that favours educational sport over high-performance sport, what has occurred is exactly the opposite, as more money has been allocated for the funding of high-performance programmes. Most notably, the Pan-American Games of Rio in 2007, along with the bidding process for the 2016 Rio de Janeiro Summer Olympic Games. Over the last decade, Brazil has emerged not only as the most important player within Latin America, but also as a strong economic power worldwide. Therefore, the justification to support high-performance sport is almost natural.

In this context, also noteworthy is the role played by the Brazilian Olympic Committee. While the BOC has been legally recognised since 1935, it has been in existence since 1913 (Abreu, Hecksher, Franceschi & Rajman, 2006). In addition, since the 1920s, several Brazilians have filled positions within the IOC executive committee. The IOC has also kept two members from Brazil, which is a privilege that few countries have. The role played by current BOC president, Carlos Arthur Nuzman, is equally important. For many, Nuzman is credited with not only successfully winning the bid for the 2016 Summer Olympic Games in Rio de Janeiro, but also with taking Brazilian sport to the highest visible level since the reigning days of Brazilian football at the World Cup. Nuzman, a former volleyball player who played for the Brazilian national team, is considered the architect for the success of the 2007 Pan-American Games and the rise of Brazilian volleyball. During his tenure as president of the Brazilian Volleyball Confederation, Brazilian national teams not only achieved numerous world titles, but also contributed to the overall growth and popularity of volleyball in Brazil. The rise and growth of the CBV serves as a case study to illustrate the organisational changes occurring in a NGB that, for many years, had minimal impact until it became the second most powerful NGB in Brazil after football. Key factors in this transformation were the influence of their leaders, the application of sound business principles, and being the recipient of public subsidies that rewarded achievement in high performance sport.

Case study: The Brazilian Volleyball Confederation

Volleyball first arrived in Brazil at the YMCA of São Paulo in 1916. Until the 1960s, the sport was practised primarily as a recreational pastime, mostly at the elite clubs in Rio de Janeiro, São Paulo and Belo Horizonte. Although throughout this time it become highly accepted in schools, the absence of an effective mechanism that allowed continuing practice at schools and the clubs impeded its growth at a faster pace (Marchi Júnior, 2004). It was not until the 1980s that Brazilian volleyball reached world-class status. Marchi Junior (2004) noted that innovative coaching methods, introduced during the 1960s and 1970s, and the arrival of Carlos Nuzman as president of the Brazilian Volleyball Confederation, are plausible explanations about the change and subsequent growth of volleyball in Brazil. The occurrence of these two events acted in a symbiotic manner and influenced not only the structure of the CBV, but also the popularity of volleyball in Brazil.

The Brazilian Volleyball Confederation was created in 1954. Its purpose was to group, under one governing body, all the state federations that existed at that time. Prior to this date, volleyball was under the jurisdiction of the Brazilian Sport Confederation (CBD). Nuzman is credited as the trailblazer that revolutionised not only volleyball, but also as the man who changed the way sport was administered in Brazil. In fact, one of his most visible accomplishments was to bring private sponsors to sport. To accomplish this he was able to influence important changes in the Brazilian sport legislation, which until 1980 restricted the use of sponsorship in certain sports (Vlaustuin, Almeida & Marchi Júnior, 2008). The need to bring in sponsors was driven by the need to provide more resources to improve and raise the overall standards of volleyball including its tournaments. It was also a call to alert politicians and sport bureaucrats that professionalisation was the only way to retain top Brazilian talent in Brazil. As a result, the first professional sport clubs fully sponsored by private companies were born.

Today, the Brazilian Volleyball Confederation follows the same goals as the ones established in 1954. However, its structure, style of management, type and numbers of programmes offered and level of success achieved, is significantly different. According to the CBV statute of 2006, the CBV is a private not-for-profit sport organisation with the aim to rule, administer, control, promote and foster the practice of volleyball at all levels of performance all over Brazil. The CBV is affiliated with the International Volleyball Federation (FIVB) and the Brazilian Olympic Committee, and according to Article 217 of the Federal Constitution of

1988, the CBV is an autonomous entity free to administer and organise its assets without government interference. Membership in the CBV is represented by each state federation that acts as a branch of the CBV at the state level. Although each state federation acts autonomously, its membership and continuity is defined by their adherence to the statutes of the CBV. Currently, there are 27 volleyball federations in Brazil, so each of the 26 state and the capital of Brasilia are all represented in the CBV.

In terms of governance, there are four main powers in the CBV: the general assembly, office of the presidency, the board of directors, and the audit board. The general assembly is the ultimate power in the CBV and is represented by each of the 27 federation members. The office of the presidency is represented by the president and the vice president. They both act as administrators of the decisions and resolutions approved by the general assembly under the advice of the board of directors. Among the main responsibilities of the president are: to adhere to the rules and policies as established in the statute of the CBV; preside over the general assembly; be responsible for personnel of the CBV; approve marketing and media contracts to commercialise events sanctioned by the CBV; nominate members to the board of directors; and, represent the interests of the CBV to the BOC. The board of directors assist the president by working in seven key areas including: administration, finance, volleyball, international relations, public relations, development, social affairs, and administrative support. The audit board has the responsibility to audit the financial state of the CBV (CBV, 2006).

Ary Graça led the CBV from 1997 to 2012. Prior to his presidential tenure in the CBV, he was president of the South American Volleyball Confederation, vice president of the International Volleyball Federation (FIBV) executive committee, vice president of the Pan-American Union of Volleyball; and a member of the BOC executive committee. Currently, he serves as the FIVB president. From 1975 to 1983, he served as vice president of the CBV during Nuzman's presidency (Graça, 2012). Once he took office in 1997 he not only continued with Nuzman's work, but he also took it to a whole new level. Graça's main innovation within the CBV was to implement a managerial model that treated each department as a business unit. This model has been praised both inside and outside the world of sport. For example, in 2003, the CBV became the first sport governing body worldwide to receive an ISO–9001: 2000 certification from the International Organisation for Standardisation (Ministério do Esporte, 2012a). This credential recognises not only the CBV's unique business model, but also its reputation as a credible and effective organisation (Ministério do Esporte, 2012a).

The current structure of the CBV includes a three-level model of management: strategic, tactical and operational. At the strategic level is the president followed by two main units, chief of staff and technical staff. The chief of staff unit oversees three departments all acting at the operational level: institutional relations; special projects; and media relations. The technical unit deals exclusively with technical matters related to volleyball. Below these strategic units are two executive superintendents acting at the tactical level. The first superintendent oversees six departments: general administration, sponsorships, purchasing, legal affairs, management of the Aryzão high-performance centre, and the Viva Volei programme. The second superintendent also oversees six departments, but only on matters directly related to volleyball: referees, coaches, management of the national teams (indoor and beach volleyball) and management of tournaments (indoor and beach volleyball). Each of these departments acts at the operational level (CBV, 2010). As a result, long-term and strategic planning at the CBV is carefully managed by the apex structure in coordination with each superintendent and each department.

The outcome of the managerial model implemented by the CBV has resulted in many world and Olympic titles for Brazil. It has also shown that a sport governing body can be managed no differently than any other business. According to the 2012 FIVB ranking of indoor volleyball, Brazil led the group in men's and was second in women's and the same applies for the men's and women's beach volleyball teams. In the last decade, the men's national team has achieved eight first places in the indoor world league. At the indoor World Cup, the men's team won in 2003 and 2007, and the women's team achieved second place during the same years. At the Summer Olympics, the men's indoor teams have achieved one gold (2004) and two silvers (2008 and 2012) since 1996; while the women's indoor teams obtained two golds (2008 and 2012) and two bronzes (1996 and 2000). Men's beach volleyball teams won one gold (2004), three silvers (2000, 2008 and 2012) and one bronzes (2008) while women's teams achieved one gold (1996), three silvers (1996, 2000, and 2008) and one bronze (2012).

Capitalising on the sporting results of the last 15 years has allowed the CBV to increase its brand equity inside and outside Brazil. In terms of marketing, it has allowed the CBV to position the sport of volleyball in the Brazilian market as a high value commodity. According to Global Sports Network (GSN, 2011), Brazilian volleyball and its many sub-products (e.g., indoor volleyball, beach volleyball, club teams, national teams, the super league, etc.) have permitted companies not only to reach specific target groups and multiply their exposure, but also has allowed them to be associated with concepts like excellence, youth, success and leadership. In 2010, Nestlé and its product Sollys (based on soy) sponsored the Osasco women's team of São Paulo. This partnership was established as a way to position the brand Sollys with the female audience. Similarly, Banana Boat and its sunscreen products also decided to sponsor women's volleyball as a way to reach that particular market.

Companies have also decided to invest in volleyball in order to strengthen its corporate image with a specific community or region. That was the case of the Italian carmaker Fiat in 2007 and 2008 when they sponsored the team Minas Tênis Clube, in the state of Minas Gerais. (Fiat has a plant in the same state). However, the most iconic case between a corporate brand and volleyball is the association that Banco do Brasil (BB) established with the CBV in 1991. A main goal in this partnership was to reach a new and younger clientele for the bank. The bank not only succeeded in expanding its base of clients but also it reached its target group effectively. Once the teams achieved world status and players became well-known all over Brazil, the bank also was able to reconnect with the more mature audience. In past years, marketing studies conducted in Brazil have ranked BB as the most remembered brand among the top 15 brands in the country (Vlaustuin, Almeida & Marchi Júnior, 2008). In 2012, BB renewed its contract with the CBV until 2017. Because its status as a credible, effective and successful NGB, the CBV has not only been extremely successful in securing resources from the private sector, but also it has been the recipient of important public subsidies as well. Thus, between 2005 and 2008, it received the highest percentage of subsidies among all the national governing bodies that received funding derived from the Law Agnelo–Piva of 2001 (Almeida & Marchi Júnior, 2011).

The growth and success achieved over the past two decades has made the CBV the shining star of not only all the NGBs of the BOC, but perhaps of the entire Brazilian sport system. Certainly, the application of sound managerial principles, effective leadership, and government subsidies has made it possible for the CBV to achieve world status as one of the most successful NGBs in the world.

Summary

Sport clubs in Brazil represent the keystone of its entire sport system. Although most sport clubs are private organisations, their development and growth have been highly dependent on sport policies enacted at the federal level. The first legislation related to sport dates back to 1941 with Law 3199. This law established the basis for organising the sport system in Brazil. However, it was not until the late 1980s that significant changes occurred with the most significant being that in 1988 sport achieved constitutional status. The Federal Constitution of 1988 stated that government must give priority to allocating public resources to educational sport, yet most policies discussed throughout the 1990s and 2000s have focused on professional football and funding for high-performance sport. Considering the significant economic growth of the country over the last decade, the justification to support high performance sport was a good one.

The Constitution of 1988 and further sport policies enacted during the 1990s provided greater autonomy for sport organisations. While this should have resulted in less financial dependency from government, the past decade has witnessed that most NGBs remain heavily dependent on public funding. Perhaps an exception to this trend is the Brazilian Volleyball Confederation (CBV) which for over two decades has applied business principles to its administration. Today, the CBV follows the same goals as the ones established in 1954, however, its structure, style of management, type and numbers of programmes offered and level of success achieved, is significantly different. The current structure of the CBV includes a three-level model of management. The outcome of this model has resulted in several world and Olympic titles. It has also shown that a sport governing body can be managed no differently than any other business. The application of sound managerial principles, effective leadership, and government subsidies has made it possible for the CBV to achieve world status as one of the most successful NGBs in the world. This has allowed the CBV not only to increase its brand equity as a NGB but also to position volleyball as a valuable commodity within the Brazilian market.

Review questions

1   In what capacity has the Federal Constitution of 1988 influenced current sport policies?
2   What factors have influenced the priorities to provide public funding for sport?
3   What managerial and business mechanisms have been adopted by the Brazilian Volleyball Confederation to achieve success?

Further reading

Bramante, A.C., Valente, E. F., Santos, J. N., DaCosta, L. P., Dias, M. L. & Matsudo, V. (2002). Brazil: Developing sport for all from public recreation (1920s) to leisure (1970s) and health promotions (1990s). In L.P. DaCosta & A. Miragaya (eds), *World experiences and trends of sport for all* (pp.675–704). Oxford: Meyer & Meyer Sport.
Bravo, G., Orejan, J., Vélez, L. & López de D'Amico, R. (2012). Sport in Latin America. In M. Li, E. Macintosh & G. Bravo (eds), *International sport management* (pp.99–133). Champaign, IL: Human Kinetics.
DaCosta, L. P. (1996). The state versus free enterprise in sports policy: The case of Brazil. In L. Chalip, A, Johnson & L. Stachura, *National sports policies* (pp.23–38). Westport, CT: Greenwood Press.
Graça, A. S. (2012) *Institutional strategy of sports in Brazil. Strategic thoughts to consolidate a democratic and responsible sports policy* (preliminary version). Confederação Brasileira de Voleibol. São Paulo: Mbooks. Available online at: http://www.cbv.com.br/v1/institucional/publicacoes/institutional/index.html

Websites

Brazilian Volleyball Confederation: http://www.cbv.com.br
Ministry of Sport of Brazil: http://www.esporte.gov.br

References

Abreu, N., Hecksher, R., Franceschi, M. & Rajman, B. (2006). Comitê Olímpico Brasileiro – COB. In L. DaCosta (ed.). *Atlas do esporte no Brasil*, Rio de Janeiro: CONFEF.
Aidar, A. C., Bueno de Almeida, C. & Miralla, R. G. (2004). Recent history of Brazilian soccer. In R. Fort & J. Fizel (eds). *International sports economics comparison* (pp.245–261). Westport, CT: Praeger.
Almeida, B. S., & Marchi Júnior, W. (2010). O financiamento dos programas federais de esporte e lazer no Brasil (2004 a 2008). *Movimento*, 16(4), 73–92.
Almeida, B. S., & Marchi Júnior, W. (2011). Comitê Olímpico Brasileiro e o financiamento das confederações brasileiras. *Revista Brasileira de Ciências do Esporte*, 33(1), 163–179.
Bastos, F.C. (2011). Apontamentos sobre a participação da sociedade no desenvolvimento de políticas de esporte no Brasil. *Revista Intercontinental de Gestão Desportiva*, 1(1), 44–59.
Bravo, G., Orejan, J., Vélez, L. & López de D'Amico, R. (2012). Sport in Latin America. In M. Li, E. Macintosh & G. Bravo (eds). *International sport management* (pp.99–133), Champaign, IL: Human Kinetics.

154   *Gonzalo Bravo*

Bueno, L. (2008). Políticas públicas do esporte no Brasil: Razões para o predomínio do alto rendimento (Unpublished doctoral dissertation). Escola de Administração de Empresas de São Paulo da Getúlio Vargas, Brazil.

CBV (2006). *Estatuto*. Confederação Brasileira do Voleibol. Available online at http://www.cbv.com.br/v1/institucional/Estatuto_CBV.pdf

CBV (2010). *Balanço social 2009–2010*. Confederação Brasileira do Voleibol. Available online at http://www.cbv.com.br/v1/institucional/balancos/BalancoSocial-2010.pdf

Constituição da República Federativa do Brasil (1988). Brasilia: Senado Federal. Available online at http://www.senado.gov.br/legislacao/const/con1988/CON1988_05.10.1988/CON1988.pdf.

DaCosta, L. (2006a). Cenário de tendências gerais dos esportes e atividades físicas no Brasil. In L. DaCosta (ed). *Atlas do esporte no Brasil*. Rio de Janeiro: CONFEF.

DaCosta, L. (2006b). Clubes esportivos e recreativos. In L. DaCosta (ed). *Atlas do esporte no Brasil*. Rio de Janeiro: CONFEF.

DeMelo Neto, F. P., & Feitosa, M. (2006). Marketing esportivo. In L. DaCosta (ed). *Atlas do esporte no Brasil*. Rio de Janeiro: CONFEF.

Graça, A. (2012). Um gestor de ouro para o esporte. Available online at http://arygraca.com/queme_carreira.php

GSN (2011). Estrategia de marketing esportivo no voleibol brasileiro. Rio de Janeiro: Global Sports Network. Available online at http://www.slideshare.net/GSNsports/gsn-marketing-no-voleibol-brasileiro-7742081

Kasznar, I. & Graça, A. S. (2002). *O esporte como indústria: Solução para criação de riqueza e emprego*. Rio de Janeiro: Confederação Brasileira de Voleibol.

Marchi Júnior, W. (2004). *Sacando o voleibol*. São Paulo: HUCITEC.

Melo, V. A. de (2006). Remo, modernidade e Pereira Passos: Primórdios das políticas públicas de esporte no Brasil. *Esporte e Sociedade*, 1(3), 1–21.

Mezzadri, F. M., DeCamargo Preste, S. E., Capraro, A. M., Cavichiolli, F. R. & Marchi Júnior, W. (2011). As interferências do Estado brasileiro no futebol e o estatuto de defesa do torcedor. *Revista Brasileira de Educação Física e Esporte*, 25(3), 407–16.

Ministério do Esporte (2012a). Confederação Brasileira do Voleibol. Available online at http://www.esporte.gov.br/cen/detalhesEntidades.do;jsessionid=C1EE0A4B3CE0876AFB23306815EBA78E?idEntidade=2

Ministério do Esporte (2012b). *Programas e projetos*. Available online at http://www.esporte.gov.br/institucional/secretariaExecutiva/programasSecretaria.jsp

Presidência da República (1993). Lei nº 8672 de 6 de julho de 1993. Institui normas gerais sobre desporto e dá outras providências. Brasilia: Casa Civil. Subchefia para Assuntos Jurídicos. Available online at https://www.planalto.gov.br/ccivil_03/leis/L8672impressao.htm

Presidência da República (2004). Lei nº 10891 de 9 de julho de 2004. Institui a bolsa-atleta. Brasilia: Casa Civil. Subchefia para Assuntos Jurídicos. Available online at https://www.planalto.gov.br/ccivil_03/_Ato2004-2006/2004/Lei/L10.891compilado.htm

Presidência da República (2006). Lei nº 11438 de 29 dezembro de 2006. Dispõe sobre incentivos e benefícios para fomentar as atividades de caráter desportivo e dá outras providências. Brasilia: Casa Civil. Subchefia para Assuntos Jurídicos. Available online at https://www.planalto.gov.br/ccivil_03/_Ato2004-2006/2006/Lei/L11438.htm

Queiroz, A. (2006). Ministério do esporte. In L. DaCosta (ed.) *Atlas do esporte no Brasil*, Rio de Janeiro: CONFEF.

Tesche, L. & Rambo, A. B. (2001). Reconstructing the fatherland: German turnen in southern Brazil. In J.A. Mangan (ed.). *Europe, sport world. Shaping global societies*, (pp.5–22). London: Frank Cass.

Tubino, M. (2001). *Política nacional do esporte. Análise da proposta elaborada pela Câmara Setorial do Esporte.* Available online at http://www.tubino.pro.br/ PoliticaNacionalEsporte.pdf

Vlastuin, J., Almeida, B. S. & Marchi Júnior, W. (2008). O marketing esportivo na gestão do voleibol brasileiro: Fragmentos teóricos referentes ao processo de espetacularização da modalidade. *Revista Brasileira de Ciências do Esporte*, 29(3), 9–24.

World Bank (2012). *World development indicators database.* World Bank, 18 September 2012. Available online at http://databank.worldbank.org/databank/download/GDP_ PPP.pdf

Zakaria, F. (2009). *The post-American world.* New York: W.W. Norton & Co.

10 The Middle East

James M. Dorsey

Topics

- Middle East and North Africa
- Politics
- Women
- Fans.

Objectives

- To portray the use of soccer by autocratic regimes in the Middle East and North Africa
- To portray the role of soccer in nation building
- To portray the role of soccer in the projection of nationhood
- To highlight the need for separation of politics and sport.

Key terms

Middle East and North Africa   A swath of land that stretches from the Gulf to the Atlantic coast of Africa that includes the 22 members of the Arab League as well as Iran and Israel.

Sports governance   The transparent, accountable and democratic management of sport.

Fans   Supporters of soccer clubs who have political agendas and play a role in the popular revolts sweeping the Middle East and North Africa.

Overview

This chapter explores how autocratic regimes in the Middle East and North Africa prevent good governance by seeking to control soccer for political purposes. Boards of soccer associations are, by and large, populated by government appointees, often under the guise of elections that serve to satisfy nominal demands for transparency by the Fédération Internationale de Football Association (FIFA), or members of royal families. The boards are often tasked with furthering the regime's interests rather than the game for the sake of the game. These interests include shoring up the regime's tarnished image by associating itself with the region's most popular sport, preventing the soccer pitch from becoming a venue for the expression of political dissent or independent civil society organisations and distracting public attention and manipulating national emotions. Defending those interests has run the gamut from the brutal excesses of the sons of Saddam Hussein and Moammar Qaddafi to corruption and match fixing (Dorsey, 2011a). Nonetheless, the winds of change blowing through the Middle East and North Africa are being felt in sport. Jordan has emerged as a regional model of sport governance (Dorsey, 2012a). Soccer association elections in Iraq and Oman have been challenged in court and Saudi Arabia is gearing up for its first ever association election that could for the first time produce a non-royal president.

Rudimentary beginnings

Sport governance in the Middle East and North Africa is marked primarily by the lack of, or at best the rudimentary beginnings of, understanding of what the concept entails in terms of procedure, transparency and accountability. While the demands for rooting out corruption and nepotism in sport in post-revolt nations like Egypt may be loudest, it is sport in nations that have not experienced a radical change of regime that are feeling the pressure the most, sparked either by a willingness of elites to challenge the status quo, ethnic and sectarian power struggles, newly found fan assertiveness or changing autocratic perceptions of the risk of direct regime control.

Ahmed Eid Saad Alharbi, a lanky former Saudi soccer mid-fielder and proponent of women's soccer, credited fan pressure for his recent appointment as head of the Saudi Football Association tasked with organising the body's first ever election. Alharbi was appointed in early 2012 after Saudi Prince Nawaf bin Faisal stepped down following Saudi Arabia's defeat in a 2014 World Cup qualifier against Australia. Prince Nawaf's resignation was historic in a nation governed as an absolute monarchy and a region that sees control of soccer as a key tool in preventing the pitch from becoming a venue for anti-government protests, distracting attention from widespread grievances and manipulating national emotions. It also marked the first time that rulers saw direct association with a national team's failure as a risk to which they traditionally responded by firing the coach or in extreme cases, like Saddam Hussein's Iraq or Moammar Qaddafi's Libya, brutally punishing players. By resigning, Prince Nawaf was disassociating himself and the ruling family from the national soccer team's potential failures.

While Alharbi hoped to incorporate new standards of governance in the statutes of the reorganised federation, Saudi Arabia was, despite the election, unlikely to emerge as a beacon of governance. The ruling Al Saud family retains its grip on sport with Prince Nawaf staying on as head of the Saudi Olympic Committee and president general of youth welfare on which the SFA depends, alongside television broadcast rights, for funding. Major soccer clubs moreover remain the playground of princes who at times micro-manage matches by phoning their team's coaches mid-game with instructions of which players to replace.

In addition, sport remains a male prerogative in the arch-conservative kingdom despite the fact that Saudi Arabia fielded two female athletes at the 2012 London Olympics after being threatened with exclusion if it continued to insist on an all-male team. Saudi Arabia had initially hoped to evade the problem by arguing that one of the women slated to compete, equestrian Dalma Rushdi Malhas, had been disqualified by the International Equestrian Federation (FEI). Saudi female athletes have expressed concern that they would be penalised for the pressure exerted on the kingdom by the International Olympic Committee and human rights groups to allow women to compete. Saudi Arabia underlined its lack of intention to develop women's sport by last year engaging Spanish consultants to develop its first-ever national sport plan for men only (Dorsey, 2011a).

By contrast to Saudi Arabia or legal challenges to Iraqi and Omani soccer association elections, Egypt's military rulers fired President Hosni Mubarak's long-standing associates on the board of the Egyptian Football Association (EFA) only a year after Mubarak was toppled in 2011 by anti-government protests. They were dismissed after 79 people died in a brawl in the Suez Canal town of Port Said that is widely believed to have been an effort to penalise militant soccer fans for their role in the overthrow of Mubarak and their opposition to military rule.

The highly politicised, well-organised, street-battle-hardened fans, the second largest civic group in Egypt after the ruling Muslim Brotherhood, have been at the forefront of an increasingly successful, at times violent, campaign to root out corruption in Egyptian soccer and hold Mubarak-era officials accountable. Two candidates for the presidency of the Egyptian Football Association, FIFA executive committee member Hani Abou Reida – an associate of the disgraced former FIFA vice president and Asian Football Confederation (AFC) president Mohammed Bin Hammam – and former Cairo club Al Ahly SC goalkeeper and popular television show host Ahmed Shobeir, were forced to withdraw their candidacies because of their links to Mubarak. The Illegal Gains Authority (IGA) froze an estimated US$82 million in assets and banned Al Ahly chairman Hassan Hamdy from travel because he could not explain how he had accumulated his wealth. Hamdy doubled up for much of his Al Ahly chairmanship as head of the advertising department of Mubarak's flagship, state-owned Al Ahram publishing house (Dorsey, 2012b).

The fans' fight against corruption extends beyond narrowly defined confines of sport to include demands for reform of the corrupt police and security forces, Egypt's most despised institutions because of their role in implementing the Mubarak regime's repression, and the holding to account of those responsible for the death of protesters and the 79 fans in Port Said. The fans' threat of violence prevented the resumption in the fall of 2012 of professional soccer matches suspended since the Port Said incident, who demand that the perpetrators of Port Said first be brought to justice. The fans are frustrated with the slow progress of the trial of 73 people on charges of involvement in Port Said and the fact that only nine mid-level security men are among those charged rather than higher figures who had allowed the brawl to take place (Dorsey, 2012b).

As the region struggles to emerge from decades of autocratic rule, it could well take the rise of a younger generation of reformers to put the Middle East and North Africa on the path towards good governance. Headed by Jordanian Prince Ali Bin Al Hussein, at 32 world soccer body FIFA's youngest ever vice president, the 16-member West Asian Football Federation (WAFF) and the Jordanian Football Association (JFA), the only Arab soccer association with FIFA-approved professional rules and regulations, have become regional models of good governance. Not surprisingly, the fundamental motive underlying Jordanian reform is akin to the region's urge for control. 'Sport plays a major role in a society with relative unemployment. It eases social tensions' said Mohamed Alayyan, JFA president and publisher of Jordan's largest daily newspaper (personal communication).

The JFA focused on ensuring a separation of its administrative and judicial functions and weaning clubs away from the notion that it would allow politics to dominate its administrative decisions. In doing so, it relied heavily on the statutory and organisational models of FIFA and the Asian Football Confederation (AFC) with the creation of a disciplinary and an appeals committee as well as committees for marketing, human resources, competitions, player status and revenue generation, and the shifting of responsibilities from the FA to the member associations by insisting that they separate their executives from their administrative bodies. The JFA has taken the process a step further with plans for the creation of a league governing body designed to increase accountability and force clubs to come to grips with stadium management and efforts to persuade clubs to transfer their assets to newly founded commercial entities. The league governing body would be responsible for distributing 80 % of sponsorship income equitably among the competing clubs.

> Clubs need to feel that they have to work, have proper corporate governance and are accountable to the sponsor. The incentive for the clubs is that it opens the door to playing in the Champions League. We are telling the clubs that we are forced to impose these changes by FIFA and the AFC
>
> (Khalil Salem, a former investment banker turned JFA general manager, personal communication)

The JFA's next step is club licensing. The association recently appointed a licensing manager tasked with building the administrative infrastructure including an appeals body.

Case study: Iraq – a reign of terror and abuse

The Jordanian push for reforms contrasts starkly with notions of good governance elsewhere in the region. For Iraqi sport managers, for example the country's golden age in terms of management was the period of Kerim Mullah, Iraq's longest-serving minister of youth and sport, despite his association with Saddam's regime and the fact that he served even after Saddam's feared and sadistic son Uday took control of the country's sport sector. Sport officials and former athletes revere him, not because he adhered to international standards of transparency, accountability, independence and participation, but because he listened in contrast to Uday who tolerated nothing but total subservience and obedience. In fact, the managers praise Mullah for attempting to keep politics out of sport, ensuring that sport associations dealt with issues on their merits and organising competitions between youth centres that could build national and international networks of their own. To be sure, boards were not elected but appointed by Mullah, but in the words of former Iraqi body-builder and Kurdish culture and youth ministry official Taher Saber Said, 'the system wasn't perfect but it worked' (personal communication).

The former headquarters of the National Olympic Committee of Iraq (NOCI) on Baghdad's Palestine Street symbolised the difference between Mullah and Uday's rule and said much about the nature of sport governance and the lengths to which Middle Eastern and North African autocrats were willing to go to harness sport to their political interests. While the excesses of the Saddam regime were perhaps rivalled only by those of Moammar Qaddafi in Libya, the two regimes, where cruel sons of the dictators took a personal interest in the management and performance of sport, the underlying principle of sport in general and soccer in particular as a tool to enhance the prestige of the regime and serve as a modern day opium for the people and morale booster for populations demoralised by war, repression and unemployment as well as collective and individual humiliation was shared by rulers across the region. Governance in a swath of land stretching from the Atlantic coast of Africa to the Gulf meant little more than regime control and subjection to the regime's whims and political designs.

In Iraq, sport governance was determined by the role of sport in the indoctrination of youth. The aim of youth centres was

> at organising youth activities, exploding youth hidden energies to use them for the benefit of progress and building process, planting revolutions' genuine principles and values in the youth brains, and deepening the youth belonging to the country and helping them to get rid of negativism and indifference within a framework of unity and intellectualism, and aim braised on sound morality and balanced emotions. The youth centres embody the programs of the Directorate General though youth practices which are organized in the centres for the sons of Saddam Qadisiyah (Hussein), the new generation of the revolution. There are various sports games such as football, basketball, volleyball, handball, table tennis, boxing, wrestling, athletics, shooting, martial arts, karate, judo, taekwondo, fencing, swimming, mass sport.
>
> (Ministry of Youth, n.d.)

The Olympic flag fluttering above the walls and bulletproof glass windows of the NOCI building that symbolised the movement's humanitarian goals constituted little more than a fig leaf for a system that violated not only international standards of sport governance but also human rights. The rise of Uday as Saddam's youth and sports czar in the guise of head of the NOCI, as well as the Iraqi Football Association (IFA), demolished whatever semblance of governance Iraq had known and made the rule of Karim Mullah look like a golden age that many, even in post-Saddam Iraq, would be happy to return to. Uday who nicknamed himself Abu Sarhan (Father of a Wolf), and was dubbed by his detractors 'the butcher's boy', tightened his grip on sport by side-lining the ministry in charge of sport and shifting its responsibilities to the NOCI. Crippled in 1996 at age 32 in an assassination attempt, Uday employed sadism and cruelty rather than national pride and ambition as drivers of performance. It was a strategy that backfired as the performance of athletes and national teams nosedived under his rule.

The layout of the NOCI headquarters said much about Uday's concept of governance. The basement was reserved for Uday's expansive collection of expensive cars that he enjoyed driving at high speed in the Iraqi capital. A huge 300-seat conference room occupied much of the first floor behind which there were up to 30 prison cells for sportsmen who had failed to perform, as well as others who had run afoul of Uday.

One floor up housed the offices of Uday's bodyguards, members of Al Fidaiyyin (The Redeemers), his brutal security force who doubled as NOCI board officials and heads of sport associations. The third and fourth floors were home to the offices of Uday and the NOCI administrative staff, the closest thing to the building blocks of proper sport governance and management. The editorial staff of the ruling Al Ba'ath party's sport newspaper worked on the sixth floor while the top floor was reserved for Uday's parties and womanising.

Those that lived to tell the tale of their incarceration in the NOCI headquarters, or public humiliation in Baghdad's People's Stadium, and on national television, were the lucky ones. 'Being a well-known athlete (could) get you killed', said former athlete Issam Thamer al-Diwan, who suffered permanent damage to two of his neck vertebrae and a knee at the hands of Uday's goons. He maintains a list of 52 athletes and sport officials he asserts were executed on Uday's orders including the son of his predecessor as NOCI head, General Faleh Akram Fahmi, an accomplished track and field champion and captain of the Iraqi national basketball team, for allegedly cursing Saddam. Al-Diwan was imprisoned twice: in 1986 because his national volleyball team ended only third in an Arab championship, and in 1990 when he refused to join an NOCI delegation dispatched to Kuwait, which had been occupied by Iraqi troops, to bring all Kuwaiti sport assets to Baghdad.

With little real pressure from international sport bodies, such as the IOC and FIFA, for the introduction of proper sport governance and management, Middle Eastern and North African governments had little incentive to change their ways. In 1997, FIFA sent investigators to Baghdad to look at allegations that national soccer team players had been caned after losing a World Cup qualifier to Kazakhstan. Unable to interview players and officials in confidence and privacy without representatives of the security service present in meetings, the investigators conceded that they had little choice but to exonerate the IFA (Farrey, 2004). FIFA however, exerted little, if any pressure, to ensure that the investigation was conducted under free and fair conditions.

Sharar Haydar, a star who missed the game against Kazakhstan because of an injury, and fled to Britain a year later after playing 40 international matches, was not among those interviewed by the FIFA investigators. 'Did the torture of those players happen? Absolutely. But when you interview athletes who are under Uday's control, what else do you expect them to say?' he says describing how he was flogged, caned, dragged over pavements and concrete with his feet and hands tied and his torso bared and then thrown into raw sewage (personal communication).

Uday regularly threatened players with blowing their aircraft out of the sky if they were en route home after losing a match abroad. Players were never beyond his reach. Using a direct telephone link from his office, Uday would curse, abuse and threaten players in their dressing room. Often they would be held in the dressing room for hours after a match uncertain what Uday had in mind for them. Uday's prestige was vested in Al-Rasheed SC, a Baghdad club originally named Al Kharq SC, which he took over. The club's players were largely national team players handpicked by Uday. Referees were advised what the outcome of Al Rasheed matches should be as a result of which the club regularly won national and Arab competitions in the 1980s.

Little effectively changed in Iraq's concept of sport governance in the 1990s when the country was hit in the wake of its 1990 invasion of Kuwait by international sanctions, isolation and shortages; even if the excesses of Uday's warped sense of sport management vanished with his gradual demotion following his killing of Saddam's valet for shooting in the air at a party at which he was hosting the wife of Egyptian President Hosni Mubarak. The international pressure on Iraq coupled with Uday's loss of power, however, marked the beginning of an era in which Iraq was almost absent from the international sport scene until the fall of Saddam. Al Rasheed's dependence on Uday's match fixing became evident as it failed to perform once its mentor no longer was in a position to ensure its success.

Similarly, little has changed since the downfall of Saddam in the ownership structure of Iraqi premier league teams and the political involvement that comes with it. Much like in various Middle Eastern and North African nations, at least seven of Iraq's 20 premier league clubs are owned by government entities, including the police, the military and public enterprises. These include the border guards (Al Hedood), the police (Al-Shorta), the air force (Al Quwa al Jawiya), the industry ministry (Al Sinaa), the electricity ministry (Al Kahrabaa), the Basra port (Al Minaa), and the oil ministry (Al Naft). Ownership changed only where it involved individual associates of Saddam, as in the case of the soccer club in the Iraqi leader's hometown of Tikrit, that when it was controlled by his half-brothers suddenly emerged as a champion, or the army team that was backed by his son-in-law General Hussein Kemil (Goldblatt, 2008, p.865). Much like Uday, Mullah commandeered national team players when he needed them to enable his team to shore up morale of a military that was struggling to beat Iran on the battlefield.

The Iraqi regime's tight control of sport prompted the Coalition Provisional Authority (CPA), established by a US-led coalition immediately after the overthrow of Saddam to lead the country to democracy, to dissolve the NOCI as part of its de-Baathification programme (Amara, 2012, p.155). The CPA made the construction and rehabilitation of soccer stadiums and clubs a priority in its 2004 budget by allocating 22.4 billion Iraqi dinars to sport in its first year and raising that amount to 93.2 billion dinars in 2005 and 2006. 'Soccer stars are more highly regarded than government leaders. That's why sporting events are so important. It will bring this society back to life' said Donald Eberly, a former deputy director of the White House of Faith-Based and Community Initiatives who served as a senior advisor to the Iraqi youth and sport ministry in the wake of the dissolution of the NOCI (Quinn, 2003). Coalition officials, moreover, saw soccer and sport as a way of thwarting efforts by terrorists, militant Islamic groups and criminal gangs to recruit idle youth. 'If they are not at school or playing sports they will be targeted by terrorist organisations, religious fundamentalists or other criminals', said former Scottish rugby player and lawyer Mark Clark who supervised the rebuilding of sport infrastructure on behalf of the CPA until 2008 (*The Scotsman*, 2004).

Sport furthermore served as a soft diplomatic tool as part of the US campaign to win hearts and minds in a country that was spiralling towards civil war. The election of Iraq's first post-Saddam Olympic Committee in the presence of International Olympic Committee representatives was heralded as Iraq's return to the global sport family.

> The elections were held as part of the day-long General Assembly event for the establishment of a new National Olympic Committee for Iraq organized by the Interim Committee to Administer Sport and supervised by the International Olympic Committee ... With the democratic election of Iraq's new National Olympic Committee we have taken a critical step towards ensuring our participation on the world stage at the Olympic Games in Athens 2004. The International Olympic Committee's validation of those elections has sent a clear and unmistakeable message around the world – A free Iraq has arrived.
>
> (Amara, 2012, p.156)

The symbolism notwithstanding, recreating Iraqi sport from the wreckage and trauma that Uday had left behind proved to be less immune to Iraq's increasing sectarian and political divisions than the country's US administrators had expected. Those divisions were compounded by the US view of sport as a tool and Iraqi officials' insistence on looking at sport in sectarian and political terms – an approach that has survived until today. Al-Samarrai and three other Olympic committee members were kidnapped in 2006. The IOC suspended the NOCI after the government dissolved the committee and appointed a group of its own headed by the minister of sport. FIFA twice suspended the Iraqi soccer body in 2008 and

2009 after police raided its offices and dissolved the federation on charges of having ties to the Saddam regime.

As he looked back at his experience in Iraq, Eberly was candid about the intersection of sport and politics, raising questions about the country's post-Saddam sport governance.

> We had to hobble together a new national ministry, reorganise hundreds of community centres across Iraq, and resupply sports clubs with equipment from some of the donations that were pouring in ... This required completely replacing the old abused system of Uday Hussein with a nationally representative temporary committee to reorganise sport and put the pieces together of a new organisation in accordance with international procedures. This required that we preside over hundreds of club elections all across Iraq, all within five months, and in an insecure environment. Only after that step was completed could a national assembly be convened that would produce a legitimately elected National Olympic Committee of Iraq. Iraqi sport teams were prepared to make a heroic effort on the field; it would fall to us to carry the organising task, legally and diplomatically.
>
> (Eberly, 2009, p.3)

He described the donation of 80,000 soccer balls to Iraqi kids as 'a powerful gift ... in reaching the hearts and minds of the youth' (Eberly, 2009). Eberly recognised the importance of sport to Iraqis and noted that soccer stars are more highly regarded than government leaders.

Detailing the challenges in barring Saddam-era officials, getting a woman to be an NOCI member, maintaining an ethnic balance on the committee, and accounting for Kurdish efforts to effectively build a state of their own, Eberly acknowledged that

> we could use our power to eliminate people, but we could not use that same power to dictate who would replace them ... We claimed the right to remove past sports officials, even though, under the IOC, sports are supposed to be independent of government. However, we could not simply and arbitrarily put new people in place.
>
> (Eberly, 2009, p.222)

Summary

This chapter looks at the devastating effect of politics and autocratic rule on sport governance in the Middle East and North Africa, a part of the world in which sport was subservient to the needs of the region's rulers. It details the emergence of Jordan as an example of good governance in a region still struggling to come to grips with notions of governance, transparency and accountability. It also looks at Iraq as an example of the abuse of sport by autocratic leaders and the problems it encounters in seeking to build a post-autocratic sport centre.

Review questions

1   What impact does political interference have on building a sport sector on principles of good governance?
2   What steps and reforms are needed to restructure sport developed under autocratic rule so that it becomes an independent sector driven by proper regulations, merit and performance?
3   How can sport be separated from politics?

Further reading

Amara, M. (2012). *Sport, politics and society in the Arab world.* New York: Palgrave Macmillan.

Foer, F. (2010). *How soccer explains the world: An unlikely theory of globalization.* New York: Harper Perennial.

Goldblatt, D. (2008). *The ball is round: A global history of soccer.* New York: Riverhead Books.

Kuper, S. & Szymanski, S. (2009). *Soccernomics: Why England loses, why Germany and Brazil win, and why the U.S., Japan, Australia, Turkey and even Iraq are destined to become the kings of the world's most popular sport.* New York: Nation Books.

Website

The turbulent world of Middle East soccer: http://mideastsoccer.blogspot.com

References

Al-Diwan, I. T. (2002). Being a well-known athlete can get you killed. ESPN. Available online at http://a.espncdn.com/oly/s/2002/1219/1479675.html

Amara, M. (2012). *Sport, politics and society in the Arab world.* New York: Palgrave Macmillan.

Dorsey, J. M. (2011a). Syria's Latakia stadium joins long list of region's politically abused soccer pitches: The turbulent world of Middle East soccer. Available online at http://mideastsoccer.blogspot.sg/2011/08/syrias-latakia-stadium-joins-long-list.html

Dorsey, J. M. (2011b). Saudi Arabia to send token woman to Olympics to evade sanctions. Available online at http://mideastsoccer.blogspot.com/2011/11/saudi-arabia-to-send-token-woman-to.html

Dorsey, J. M. (2012a). Sports governance: Altering basic attitudes. Available online at http://mideastsoccer.blogspot.sg/2012/07/sports-governance-altering-basic.html

Dorsey, J. M. (2012b). Ultras force indefinite suspension of Egyptian soccer league. Retrieved from http://mideastsoccer.blogspot.co.nz/2012/10/ultras-force-indefinite-suspension-of.html

Eberly, D. (2009). *Liberate and leave: Fatal flaws in the early strategy for post-war Iraq.* Minneapolis, MN: Zenith Press.

Farrey, T. (2004). Former athlete concerned about Uday connection. *ABC News*, August 4.

Foer, F. (2010). *How soccer explains the world: An unlikely theory of globalization.* New York: Harper Perennial.

Goldblatt, D. (2008). *The ball is round: A global history of soccer.* New York: Riverhead Books.

Kuper, S. & Szymanski, S. (2009). *Soccernomics: Why England loses, why Germany and Brazil win, and why the U.S., Japan, Australia, Turkey and even Iraq are destined to become the kings of the world's most popular sport.* New York: Nation Books.

Ministry of Sports and Youth (undated). The Ministry of Youth in the era of revolution. Retrieved from http://www.mosy-krg.org/index.php?option=com_content&view=article&id=45:the-ministry-of-sports-and-youth-launching-youth-roadmap-&catid=16:common&Itemid=31

Quinn, J. (2003). Rebuilding Iraq: 'What in the world have I gotten myself into?'; East Hempfield resident Don Eberly helps United States rebuild Iraq, *Lancaster New Era/Intelligencer Journal,* July 16.

The Scotsman (2004). MBE for getting Iraq back in play. December 4.

11 Scandinavia

H. Thomas R. Persson

Topics

- The Scandinavian model of sport governance
- The organisational structures of Scandinavian sport
- The philosophy and reality of Scandinavian sport governance
- Sport and social responsibility
- Good governance and corporate social responsibility (CSR).

Objectives

- To introduce the reader to Danish, Norwegian and Swedish sport governance
- To describe the organisational structures of Scandinavian sport governance
- To describe the philosophy and reality of Scandinavian sport governance
- To describe the Scandinavian social responsibility discourse in sport governance
- To discuss good governance and CSR in Scandinavian football governance.

Key terms

Danmarks Idræts-Forbund (DIF)   The National Olympic Committee and Sports Confederation of Denmark.

Norges idrettsforbund og olympiske og paralympiske komité (NIF)   The Nowegian Olympic and Paralympic Committee and Confederation of Sports.

Riksidrottsförbundet (RF)   The Swedish Sports Confederation.

Good governance   The clarification of the overall picture of the relationships between different organisations, between different levels within organisations and between organisations and their members, as well as the methods and instruments to sustain these relationships in an ethical manner.

Corporate social responsibility (CSR)   CSR is defined as,

> ... to have in place a process to integrate social, environmental, ethical, human rights and consumer concerns into the sport organisation's business operations and core strategy in close collaboration with their stakeholders,

with the aim of maximizing the creation of shared value for their owners/ members/stakeholders and other stakeholders and society at large, as well as identifying, preventing and mitigating their possible adverse impacts.

(adapted from COM, 2011, p.6)

Overview

It has long been argued that that there is a common Scandinavian way of organising sport, which is closely related to the development of the Scandinavian social-democratic welfare model and civic sector. In time of reorganisation or reduction of the welfare state and growing doubt about sport's inherent capacity to deliver towards the public social-policy agenda – solving social integration and public health problems, such as growing problems with obesity-related illnesses – the topic of social responsibility has become increasingly important to sport (Persson, 2008, 2011a). While introducing the reader to Scandinavian sport governance and the central issues facing sport governance in Scandinavia, football governance in the three countries will be used to discuss the development of good governance and social responsibility or corporate social responsibility.

The Scandinavian model of sport governance

Sport and society is part and product of its current and historic dialogic relationship where the two relate and respond to each other, in a Bakhtinian sense (Bakhtin, 1990). With a population of more than 20 million inhabitants, a common history, languages similar to the extent of resembling different dialects; the Scandinavian countries, Denmark, Norway and Sweden, have in many ways a common past where the geographical territories and the ruling power have changed between the different countries over time. The relations remain close and it has been argued that the similarities often outweigh the differences between the countries, such as the development of Scandinavian welfare states as models of institutional solidarity (Esping-Andersen, 1988), with large public sectors and largely publicly funded welfare systems for all (Klausen & Selle, 1996). Hence, sport in the Scandinavian countries is to a great extent governed according to similar democratic and philosophical principles. The central characteristics of Scandinavian sport as a large popular movement, anchored in a legacy of voluntarism and idealism, upheld by voluntary club structures and sport governing bodies (SGBs), which are mobilised in unified confederations, understood as cultural and political features specific to the neighbouring countries (Bergsgard & Norberg, 2010).

The Scandinavian sport tradition as a popular movement dates back to 1861 and has its origin in Norwegian and Danish Rifle Associations: the Norwegian Central Federation for Promotion of Bodily Exercise and Weapon Use and the Danish Central Committee for Establishment of Rifle Association, and popular willingness and ability to defend the respective country against foreign military powers (Breivik, 2007; Korsgaard, 1986). While rifle shooting was the main activity of these early sport manifestations, gymnastics had a central role in building a strong and healthy defence. Gymnastics was also central to the origin of sport in Sweden where Gothenburg's Gymnastic Association founded in 1891 is accredited as the earliest Swedish popular sport movement (Norberg, 2004) followed only four years later by the Swedish Sports Association. Although sport as a popular movement and the creation of sport clubs took off during the 1880s, earlier examples of sport have been recorded. A one-off occasion of horseracing in Denmark took place in 1771 to become a more established phenomena during the 1820s. In Sweden, the Uppsala Swimming Association was founded in 1795 and in Norway the Christiania Ice Skating Club in 1864.

The relationship between the state and sport movements

That the state is supposed to be the largest sponsor of the national sport movements is an unquestionable dogma in Scandinavia, based on common beliefs in sport's intrinsic values and benefits to public health and social integration. Steeped in the social-democratic welfare model, the general ideology of unity carries a belief that all citizens are best served when all is organised under one umbrella SGB: mass; elite; dis/abled bodied; women; children; youth; adults and elderly. Hence, the national systems are similar in nature with large public support channelled via the national umbrella organisation(s), with only Denmark standing out as somewhat different due to its divided organisational structure. The origin of the finance has, however, differed over time and between the countries. Norway and Denmark have primarily used the surplus of their national gambling markets, while the Swedish support has been part of the national budget with exceptions of some brief periods where it also has been tied to the gambling market (Norberg, 2011). Yet, even in Scandinavia times are not standing still and the amounts allocated to sport are negotiated and renegotiated over time. Currently, the total public support to sport differs between the three countries and a comparison of public support per capita shows that the Swedish state is presently slightly more generous than its neighbours with € 21 million (Regeringen, 2011; SCB, 2012b), followed by Norway's € 15.2 million (Regjeringen, n.d.; SSB, 2012) and Denmark's € 12.8 million (DST, 2012; KUM, n.d.). However, it must be considered that no comparison is straightforward due to ever-so-small organisational differences of sport as well as funding. That which in one case may be seen as public support to sport, may in another case be seen as beneficiary to several sectors of society; that which is state-based in one case, may be municipality-based in another; and that which is allocated to different organisations may in the end have the same addressee. In addition, if wanting to make larger international comparison, consideration must be given that the Scandinavian sport movement is largely supported by its volunteers, which for example in Swedish adds up to 70,000 full time jobs, or in the Danish case, 360,000 individual volunteers (RF, 2012a).

Despite having received financial support from the very beginning and being entrusted with autonomy to run itself and its activities, sport is, and has on and off, been a topic of political debate, while the states on other occasions of disputes internal to sport have chosen to step in as mediator (Enjolras, Seippel, & Holmen-Waldahl, 2012). Some of the more prominent topics attracting attention over the years have been defence, public health, soundness and the nurturing of children, sport values, social integration, voluntarism and identity building. Although Enjolras *et al.* (2012) argue that these political topics have more or less appeared in the order presented, looking at the general, and more specifically the SGB's, discourse in particular, they all seem to carry similar immediacy today, except for the topic of national defence. Despite mentioned autonomy, the financial tradition of supporting sport in Scandinavia should be understood as what Henry and Lee (2004) refer to as political governance. That is:

> the processes by which governments or governing bodies seek to steer the sports system to achieve desired outcomes by moral pressure, use of financial or other incentives, or by licensing, regulation and control to influence other parties to act in ways consistent with desired outcomes.
>
> (Henry & Lee, 2004, pp.26-27)

Philosophy and reality

With a starting point of the social-democratic welfare model supported by broad volunteerism, Scandinavian sport is firmly anchored in a philosophy of sport for all. Active participation in sport clubs and associations is an equally common phenomenon in all three countries and relatively high in the European context. According to the national SGBs, sport is supposed to be about enjoyment, everyone's right to participate, fair play, democracy and participation. Moreover, this is expressed as the promotion of sport development, democracy, gender equality, universal right to participate, respect for others, voluntary commitment, fair play, good health, sound finances, environmental awareness and professionalisation of employees and volunteers (DIF, 2011a; NIF, 2011a; RF, 2012b). Although neither of the countries may come out poorly in an international comparison of their commitment to sport for all, while sport primarily is a children and youth activity, all of the Scandinavian countries are facing a high degree of dropout in early teenage years. Although 75 per cent of all 13-year-olds in Sweden participate in sport, this is reduced to 35 per cent of females and 40 per cent of males when reaching age 19. The same figures for Norway are approximately 50 per cent at age 13 and 25 per cent at age 19. The tendency is the same for Danish youth (Skille, 2011). Furthermore, in all age groups women's participation is lower than that of men, only making up approximately 40 per cent of the total number of registered members. Looking at the gender makeup of decision-making positions, it can be described as a homosocial sphere, or as women representatives on male boards (Fundberg, 2009; Hovden, 2011). Although the composition occasionally may reach 50–60 per cent men and 40–50 per cent women, chairpersons are predominantly male. Comparing ethnic composition, the numbers are far worse with the main focus within the SGBs, as well as in research, still being on integrating immigrants or minorities in sport into clubs and teams (Agergaard, 2011; Fundberg, 2012; Fundberg & Lagergren, 2010; Walseth, 2006, 2011) and with very little written and less done in terms of decision-making positions (Fundberg, 2009, 2012).

Scandinavian sport: organisational structure

Sport is no doubt organised differently in different countries. In the Scandinavian countries sport is organised as an independent voluntary movement. As such, a history of collaboration between central government, local authorities and the sport movement has, over time, resulted in mutual trust and sport organisations being entrusted with relatively large amounts of autonomy to organise sport with financial support from states and local authorities. Sport is organised in a pyramid shape, where local grassroots clubs are seen as the foundation of all organised sport and the role of SGBs on national, regional and local levels is to create the essential conditions for successful club activities. The national confederations are found at the top organising and managing individual sports and regional confederations and federations serving as the extended arm of the national confederation and federations respectively. The regional or district levels, comparable to county or provincial levels, function as the collective bodies for support of sport and individual clubs, organising local leagues and offering different courses, and assistance to the clubs in their everyday business.

Denmark

Founded in 1896, the Danish Sporting Federation, since 1993 the Danish Sport Confederation, (DIF, short for the National Olympic Committee and Sports Confederation of Denmark) is the largest Danish umbrella sport organisation (DIF, n.d.-a; Jørgensen, 1997; Korsgaard, 1986). Although the DIF is the main governing body, the Danish sport movement is made up of four different confederations: the DIF, the Danish Gymnastics and Sports Associations (DGI), the Danish Federation of Company Sports (DFIF) and Team Denmark. On a national level the 14,900 sport associations and clubs are organised in the three main organisations; the DIF, the DGI and the DFIF, but many of the clubs have multiple memberships. In addition to this, Team Denmark is exclusively responsible for the development of Danish elite sport (DIF, n.d.-c).

The DIF is the umbrella organisation for 61 sport federations with 1.7 million members in 10,700 clubs. The DGI dates back to 1861 and is a direct descendant of the Danish Central Committee for Establishment of Rifle Associations and took its current name and shape in 1992 after a merger between the Danish Gymnastics and Youth Associations and the Danish Rifle, Gymnastics and Sport Associations.

The DGI, which organises 17 sports/activities, is both a sport and cultural organisation with approximately 1.3 million members (and for historic reasons 12,000 German members) in 5,100 sport clubs (DGI, n.d.-a, n.d.-b, n.d.-c).

The DFIF works to promote sport and exercise primarily through the workplace. The Association is the third largest sport organisation in Denmark and organised regionally via 14 districts, 92 local sport associations and approximately 6,200 company sport clubs with approximately 319,000 members (DFIF, n.d.).

Norway

In Norway, the Norwegian Olympic and Paralympic Committee and Confederation of Sports (NIF), is the national umbrella organisation for all national sport federations. NIF consists of approximately 2.1 million members and more than 11,900 clubs organised in 54 national federations, 19 regional confederations (NIF, n.d.). NIF was established in 1893 as the Central Federation for Promotion of Bodily Exercise and Weapon Use. After several incorporations and mergers, such as with the Worker's Sport Federation, the Norwegian Olympic Committee and the Norwegian Disability Sport Confederation, it took its current name, the Norwegian Olympic and Paralympic Committee and Confederation of Sports in 2007.

Sweden

The Swedish Sports Confederation (RF) was founded in 1903 as the National Association of Gymnastics and Sport Clubs (RF, n.d.), which stemmed from the Swedish Gymnastics Association which was founded in 1891. Today the RF is the national umbrella organisation for Swedish sport and consists of approximately 3.4 million members and 20,000 clubs organised in 69 national federations, 21 regional confederations and 1000 special sport district federations (RF, 2012b). RF is the main sport organisation, which in similar fashion to Norway but different to Denmark, includes the Swedish Federation of Company Sports (Korpen). Parallel to the RF, the SOK and the Swedish Olympic Committee (SOC), are in charge of and responsible for Swedish Olympic representation. SOC is made up of 36 permanent member federations and an additional 14 by the IOC recognised sport federations currently not represented in the Olympic Games (SOC, 2008), which means that some sport federations have double membership.

Case study: Sport and social responsibility

While there is no doubt that Scandinavian sport governance is firmly anchored in a philosophy of sport for all, it is clear that the sport movement still has some way to go before realising its goals. The work of the SGBs described is divided between competitiveness amongst elite as well as grassroots athletes and sport as a leisure activity for all. This can be traced back to ideas about success and gold medals resulting in more sport participants and the more participants (read children and youth) the greater success and medal count. It has elsewhere been argued (Skille, 2011) that the division between the competitive side and the leisure activity side of sport, or more to the point the lack of realising how central competing is to sport, is part of the problem of realising sport for all policy goals. One solution for sport for all policies, according to Skille, would be to turn to other SGBs then such as the DIF, the NIF and the RF, however, this is still yet to happen.

What is taking place is that the entire sport movement, directly or indirectly, is gradually being put under greater pressure to live up to the sport for all policy goals. A strong focus on the promotion of health and social integration in the

Scandinavian countries has resulted in the states' increasing expectations that sport associations should deliver a social policy agenda matching sport for all policies (Breivik, 2011; Persson, 2008, 2011b; SOU, 2008). This should be understood as a new role for the SGBs and a new relationship or partnership between the states and the SGBs, comparable to governmental franchising. Although not new to the civic sector, to a popular movement made up of almost exclusively volunteers it may be interpreted as controversial when the line between volunteering and explicit mission is being blurred (Milling, 2008).

Nevertheless, from traditionally asserting that practising sport is a goal in itself and not the means to solve social, health or other societal problems (Persson, 2008), the current SGBs discourse is gradually meeting the external pressures with statements such as: 'The public authorities and the sport community have a range of common national goals on all administrative levels' (NIF, 2011a, p.7, author's own translation (a.o.t.)), 'We want to acknowledge sport's social responsibility and improve and strengthen the Danish society within those areas where sport can make a difference' (DIF, 2011a, p.5, a.o.t.) and 'The sport movement shall also offer older people age adapted activities' (RF, 2009, p.31, a.o.t.).

Although the pressure might have increased, the topics seem to have remained the same with (public) health and social integration at the top. The former is connected to soundness and nurturing of both children and the elderly (third age) and the latter to (national/regional/local) labour market integration through social integration. A growing ageing population – Sweden having 20 per cent of its population above 65, a life expectancy for men of 79.4 and 83.4 for women (SCB, 2012a) – makes public health into a central urgent issue for the Swedish government. The situation is similar in Denmark and Norway, albeit somewhat fewer above the age of 65 and a marginally shorter life expectancy. From the position of any government and state, it is important to have a healthy population. This applies to the labour force just as it does to the retired part of the population. In terms of social integration for people with an immigrant background as well as for the remaining population, age, sex/gender, class, employment tends to be seen as central to integration and economic independence. Nevertheless, the vulnerability is greater for those with an immigrant background due to being subject to discrimination and with few contacts within the labour force; social networks are increasingly proving to be the entrance port to the labour market (Villund, 2010). Here, according to political and popular views explicitly or implicitly tied to social capital theories of Putnam and others (Helliwell & Putnam, 2004; Putnam, 2007), sport plays, or at least could play, a central role as a natural arena for social integration between people with different social and socioeconomic backgrounds (Enjolras *et al.*, 2012). Consequently, the popularity amongst ministries to (co)finance social integration sport projects, such as 'Get2sport' in Denmark (DIF, n.d.-b), has increased over the last decade(s).

Football governance

Football, the single biggest sport activity in all three countries followed by gymnastics and swimming in Denmark, skiing and golf in Norway, and gymnastics and floorball in Sweden, should be a suitable candidate for furthering a discussion around what is and what is not done to meet this new situation facing sport governance, i.e. the need to deliver towards a social policy agenda (RF, 2011). As such, it is probably true to say that while it may not be representative of all sports, it is plausible to assume that it should be at the forefront reacting to governance trends (Persson, 2008). When comparing football governance among the Scandinavian countries, the similarities and differences become both obvious and of obvious importance. Like many football associations they have a long history. The Danish FA is the oldest of the three FAs, founded in 1889, followed by the Norwegian in 1902 and the Swedish in 1904. Denmark and Sweden were also among the seven founding members of FIFA in 1904. Today, the Danish FA (DBU) has more than 350,000 members or 21 per cent of the total number of DIF's members, out of which 22 per cent are girls/women (DIF, 2011b). The Norwegian FA (NFF) consists of just above 365,000 members, or 17 per cent of the total number of NIF's members, out of which 29 per cent are girls/women (NIF, 2011b). The Swedish FA (SvFF), has approximately 571,000 members, or 25 per cent of the total number of RF's, out of which 27 per cent are girls/women (RF, 2011).

Scandinavian top-level football has supported amateurism longer than most other European leagues (Andersson & Carlsson, 2009). While Sweden lifted its amateur rule in 1967 and Denmark theirs in 1978, Norway waited until 1991 to do the same. However, none of the leagues had fully professional teams until Danish Brøndby and Swedish Malmö turned professional in 1986 and 1989 respectively. Although the forms of professionalisation have taken slightly different shapes in the three countries, in different ways they all have kept one foot firmly anchored in the Scandinavian mixed-market economy and welfare state while still striving for increased professionalisation and commercialisation. Consequently, it has been described as an amalgam of commercialism and volunteering (Andersson & Carlsson, 2009; Gammelsæter, Storm, & Söderman, 2011). Despite the natural tension between commercialised elite football and traditions of amateurism and grassroots football, there is said to be a widespread consensus that the top needs the bottom to secure a rich talent supply. Hence, the preferred and chosen organisational structure is one that includes the entire football community (Andersson, 2011; Gammelsæter *et al.*, 2011; Persson, 2011b). According to democratic fashion and in practical terms, this means that the district FAs that represents grassroots football are in majority when resolutions are to be passed. In some ways this balances commercial aspects with grassroots aspects.

Football: good governance and social responsibility

It has been argued that one needs to view domestic sport governance from a perspective of multi-level governance to understand the current situation and the development of SGBs in terms of a social policy agenda of health and social integration (Persson, 2011b). This is certainly true when looking at the national football associations' need to adhere to UEFA and FIFA (and the EU) on an international level and its membership, local, regional and national federations, and indirectly the state. Besides the already mentioned increased pressure from the states, FIFA and UEFA have for some time also been arguing for the importance of CSR and good governance, with focus on openness, democracy, transparency and social responsibility (FIFA, n.d.; UEFA, 2012a, 2012b). Likewise, this is high on the agenda of the Council of Europe (CCSEM, 2012). Without evaluating FIFA and UEFA's ability to live up to their own goals, but with these goals in mind, the chapter turns to discuss Scandinavian football governance response to questions of good governance and CSR.

Good governance, in the context of this chapter, refers to the clarification of the overall picture of relationships and ethical standards of these relationships. It refers to the relationships between different organisations, different levels within organisations and organisations and their members, as well as the methods and instruments to sustain these relationships (Persson, 2011b). To define CSR in a European context, the EU's official definition is used, which refers to having a process in place to integrate social, environmental, ethical, human rights and consumer concerns into the sport organisation's business operations and core strategy in close collaboration with stakeholders, with the aim of maximising the creation of shared value for their owners, members/stakeholders and society at large, as well as identifying, preventing and mitigating possible adverse impacts (adapted from COM, 2011). Good governance, as a general guiding principle set out by UEFA, is hard to object to. To pressure professional sport clubs to a CSR engagement similar to that of any other business should, for the same reasons, be uncontroversial. When discussing the CSR engagement of football associations in the context of this chapter, the argument relies on the wealth of the football associations that on top of their own commercial revenues also receive tax-financed support. Consequently, taxpayers should be on the list of stakeholders, something stated by the DBU in conjunction with their launch of an Ethical Committee in 2008. At the time they stated that their stakeholders were not only active practitioners, but also trainers, coaches, referees, entire clubs, umbrella and international organisations, organised crowds and fans, state and municipalities, private companies in the shape of established and potential sponsors and partners, media and the entire population (Persson, 2008). Moreover, the aforementioned philosophical stance of democracy, development, gender equality, universal right to participate, respect for others, voluntary commitment, fair play, good health, sound finances, environmental awareness and professionalisation together with law and order, transparency and a concept of social responsibility as central to the development of governance, could all be argued as part of building and/or rebuilding trust. With this as the baseline, viewing the governance practices of the three Scandinavian FAs through a lens integrating good governance, CSR and social capital in the context of multi-level governance, should give an idea of how good governance and CSR are embedded in the context of both economic action and social relations in and with society at large (see Carroll, 1979; Persson, 2011b).

Considering the centrality of the concept of transparency in terms of good governance, closely related to accessibility of information, the first step was to search each FA's web page with the help of its own search engine. Since the concepts in focus are generally used in their original form and language, the key words used were good governance and corporate social responsibility or CSR. Before presenting the results of the search, it should be made clear that there was no doubt about the fact that all three FAs do not only follow the local laws regulating financial reporting, but produce and publish administrative and activity reports, as well as vision and policy documents (DBU, 2011, n.d.-c; NFF, 2011a, 2012; SvFF, 2011b, 2011c, 2011d). This provides a degree of transparency towards good governance.

Searching the DBU's web page for documents mentioning good governance, everything from disciplinary cases (the local premier league), annual reporting, the launch of five 'good governance groups' (including the Ethical Committee, the Medical Group, the Fair Play Group, the CSR Group and the Society Group), to the mentioning of having been given the responsibility for putting together the much questioned and criticised FIFA Transparency and Compliance Board, was listed (DBU, n.d.-b). The same search on NFF's and SvFF's web pages did not provide any such hits. Using the Norwegian term of good governance (*god styring*) provided one hit mentioning and discussing the topic of good governance in the context of a democratic, competent, responsible organisation with a focus on society (NFF, n.d.). While the 2008–2011 Policy Programme came up, the search engine missed the 2012–2015 Policy Programme. The latter provides a detailed description of good governance in connection to individual clubs (NFF, 2012). The Swedish translation (*god styrning*) provided no similar hits (SvFF, n.d.).

Switching the focus to CSR, a search on the DBU's web page resulted in a smaller number of hits mentioning or discussing CSR. These included lists of staff and each staff member's responsibility, trainers' courses for socially vulnerable people, a longer summary of the 2011 Annual Report, and information on the launch of the five 'good governance groups' (DBU, n.d.-b). The same search on NFF's and SvFF's web pages did not provide any similar hits. Using the Norwegian and Swedish translations for (corporate) social responsibility in order not to miss information covering the topic of interest did provide several hits, but not on subjects matching the aforementioned definition of CSR (NFF, n.d.; SvFF, n.d.).

To be sure not to paint an incorrect picture of the three FAs, for example due to using incorrect key words, emails explaining the research topic were sent to the person listed as responsible for one or several of the topics in focus. When no such position was listed, the same email was sent to the Administrative Director. While the Danish FA had a person listed as responsible for CSR and public affairs in their Communication Department (DBU, n.d.-a), in the Norwegian and Swedish cases the appropriate contact was conveyed with the help of the Administrative Directors. In the former it was the Director of Competition and in the latter the Head of Communication. In addition to summarising the material already available on the DBU web page, the CSR and Public Affairs at the DBU shared documentation discussing and outlining an update of the FA's strategy for CSR from a more ad hoc engagement with NGOs to a more professional, defined and planned agenda and effort; a draft on the cooperation between Save the Children and the DBU; and strategy for selecting an maintaining CSR partnerships visualised with the help of a partnering cycle (DBU Communication Department, email communication, 28 February–1 March 2012).

In the Norwegian case, in similar fashion to the Danish representative, the Director of Competition summarised that which could be read or downloaded from its web pages on the topic of good governance. Here, the FA underlines that they work actively to strengthen sustainability at the club level and especially in relation to economic issues under the heading of Economic Fair Play, but also in terms of education programmes strengthening the management of clubs. In terms of CSR, where the search produced no results, the Director of Competition stressed that the FA works actively with their amateur sections in terms of social development, especially in terms of social inclusion and on an international level in collaboration with Norwegian authorities in development projects in the Middle East, Vietnam and the Balkans (NFF Director of Competition, email communication, 22 February–11 April 2012). Furthermore, the email conversation included links to web pages and web publications, such as the regulations of commercial and/or administrative collaborations between club and association by the Association Board (NFF, 2011b), club license statutes (NFF, 2010), fair play in top football (NFF, 2009), and Proposal for Action Plan 2012–2015 (NFF, 2012). Despite the lack of explicit references in all but one of these web pages and publications, they indicate support for a good governance approach.

From the Swedish FA's Head of Communication the answer was, in comparison to the NFF, more exhaustive and convoluted. It stressed that the SvFF, first and foremost, collaborates with UEFA on the issues in focus and that it, on more than one occasion, applied for financial support regarding different good governance projects, such as democracy and social inclusion, and solidarity and antidiscrimination. Also, the Head of Communication listed some of the work carried out by the SvFF in regards to transparency, solidarity and antidiscrimination, rule of law, democracy and inclusiveness, and effectiveness and efficiency. In terms of CSR and sustainability, the SvFF has less explicit information to contribute. While stressing that they are under strain due to international events such as the Olympics and the European championships, the Head of Communication also admitted that they have not done enough to make their efforts visible (SvFF Head of Communication, email communication, 5–13 March 2012). Web accessible publications: *Unity – A Cornerstone in Swedish Football Today and in the Future* (SvFF, 2011a) and *Onside or Offside – A Magazine about the Values of Football* (SvFF, 2006), were made available fit with the aforementioned definitions of good governance, without expressing it explicitly. The former explains the SvFF's different national and international memberships and implications, responsibilities and democracy in Swedish football. It presents the common foundation pillars of the SvFF as a coherent league system based on sport principles, member clubs accepting the bylaws, equal treatment of clubs, association and representative meetings as checkpoints, each segment being responsible for its costs and keeping its revenues, and the observance of rules and laws on all levels. The latter document discusses zero tolerance in terms of swear words, fair play, UEFA's 10 commandments, integration vs. racism, homophobia, elite and grassroots in collaboration, finance. In terms of CSR, but without using any of the associated terms, *Onside or Offside* mentions SvFF work with the Swedish Church and their Lutheran Aid projects as well as IOGT-NTO and the National Alcohol Committee (ended 2009).

Summary

There should be no doubt that the Scandinavian football associations live up to at least the minimum levels of all aspects of good governance. They all, according to the available documentation, albeit with different levels of clarity, work according to a philosophy of transparency in terms of the relationships between different organisations, between different levels within organisations and between organisations and their members, as well as the methods and instruments to sustain these relationships in an ethical manner. Furthermore, and central to both good governance and CSR, they all stress the importance of democracy, development, gender equality, universal right to participate, respect for others, voluntary commitment, fair play, good health, sound finances, environmental awareness and professionalisation, together with rules and regulations. In this way and in relation to the increased pressure to live up to the social policy agenda of the day, they could be described as working towards building and rebuilding trust in terms of acknowledged stakeholders, sometimes framed as social capital (Persson, 2011b).

Nevertheless, when scrutinising the DBU's, NFF's and SvFF's web pages, it is clear that the Danish FA is at the forefront in terms of explicitly communicating their approach and philosophy behind good governance and CSR policy. This is an important assertion, specifically in terms of good governance, due to the centrality of explicit and clear communication in terms of achieving full transparency. This is not about criticising or revealing the reasons behind why the NFF and SvFF have chosen different approaches to that of the DBU. In fact, they have not done anything wrong by choosing their individual approaches. Instead, the intention is to raise the awareness and interest in comparing and scrutinising the difference in governance approaches and to look at the how and when these approaches (un)intentionally or (un)consciously (mis)match, support or clash and whether they fulfil and live up to existing regulations and intentions. The next step for the interested is to ask the 'why' question.

Review questions

1   Two out of the three umbrella SGBs had similar origins. Explain which and discuss how this may or may not have influenced the current state of sport.
2   Two types of sport governance are mentioned and discussed in this chapter. How are they defined and how may they relate to corporate social responsibility?

3   The description of the current state of football governance in Scandinavia shows that although they are very similar in terms of history and context they may not be in sync in terms of good governance and CSR. Compare this situation with the SGB of your choice by searching its web page for good governance and CSR.

Further reading

Carlsson, B., Norberg, J.R. & Persson, H.T.R. (eds) (2011). Special Issue: The governance of sport from a Scandinavian perspective. *International Journal of Sport Policy and Politics*, 3(3), 305–420.

Gammelsaeter, H. & Senaux, B. (2011). *The organisation and governance of top football across Europe: An institutional perspective*. London: Routledge.

Groeneveld, B., Houlihan, B. & Ohl, F. (eds) (2011). *Social capital and sport governance in Europe*. London: Routledge.

Hassan, D. & Lusted, S. (eds) (2012). *Managing sport: Social and cultural perspectives*. London: Routledge.

Websites

The National Olympic Committee and Sports Confederation of Denmark: www.dif.dk

The Norwegian Olympic and Paralympic Committee and Confederation of Sports: www.nif.no

The Swedish Sports Confederation: www.rf.se

References

Agergaard, S. (2011). Development and appropriation of an integration policy for sport: How Danish sports clubs have become arenas for ethnic integration. *International Journal of Sport Policy and Politics*, 3(3), 341–53.

Andersson, T. (2011). *Spela fotboll bondjävlar!* Stehag: Symposion.

Andersson, T., & Carlsson, B. (2009). Football in Scandinavia: A fusion of welfare policy and the market. *Soccer & Society*, 10(3-4), 299–304.

Bakhtin, M. M. (1990). Author and hero in aesthetic activity (1920–1923). In M. Holquist & V. Liapunov (eds), *Art and answerability: Early philosophical essays* (pp.4–256). Austin, TX: University of Texas Press.

Bergsgard, N. A., & Norberg, J. R. (2010). Sport policy and politics – the Scandinavian way. *Sport in Society*, 13(4), 567–82.

Breivik, G. (2007). Idrettens utvikling og historie: Speilbilde eller motkultur? In A. Hompland (ed.), *Idrettens dilemmaer* (pp.11-27). Oslo: Akilles.

Breivik, G. (2011). Norges Idrettsforbund som ideologisk maktfaktor og aktivitietskaper. In D. V. Hanstad (ed.), *Norsk idrett: Indre spenning og ytre press* (pp.11–27). Oslo: Akilles.

Carroll, A. B. (1979). A three-dimensional conceptual model of corporate performance. *Academy of Management Review*, 4(4), 497–505.

CCSEM. (2012). Good governance and ethics in sport. Doc. 12889. Report to the Parliamentary Assembly, Council of Europe, by the Committee on Culture, Science, Education and Media. Rapporteur: Mr Francois Rochebloine. Available online at http://www.assembly.coe.int/ASP/Doc/XrefViewPDF.asp?FileID=18099&Language=EN

COM. (2011). *A renewed EU strategy 2011-14 for corporate social responsibility.* Communication from the Commission to the European Parliament, the Council, the European Economic and Social Committee and the Committee of the Regions. 681 final. Available online at http://ec.europa.eu/enterprise/policies/sustainable-business/files/csr/new-csr/act_en.pdf

DBU. (2011). Årsberetning 2011. Available online at http://www.dbu.dk/~/media/Files/DBU_Broendby/aarsberetningen/aarsberetning_2011.pdf

DBU. (n.d.-a). Afdelinger og ansatte i DBU. Available online at http://www.dbu.dk/oevrigt_indhold/Om DBU/ansatte_i_DBU.aspx

DBU. (n.d.-b). DBU. Available online at http://www.dbu.dk

DBU. (n.d.-c). Om DBU. Available online at http://www.dbu.dk/oevrigt_indhold/Om DBU.aspx

DFIF. (n.d.). Om Dansk Firmaidrætsforbund. Available online at http://www.firmaidraet.dk/om-dansk-firmaidraetsforbund.aspx

DGI. (n.d.-a). DGIs historie fra 1800-tallet til 1930. Available online at http://www.dgi.dk/OmDGI/Fakta   og   tal/Historie/nyheder/DGIs_historie_fra_1800-tallet_til_1930_%5Ba10554%5D.aspx

DGI. (n.d.-b). DGIs historie fra 1930 til 1965. Available online at http://www.dgi.dk/OmDGI/Fakta   og   tal/Historie/nyheder/DGIs_historie_fra_1930_til_1965_%5Ba10556%5D.aspx

DGI. (n.d.-c). DGIs historie fra 1965 til i dag. Available online at http://www.dgi.dk/OmDGI/Fakta   og   tal/Historie/nyheder/DGIs_historie_fra_1965_til_i_dag_%5Ba10557%5D.aspx

DIF. (2011a). Idræt for alle – Danmarks Idræts-forbunds politiske program for perioden 2011 til 2014. Available online at http://www.dif.dk/OEKONOMI_OG_POLITIK/politik/DIFs politikker.aspx

DIF. (2011b). Medlemstal i tal. Available online at http://www.dif.dk/da/STATISTIK/Medlemstal_i_tal.aspx

DIF. (n.d.-a). DIF›s historie. Available online at http://www.dif.dk/OM_DIF_OG_FORBUNDENE/historie/difs historie.aspx

DIF. (n.d.-b). Get2sport. Available online at http://www.get2sport.dk

DIF. (n.d.-c). Idrættens organisering. Available online at http://www.dif.dk/OM_DIF_OG_FORBUNDENE/organisation/idraettens organisering.aspx

DST. (2012). Folketal. Available online at http://dst.dk/da/Statistik/emner/befolkning-og-befolkningsfremskrivning/folketal.aspx

Enjolras, B., Seippel, Ø., & Holmen-Waldahl, R. (2012). *Norsk Idrett: Organisering, fellesskap og politik.* Oslo: Akilles Forlag.

Esping-Andersen, G. (1988). *Politics against markets :The social democratic road to power.* Princeton, NJ: Princeton Univ. Press.

FIFA. (n.d.). About FIFA's CSR. Available online at http://www.fifa.com/aboutfifa/socialresponsibility/about.html

Fundberg, J. (2009). *Vilka är idrottens valda makthavare: Om rekrytering till styrelser inom svensk idrott.* FOU-rapport 2009:6. Stockholm: Riksidrottsförbundet.

Fundberg, J. (2012). En etnisk tackling mot ett kompakt försvar? En kunskapsöversikt om idrott och etnicitet. In C. Dartsch & J. Pihlblad (eds), *Vem platsar i laget? En antologi om idrott och etnisk mångfald* (pp.13–63). Centrum för idrottsforskning 2012: 3. Stockholm: Centrum för Idrottsforskning.

Fundberg, J., & Lagergren, L. (2010). *Etnisk mångfald inom svensk elitidrott: Om förändring över tid och en nulägesanalys.* FoU-rapport 2010:4. Stockholm: Riksidrottsförbundet.

Gammelsæter, H., Storm, R. K., & Söderman, S. (2011). Diverging Scandinavian approaches to professional football In H. Gammelsæter & B. Senaux (eds), *The organisation and governance of top football across Europe: An institutional perspective* (pp.77–92). London: Routledge.

Helliwell, J. F., & Putnam, R. D. (2004). The social context of well-being. *Philosophical Transactions of the Royal Society London B*, 359(1449), 1435–46.

Henry, I., & Lee, P. C. (2004). Governance and ethics in sport. In J. Beech & S. Chadwick (eds), *The business of sport management* (pp.25–42). Harlow: Pearson Education.

Hovden, J. (2011). Kjønn og leiarskap i norsk idrett. In D. V. Hanstad (ed.), *Norsk idrett: Indre spenning og ytre press* (pp.299–315). Oslo: Akilles.

Jørgensen, P. (1997). *Ro, Renlighed, Regelmæssighed: Dansk Idræts-Forbund og sportens gennembrud ca. 1896–1918*. Odense: Odense universitetsforlag.

Klausen, K. K., & Selle, P. (1996). The third sector in Scandinavia. *Voluntas: International Journal of Voluntary and Nonprofit Organizations*, 7(2), 99–122.

Korsgaard, O. (1986). *Kampen om kroppen – Dansk idræts historie gennem 200 år*. Copenhagen: Gyldendal.

KUM. (n.d.). Tips- og lottomidler til idaetten. Available online at http://kum.dk/Kulturpolitik/Idraet/Tips--og-lottomidler/

Milling, H. B. (2008). Urealistiske forventninger til foreningerne. *Idrætliv* (4), 8.

NFF. (2009). Fair Play i toppfotballen. Available online at http://www.fotball.no/nff/Fair-Play/Fair-Play-i-toppfotballen/

NFF. (2010). Klubblisensreglement. Available online at http://www.lovdata.no/nff/klubblisensreglement.html

NFF. (2011a). Årsrapport 2011. Available online at http://www.fotball.no/Documents/PDF/2012/NFF/NFF_Aarsrapport_2011_endelig_LAV.pdf

NFF. (2011b). Forbundsstyrets bestemmelser om kommersielt og/eller administrativt samarbeid mellom klubb/idrettslag og selskap. Available online at http://www.fotball.no/Documents/PDF/2010/NFF/AS-bestemmelser – endelig pr 01.01.11.pdf

NFF. (2012). Handlingsplan: 2012-2015. Available online at http://www.fotball.no/Documents/PDF/2012/NFF/Handlingsplan2012-2015_WEB_enkel.pdf?epslanguage=en

NFF. (n.d.). NFF. Available online at http://www.fotball.no

NIF. (2011a). *Idettspolitisk dokument 2011–2015*. Available online at http://www.nif.no/omnif/ipd/Documents/Idrettspolitisk_dokument2011_2015.pdf

NIF. (2011b). *Norges idrettsforbund og olympiske og paralympiske komité – Årsrapport 2011*. Available online at http://www.idrett.no/omnif/Documents/NIF_Aarsrapport_2011_LR_Smaller.pdf

NIF. (n.d.). Om NIF. Available online at http://www.nif.no/omnif/Sider/forside.aspx

Norberg, J. R. (2004). *Idrottens väg till folkhemmet: Studier i statlig idrottspolitik 1913–1970*. Stockholm: SISU Idrottsböcker.

Norberg, J. R. (2011). A contract reconsidered? Changes in the Swedish State's relation to the sports movement. *International Journal of Sport Policy and Politics*, 3(3), 311–25.

Persson, H. T. R. (2008). Social capital and social responsibility in Denmark: More than gaining public trust. *International Review for the Sociology of Sport*, 43(1), 35–51.

Persson, H. T. R. (2011a). Danish sport governance: Tradition in transition. In M. Groeneveld, B. Houlihan & F. Ohl (ds.), *Social capital and sport governance in Europe* (pp.63–84). London: Routledge.

Persson, H. T. R. (2011b). Good governance and the Danish Football Association: Between international and domestic sport governance. *International Journal of Sport Policy and Politics*, 3(3), 373–84.

Putnam, R. D. (2007). E Pluribus Unum: Diversity and community in the twenty-first century. The 2006 Johan Skytte Prize Lecture. *Scandinavian Political Studies*, 30(2), 137–74.

Regeringen. (2011). Budget och mål för Kulturdepartementet. Available online at http://regeringen.se/sb/d/13574

Regjeringen. (n.d.). Tilskudd til Norges idrettsforbund og olympiske og paralympiske komité. Available online at http://www.regjeringen.no/nb/dep/kud/tema/idrett/tilskudd_til_lokale_lag_og_foreninger/tilskudd-til-norges-idrettsforbund-og-ol.html?id=426590

RF. (2009). Idrotten vill: Idrottsrörelsens idéprogram. Available online at rf.se/ImageVault/Images/id_2473/ImageVaultHandler.aspx

RF. (2011). 2011Verksamhetsberättelse med årsredovisningar. Available online at http://rf.se/ImageVault/Images/id_24517/scope_0/ImageVaultHandler.aspx

RF. (2012a). Sport in Sweden. Available online at http://rf.se/ImageVault/Images/id_23441/scope_0/ImageVaultHandler.aspx

RF. (2012b). Sport in Sweden. Available online at http://rf.se/ImageVault/Images/id_23441/scope_0/ImageVaultHandler.aspx

RF. (n.d.). Sports in Sweden. Available online at http://www.rf.se/ImageVault/Images/id_166/scope_128/ImageVaultHandler.aspx/

SCB. (2012a). Befolkning: Minskat barnafödande under 2011. Available online at http://www.scb.se/Pages/PressRelease____331064.aspx

SCB. (2012b). Population. Available online at http://www.ssd.scb.se/databaser/makro/Visavar.asp?yp=bergman&xu=scb&omradekod=BE&huvudtabell=BefUtv1749&omradetext=Population&tabelltext=Population+and+population+changes+in+Sweden.++Year&preskat=O&prodid=BE0101&deltabell=&deltabellnamn=Befolkningsutvecklingen+i+riket.++%C5r&innehall=Doda&starttid=1749&stopptid=2011&Fromwhere=M&lang=2&langdb=2

Skille, E. Å. (2011). Sport for all in Scandinavia: Sport policy and participation in Norway, Sweden and Denmark. *International Journal of Sport Policy and Politics*, 3(3), 327–39.

SOC. (2008). The Swedish Olympic Committee. Available online at http://www.sok.se/inenglish.4.18ea16851076df63622800010832.html

SOU. (2008). *Föreningsfostran och tävlingsfostran – En utvärdering av statens stöd till idrotten.* SOU 2008:59. Idrottsstödsutredningen. Kulturdepartementet. Stockholm: Fritzes Offentliga Publikationer.

SSB. (2012). Population statistics. Available online at http://www.ssb.no/folkendrkv_en/

SvFF. (2006). *Onside eller offside – En tidning om fotbollens värderingar* Available online at http://fogis.se/ImageVault/Images/id_57626/scope_0/ImageVaultHandler.aspx

SvFF. (2011a). *Enighet – En grundpelare i svensk fotboll i dag och i framtiden.* Available online at http://fogis.se/ImageVault/Images/id_61142/scope_0/ImageVaultHandler.aspx

SvFF. (2011b). Verksamhetsberättelse 2011, Del 1. Available online at http://fogis.se/ImageVault/Images/id_73399/scope_0/ImageVaultHandler.aspx

SvFF. (2011c). Verksamhetsberättelse 2011, Del 2. Available online at http://fogis.se/ImageVault/Images/id_73400/scope_0/ImageVaultHandler.aspx

SvFF. (2011d). Verksamhetsberättelse 2011, Del 3. Available online at http://fogis.se/ImageVault/Images/id_73401/scope_0/ImageVaultHandler.aspx

SvFF. (n.d.). SvFF. Available online at http://www.svenskfotboll.se

UEFA. (2012a). *Financial Report: 2010/11.* Available online at http://www.uefa.com/MultimediaFiles/Download/EuroExperience/uefaorg/Finance/01/77/26/16/1772616_DOWNLOAD.pdf

UEFA. (2012b). *Report of the President and Executive Committee: UEFA Administration Report 2010/11*. Available online at http://www.uefa.com/MultimediaFiles/Download/EuroExperience/uefaorg/President/01/77/26/05/1772605_DOWNLOAD.pdf

Villund, O. (2010). *Overkvalifisering blant innvandrere: En registerbasert undersøkelse for perioden 2007-2009*. Rapport 2010:28. Oslo: Statistisk sentralbyrå.

Walseth, K. (2006). *Sport and integration. The experience of young Muslim women*. Oslo: Norges Idrettsøgskole.

Walseth, K. (2011). Minoritetjenter i idretten: Status og utfordringer. In D. Vidar-Hanstad (ed.), *Norsk idrett: Indre spenning og ytre press* (pp.355–69). Oslo: Akilles.

12 Greece

Shayne Quick and George Costa

Topics

- The linkage between Greek sport and politics
- The relationship between sport and the government of the day
- Sport and the law
- The General Secretariat of Sport
- The impact of economic crises on state funded sport.

Objectives

- To comprehend political interventions in the sporting landscape of Greece
- To assess the impact of the dependency of sport on state funding
- To critically appraise the governance of sport in Greece
- To determine the utility of the bureaucracy in contribution to successful sport delivery in Greece
- To examine the relationship between professional and amateur sport organisations.

Key terms

PASOK (PanHellenic Socialist Movement)   Political party of the left.
Néa Dimokratía (New Democracy)   Political party of the right.
GGA (General Secretariat of Sport)   Bureaucracy responsible for the implementation of government sport policy in Greece.
PAOK (Panthesalonikian Athletic Club Konstantinoupolis)   A multi-sport club based in Thessaloniki, Greece.
Political clientelism   A mechanism whereby political support is offered in exchange for resource allocation.

Overview

This chapter explores the major stages of governance in sport in Greece from 1974 to present time. It will examine sport governance from four perspectives. These are professional sport, youth sport, sport for all and the Olympic movement in Greece. Such perspectives will be contextualised against a backdrop of changing political and cultural forces and will illustrate how sport in Greece is inextricably linked to the prevailing government agenda. PAOK, a regional sport club with both professional and non-professional teams, will be used as the case study to exemplify contemporary sport governance in Greece.

As a caveat, it must be acknowledged that this chapter on the governance of sport in Greece is being written at a time of great upheaval and uncertainty in a country often regarded as the cradle of democracy and the birthplace of both the modern and ancient Olympics. Debt-laden, politically in a state of disarray and socially pessimistic, the governance of sport is the last thing on the mind of a traumatised citizenry and an economically and strategically bankrupt government.

Helen Smith (2012) writing for *The Guardian* states that

> as London makes its final preparations for this year's Olympics ... Athens Olympic Park, once billed as one of the most complete European athletic complexes, is not testimony to past glories. Instead it is indicative of misplaced extravagance, desolation and despair.

She further indicates that

> no one knows how much the Olympics cost Greece – although many think they played a major role in producing the debt that spurred the country's economic downfall.

She concludes that

> a bankrupt Greece cannot even afford the €600 million needed as basic upkeep to operate and maintain the [Olympic] sites [and that] fed up with shoddy facilities Greek Olympians now invariably go to Cyprus to train.

Writing for *Time* Josh Sanburn (2012) argues that as 'the country grapples with the destabilizing effects of the European economic crisis, many Greeks now look back on those games with regret rather than pride'. Moreover, he argues that the 2004 Olympics 'were a microcosm of Greek economic dysfunction: missed budget estimates, poor planning, financial mismanagement'.

While neither Smith nor Sanburn provide hard evidence for their assertions, and as such the link between reality and rhetoric is somewhat blurred in their analysis of the governance and management of Greek sport, for those that have seen the Olympic facilities in Athens post-2004 it is hard not to share their conclusions.

Perhaps more telling is the fact that the Hellenic Amateur Athletic Federation (SEGAS) ceased all operations in April 2012 in protest of the reduction in government funding. Turnbull (2012) suggested that the Greek government had cut athletic funding by one-third in each of the previous years and that national coaches had not been paid since mid-2011. Yet, while Greece's 2012 Olympic preparation and participation may be the most obvious and public example of the impact of the country's economic decline on the successful governance of sport, it is by no means unique. Even the professional sport leagues have felt the pinch.

Ken Maguire, reporting for SI.com on how the Greek financial crisis was affecting the Greek basketball league, commented that 'most teams could not afford to pay their salaries, FIBA had banned some teams from signing players and others were fleeing the league'. In the same article Maguire's dire comments were supported by Rethymno owner Costi Zombanakis, who believed that 'the Greek league is just a reflection of what is going on in Greece [and that the league was] in a precarious position because the owners don't have any money' (Maguire 2012).

Hence, while ostensibly this chapter is a contribution to an edited collection on national sport governance, what Greece has amply demonstrated mid-2012 is that sport is inexorably linked to and affected by the political, economic and social conditions of the time. Moreover, nowhere is this more telling than in a state-supported sport system, such as that which exists in Greece.

Margaratis (2012a) contends that sport in Greece is protected under the Greek constitution with Article 16 (9) stating that 'athletics shall be under the protection and ultimate supervision of the State and that the State shall make grants to and control all types of athletic associations'. Moreover, he continues that 'every citizen has the right to participate in the sport of his [sic] favour and the State is obliged to provide them with the necessary facilities for their sporting activities'. Significantly, especially in the current economic climate, the Constitution states that 'the State is required to finance sporting associations in order for them to achieve the purposes of their establishment'. Margaratis also comments that the law pertaining to sport in Greece (2725/1999) has been revised on a number of occasions and that:

> The law consists of 140 articles and is divided into 5 parts which deals with the organisation of sport at an amateur and professional level, and the way that the state can control the associations according to the Constitutions and competent authorities.
>
> (Margaritis 2012a)

Hence, while in a time of plenty, national sport would seriously benefit under such a constitutional enactment, in times of austerity and crisis such as that which has existed in Greece in recent years, sporting organisations that have become reliant on state funding find that their capacity to provide support, programmes and sporting infrastructure significantly diminished when that funding dries up. Moreover, Grohmann (2012) suggests that 'apart from the massive budget cuts for all Greek sporting federations, gone are all the state incentives to success on the world stage'.

As a final segue into our understanding of the governance of sport in Greece, the work of Henry and Nassis (1999) is acknowledged and referred to. While specifically focusing on the 12-year period, 1981–1993, which gave Greece two PASOK (socialist) governments (1981–5, 1986–9), a 10-month coalition government, and a neoliberal New Democracy government (1989–1993), the underlying philosophy of political clientelism was, and is, systemic in Greek life and its impact on sport governance is keenly felt. According to Henry and Nassis (1999) political clientelism 'involves the disbursement of financial, employment or other forms of patronage in exchange for political support' (p.43). Their research indicated that a determining variable for support was the political affiliation of the members of the boards of the particular national governing body (NGB) [Federations]. Moreover, they clearly stated that 'where key members of the board identified themselves as affiliated to a particular party, the NGB was identified as a particular beneficiary' (p.49). As a result certain sports benefited, or were disadvantaged, by changes in government depending on political affiliation. Consequently, in return for their support, national governing bodies are significant benefactors of state aid to their sporting organisations. Indeed Henry and Nassis (1999) state 'that NGBs are very heavily dependent (and in one case virtually wholly dependent) on state funding' (p.50).

If ever there was required an unequivocal example of the interrelationship between sport, economics, politics and society, Greece in 2012 provides a compelling case study. However, even in such turbulent times, the management and governance of sport must continue, even if in a volatile and uncertain environment.

Sakka and Chatzigianni (2012, p. 7) state that,

> The Standing Committee of Educational Affairs is a corporate body of the Greek parliament with an important role in planning and directing sport in Greece and setting the legislative framework for sport. In this context it is responsible for supervising the implementation of policies and programs of the Ministry of Culture and it agencies such as the General Secretariat of Sport (GGA).

The General Secretariat of Sport (GGA)

As indicated, the General Secretariat of Sport is a portfolio of the Ministry of Culture and, according to its website (GGA n.d.-a), it is responsible for the country's sport policy. The GGA's stated mandate is to formulate and administer, based on national sporting interest and the principles of the Olympic ideal, a strategic programme of sport policy.

The mission of the GGA is:

- [To ensure] the systematic cultivation, propagation and consolidation in the social consciousness of sportsmanship
- [To] safeguard the values of Olympism and its dissemination at national and international level by any means
- [To] diagnose and document the sporting needs of the country and change sport strategy policy accordingly
- [To provide] specialisation in operational and tactical plans, actions, and projects

- [To] organise, administer and monitor the implementation of sport services to ensure effectiveness, efficiency, and quality
- [To] evaluate policy outcomes
- [To] supervise and control any kind of legal persons subject thereto, in accordance with the applicable provisions and based on the strategic planning of sport policy [sic]

(GGA n.d.)

The GGA comprises three major areas under the political leadership of the minister, the deputy minister, the secretary of state and the General Secretary of Sports. The areas are the General Directorate of Sports, Sports General Directorate of Support, and departments and independent offices.

The General Directorate of Sports

The General Directorate of Sports consists of four departments. They are Sports Promotion, Competitive Sports, Board (an internal department that is primarily responsible for resource and personnel management), and Quality and Efficiency. These departments are responsible for activity planning and for coordinating the individual service units within each department.

The General Directorate of Sports Support

The General Directorate of Sports Support comprises the following divisions and offices. They are the Sport Studies Project, Construction and Maintenance, Economics, and the Offices of Sports Planning, Real Property and Agricultural Studies, and Projects.

Departments and independent offices

The departments and independent offices include the offices of parliamentary control and press which are under the control of the deputy minister and the offices of legal counsel, personnel training, policy planning, emergency, seizure and legal documentation, athletic guidance, truce, national spatial athletic works, and finally, maintenance. The latter offices are under the direct supervision of the secretary general.

Moving beyond the central bureaucracy, the General Secretariat of Sport is supported by, and in turn supports, the Hellenic Olympic Committee and national federations, along with other sport clubs and agencies.

The Hellenic Olympic Committee and the Olympic movement in Greece

The Hellenic Olympic Committee engages in similar activities to other national olympic committees (NOCs) in that its fundamental mandate is, in general, to promote the concept of Olympism and support the initiatives of the IOC (http://www.hoc.gr/). A unique addition to the Hellenic Olympic Committee's responsibility is ensuring the lighting of the Olympic torch for the summer and winter Olympics and it holds the exclusive rights for this ceremony.

Greece has a proud tradition with respect to the Olympic movement. It is one of only four countries that have been represented at every occurrence of the modern summer Olympic games and although historians may debate some of the finer points of fact, there is little doubt that the country has a strong connection to both the modern and ancient games. Yet in 2012 only 103 athletes represented the country at the London Olympics, which was nearly 50 less than the country sent to Beijing in 2008 and a far cry from the halcyon days of 2004 when Greece had 441 athletes competing.

Moreover, Sanburn (2012) states that,

> The Helliniko Olympic Complex in Athens was supposed to be thriving long after the 2004 Summer Olympics ended ... There were big plans to turn much of the complex into the largest metropolitan park in Europe but that never happened, largely because of the bureaucracy that hampers much of Greek development. Today, the complex sits amid overgrown weeds, virtually deserted.

It must be acknowledged that Greece is not alone in failing to arrive at a financial management strategy for post-Olympic facility use. However, it is probably the most telling.

To fully appreciate the decline in representative numbers of Greek athletes between the 2004 and 2012 Summer Games, and to develop an understanding of the post-2004 Olympic decline in Greek sporting infrastructure, the connection between the state, the sporting federations and the Hellenic Olympic Committee has to be acknowledged and understood.

National federations

Margaritis (2012a), when discussing Greek sports law, defines a sport federation as,

> A superior sport organisation at a national level. Only one federation can be established for a particular sport and the main aim of a federation is to advance the sport it represents at a national level and promote the country's sport culture abroad.

Panagiotopoulos (1995) states that that the federations have a dual function under the law which are 'to contribute to the development of sport on a lower level and to function under the supervision and control of the state at a higher level' (p.245).

Papadimitriou and Taylor (2000) have examined the organisational effectiveness of Hellenic national sporting organisations using a multiple constituency approach. Their sample consisted of 20 Hellenic NSOs which [had] a permanent office location and employed at least two administrative staff. All the organisations sampled [were] controlled and managed by powerful boards of directors and most of their financial resources [were] generated from the General Secretariat of Sport (GGA).

(Papadimitriou & Taylor, 2000, p.29)

They concluded that 'Hellenic NSOs need to pay more continuous attention to exploring the role of multiple constituencies in their organisations. More importantly, they need to identify the most important constituencies and determine their relationships with the outputs of their organisations' (p.43). While theoretically such an observation is apropos, the political machinations of Greek sport organisation militates against such a logical path of activity.

With respect to structure and governance of national federations, the GGA list 51 federations, three disabled sport federations and eight judges' and referees' associations. As an aside, Stergioulas and Triploitsioti (2007, p 55) believe that

despite the recognition of people with disabilities in Greece in all walks of life may lag some way behind their contemporaries in other developed countries, a lot has been done in the field of sports to support and encourage participation.

The Greek Federation of Sports for the Deaf was established in 1988, the Wheelchair Federation in 1994, and the Greek Paralympic Committee and the National Athletic Federation of People with Disabilities in 2002.

The national federations are categorised under a 2010 sport classification system as 1) priority national sports; 2) national interest sports; 3) state-supported sports; 4) private initiative sports with targeted state assistance; 5) recognised private sports; and 6) local significance sports. The sports in the first two categories are either Olympic or Paralympic sports while sports in category three, although still being state-supported, have greater reliance on private investment. While in the main, sports in category three are still Olympic sports, this group does include chess. Category four sports have to rely almost solely on private activities and include a mix of Olympic and non-Olympic sports. Category five sports rely totally on private investment and are mainly non-Olympic or infrequent Olympic sports. The final category currently has one sport listed, that being cricket. Interestingly the Hellenic Cricket Federation has 21 clubs with the majority on the island of Corfu. All federations are currently listed on the GGA website under supervised institutions with links in most cases to the individual federations (GGA n.d.-b).

When Panagiotopoulos (1995) argues that 'as federations function in a way to serve the public interest, the State [according to the Constitution] ought to offer protection to the Federation by financing it, checking its legality and expediency and helping it survive', the relevance of Nassi and Henry's (1999) 'political clientelism' becomes evident. Sports that support contemporary government ideology, whoever they may be, are far more likely to receive appropriate funding than those that are aligned with alternative power structures.

Sport for all

Although it is commonly mooted that 'sport for all' is an important part of the Greek sporting fabric, there is acknowledgement but little commentary about this concept on the GGA website other than it is a 'systematic social investment, essential to improve the quality of life, help prevent degenerative trends, develop interpersonal relationships and [establish] a better relationship between man and the natural environment' (GGA n.d.-c).

Harahousou and Kabitsis (2002) contend that while ' the starting point for "sport for all" in Greece was the sport camping facilities established in 1911 in different parts of the country for leisure and vacation activities' (p.551), the landmark moment for its development in Greece was the establishment of the General Secretariat for Sport in 1958. With the support of OPAP (Organisation of Football Prognostics – a state-based lottery system) a five-year development programme was established with funding priorities directed towards facilities development.

In the subsequent decades while the GGA has remained the main organisation responsible for the development and management of sport in Greece, much of the 'sport for all' activity has been devolved to local prefectures, councils, and organised groups. The role of the GGA in such activity has mainly been one of financier of programmes and activities.

The range of groups targeted for such activity has included all those in the school system (from preschool to university students): the elderly; those with special needs; and numerous subgroups within each category. It is interesting to note that historically many ministries have been involved in 'sport for all' programmes. Such ministries have been National Security; Justice, Health and Welfare; Agriculture; Education; and Tourism. All have been charged with providing services, programmes or access to sport for their constituent groups.

The concept of 'sport for all', especially at the government level, seems to be a particularly European concept. Over the last century Greece has clearly attempted to provide a range of programmes and activities to their citizenry, and as in all cases, funding is an issue but the commitment to the philosophy is unwavering. It is for that reason it is included as one of the four pillars of sport governance in Greece.

Professional sport

According to Margaritis (2012b) 'professional sport leagues [in Greece] are established under a ministerial decision from the Minister of Cultural Affairs [upon] receiving an application from the representative sports federation'. Margaritis (2012b) goes on to suggest 'the concept of the Sports Law which reflects the general policy about sports in Greece is that all sports private actors are under the supervision of the State'. However, Margaritis (2012b) also suggests that the Sports Law goes too far making the administration of sport unnecessarily complicated with too much governance and too little competence giving rise to an over bureaucratic sports system.

However, while the leagues are established by the state and controlled under Sports Law, the clubs themselves are prohibited by legislation from becoming public companies and Anagnostopoulos (2011) suggests that 'this has consequences for both accountably and decision making' (p.254). It is in this environment that professional sports in Greece operate.

The GGA list the Greek Football Federation (HFF), Superleague (the teams that make up the league); the Greek Basketball Federation, the Association of Greek Contracting Companies Basketball (the teams that make up the league); the Greek Volleyball Federation and the Unions' paid Volleyball Association (the teams that make up the league) as professional sport organisations. Although this chapter is not suggesting the case of professional football in Greece is generalisable to other professional sports, i.e. basketball and volleyball, the relationship between the sport, in this case football, and the parent club most likely is.

According to Anagnostopoulos (2011) the smallest unit of organised sport in Greece is the sport club, the majority of which are multisport organisations 'and are represented by NSF's and the NGBs for each of the sport they serve' (p.257). At this time it is important to remember the relationship between these entities and the GGA and, by extension, the Ministry of Culture. Thus the situation has arisen that a football club, e.g. PAOK, a limited liability company with shares held by owners, has a multisport parent club to which it must by law pay a percentage of its revenues. Anagnostopoulos (2011) argues that given the business of football, it is hardly surprising that conflict has arisen around the size of the contribution back to the parent club. More significantly, he suggests that

> the social role and nature of the sporting clubs have often become the vehicle for public monies to be floated into the professional clubs, while the local authorities either 'turn a blind eye' or even assist such practices.
>
> (Anagnostopoulos, 2011, p.258)

To further explicate this relationship a case study of PAOK is offered.

Case study: Panthesalonikian Athletic Club Konstantinoupolis (PAOK)

PAOK is a popular multisport club located in Thessaloniki, Greece. PAOK FC is the associated football club which competes in the Superleague, the highest professional football league in Greece. PAOK FC is arguably the largest supported football club in the country. The original team colours are black and white; black symbolising the tragic history of the Greeks and the 'the lost country' while white, the colour of optimism, signifies 'hope for the future' along with their struggle for tomorrows and hoped for victories.

History

PAOK is the historical succession from the Hermes Sports Club, originally founded in 1875 by a Greek community living in Konstantinoupolis, known today as Istanbul. In 1922 after the Greco-Turkish War and the subsequent population exchange between Greece and the newly established Turkey, many of the club members were forced to emigrate. Many of those who fled Turkey settled in Thessaloniki and PAOK was officially founded on 20 April 1926. The first official football game took place on 26 July 1926 against another Thessalonikian team named Iraklis (Hercules).

POAK's first emblem adopted in 1926 consisted of a four leaf clover and a horseshoe. However, in 1929 PAOK merged with AEK (Athletic Union of Constantinople), a local rival team of immigrants. As a result, a new emblem was developed which contained a double headed eagle symbol. This Byzantium eagle symbolises the origins of the PAOK club and its return to its roots and the legacy of the refugees of the Byzantine Empire and Constantinople.

On 5 September 1928 the team signed the first professional contract with a football player. The athlete's name was Etien and his salary was 4,000 drachmas per month, the present-day equivalent of 12 Euros. From 1931 to 1932, PAOK had its first professional coach, Rodolfo Ganser from Germany.

After the Second World War and the German occupation of Greece, PAOK became very popular and competitive in the Greek championship league under the coaching direction of Austrian Willi Sevtsik. In 1951 PAOK played its first final for the Greek Cup and won the Thessaloniki championship three years in a row. Subsequently, the team's management envisioned a new football ground worthy of their incredible performance. After two years of planning and construction, the first stadium, Syntrivaniou Football Ground, otherwise known as Toumba Stadium, was officially opened. It was built on land belonging to the National Defence Fund in Toumba, a neighborhood closely associated with refugees from Asia Minor where today's Syntagma Square (Square of the Central Water) is located. In 1959 the stadium was opened by the Minister of National Defence and the first game was played. To this day, it remains the team's home field and is possibly the most valuable asset the team has.

Throughout the 1960s the team did not have any extraordinary performances. Presumably, they were in the process of building for the next decade of success. In 1972 and 1974 PAOK won the Greek Cup, followed by the championship in 1976. By this time, the team had become legendary across Greece and was spreading to become a European-wide phenomenon. In July of 1979, professional sport was made official in Greece and the PAOK club was divided into two parts: the Professional Football Club and the Amateur Association of PAOK. PAOK's excellent performance continued through the 1980s, although the next 20 years were marked by the typical ups and downs of a professional sport team.

Facilities

In 2000, the PAOK Sports Arena was built on land donated by Ioannis Dedeoglou and is the largest privately owned basketball stadium in Greece. With a capacity of around 8,500 seats it is the home of the PAOK Basketball and Volleyball Clubs and hosts basketball and volleyball tournaments as well as a number of concerts.

Toumba Stadium

In the 1970s, the stadium with an original capacity of 20,000 was expanded to a total of 45,000. However, in the mid-1990s the capacity of the stadium was reduced with the installation of seats in the place of the terraces. In 2004, the stadium was slightly renovated to include VIP facilities. Interestingly, the PAOK Football Club continues to use the facilities at Toumba Stadium, which it shares with other amateur clubs. Current capacity is just over 28,000 seats. Rather than paying rent, the professional clubs provide usage of food corners in the stadium on game days to the amateur clubs which is a strong revenue source for the latter. Professional clubs also undertake advertising within the surrounding area. The professional clubs are responsible for stadium renovations and meeting all the standards and requirements for international games.

Iannis Dedeoglou, the man who donated the land that the current PAOK Sports Arena was built on, has also offered to donate the land beside the stadium to build a new stadium to seat over 40,000. However, the management team at PAOK has shown no interest, declaring their preference to stay at the original Toumba Stadium.

Organisational structure

Today there are three men's professional sports clubs, football, basketball, and volleyball, associated with PAOK. PAOK has expanded to be a diversified sport club that involves many other teams. These include:

- water sports: swimming club, men's water polo club, women's water polo club, technical swimming club, swimming lessons and a department to manage the pool;
- heavy sports: separate men's and women's clubs and youth programmes for weight lifting, boxing, wrestling, and Tae Kwon Do;
- football: women's club;
- basketball: women's club and youth programmes;
- volleyball: women's club and youth programmes;
- handball: men's and women's clubs;
- athletics: men's and women's clubs;
- cycling: men's and women's clubs;
- hockey: men's and women's clubs.

Organisationally PAOK is governed by a president, titled President of the Council, and four vice presidents (see Figure 12.1):

1   Vice President A liaises with the professional football club;
2   Vice President B liaises with the professional basketball club;
3   Vice President C responsible for legal aspects and is a lawyer;
4   Vice President D liaises with the amateur clubs and the General Secretary.

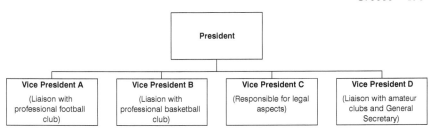

Figure 12.1 PAOK Organisational Chart

There are also 10 administrative positions within the PAOK organisation and these are:

1 General Secretary
2 Treasurer
3 Special Secretary responsible for basketball and youth programmes
4 Facility manager responsible for the football and basketball stadia and the swimming pool
5 Water sport manager
6 Handball manager
7 Administration building manager
8 Manager for competitive sports
9 Marketing and communication manager
10 Person responsible for liaison with the organised fan clubs.

Professional sport clubs

The sources of income of the three PAOK professional sport clubs include:

- Television rights: in 2008, PAOK along with 13 other Superleague teams, signed a collective television deal with Forthnet/SKAI TV for three seasons (2009–2012). As part of the deal, PAOK received €4.55 million per season.
- Sponsors: PAOK has had many sponsors over the years, most recently with Pame Stoihima as their shirt partner and Puma as the kit manufacturer.
- Ticketing and merchandise: other sources of income come from ticketing and merchandise.

Amateur organisations

The amateur organisations receive their income from a variety of sources in a number of ways:

- Government: due to their continued support of Olympic sports and for organising sport development programmes for men, women, and youth.

- Concessions: the professional clubs have a special agreement to contract out the food kiosks and advertising locations.
- Programme services: organisation of youth sports programmes for which they charge a fee.

It has probably become quite clear that it is the professional clubs who generate revenue, which in part, supports the initiatives of the parent club. While this can often be a cause of tension between the parties as to how the revenue split is determined, it does appear to be an effective mechanism by which professional clubs can make an ongoing contribution to sport development and programming in their local communities.

Summary

As has been demonstrated, sport in Greece is an important part of the social fabric of the country with the Government recognising the need to support activities and provide facilities appropriate to the needs of the community. While much has been said of the decline of Greek sporting facilities in the years following the 2004 Olympic Games, it could be argued this has not been as a result of any lack of desire, but rather a lack of funding, the causes of which have been well documented. Interestingly, while many governments, e.g. former USSR, former GDR, China and even Australia, pour money into sport hoping to demonstrate national superiority on the international stage, internal political mechanisms drive the funding and governance of Greek sport. As Greece recovers from its current economic crises, so by association will its sport organisations. While the governance of Greek sport may be somewhat labyrinthine they at least recognise the importance of a broad approach to the sport environment and endeavour to provide support to all.

Review questions

1   What are the benefits and limitations of the governance of sport in Greece?
2   What are the advantages and disadvantages or 'political clientelism' as it relates to the Greek context?
3   In what ways does the Sports Law hinder the development of sport in Greece?
4   What additional process can be put in place in the relationships between professional and amateur clubs in PAOK, which would benefit all involved?
5   In what ways can Greek sport be funded in the future which would move away from the reliance on state funding?

Further reading

Dimitropoulos, P. (2010). The financial performance of Greek football clubs. *Choregia – Sport Management International Journal,* 6(1), 5–27.
Kamberidou, I. & Patsadaras, N (2007). A new concept in European sport governance. *Biology of Exercise,* 3, 21–34.

Papadimitriou, D. (2007). Conceptualizing effectiveness in a non-profit organisational environment. *International Journal of Public Sector Management,* 20(7), 571–87

Papadimitriou, D. (2002). Amateur structures and their effects on performance: the case of Greek voluntary clubs. *Managing Leisure,* 7, 205–19

Siekmann, R & Soek, J. (2010). Models of sport governance in the European Union. *The International Sports Law Journal,* 3(4), 93–102.

Websites

ekathimerini.com Sport News: http://www.ekathimerini.com/ekathi/sports

Panthesalonikian Athletic Club Konstantinoupolis: http://www.paokfc.gr/

General Secretariat of Sport: http://www.sportsnet.gr/

References

Anagnostopoulos, C. (2011). Stakeholder management in Greek professional sport: Identification and salience. *Soccer & Society,* 12(2), 249–64.

Greek General Secretariat of Sport (n.d.-a) Greek General Secretiat of Sport. Available online at http://www.sportsnet.gr/

Greek General Secretariat of Sport (n.d.-b) 'Sports federations' Available online at http://www.gga.gov.gr/index.php/epopteyomenoi-foreis/omospondies

Greek General Secretariat of Sport (n.d.-c) 'Sport for all' Available online at http://www.gga.gov.gr/index.php/athlitismos/athlhsh-gia-olous

Grohmann, K. (2012). *From heaven to hell: Greek sport in freefall.* Ekathimerini. 6 February. Available on line at http://www.ekathimerini.com/4dcgi/_w_articles_wsite5_1_06/02/2012_426290.

Harahousou, Y. & Kabitsis, C. (2002). Greece: Sport for all as a government commitment. In L. DaCosta & A. Miragaya (eds) *Worldwide experiences and trends in sport for all.* Oxford: Meyer & Meyer Sport

Henry, I. & Nassis P. (1999), Political clientelism and sports policy in Greece. *International Review for the Sociology of Sport,* 34, 43–58.

Maguire, K. (2102). Greek basketball league crumbling amid country's financial crisis. SI.com., 12 April. Available online at http://sportsillustrated.cnn.com/2012/writers/the_bonus/04/12/greek.league/index.html.

Margaritis, K. (2012a). Greek sports law: Sport and the state – Part 1. *Sports Law and Business.* Available online at http://www.lawinsport.com/articles/regulation-a-governance/item/greek-sports-law-sport-and-the-state-part-1.

Margaritis, K. (2012b). Greek sports law: Professional sport – Part 2. *Sports Law and Business.* Available online at http://www.lawinsport.com/articles/regulation-a-governance/item/greek-sports-law-professional-sport-part-2.

Panagiotopoulos, D. (1995). The institutional problem of the Greek Sport Federation: Structure organization and legal function. *Marquette Sports Law Review,* 5(2) Spring, 243–50.

Papadimitriou, D. & Taylor, P. (2000). Organisational effectiveness of Hellenic National Sporting Organisations. *Sport Management Review,* 3, 23–46.

Sakka, S. & Chatzigianni, E. (2012). Europeanizing the social aspects of the Greek Sport Policy. *Journal of Sport and Social Issues,* 36, 195–222.

Sanburn, J. (2012). Was it worth it? Debt-ridden Greeks question the cost of the 2004 Olympics. *Time.* Available online at http://olympics.time.com/2012/07/09/

amid-economic-turmoil-some-greeks-look-back-at-2004-olympics-as-losing-proposition/?iid=tsmodule.

Smith, H.(2012). Athens 2004 Olympics: What happened after the athletes went home. *The Guardian*. 9 May. Retrieved from http://www.guardian.co.uk/sport/2012/may/09/athens-2004-olympics-athletes-home?INTCMP=SRCH

Stergioulas, A. & Triploitsioti, A. (2007). Sport organization for the disabled in Greece. *Choregia – Sport Management International Journal*. 3(2), 49–55.

Turnbull, S. (2012). The last word: The Greeks must go to the Games even if they are not very likely lads. *The Independent,* 8 April. Available online at http://www.independent.co.uk/sport/olympics/the-last-word-the-greeks-must-go-to-the-games-even-if-theyre-not-very-likely-lads-7626943.html.

13 Ireland

Ryan Feeney, Ian O'Boyle and Paul Cummins

Topics

- Governance complexities
- The Gaelic Athletic Association (GAA)
- Modernisation
- Strategy and governance
- Financial governance.

Objectives

- To examine the governance structure within the GAA
- To analyse the relationship between governance and funding
- To understand the development of the Ulster GAA within Ireland
- To demonstrate who are the major actors within sport in Northern Ireland
- To understand the emerging challenges facing the GAA in Ireland.

Key terms

Modernisation   The evolution of an organisation from a volunteer-led entity to a more professional approach.

Provincial councils   Regional bodies within the GAA made up of a number of county representations.

Central Council   Consists of all the provincial and central directors reporting to the Director General.

GAA Annual Congress   The GAA Congress is the main policy setting forum of the GAA consisting of GAA representatives from all aspects of the organisation.

Overview

This chapter will review the changing role, structure and governance procedures of Ulster GAA – one of the Provincial councils within the Gaelic Athletic Association in Ireland. This includes an overview of the entire GAA structure, focusing on the governance structure within the organisation. The chapter will highlight the significant change the Ulster GAA has undertaken over the past decade and outline its now significant links with government.

> Nobody could have designed the coalition that is the GAA (Gaelic Athletic Association); it brings together, in a common purpose, so many shades of opinion, so many 'states of mind', so many different political, social and cultural perspectives, such a combination of radicalism and conservatism, of urban and rural, some might even say of the urban and the ingenuous, that, theoretically, it should not survive never mind thrive. But that is its strength; it tolerates – it even cherishes – diversity and it succeeds, not in spite of that but because of that.
>
> (Peter Quinn (GAA President 1991–1994), 2002)

The Gaelic Athletic Association

The Gaelic Athletic Association (GAA) is Ireland's largest sporting, cultural and community organisation. Founded in 1884, the Association has grown to have over one million members representing 1,650 clubs.

The vision of the GAA as defined in its *Strategic Action Plan and Vision Plan 2009–2015* is 'that everybody has the opportunity to be welcomed to take part in our games and culture, to participate fully, to grow and develop and to be inspired to keep a lifelong engagement with our Association' (GAA, 2008a, p.15).The aims of the GAA are:

a.   The strengthening of the national identity of a 32-county Ireland through the preservation and promotion of Gaelic games and pastimes.
b.   The Association shall actively support the Irish language, traditional Irish dancing, music, song, and other aspects of Irish culture. It shall foster awareness and love of the national ideas in the people of Ireland, and assist in promoting a community spirit through its clubs.
c.   The Association shall promote its aims amongst communities abroad through its overseas units.
d.   The Association shall support the promotion of Camogie and Ladies' Gaelic Football.
e.   The Association shall support Irish industry. All trophies and playing equipment shall be of Irish manufacture. Penalty for non-observance is €200. Irish paper shall be used for all official documents and correspondence. Documents not complying shall be ruled out of order.

The GAA promotes the following sports:

- Gaelic Football
- Hurling
- Handball
- Rounders.

The Association at central level also has strong links with the Ladies' Gaelic Football Association and the Camogie Association which govern the female versions of both Gaelic Football and Hurling.

The GAA's mission as outlined in its most recent strategic plan is:

The GAA is a community-based volunteer organisation promoting Gaelic games, culture and lifelong participation. The GAA is a volunteer organisation. We develop and promote Gaelic games at the core of Irish identity and culture. We are dedicated to ensuring that our family of games, and the values we live, enrich the lives of our members, families and communities we serve. We are committed to active, lifelong participation for all, and to providing the best facilities. We reach out to and include all members of our society. We promote individual development and well-being, and strive to enable all our members achieve their full potential in their chosen roles.

(GAA, 2009, p.15)

Values are very important in the GAA; the organisation operates almost completely on a voluntary and amateur basis, and while the GAA has a small number of professional staff, its members and players participate in the association's activities without financial reward. GAA Director General, Paraic Duffy, highlights the importance of values:

Each of the one million GAA volunteer members are 'owners' of the GAA. These members carry out the work of the Association on a voluntary and democratic basis. As such, the executive staff and leadership of the Association have a responsibility to adhere to a clear set of values and principles.

(Duffy 2011)

The issue of values also applies to volunteer members and in some cases there are reports of members breaching the rules and values of the GAA with individuals receiving illegal payments to coach and manage teams. This is against the rules of the GAA and something which the leadership is strongly against.

GAA structure and governance

The GAA's governance structure is unique and comprises the following democratic units:

- Clubs (1,650)
- County committees (32)
- Provincial councils (5)
- Central council (1)
- Annual congress.

One of the key elements of the GAA is that the association's structures are hugely energised by place and attachment to that place. In the vast majority of cases, a club catchment area will be based on the Roman Catholic parish area, with the English applied county model serving as the basis for catchment areas for county committees, and the four provinces of Ireland serving as the catchment areas for the provincial councils.

The GAA club

The club is the basic unit of the association and organises GAA games and activities on a local level. Membership of the GAA is operated through the club structure, and so you cannot be a GAA member unless you are member of a GAA club. Each club elects its management committee at the annual AGM. The makeup of management committees may vary, however, officers usually include chairperson, vice-chairperson, secretary, treasurer, public relations officer, cultural officer, children's officer, youth officer, coaching officer, players' representative, delegate to county committee, and no more than five committee members without portfolio. The delegate to county committee speaks and votes for the club on the county committee, and it is good practice that the club chairperson also holds the role of delegate to the county committee (although this is not mandatory).

The GAA county committee

A county committee is a geographic region of control in the GAA based on the relevant county of Ireland. The county committee is responsible for organising GAA club fixtures, the promotion of GAA games and activities at county level, including the management and organisation of county teams. The county committee elects officers to be members of a county management committee, which has executive responsibility for the governance of the GAA in the county.

Officers of a county committee who are elected at the annual county convention include chairperson, vice chairperson, secretary (full-time official non-voting), treasurer, public relations officer, delegate to the GAA central council, two delegates to the provincial council, coaching officer, development officer, and youth Officer. The management committee meets on a monthly basis, can take decisions on day-to-day issues, and make recommendations on major decisions to the larger county committee (with representatives of each of the county's clubs) which usually meets on a bi-monthly basis.

In most cases the county secretary is a full time post, appointed by the county committee, who operates as a defacto chief executive officer for the GAA in the county. The county secretary is responsible to both the county committee and has a broken line of responsibility to the director of the relevant provincial council.

Provincial councils

Provincial councils are organisational regional bodies within the GAA and are comprised of several GAA county committees. The provincial council is responsible for the organisation of club and inter-county competitions, and the promotion of

GAA games and activities within their region. There are five provincial councils: Connacht, Leinster, Munster, Ulster and Britain. The European county committee is also aiming to become a full provincial council in due course.

The core functions of a provincial council are:

- Management of inter-county and club championship fixtures programmes
- Coaching and games development
- Club and community development
- Educational sector development
- Training of volunteer county and club officials
- Development of physical projects to enhance the Gaelic games
- Public affairs (only relevant to the Ulster Council).

(Quinn, 2002, p.245)

Each provincial council comprises two county committee delegates, delegates from the GAA education sectors (primary, two at secondary level and tertiary level), and delegates from ladies' Gaelic football, camogie, handball and rounders. A provincial management committee oversees the day-to-day affairs of a provincial council, and comprises the following officers elected at the provincial convention: chairperson, vice chairperson, provincial director and secretary (full-time post non-voting), treasurer, and public relations officer. The president can also appoint three more members of the council as voting members of the management committee. The provincial director is the chief executive and accounting officer of the council, and also acts as a member of the GAA central executive committee.

Central council

The central executive committee consists of all the provincial and central directors reporting to the director general, who is the chief executive of the overall GAA. Between annual congresses, responsibility for the ongoing operation and development of the GAA is vested in the central council. The main role of the central council is to oversee the implementation of policy on behalf of the members, provide leadership and direction to the association, direct operations, manage and develop resources, and facilitate communications with provincial councils, county committees, and clubs. Day-to-day responsibility for the running of the GAA is delegated to a management committee chaired by the president (who is elected for a three-year term at congress and acts in the same role as non-executive chairman). The management committee also serves in the same role as a board of directors in a public company overseeing the work of the association and with central council setting policy. On a day-to-day basis the president oversees the work of the director general, who is the chief executive of the association.

Each county committee (in Ireland and overseas) has a voting delegate on the central council, in addition to the GAA educational sector (primary, two at secondary level and tertiary level). Members of the management committee of the GAA also sit as members of central council.

Each provincial chairperson sits as an ex-officio member of the central council management committee, which also consists of the president (who is chair), director general (non-voting), two representatives of congress (elected for a three-year term), four members of the central council representing each province, and two members of the GAA appointed by the president.

The central council has a range of sub-committees to develop GAA policy and oversee initiatives. The chairperson, secretary and members of each sub-committee are appointed by the president subject to ratification by the central council.

As chief executive of the GAA, the director general is responsible to the GAA management committee and central council, and oversees the work of the staff of the GAA as directed by an executive committee (senior management team of the association). The executive committee of the GAA includes the director general (chair), director of finance, director of games, marketing and commercial director, director of communications, Croke Park Stadium director, Ulster provincial director, Munster provincial director, Leinster provincial director, and Connacht provincial director. Consideration was given to appointing two additional directors namely an operations director to support the role of the director general and director of strategic development to oversee the ongoing strategic agenda within the Association. It was decided following the appointment of Paraic Duffy as director general to redefine the operations director role to an operations manager who acts as a direct assistant to the director general, dealing with day-to-day association issues. The strategic director appointment was not made due the current economic situation however it is a post that the GAA plan to proceed with in the near future.

Annual GAA congress

The GAA congress is the main policy-setting forum of the GAA. The functions of Congress are:

- Report to members on the stewardship of the association during the preceding twelve months.
- Election of a president of the association every three years.
- A forum for debate on the issues affecting the association which should inform central council in its decisions on strategic issues.
- Determination of policy for the association in relation to specified reserved rights, such as:
  - The strategic direction and role of the association including its ethos – especially its voluntary ethos.
  - The structure and administration of the games.
  - Playing rules.

(Quinn, 2002, p.245)

Case Study: The Ulster Council of the Gaelic Athletic Association

> The Ulster Council is the most progressive, well-organised unit of the GAA, and it has introduced the culture of strategic planning to the overall Association.
>
> (Paraic Duffy, 2011)

The Ulster Council is the second largest provincial council in the GAA, and it consists of nine counties: Armagh, Antrim, Derry, Donegal, Down, Cavan, Fermanagh, Monaghan and Tyrone. The Ulster Council is unique as it is the only provincial council in Ireland which operates in both the northern and southern government jurisdictions, and is recognised as the official governing body for Gaelic games in Northern Ireland.

> The GAA in Ulster is both deep-rooted and robust. Nine counties, over 550 clubs, 90,000 active players, 250,000 members, and match attendances of up to 70,000 at a time contribute to the Association's breadth, depth, and strength. Whilst Gaelic games underpin the GAA, it has parallel interests in culture, heritage, community development and community well-being.
>
> (Ulster GAA, 2006, p.5)

The council was founded in 1903 in Armagh, and has grown into the most progressive governing body of sport in Northern Ireland according to Professor Eamonn McCartan, chief executive of Sport NI: 'The Ulster Council is one of, if not the best governed and most forward-thinking governing body of sport' (McCartan 2009).

Modernisation: From the kitchen table to the boardroom

Modernisation of the Ulster GAA coincided with the restoration of devolution, the resurrection of the Northern Ireland Executive and Assembly, and the election of a new president and management committee of the Ulster Council on a three-year term. Tom Daly who had served as both vice president and treasurer was elected Chairman in 2007. Daly is from a professional background and is employed by the Health Service Executive as a senior manager. Daly has extensive experience in corporate governance and public affairs and was able to put this experience to good use during the review of the modernisation process.

A review concluded that the modernisation process had presented Ulster GAA with several problems but, in general, had been successful. The introduction of new staff had assisted in raising the overall capacity of the GAA in Ulster. As the funding for the posts was to cease in March 2009, there was also a need to review the expected decrease in government funding, and highlight what the future needs of the council would be up until 2014.

The management committee established a working group to develop a proposal on how the council would move forward after 2009. The group presented its findings in September 2007 in a document titled *The next steps: Moving forward with modernisation,* and outlined the steps that the council needed to take to ensure it could build on the success of the first phase of modernisation; it needed a clear plan on how to sustain an appropriate level of investment from government.

What was clear was that Ulster GAA had become dependent on a sizable number of staff in order to deliver its objectives. As such, the 2007 document suggested that in late 2008, the council should commence developing a third strategic plan, which would be completed in March 2009. In the interim, the council should lobby all areas of government in order to secure the necessary revenue funding required to sustain a suitable and appropriate staff structure. It was also suggested that the Ulster Council core-fund some posts, and seek funding from central council for others (Ulster GAA, 2007).

Finally, it was highlighted that there would be no ring-fenced government capital funding for specific GAA projects, and so it was suggested that specific projects be identified for capital funding, brought up to an appropriate state of readiness to secure government funding from Sport NI capital projects. A new senior staff post would be established to coordinate the lobbying and oversee the development of the new strategic plan.

It was also agreed that the capacity building and diversity initiatives for which the integration officers had responsibility would be merged into the new senior staff role. The role of community development and public affairs manager were also established, as following an internal trawl, one of the integration officers was promoted to the new post.

The third Ulster GAA strategy outlined a new staff structure which would be affordable and appropriate, incorporating all the areas of responsibility of Ulster GAA. The strategy, which was for a six-year period from 2009–2015, envisaged a new structure with five departments:

- Provincial director's office: The provincial director's office is responsible for the administration of the office of the provincial director, coordination of the day-to-day operations of Ulster GAA, fixtures, event coordination, information communications, child protection, ICT, and general administrative support.
- Coaching and games development: The coaching and games development staff are responsible for the development of all Gaelic games. This includes implementation of strategies to increase overall participation, hurling development, football development, ladies Gaelic football development, camogie development, handball development and rounders development. Continuing professional development of coaches and players, regional development, disability games, third-level development, high performance, referee development, staff development, primary schools project management, and coach education and development.
- Community development and public affairs: The community development and public affairs department is responsible for club and community development, volunteer development, strategic development, public affairs and communications, health and wellbeing, community outreach and

diversity initiatives, urban project development, culture and heritage, and the administration of the GAA's 125th anniversary celebrations.

- Operations and infrastructure: The operations staff are responsible for overseeing infrastructure programmes, project management of Ulster Council capital projects, health, safety and compliance issues, commercial activities and marketing and match event control.
- Finance and business development: The finance and business development staff are responsible for the financial control and compliance of the Ulster Council, including financial-planning, budgets, business-planning, human resources and general administration department or section would have a lead officer as 'head of section'. The director of coaching and games was already head of the coaching and games department, and three new internal appointments would be made for a head of community development and public affairs, head of operations and infrastructure, and head of finance, HR and business development. The provincial director and each of the heads of section would together form the new senior staff (senior management team). The hurling development manager, football development manager, and the new posts of coaching development manager and health and wellbeing manager would form a middle management team to assist senior staff with their work. The annual cost of this staff structure amounts to approximately €1.8 million.

Following a long and sometimes difficult process of lobbying, the Ulster Council secured a cocktail of funding from Sport NI, central council, and its own resources sufficient to progress the new structure. The strategy was also successful in securing funding from the Department of Education (DENI) for an additional 32 coaching staff, who would focus on promoting the games at primary school level. This was a clear endorsement of the modernisation process and strategic planning of Ulster GAA, as it was the Department of Education which approached the Ulster GAA to request a partnership.

The Department of Social Development also invested by employing two new staff for the newly established community development and public affairs department. One of these new officers would focus on capacity building and diversity work, and the other on volunteer and strategic development.

The establishment of both the community development and public affairs and the finance and business planning departments highlight the changing remit, and thereby the changing governance procedures and structures, of Ulster GAA.

The constantly increasing revenue stream of Ulster GAA from public funds and commercial revenue resulted in an organisation with a turnover of approximately £8 million per year. It was no longer viable or appropriate for a volunteer finance committee led by a volunteer treasurer to handle the finances of the organisation. Ulster GAA took the decision in 2004 to appoint a full time finance officer to handle the day to day finances of the association.

However, following a series of meetings with the Department of Culture, Arts and Leisure and Sport NI, both bodies agreed to fund a full-time business development manager with responsibility for finance, business development and human resources, and the Ulster GAA decided that it was necessary for the holder of this post to be a chartered accountant.

The Ulster GAA also made changes to the operations of its financial governance, giving the provincial director/secretary the role of chief accounting officer, who has direct responsibility for the finance and business development manager. Both staff members report to the volunteer finance committee and the management committee on the financial affairs of Ulster GAA on a monthly basis. A finance administrator was also appointed in 2007 to support the role of finance and business development manager.

By 2008, Ulster GAA was receiving funding from the following government Departments:

- Department of Culture, Arts and Leisure (DCAL)
- Sport NI
- Department of Social Development
- Department of Foreign Affairs
- Department of Education.

The appointment of the new finance staff was a success as Ulster GAA achieved the highest level of audit assurance from DCAL in 2008 and unqualified audited accounts since 2006. Ulster GAA received the largest allocation of £565,298 from the Sport NI Performance Investment programme, which will secure 11 jobs in the Association for the future.

Case study conclusion

Due to the involvement and funding of government, the role and remit of Ulster GAA has significantly changed. This has been one of the results of the expansion of the role of the sporting sector.

The structure and remit of the organisation has evolved rapidly over the last decade. From the early 1980s, Ulster GAA has had some kind of government funding input, although the funding allocation until 1998 focused on the employment of one post, a hurling development officer, and some support for coach education. The requirements for this funding were limited, not strategic, and involved the submission of a simple application every three years.

In 2004, the Ulster Council recruited 24 staff in the space of four months; this was a 500 per cent increase in staffing in Ulster GAA, which put massive pressure on the internal structures. It required an almost immediate change in organisational culture. A range of issues arose, ranging from structural problems, human resources capacity, office accommodation, and the role of the new staff in contrast to the role of the volunteer. The management committee and the provincial director made a sensible decision when it was agreed to appoint the business development manager first so that the financial and HR requirements would be in place before the majority of the new staff commenced employment. Ulster GAA also employed a project manager to oversee the facilities modernisation process and to assist with the recruitment process. This role evolved into the operations and infrastructure role.

Modernisation in the Ulster GAA

Modernisation has been a relatively positive experience for Ulster GAA, as the profile and public perception of the organisation has increased significantly and participation figures in the six Gaelic games have enjoyed a substantial increase.

The council also took some very wise decisions regarding the outworking of the modernisation process, having the foresight to realise that an increase in participation at all levels would require an increase in the association's capacity in terms of governance, volunteer input, facilities and finance. A range of non-games-related programmes have been developed in this area and have proved successful.

It is clear that, after many years of significant change in Ulster GAA, a new, permanent and sustainable staff structure is now in place. Despite initial issues arising between the volunteer members and the staff, clear and agreed protocols have allowed both sets of personnel to work together.

As already stated, modernisation has seen a significant increase in the remit of Ulster GAA. The GAA charter highlights that the primary role of the association is to promote Gaelic games, with a secondary aim to promote Irish culture. While the council still undertakes both these roles, it has increased its operations to include health and wellbeing, community development, and diversity programmes. While some criticism has been levelled at Ulster GAA that these are areas outside the sphere of responsibility for the association, it is clear that they have complemented the primary participation and culture aims thereof. By promoting strong capacity building programmes, the majority of clubs and county committees can cope with the significant increase in the playing membership. Additionally, Ulster GAA's work in these areas has been so successful that Sport NI uses the programmes as examples of best practice, and the GAA at central level has taken the programmes in order to roll them out across the entire association. Ulster GAA's governance systems are also very strong, with Sport NI again highlighting the Ulster Council as a role model for other governing bodies of sport.

Summary

Traditionalists would argue that Ulster GAA has become too large and that in some cases it has exceeded the normal remit of a provincial council of the GAA. Further criticism would include the view that the employment of staff is discouraging personnel from becoming active GAA volunteers and that in some cases the governance requirements of Ulster GAA are putting additional pressure on club and county committee volunteers.

However, research commissioned by the GAA at central level to assist the association in the development of its new branding guidelines showed that Ulster GAA had a very positive standing among club members in Ulster. The research highlighted the supporting role that the provincial council had with clubs and the positive profile that Ulster GAA enjoys (GAA, 2008a, p5).

One issue that may continue to cause significant problems for the GAA is that the professional outlook and remit of the association is causing problems with the amateur ethos of the organisation. All players, managers, coaches and officials (apart from the full-time coaching staff and administrators) are volunteers, and the continued increase in coaching resources and techniques has at times encouraged a professional standard of training and high performance with county-level players.

An indirect result of this has been the establishment of a Gaelic Players Association (GPA), formed in 1999. This association focuses on the needs of elite players, and suggests that the 1,800 county players should receive preferential treatment and funding over club-level players and grass-root GAA members. While it claims not to seek a change from the GAA's amateur status to professionalism, its motives thus far have clearly indicated that a professional GAA at county level is its final goal. At the time of writing, the GPA is seeking recognition and substantial finances from the GAA, along with an annual 5 per cent of the GAA income, which amounts to around €2.5 million.

The vast majority of GAA members are content with the current volunteer ethos of the GAA, and GPA's aims are seen by many as directly conflicting with the aims and values of the association. Clearly, if the GAA moves to a professional model, it will be unable to sustain any of its participation, health, or community programmes, and the contribution that the association makes to the provision of social capital on the island of Ireland will eventually disappear. This view can be supported when reviewing the progress of Irish rugby which became a professional sport in the early part of this decade, club rugby, participation and grassroots development has been severely affected with entire focus of the sporting body shifting to funding and supporting the elite.

Review questions

1   Describe the structure of governance that operates within the GAA from the club level up to annual congress.
2   Discuss the various sources of funding that the Ulster GAA receives and how modernisation played a key role in the current structure of the organisation.
3   Discuss the current challenges facing the GAA in relation to a call for the game to turn professional.

Further reading

Bairner, A. (2004). Creating a soccer strategy for Northern Ireland: Reflections on football governance in small European countries. *Soccer & Society*, 5(1), 27–42.

Cronin, M. (1999). *Sport and nationalism in Ireland: Gaelic games, soccer and Irish identity since 1884.* Dublin: Four Courts.

Hassan, D. (2010). Governance and the Gaelic Athletic Association: Time to move beyond the amateur ideal? *Soccer & Society,* 11(4), 414–27.

Websites

Gaelic Athletic Association: http://www.gaa.ie/
The Irish Sports Council: http://www.irishsportscouncil.ie/
Ulster Gaelic Athletic Association: http://www.ulster.gaa.ie

References

Duffy, P. (2009) Personal communication, Dublin 5 August.
Duffy, P. (2011). Personal communication, Dublin, 15 July.
GAA (2008a). *Strategic action and vision 2009–2015*. Dublin: GAA Press.
GAA (2008b). *The brand union: GAA identity and perception report*. Dublin: GAA Press.
GAA (2009). *Official guide: Rules and regulations*. Dublin: GAA Press.
McCartan, E. (2009) Personal communication, Belfast, 10 August.
Quinn, P. (ed.) (2002). *Enhancing community identity: GAA strategic review*. Dublin: GAA Press.
Ulster GAA (2006). *Beir Bua Nua Ulster Council GAA Strategy 2006–2010*. Belfast: Ulster GAA.
Ulster GAA (2007). *Moving forward with modernisation: Review document*. Belfast: Ulster GAA.

14 Cyprus

Mary Charalambous-Papamiltiades

Topics

- Historical background of the Cyprus sport system
- Sport policy and the supreme sport authority
- Governance problems associated with sport and football
- The role of volunteers
- Political intervention.

Objectives

- To provide a broad overview of the sport system in Cyprus
- To describe the structure of sport in Cyprus
- To highlight the main governance practices associated with sport
- To present the main sport governance problems
- To recommend several actions for improving governance practices.

Key terms

Sport governance structure   The principles used by sport organisations when setting policies and management procedures.

Board–management relationships   The relationships and communication between board members and staff.

Sport volunteerism   The action of choosing to serve a sport organisation on a voluntary basis; that is, giving time, effort and talent to a sport organisation without profiting monetarily.

Accountability and responsibility   The acknowledgment and assumption of responsibility for actions, decisions and policies.

Independence   Decisions and actions free from dependence, interference, control and direction.

Overview

This chapter contains a general overview of the development of the sport sector in Cyprus and focuses on the role of the Cyprus Sport Organisation (CSO), which is the umbrella organisation under which all national federations and associations operate. Special emphasis will be given to the sport governance problems that the sport system in Cyprus experiences. Issues identified involve board–employee relationships, independence, accountability and audit, fairness and democracy in elections and appointments, board roles and responsibilities, performance measurement, solidarity, transparency and communication.

The sport sector

The prominent role of sport in the cultural life of Cyprus is not a recent phenomenon. There is much archaeological evidence, such as the gymnasium of Salamis and the stadium of Curium, demonstrating that athletics played an important role in ancient Cyprus (CSO, 1986). By 1900, several gymnastic and athletics clubs were founded initiating sport development in Cyprus as well as sporting events and competitions. At about the same time, team sport was organised in a more formal way, through the establishment of sport regulatory bodies (CSO, 1986).

Although there are no records on the sports gross domestic product (GDP), according to the last Census of Establishments conducted by the Department of Research and Statistics of the Republic of Cyprus in 2010, there are 503 sport enterprises operating in Cyprus. Most of them are small, employing only one person, while three are mid-sized employing 50 to 249 employees. Only the Cyprus Sport Organisation employs more than 249 staff. Moreover, there are 132 sport clubs and 205 fitness centres, a number that is regarded as large considering the size of the Cyprus.

Sport policy

State intervention into sport development began in the nineteenth century through sport and physical education programmes introduced in the school curriculum. The political situation, however, and the independence Cyprus achieved in 1960, led to a stronger and more systematic approach to the development of sport in the country. State intervention continues to influence sport today. Although there is not a council or ministry devoted to sport, the development of sport policies is carried out through the CSO, which is under the umbrella of the Ministry of Education and Culture.

Cyprus Sport Organisation: the supreme sport authority

The Cyprus Sport Organisation was established in 1969 as a non-profit, semi-governmental organisation acting as the supreme authority in the Republic of Cyprus, responsible for the development of sport. Since then, every athletic and developmental activity comes under the jurisdiction of the CSO (CSO, 2004). The organisation is governed by a board of administration, whose members are appointed by the president of the Republic of Cyprus. This practice has traditionally generated concerns since the main criterion used for the appointment of the members is their political orientation. This factor, combined with the fact that the members are acting on a voluntary basis, are regarded as sources of the major problems that the organisation is faced with. The CSO is often used by the board members as a means to serve political interests. This, and the political dimensions and implications of their decisions, are major issues which generate much criticism. Transparency of decision making in the whole sport system is a major concern today (Kartakoullis, 2008). Moreover, voluntary involvement of the members usually indicates a lack of time (Charalambous-Papamiltiades, 2006) as most of the members have their own profession or business where they devote the majority of their time. Many of them lack the qualifications necessary for effective governance. Some of the board members are former athletes or former coaches who, although they have competed successfully in the field, have no educational background in the management of sport organisations, something that impacts upon the efficiency and effectiveness of the CSO.

Some additional problems that the CSO is faced with concern the relationship between executives and professionals, and primarily involve communication difficulties, trust problems, and a power struggle that leads to conflict and ineffective performance (Charalambous-Papamiltiades, 2006). This is in line with international research examining the governance of voluntary sport organisations (Hoye & Cuskelly, 2003; Kikulis, Slack, Hinings & Zimmerman, 1989; Searle, 1989).

Despite the problems and difficulties that the CSO has been experiencing, sport policy initiatives undertaken are noteworthy. These include the establishment of national federations, sport development through the construction of several stadia, sport halls for indoor events, swimming pools and other facilities, provision of grants and subsidies to sport associations, clubs and other athletic bodies, promotion of its international relationships, and introduction of schemes covering the needs of athletes after they retire from high level sport (CSO, 2004). At the same time, and according to CSO, mass sport continues to be a priority. The main platform for promoting mass sport is the 'Sports for All' programme aimed at the adoption of a healthy lifestyle for people of all ages. Although the CSO deserves credit for the development of mass sport programmes, it is noteworthy that its overall financial policy does not depict the alleged emphasis on mass sport. According to the Mass Sports Department, only €1,782,000 was devoted to the 'Sports for All' Programme in 2008 whereas during the same year competitive sport enjoyed financial support of €15,846,954.

Competitive sport development: Cyprus Olympic Committee, sport federations and clubs

The CSO has traditionally demonstrated an overwhelming commitment to the development of competitive sport. The government subsidy granted to sport clubs and federations in 2009 was €11,377,000 (CSO, 2009) and in 2008, the subsidy for competitive sport was €9,858,630 (CSO, 2008) but, according to internal financial data, the total support granted to competitive sport reached €15,846,954. The biggest part of this financial support, €5,561,391, was absorbed by the most popular sport in Cyprus, football. The remaining amount was utilised by the 52 sport federations that regulate competitive sport in Cyprus.

Another sport body responsible for competitive sport is the Cyprus Olympic Committee (COC), which was founded in 1974 and became a member of the International Olympic Committee in 1978. The COC is the main body responsible for athletic representation at the Olympic Games. Among the basic objectives of the COC is encouraging interest in the Olympic Games, fostering the aims and ideals of the Olympic movement, observing and enforcing the rules as laid down in the Olympic Charter, and organising, together with the respective national federations, the preparation and selection of athletes for the Games.

The role of volunteers

In line with the broader sport context, the executive board of the COC and the boards of the national sport federations are volunteer-driven. The boards of these organisations are not appointed but elected through a voting procedure. A study examining the administration and management roles and activities of sport organisations in Cyprus revealed that the sport system relies heavily, if not exclusively, on volunteers (Charalambous-Papamiltiades, 2006). The study focused on 'policy volunteers' (Inglis, 1997) or 'leadership volunteers' (Ridley & Barr, 2006), who primarily form the decision-making bodies and are responsible for setting strategic initiatives and policies of sport organisations.

The results indicated that 97 per cent of the decision-making positions of the federations (executive boards, committees and sub committees) are held by volunteers. Another issue that deserves consideration is the fact that the vast majority (88 per cent) of these volunteers are male. With regard to board volunteers, the dominance of the male volunteer is even bigger, reaching 93 per cent, illustrating the strong male-dominated sport culture that exists in Cyprus. This culture corresponds to the broader picture of the Cyprus sport sector, as female sports are clearly downgraded, not just in terms of participation and performance, but also in terms of investment and allocation of resources.

As the policy volunteer represents 97 per cent of the members of the decision-making bodies, then the remaining 3 per cent represents the professionals whose role is to assist and are therefore not central in the administration and management of sport organisations. Only 35 per cent of Olympic sport federations employ at least one professional, while the majority (65 per cent) rely solely on volunteers (Charalambous-Papamiltiades, 2006). Lack of professionalism and reliance on voluntary work, however, are regarded as the main factors contributing to management deficiencies and poor governance of sport organisations, which in turn is considered as the most severe problem for sport governing bodies.

The management deficiencies may result from a lack of sport-management knowledge or from a lack of interest in the healthy growth of sport organisations, as the motives behind involvement in these highly prestigious positions is questioned. Many of these volunteers may be driven by factors other than an altruistic, sheer interest in the sport itself. Research to date (Cuskelly & Harrington, 1997; Inglis, 1994; Kikulis, 1990; Shilbi, Taylor, Nichols, Gratton, & Kokolakakis, 1999) indicates that people are particularly drawn to volunteering for sport executive committees for egoistic reasons, such as the development of personal and professional growth, future professional opportunities, image enhancement, social recognition and social relations. Research examining board member motivation revealed that 'people will maintain their involvement so long as they see their needs being met and the costs of involvement (e.g. time, money, effort), is not in excess of the benefits' (Searle, 1989, p.363).

Whatever the motives of volunteers may be, the central role of policy volunteers in Cyprus is accompanied by several problems and conflicts at the decision-making level, which results in poor management and ineffective governance of sport organisations. Reliance on volunteerism acts as an obstacle to the professionalism of sport in the country and raises several corporate governance concerns. The lack of educational and professional backgrounds of volunteers holding key management positions, cultural and conceptual differences between professionals and volunteers, undefined roles and responsibilities, and communication difficulties result in dire relations with professionals that hamper effective management (Charalambous-Papamiltiades, 2006).

Football in Cyprus

Although amateurism characterises the overall sport industry, the only sport that is escaping this reality is football. Football is the only sport in Cyprus that is regarded as professional. There are 16,000 registered youth players in academies all over the island and the football industry in financial terms during the 2004–2005 period was calculated to be worth €223,826,788, which represents 1.84 per cent of the gross domestic product (Kartakoullis & Theophanous, 2007). The football industry provides employment to 10,200 people, which represents 3.3 per cent of the country's workforce (Kartakoullis & Theophanous, 2007).

The initial stages: the role of politics in the development of football

Football was introduced to Cyprus early in the twentieth century when the island was a British colony. British immigrants played a pioneering role in the development and spread of football, which seems to have been introduced in the English school system. Evidence indicates that the first football match was held between the British and Cypriots in 1900 (Peristianis, Kapardis, Loizou, Fakiolas, & Puloukas, 2002). The sport proved hugely popular and a number of clubs were duly formed.

The first clubs founded were initially cultural clubs and contributed to the development of ethnic consciousness and the national struggle, which culminated in the 1955 anti-colonialist uprising. The ideological goal of this struggle was the political unification with Greece, and football clubs established at that time were considered as sport departments of those cultural clubs. The first football club formed was ANORTHOSIS (Ammohostou) in 1911 and, based on the same platform, APOEL (Nicosia) was founded in 1926, followed by AEL (Limassol) in 1930. The need for an official regulatory body emerged that resulted in the creation of the Cyprus Football Association in 1934 and subsequently the establishment of official football leagues. The top-tier football league competition is the Cypriot Championship – First Division, presently comprising 14 clubs. The second most important football competition is the Cypriot Cup which began in 1934. Football competitions are growing in popularity every year and attract overwhelming spectator support.

The history of Cyprus football has been marked by the civil war in Greece (late 1940s) between the nationalists and the communists, which had a great impact on all domains of life on the island, including sport. The political situation has given football political dimensions, which in turn has resulted in the segregation of football clubs into left and right, according to political parties (Charalambous-Papamiltiades, 2011).

The politicisation of football is further illustrated in the anti-colonialist uprising of Cypriots in 1955 with many athletes having an active role in the struggle against the British. Cyprus became an independent state in 1960, however the politicisation of football has continued to this present day.

Challenges for the football industry

The politicisation of football is still part of the fans' culture and it is expressed in the several political slogans that the rival teams' fans exchange in the field. In recent years the politicisation of football is weakening, possibly due to the diminution of ideological differences between right and left. Conversely, localisation is replacing the dominant role of politics in the fans' culture (Peristianis *et al.*, 2002). The main result associated with localisation and politicisation of football is violence and hooliganism (Puloukas & Kartakoullis, 2004), which, if not controlled, could lead to the financial collapse of the football industry (Aristotelous & Puloukas, 1996; Peristianis *et al.*, 2002).

Furthermore, poor management and governance are major characteristics of the industry and so it is no surprise that most football clubs are in severe financial crisis. Often proper financial records are not kept by clubs, a practice that is common in many countries (Kartakoullis, 2005). The introduction of UEFA (Union des Associations Européennes de Football), the European football governing body, club licensing system assisted and contributed to sorting out of the football clubs' finances, as clubs were forced to prepare financial statements, accounts, and budgets that were to be submitted to the Cyprus Football Association. If not, permission would not be granted to compete in national and European competitions. The documentation gathered revealed that clubs were in a very bad financial situation and were struggling for survival as they were in severe debt (Kartakoullis & Theophanous, 2007).

Ineffective management has a great impact on sponsorship potential. The football clubs' approach to sponsorship recruitment and development is clearly in the preliminary stages and is seen as a philanthropic activity. Club officials need to realise that the days when companies donated money to football clubs in the form of charity are gone (Kartakoullis, 2007), that sponsorship is a vital promotional activity through which the sponsor's organisational objectives can be realised (Fahy, Farrelly & Quester 2004; Gardner & Shuman, 1987; Meenaghan, 1983), and that they have a golden opportunity to capitalise on the new sponsorship culture that is developing to assist in overcoming the financial difficulties they currently face.

Despite the severe financial crisis they experience, it is surprising that clubs increase their budgets annually with the result that the football industry is becoming too big and risky for the country. This indicates ineffective management and poor governance of football clubs, something that aligns with the overall picture of the sport industry described earlier. Voluntary work, lack of knowledge and professionalism, as well as the questionable motives that intervene in decision making, are regarded as responsible for the lack of strategic direction and future developmental plans.

Another major issue that needs to be urgently addressed is the lack of competitive balance in the national league, something that further nurtures the financial crisis of the industry. Competitive balance is a critical success factor for the football industry (Michie & Oughton, 2004; 2005). A result of the competitive imbalance was the reduction of interest in the football industry, which in turn further reduced the income of the football clubs.

Case study: Governance in sport – a survey of Cyprus national sport governing bodies

Given the governance problems that the sport system in Cyprus seems to be confronted with, a multi-case study was conducted to identify and highlight several governance issues that deserve consideration. The Governance in Sport Working Group (2001) suggested that the roles and responsibilities of a sport organisation need to be performed and achieved through 'ensuring that the principles of democracy, independence, fairness, solidarity and transparency are respected' (p.4). Thus, the objective of the study was to analyse Cyprus sport governing bodies' standards of governance and provide recommendations on the application of good governance principles that could improve the effectiveness of the sport system in Cyprus and eventually the value of sport itself.

The research took place between April and June 2012 through the administration of a survey consisting of 50 questions based on the nine pillars of good governance as identified in the Statement of Good Governance Principles developed by the Governance in Sport Working Group (2001) and the Cyprus Corporate Governance Code (Cyprus Stock Exchange, 2006) for profit and non-profit making organisations. The sample consisted of registered sport federations ($n=52$), the Cyprus Sport Organisation and the Cyprus Olympic Committee. In total 61 administrative staff and 43 board members of Cyprus national governing bodies completed the questionnaire.

The study presents detailed analysis of nine key areas relating to sport governance:

- board composition, size and structure
- fairness/democracy in elections and appointments
- roles and responsibilities
- performance measurement
- accountability and audit
- solidarity
- transparency and communication
- social responsibility and ethics, and
- independence.

Board composition, size and structure

Board composition and structure are regarded as essential components of good governance in sport according to the principles developed by the Governance in Sport Committee. The centrality of the principles was also identified by the Cadbury Report produced by the Cadbury Committee formed in the UK in the early 1990s. One of the most important outputs of the report was the composition of a board of directors. It suggested that the board should comprise a combination of executive and non-executive directors with a maximum term of office for non-executive directors (Committee on the Financial Aspects of Corporate Governance,1992) in order to arrive at more independent and accountable decisions. The way that boards and committees are structured can affect their ability to govern a sport organisation effectively. Large and unwieldy boards can result in ineffective decision making. Gaved and Hoehn (2001) held that simple board structures are preferred, as they promote accountability and improve the quality of decision making and communication. The results of the survey indicated that 42 per cent of boards comprised more than nine members, while 41 per cent consisted of nine board members, and 17 per cent consisted of seven members. What is extremely important, however, is that the boards of the Cyprus sport governing bodies (CSGB) did not comprise a combination of executive and non-executive directors, as all members were volunteers rather than paid executives.

Another important finding with regard to board structure is that 61 per cent of the respondents believed that the boards of the CSGBs did not comprise people with an appropriate range of skills and knowledge to ensure that the objectives of the sport organisation could be achieved. Comparison of the administrative staff and board members responses found that 71 per cent of people working for a CSGB believed that the board members did not possess the necessary skills and knowledge, while 47 per cent of board members admitted the same inadequacy with regard to their capacity to run a sport organisation effectively. An additional issue that raises concerns is the fact that 66 per cent of the respondents said that there was no maximum term of board membership, something that is regarded extremely detrimental to the independent and accountable governance of a sport organisation. This has resulted to very long term memberships and the creation of self-perpetuating sport governing bodies, discouraging and restricting the entrance of new people to the governing body. Facilitating the entrance of new members is extremely important according to the Statement of Good Governance Principles, thus it is a requirement that all key positions are subject to a fixed term of office (Governance in Sport Working Group, 2001).

Fairness/democracy in elections and appointments

Good governance is also associated with regularly contested, democratic, fair and transparent election processes involving confidential voting and published results (Gaved & Hoehn, 2001). The results of elections held by Cyprus sport governing bodies were not very encouraging with 65 per cent of the respondents indicating that the elections were not transparent and fair. Although 53 per cent of the administrative staff aspired to this view, it seems that for the vast majority of the board members (91 per cent) the elections were regarded as open, democratic and transparent. This is not surprising seeing it would be hard for a board member to admit that the election process that resulted in their placement in a certain organisation was not fair. More promising results were reported in regard to voting with 86 per cent of the respondents saying that voting was confidential but 76 per cent reported that the results were not always published.

The factors taken into consideration for the election of board members raised serious concerns regarding the reliability, capability and trustworthiness of CSGB board members. Based on the views of the whole sample, power and experience were the two main factors for their placement, followed by knowledge (Figure 14.1). It is surprising that political orientation was regarded as a more influencing factor than honesty and integrity. It is less surprising that the views of the administrative staff differed greatly from those of the board members with regard to the same issue. Honesty and integrity were much more highly rated by board members as compared to administrative staff. Only 15 per cent of the board members admitted that political reasons were responsible for their placement in a sport organisation, as opposed to a much greater percentage of the administrative staff that had the same opinion (see Figure 14.1).

The reluctance of board members to acknowledge governance problems associated with their sport governing body was also well illustrated. With regard to the hiring process of management personnel, 49 per cent of the administrative staff said that the management positions were not always openly contested while 60 per cent believed that the process of hiring management staff was not, or was hardly, based on objective, fair and transparent methods. Although 49 per cent of the board members said that the hiring process was fair and transparent, 34 per cent said that the hiring process was only slightly based on fair procedures and objective criteria.

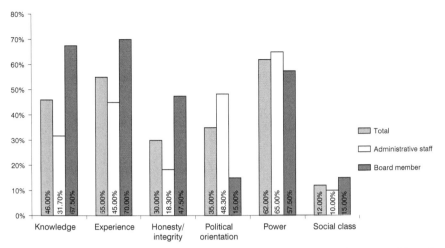

Figure 14.1 Factors taken into consideration for the election/appointment of board members

Board roles and responsibilities

The role of the board of directors is central to the governance of sport organisations. Board members are expected, and required, to clearly define and understand their roles and responsibilities. Well defined and demarcated responsibilities between the executives and the board members can ensure a more effective operation of a sport organisation. Corporate governance literature has suggested that the main roles performed by the board involve ensuring compliance and conformance by management, enhancing organisational performance, building relationships with other organisations, and securing resources to support the organisation. The Governance in Sport Working Group (2001) considered that the roles of sport governing bodies primarily involved drawing up rules for the sport, developing and promoting the sport, improving its popularity, and representing the sport and those involved in it.

Given the importance of delineating the objectives and the multiple roles that the board undertakes, it is interesting that the study revealed that 39 per cent of the sample felt that the roles, responsibilities and duties were not clearly defined in writing and 29 per cent said that the roles between management and board were not separated. This can lead to a lack of accountability and a creation of conflict which can be very counterproductive for a sport organisation. Those findings, along with the fact that 44 per cent of the respondents felt that the board was not well aware of their specific roles and responsibilities, is something that should generate concerns for people responsible for governing a sport organisation.

With regard to the functions the board performs, 38 per cent of the respondents said there was a weakness in evaluating board and the organisation performance, 35 per cent said there were shortcomings in developing sound partnerships with external stakeholders, continuing with poor monitoring of the direction of the organisation and ineffective distribution of organisation revenues to athletes, youth sport and grassroots sport. Only 60 per cent of the CSGBs had a corporate governance policy, but the vast majority of those who had a policy claimed that they did monitor and evaluate the governance practices of the organisation.

Performance measurement

Evaluating the performance of the organisation is a key issue for a sport governing body. Evaluation is important in that it provides an opportunity for the board to assess its own effectiveness, to identify areas of strength and weakness, to set standards and performance expectations based on certain criteria, and to evaluate individual member performance (Hoye & Cuskelly, 2007). Unfortunately, 37 per cent of the respondents said that there was no evaluation of board or sub-committee performance. According to 84 per cent of the respondents, in the case that evaluation was undertaken, the board was the main evaluator of the organisation and the board itself.

Accountability and audit

Evaluating the performance and the actions of a sport organisation can also ensure that the organisation shows accountability through measures that aim to protect the interests of the organisation and its stakeholders. The need for sport organisations to achieve legitimacy through accountability and transparency has also been stressed by the Governance in Sport Working Group (2001). Each governing body has a responsibility towards stakeholders to regularly review and account for activities performed by the organisation that impact their interests. However, one third of the respondents indicated that the board was not accountable for actions such as hiring, firing and promoting personnel or deciding on athletes' participation in competitions. Specific objectives and fair criteria should be set in place for all these actions to improve the accountability of the board and thus make the organisation trustworthy and credible.

There is a remarkable difference between the views and opinions regarding the financial transactions of the organisation. Although 98 per cent of the board members said that they were accountable for the financial activities of the organisation, 37 per cent of the administrative staff argued that the board did not regularly account for the commercial activities and decisions regarding the management of financial resources. The audit results were more encouraging as sport organisations seemed to be adequately audited by external auditors, and many of them seemed to provide their members with an annual report. However, it appears that the majority of the sport governing bodies (68 per cent) did not have internal audit committees, something that would be very beneficial in improving accountability, as well as in identifying and dealing with problematic areas needing consideration.

Solidarity

One of the main responsibilities of sport governing bodies is the allocation of revenue derived from the commercial exploitation of events and championships. Fair, transparent and effective distribution of financial revenue within a sport is essential to the development of talent, the maintenance of competitive balance, and attracting competition. Therefore, the financial redistribution mechanism of sport organisations should be transparent, accountable, based on clearly defined and justifiable objectives, and built upon the principles of solidarity between all levels of sport (Governance in Sport Working Group, 2001). In response to the question whether CSGBs had a formalised strategy through which the revenue of the organisation was distributed to the sport's grassroots level, 76 per cent reported that they did, even though board members reported a low degree of transparency with regard to the distribution process.

Transparency and communication

The way in which a sport governing body communicates with key stakeholders is 'a key indicator of the quality of its governance processes' (Governance in Sport Working Group, 2001, p.6). Nowadays sport organisations are required to explain their governance processes, performance, roles and responsibilities, and other information of interest to members, such as policy decisions, election processes and results, in their annual reports or on their web site. Communication and transparency are areas that need improvement as 36 per cent of the respondents stated that their sport organisation did not disclose information on financial activities while 38 per cent said that they did not provide information on governance practices, and 32 per cent said that their remuneration policy was not published in the annual report. When respondents were asked about the communication channels between the administrative staff and the board, 40 per cent of the total sample stated that there was no regular communication.

Similar findings were stated with regard to the working relationships established in the CSGBs. Poor working relationships were reported by 33 per cent of the overall sample, while the percentage of administration aspiring to this notion was 48 per cent. In the same vein, 37 per cent of the respondents said that the board was not willing to accept feedback while again the percentage of managerial personnel having this belief was greater and reached 50 per cent. Those findings provide further support that long-standing communication difficulties result in poor relations with professionals that hamper effective management (Charalambous-Papamiltiades, 2006). The results of this study are very disappointing as two-way communication channels are crucial in the development of effective sport organisations, thus it would be especially beneficial and constructive for Cyprus sport organisations to work harder to set up communication mechanisms that are conducive to the improvement of governance practices.

Social responsibility and ethics

An examination of the ethical decision making and socially responsible practices and policies adopted by sport organisations revealed rather disappointing findings. Despite the fact that social responsibility and ethics are essential components of good governance, the study demonstrated that the majority of sport governing bodies did not develop a code of ethics nor have a social responsibility policy. The majority of respondents stated that they did not have fraud or corruption policies, or a system raising concerns for inappropriate behaviour. It seems that there is an urgent need for the development of such mechanisms which are essential in preventing mismanagement and inappropriate practices that can seriously damage an organisation. When respondents were asked about any form of discrimination intervening the decision making process of the board, 26 per cent of the board members acknowledged that there were some discriminatory factors involved in making their decisions. A large percentage of the administrative staff (38 per cent) felt the boards' decisions were more heavily based on discriminatory factors, something else that raises serious concerns and urges for action to be taken.

Independence

According to the Principles of Good Governance, sport governing bodies should ensure their independence and autonomy and reduce conflict of interest. There is a need for clear distinction between the sport organisation's governance functions and any commercial activities. Almost half of the respondents reported almost non-existent degrees of independence and unbiased judgment by the board of directors. Also, 44 per cent stated that the board had substantial relationships with commercial activities of the sport organisation. Unexpectedly, 50 per cent of the board members admitted that conflicting interests intervened the decision-making process. Personal interests were identified by both management and board as having the most prevalent impact, followed by financial interests and political factors. That politics have a prevalent role in the Cyprus sport system has been clearly demonstrated. This is counterproductive and against the healthy development of sport in general. A lack of independency can result in heavily directed and guided decisions that harm sport at all levels and discourage involvement in sport.

Recommendations

Considering the abundance of governance issues identified, the following recommendations can be made:

- Appointment of independent individuals from outside the sport to boards or committees, and election or appointment of executive directors to the board
- Introduction of a maximum term of membership
- Appointment of individuals with an adequate range of skills and knowledge
- More open, fair and transparent election processes including the publication of election results

- More open, transparent and fair processes of hiring management personnel
- Demarcation of the roles and responsibilities of the board and management
- Separation of power and roles between management and the board
- Establishment of good governance policies
- Employment of evaluation mechanisms
- Improving accountability of the board through the introduction of specific, objective and fair criteria with more transparency and accountability on financial issues, hiring and promotional decisions
- More independent and transparent decision making processes on redistribution of revenue within the sport at the grassroots level
- Creation of internal audit committees
- Establishment of two-way communication channels
- Adoption of a code of ethics, social responsibility, fraud, and corruption policies, as well as systems and mechanisms raising concerns on inappropriate behaviour
- Ensuring independence and autonomy, and reducing conflicts of interest.

Summary

The role of sport has been fundamental in the Cypriot society. Although many remarkable steps have been made in terms of sport policies and initiatives, the sport industry is suffering. Problems of amateurism, accompanied by ineffective management of sport organisations, are urgent issues that need to be addressed immediately. Although the contribution of volunteers is appreciated, sport organisations need a more professional approach in order to successfully respond to the environmental challenges and effectively promote the interests of the participants from the grass roots to elite levels.

Sport authorities should place more emphasis on the individual athlete in order to provide incentives for notable competitive presence. Sport decision makers need to realise that the core of the sport system is the athlete and not the sport official. The sport system should no longer represent a political arena or the means for serving political interests. As the former president of CSO admitted in an interview in November 2008, 'There is an imperative need for the creation of a culture of transparency in our sport system' continuing to say that 'the Cyprus sports sector does not need sport officials whose goals and personal interests will expose the whole sport system to risks' (Kartakoullis, 2008). Decision makers need to realise that the policies and strategies of any sport organisation should be directed towards providing support and encouraging participation at all levels. As well, more emphasis should be placed on mobilising mass sport. Mass participation is, unfortunately, very limited, and it is even more disappointing that there is no political willingness towards encouraging mass involvement.

Furthermore, considering that the larger part of the sport sector in Cyprus involves the football industry, the main issues that it is faced with need to be addressed immediately. Football hooliganism and the lack of competitive balance in the national league are further fostering the crisis that football clubs are confronted with. It is obvious that there is an urgent need for policies and strategies that will help football overcome these challenges.

Finally, as the multi-case study demonstrated, the governance problems that sport bodies are confronted with are many. Hence, sport authorities should direct their efforts on investing in good management and corporate governance practices to develop a healthier industry that will be able to take advantage of opportunities presented and minimise the harmful effects of the threats and challenges of an uncertain and radically changing environment.

This chapter presented the main governance problems that the Cyprus sport system is faced with. The involvement of volunteers in the management of sport organisations, the intervention of politics in the system, unclear separation of power, poor communication between the board and management, the underestimated role of the professional, and lack of independency and accountability on several governance issues are some of the problems that the industry must face. There is a need for sport authorities to direct their efforts to introducing and applying good governance practices so as to develop a healthy and credible sport industry.

Review questions

1   What are the main governance problems that the sport industry in Cyprus is confronted with?
2   What are the main factors that resulted in the creation of several sport governance problems in Cyprus?
3   How do you think that the sport sector in Cyprus can improve sport governance?

Further Reading

Sobry, C. (2010). *Sport governance in the world.* Paris: Le Manuscript.
Henry, I. P. (2007). *Transnational and comparative research in sport: Globalisation, governance and sport policy.* London: Routledge.
Hoye, R., Nicholson, M., & Houlihan, B. (2010). *Sport and policy.* London: Butterworth-Heinemann.
Hums, M. A. & MacLean J. C. (2008). *Governance and policy in sport organization.* Holcomb: Hathaway Publishers.

Websites

UK Sport: http://www.uksport.gov.uk/pages/governance/
Responsiball: http://community.responsiball.org/
Play the Game: http://www.playthegame.org/news/detailed/website-on-good-governance-in-international-sports-organisations-calls-for-your-contribution-5374.html

References

Aristotelous, K., & Puloukas, S. (1996). Fan violence and football attendance in Cyprus. *Journal of Business and Society,* 9, 104–9.

Charalambous-Papamiltiades, M. (2006). Corporate governance of sports organisations in Cyprus: The role of volunteers. Paper presented at the 3rd Annual Sports Congress, December, Cyprus College, Nicosia.

Charalambous-Papamiltiades, M. (2011). The sports sector in Cyprus: Issues to be urgently addressed. In: C. Sobry (Ed.). *Sport governance in the world: A socio-historic approach* (pp.119–53). Paris: Le Manuscript.

Committee on the Financial Aspects of Corporate Governance (1992). *Report (The Cadbury Report.* London: Gee. Available online at http://www.jbs.cam.ac.uk/cadbury/report/index.html

CSO (Cyprus Sport Organisation) (1986). *CSO album.* Nicosia: Cyprus Sport Organisation.

CSO (Cyprus Sport Organisation) (2004). The sports sector in Cyprus. Research Paper presented in Vocasport Conference, May, Lyon, France.

CSO (Cyprus Sport Organisation) (2008). *2008 Memorandum for the distribution of sports subsidies.* Nicosia: Competitive Sports Department, Cyprus Sports Organisation.

CSO (Cyprus Sport Organisation) (2009). *2009 Memorandum for the distribution of sports subsidies.* Nicosia: Competitive Sports Department, Cyprus Sports Organisation.

Cuskelly, G., & Harrington, M. (1997). Volunteers and leisure: Evidence of marginal and career volunteerism in sport. *World Leisure Journal,* 39(3), 11–18.

Cyprus Stock Exchange (2006). Corporate Governance Code. 2nd edn. Available online at: http://www.cse.com.cy/en/MarketData/Data/corporate%20governance%20code%202nd%20edition%20(final).doc

Fahy, J., Farrelly, F., & Quester, P. (2004). Competitive advantage through sponsorship: A conceptual model and research propositions. *European Journal of Marketing,* 38(8), 1013–30.

Gardner, M., & Shuman, P. (1987). Sponsorship, an important component of the promotions mix. *Journal of Advertising*, 16 (1), 11–17.

Gaved, M. & Hoehn, T. (2001). Governance in sport. Paper presented at the 18th Annual Conference of the European Association of Law and Economics, Vienna, 13–15 September. Available at: http://www.competitionrx.com/documents/Sports%20Governance/Governance%20in%20Sport%20-%20EALE%20-%20Vienna%20-%202001.pdf

Governance in Sport Working Group (2001). Conference report and conclusions. The rules of the game, Europe's first conference on the Governance of Sport, February Conference, Brussels 26–27 February.

Hoye, R., & Cuskelly, G. (2003). Board–executive relationships within voluntary sport organisations. *Sport Management Review,* 6, 53–74.

Hoye, R. & Cuskelly, G. (2007). *Sport governance.* Oxford: Elsevier.

Inglis, S. (1994). Exploring volunteer board member and executive director needs: Importance and fulfilment. *Journal of Applied Recreation Research,* 19, 171–89.

Inglis, S. (1997). Roles of the board in amateur sport organizations. *Journal of Sport Management*, 11, 160–76.

Kartakoullis, N. (2005). *FUTURO III – FIFA football management programme.* Kuala Lumpur, Malaysia: FIFA.

Kartakoullis, N. (2007). Sport sponsorship – not charity! Paper presented at a Congress organised by the Cyprus Football Association and FIFA. Nicosia.

Kartakoullis, N. (2008). Sports officials and their stubbornness. Available online at http://www.sigmalive.com/sports/track/cyprus/86124.

Kartakoullis, N., & Theophanous, A. (2007). *The financial dimensions of football in Cyprus.* Research Center Intercollege in cooperation with the Center for Leisure, Tourism and Sport Research and Development, Intercollege. Commissioned report for the Cyprus Football Association. Nicosia: University of Nicosia

Kikulis, L.M. (1990). Understanding the satisfaction of volunteer sport administrators. *CAHPER Journal,* 56(4), 5–11.

Kikulis, L. M., Slack, T., Hinings, B., & Zimmerman, A. (1989). A structural taxonomy of amateur sport organisations. *Journal of Sport Management,* 3, 129–50.

Meenaghan, T. (1983). Commercial sponsorship. *European Journal of Marketing,* 17(7), 1–74.

Michie, J., & Oughton, C. (2004). Competitive balance in football: The corporate governance of football clubs 2004. Research Paper 2004, No.2. London: Birkbeck University of London.

Michie, J., & Oughton, C. (2005). Competitive balance in football: An update. London: Birkbeck: University of London.

Peristianis, N., Kapardis A., Loizou, C., Fakiolas, N., & Puloukas, S. (2002) *Football violence in Cyprus.* Nicosia: Research Promotion Foundation.

Puloukas, S., & Kartakoullis, N. (2004). Cyprus football: Opinion survey. Paper presented at a conference organised by the Cyprus Football Association, October, Nicosia.

Ridley, E., & Barr, C. (2006). *Board volunteers in Canada: Their motivations and challenges: A research report.* Toronto: Knowledge Development Centre. Available online at http://library.imaginecanada.ca/files/nonprofitscan/kdc-cdc/imagine_board_volunteers_report.pdf

Searle, M. (1989). Testing the reciprocity norm in a recreation management setting. *Leisure Science,* 2, 353–65.

Shilbi, S., Taylor, P., Nichols, G., Gratton, C., & Kokolakakis, T. (1999). The characteristics of volunteers in UK sports clubs. *European Journal for Sport Management,* 6, 10–27.

15 The Czech Republic

Dino Numerato and Libor Flemr

Topics

- Plurality of actors and associations in Czech sport governance
- Governmental and non-governmental pillars of Czech sport governance
- Main umbrella sport governing bodies
- Historical roots of sport governance in the Czech Republic
- The crisis of contemporary Czech sport governance.

Objectives

- To describe the main characteristics of contemporary Czech sport governance
- To explain how sport governance has reflected major sociocultural and political developments
- To outline major historical developments of Czech sport governance
- To explore contemporary efforts to redefine Czech sport governance
- To suggest possible future scenarios of Czech sport governance developments.

Key terms

Sokol movement Traditional sport governing body founded in 1862 that is historically connected with mass gymnastics. It has significantly contributed to the development of democratic citizenship and Czech identity.

Central planning of sport Ideologically driven and highly politicised sport governance during the communist regime between 1948 and 1989 with strong adherence to the Soviet sport model.

Democratisation The process that followed the fall of the communist regime in 1989 and during which the decision-making processes were transposed from the state to non-governmental and autonomous sport associations.

Czech Sport Association (ČSTV) The most important umbrella sport association in the Czech Republic.

Crisis of governanc The crisis of Czech sport governance is connected with the bankruptcy of Sazka in 2011. Sazka was the biggest lottery company in the Czech Republic that used to substantially support the sport movement.

As ČSTV represented the main stakeholder of the bankrupt company, the bankruptcy undermined legitimacy of the former board of the ČSTV and opened a discussion about the role of the ČSTV in Czech sport governance.

Overview

This chapter provides a general overview of sport governance within the Czech Republic. It first offers a presentation of major umbrella associations and the relationship among them. The account that follows deals with the involvement of public authorities in sport governance and describes the ways in which the sport governing bodies are interconnected with public authorities. Following this, major trends influencing contemporary sport governance and historical developments that are relevant in the Czech Republic context are explored. A brief outline about the origins of sport governance in the Czech countries during the Austro-Hungarian Empire in the second half of the nineteenth century is followed by a description of the direct impact of communist ideologies on sport governance after World War II. More in-depth attention is given to recent developments. The period of transformation from communism to democracy and capitalism is first described, and the period of crisis starting in 2011 is elaborated upon.

Contemporary Czech sport governance: a basic outline

Contemporary sport governance in the Czech Republic can be defined as a pluralised, diversified and heterogeneous system of actors and associations. Its contemporary structure has been developed since the fall of the communist regime in 1989. The 1989 Velvet Revolution was followed with a period of transformation from centrally planned and highly politicised sport governance to pluralised and decentralised sport governance. The sphere of sport was changed with a strong connection to a newly developing capitalist system. Two main processes were symptomatic for this period: a process of automony and increasing detachment of sport governance from the state, and a revival of previously banned sport movements. Moreover, the reorganisation of the system of governance was further redirected by the split between the Czech Republic and Slovakia on the 31 December 1992.

Nowadays, the governance of sport is based on two main pillars: non-governmental sport associations and governmental authorities. The first pillar, based on non-governmental organisations, has a crucial role. Because of these factors, the Czech model of sport governance can also be defined as a non-interventionist model (Chaker, 2004), in which the Czech government is not directly involved in sport governance (Novotný, 2011; Numerato, 2010a).

Non-governmental pillar of sport governance

Umbrella sport associations represent a key structural element of Czech sport governance. According to the latest official published statistics from the National

Sport Policy in March 2011, there were 2,740,094 members of Czech sport governing bodies in 2009 (MŠMT, 2011). Currently, the most important umbrella sport association in the Czech Republic is the Czech Sport Association, which in 2011 had 1,710,616 members associated with 95 sport-specific associations, either as ordinary or associate members (ČSTV, 2012). The association with most numerous members is the Football Association of the Czech Republic with 538,762 members. The most rapidly developing association is the Czech Floorball Union with 72,982 members in 2011 in comparison to only 8,316 members in 2000 (ČSTV, 2012).

The ČSTV is organised both vertically and horizontally. The horizontal division of the association is based, first, on membership of sport-specific sport associations who have their voice in decision-making processes and, secondly, on geographical division of the ČSTV. The geographical division of the ČSTV mirrors the contemporary administrative division of the Czech Republic into 14 regions. The ČSTV is further organised internally into districts, which represent former administrative units, as a legacy from the socialist geopolitical division of the Czech Republic. The continued existence of these units, whose role is even more important than the role of regional units, provides testimony of the persistence of the otherwise rejected ideologically driven forms of organisation of Czech(oslovak) sport governance. This organisational structure is not the only aspect of Czech sport governance that is a legacy of the former political regime. An overly strong bureaucratic mentality and working habits and clientelistic networks, which originated in the communist past and were transformed into allegiances between sport officials and entrepreneurs or politicians, all represent a malaise of the contemporary sport governance juggernaut.

The persistence of this legacy, together with an inability of the sport movement to cope with new challenges of transformation, represents the main causes beyond the recent crisis of the ČSTV. The crisis, which primarily rests on the lack of material resources, in turn represents a crisis for Czech sport governance overall. As is explained further in this chapter, it was mainly indifference of previous ČSTV boards and a non-transparent style of governance, favouring private interests, that contributed to the deep financial crisis of Czech sport governance. The contemporary crisis was anticipated with several waves of strong public criticism against the ČSTV. ČSTV legitimacy has been increasingly questioned over the last five years in connection with the financial crisis of Czech sport. Also due to this crisis of legitimacy, the position of the ČSTV was progressively weakened in the following months and years.

In addition to the ČSTV, the Sokol movement, a traditional sport governing body, played a significant role within Czech sport governance. The scope of activities of the Sokol movement lies beyond the sphere of sport and physical activities. It is further focused on an education for democratic development, on a promotion of Slavic and Czech national identity, and on emphasising ethics, civic engagement and wellbeing. Contrary to the otherwise low involvement of woman in mainstream sport associations (Fasting & Knorre, 2005), Sokol seeks to maintain a gender equity of the association's boards.

The movement was banned four times during its history (Černek, 2008), with the last ban revoked after the Velvet Revolution in 1989. Considering numerous barriers that undermined the official continuity of the Sokol movement, the movement still struggles to re-establish its position within the context of Czech sport governance even today. In addition to efforts aimed getting back expropriated property, the Sokol movement struggles to attract new members as it is often considered not 'modern' enough in the everyday sense of the word. Since 1990 the demand for 'modern' and grassroots sport has been satisfied by the Czech Association of Sports for All, now having the third highest number of umbrella associations in the Czech Republic. This sport governing body is considered to be the main competitor of Sokol in the area of Sports for All sport governance. In a position similar to Sokol, it has been working with the Catholic sport movement Orel since 1989, whose members had experienced political bans and property expropriation.

The position of the Czech Olympic Committee (ČOV) is rather limited. The mission of the ČOV is almost exclusively related to the organisation of elite sport and to the performance of Czech athletes in the Olympic Games. The weakening position of the ČSTV has, however, stimulated some to call for it to be absorbed under the umbrella of the ČOV, as in other countries.

Last, but not least, other umbrella associations must be listed for the sake of completeness: the Association of School Sport Clubs of the Czech Republic, the Association of Technical Sports and Activities, the Czech Shooting Federation, the Association of Sport Unions and Clubs of the Czech Republic, and the Autoclub of the Czech Republic. Table 15.1 summarises umbrella and sport associations, including their membership numbers.

Table 15.1 Umbrella and sport associations with membership numbers

Sport governing body	Membership base in 2009
ČSTV	1,533,279
The Association of the Sport Federations of the Czech Republic	272,384
Czech Association of Sports for All	261,107
Association of School Sport Clubs of the Czech Republic	238,500
Sokol	180,817
Autoclub of the Czech Republic	85,100
Czech Tourist Club	37,728
Union of the Police Sports Clubs in Czech Republic	32,248
Association of Sport Unions and Clubs of the Czech Republic	23,509
Czech Shooting Federation	18,900
Orel	17,567
Czech Paralympic Committee	15,582

Source: Usnesení vlády č. 167/2011 o Koncepci státní podpory sportu v České republice.

Public sport policy: government and local authorities

The involvement of the state in sport governance is primarily by the Department for Sport and Physical Education of the Czech Ministry of Education, Youth, and Sport (MŠMT). The governmental regulatory role on sport is defined by the Law on the Support for Sport (Act no. 115/2001) and is further specified by sport policy documents approved in 1999, 2000, 2003, and 2011. Whereas policies from the turn of the millennium were intended to fill a policy vacuum that existed in the sphere of sport after the Velvet Revolution and to define basic principles and the responsibilities of the state in the area of sport, recent national policy primarily mirrors the trends emanating on a European level and reflects the main topics in the White Paper on Sport (European Union, 2007), such as health and social wellbeing.

Due to the politically unstable situation and changes of ministers and deputies for sport since the division of Czechoslovakia into two autonomous states in 1993, there has only been weak regulation in relation to sport. Moreover, this extraordinary instability was accompanied with a lack of continuity and systematic work. From 1993 until the spring of 2012, in total 12 ministers have been in place, and the changes at the ministerial level usually entailed personnel changes in the position of the deputy for sport. These developments undermined any possibility for continuity and systematic work. This is documented by Flemr's (one of the chapter's authors) experience when he visited the MŠMT to carry out an interview related to urban planning, and sport and physical activities. Documents were requested but were not available due to personnel changes. The reason given was 'it has become quite common to completely empty out cupboards' (Flemr, personal communication, 22 May 2007).

The MŠMT is not the only organisation that provides support for sport. The Ministry of Defence and the Ministry of Interior, continuing from the communist past, provide a modest contribution to sport governance. These ministries support army and police sport clubs and provide them with equipment and facilities. Moreover, several athletes of Czech national teams are *de facto* employees of either the Ministry of Defence or the Ministry of Interior.

Sport governance is supported at a national governmental level, as well as at regional and local levels by local public authorities. The system of regional sport policy has been institutionalised since 2001 after being supported by two new legislative acts. The first act divided the Czech Republic into 14 new regions and, the second, the Law on the Support of Sport, defined the sport policy responsibilities of regions and municipalities. Regional and municipal policies are generally framed at a national level, but specific applications are quite diversified (Numerato, 2009). Although some of the regions have recently strengthened their attempts to support the decision-making process with policy and strategy documents, in some areas the regional support of sport still suffers from a lack of transparency, inadequate audit procedures and an overly strong emphasis on elite sport at the expense of recreational and amateur sports. Last, but not least, the recent financial crisis has contributed to the decline in public subsidies and funding of sport (KPMG, 2012).

Dynamics between governmental and non-governmental spheres

The Czech government and local authorities are not directly involved in sport governance. However, the spheres of sport and politics cannot be portrayed as absolutely separate and autonomous. Whilst the influence of politics on the sport movement is not as explicit, direct, ideological or formalised as during the period of socialist Czechoslovakia, with its strong adherence to the Soviet sport model (Duke, 1990; Kostka, 1978), the dynamics between sport movements and public authorities continue to play a significant role. The symbiotic relationship between politics and sport movements, on the one hand, guarantee sport governing bodies access to material resources, and who, on the other, in turn support the visibility of politicians.

In addition to informal allegiances and networks, the relationship between the state and the umbrella sport associations is mediated by the All Sport Advisory Board of the Czech Republic (Všesportovní kolegium ČR). The All Sport Advisory Board (which has a legal personality) is a formal coalition of 10 principal Czech sport governing bodies. This body was established in 1994 and until 2010 functioned as a semi-formal coalition with no legal personality. The low recognition of the All Sport Advisory Board and its weak political influence contributed to the formalisation of the coalition and its transformation into a body with legal personality.

The All Sport Advisory Board of the Czech Republic has representatives from 10 major sport umbrella associations and represents the interests of the Czech sport movement in the spheres of executive and legislative power. Its board is focused primarily on lobbying activities. Mirroring the geographical organisation of the Czech Republic and its division into regions, the board is active at a regional level in order to promote and support the needs of the sport movement vis-à-vis local authorities, principally in terms of financial support for organised sport.

The relative autonomy of sport from the Czech government can be illustrated by example of the recent struggle over the national motorcycle sport authority between a new, recently founded Czech Union of Motorcycle Sport and the traditional organisation, the Autoclub of the Czech Republic (AČR). The struggle started on the 7 October 2011 when the former Minister of Education, Youth and Sports sent a letter to the President of the Motorcycling International Federation, in which he recognised 'the Czech Union of Motorcycle Sport is the only and supreme sports authority in the field of motorcycle sport in the Czech Republic' and it 'fully replaces the powers and competence of the AČR' (MŠMT, 2011, pp.1-2). By this formal communication, the minister, Josef Dobeš, interfered with the non-governmental sector with no legal power to do so.

This letter, however, was later contested by the AČR, and the Czech Constitutional Court issued a resolution which stated that the MŠMT did not possess any power to 'determine in an authoritarian manner "the supreme authority in the field of motorcycling"' (Ústavní soud, 2012, p.4). In fact, this autonomy was later confirmed by the new Minister, Petr Fiala (MŠMT, 2012).

Case study: Czech sport governance and its historical development

The contemporary nature of the system of Czech sport governance can hardly be understood without considering its historical roots and sociocultural development. This case study therefore considers some of the milestones in Czech sport governance history. First, the origins of sport governance in the Czech countries are described. Then, major tenets of its development during the Communist regime are outlined followed by an in-depth examination of the major trends in sport governance development during the last two decades since the 1989 Velvet Revolution.

Origins of modern organised sport in the Czech Republic

The origins of the sport movement in the Czech countries are intrinsically connected with the foundation of the Sokol (Falcon) movement in 1862 by Miroslav Tyrš. Because of Sokol's strong emphasis on building a Czech national identity within the Austro-Hungarian Empire and its contribution to the rebirth of the Czech nation, its importance is not only recognised in sport and physical education, but also in cultural, educational and political spheres (Nolte, 2002; Thorne, 2011; Waic, 1997).

The Sokol movement's initiatives were clearly different from the Czech Olympic Committee founded in 1899 (Kolář & Kössl, 1994). Its founder, Jiří Stanislav Guth-Jarkovský, was one of the three principal founders of the International Olympic Committee together with Baron Pierre de Coubertin and Demetrius Vikelas (Dovalil, 2004). By emphasising wellbeing and everyday involvement in sport and physical activities, Sokol's ideas were not aligned with the Olympic focus on elite and competitive sport promoted by the Czech Olympic Committee (Černek, 2008). Furthermore, since its beginning, Sokol was unique in promoting the idea of volunteering and democratic citizenship (Nolte, 2002).

In addition to the Sokol movement and the Czech Olympic Committee, other associations attracted the support of Czech citizens. Among the most important was the Orel Association, which was founded in 1909, supported by the Catholic Church; the Social Democratic Workers Athletic Association (Dělnická tělocvičná jednota) founded in 1897; and the University Sports movement with origins in 1910 (Valjent & Flemr, 2010).

Czech sport governance flourished significantly during the period of the First Republic from the foundation of Czechoslovakia in 1918 until the beginning of World War II. The period of the First Republic was typified by the pluralisation of Czech sport governance based on democratic principles. In addition to the ideologically, politically and religiously focused sport associations, new sport-related governing bodies were founded in this period.

The era of communism: centrally planned and ideologically driven sport governance

Nazi occupation during World War II and a strong political adherence of the country to the Soviet Union and to communist ideology after 1948 both contributed to a radical shift in sport governance. These two milestones in Czech history destroyed the civic and democratic principles of sport governance. With the arrival of the Communist Party of Czechoslovakia in government, the sphere of sport was, as in other social spheres, subsumed under the communist ideology, and its organisation was unified and centralised. Sport governance was under the control of a sole strongly politicised central unit, the State Committee for Physical Education and Sport.

Sport governance was regulated by Legislative Act No. 187/1949, further augmented by Legislative Act No. 71/1952 Sb. These acts emphasised the utility of mass gymnastics for a healthy communist society. The latter act also guaranteed unprecedented material support in order to reinforce political and ideological representation of the state; it also banned the Sokol movement, which had revived for a short period after being proscribed during the Nazi occupation of Czech countries during World War II (Slepičková, 2007b). Following these regulations, the sport governance system was totally dependent materially on the state, state-owned factories and the national trade union, Revolutionary Union Movement (Revoluční odborové hnutí – ROH). The acts also regulated the relations of athletes and officials with Western, non-communist sport (Duke, 2011; Slepičková, 2007a) and limited these to the lowest necessary level around sport competitions. It was only in the late 1980s that a greater openness towards Western countries occurred. In this period, rudimentary forms of commercialisation and sponsorship started and professionalisation of players, together with transfers of athletes to Western countries – although bureaucratically regulated (Duke, 1990) – was permitted in a limited manner (e.g. transfers of football players at the end of their career).

Although being primarily an object of ideological propaganda and central planning, the sport sphere also contributed to resistance to the communist regime. Acts of resistance were not only undertaken by famous Czech athletes during major sport events, such as Czech gymnast and multiple Olympic medal winner Věra Čáslavská's silent protest during the 1968 Mexico Olympics or the so-called ice hockey protests of the Czechoslovak ice hockey team during and after the world championships in Sweden in 1969, but also at a lower level of sport governance, in everyday activities of the members of Czechoslovak sport associations (Numerato, 2010b; Uhlíř & Waic, 2001).

Sport governance in the eras of transformation and post-transformation

The political and sociocultural changes in Czechoslovakia, and later in the Czech Republic after 1992, have significantly impacted upon sport governance. The rupture with any aspect of the communist past also touched the Czech sport movement. The centrally planned and ideologically driven system of sport governance was rejected. Two new legislative acts, No. 83/1990 and No. 173/1990, redefined the position of Czech sport associations by enhancing their autonomy and non-governmental, third-sector character. Collaboration, knowledge exchange and more frequent competition with athletes from the Western countries, until then separated by the Iron Curtain, was facilitated. This related not only to transfers of professional athletes at an elite level (Duke, 2011), but also at a level of common membership of sport associations.

The new legal framework opened the door for a revival of previously banned sport associations, the most important among them Sokol and Orel. Furthermore, these legal regulations dealt with property issues. In particular, they dealt with claims of formerly banned sport associations and their rights for restitution of sport facilities and land that had been expropriated by the state in 1948.

Furthermore, they provided sport governance representatives with autonomy in decision-making and with an opportunity to manage material resources independently of the state (Slepičková, 2007b). At the same time, these processes were accompanied with new challenges brought about by wider sociocultural developments. The challenges were concerned with the difficulties of accessing material resources, with the changed relationship between politics and sport, with a decrease in volunteering, with problems related to property, and with communist legacies.

First, in regard to the material resources, public subsidies and generous public support to sport decreased. In these conditions private companies and entrepreneurs started to play an important role. On the one hand, the sport movement gained new opportunities but uneven access to resources, while on the other hand sport governing bodies risked being misused for private interests. Sport officials were not always skilful enough in deciphering conflicts of interest and allegiances of executive boards' representatives within the business environment.

Second, the relations between sport and politics have increasingly become more strategically pragmatic and less ideologically driven. The role of public authorities in sport governance was significantly weakened in terms of the state's control over sport governance and contribution to the policy-making process. In particular, during the first 10 years after 1989, the government did not provide any policy framework for sport governance, and this led to a crisis in sport development in the Czech Republic at the turn of the millennium. The critical situation was partially resolved through several policies and the Law on the Support for Sport, Legislative Act No. 115/2001.

Third, since 1989 volunteering in sport governing bodies significantly declined as thousands of officials, coaches, referees and athletes invested more time in their careers because of the introduction of capitalism. As a consequence, they dedicated less time to sport (Numerato, 2010a). The loss of volunteers from sport associations was also made worse by competition from other forms of leisure. Travel and information technologies (e.g. computer games) were often mentioned by sport officials as main causes of the decreasing engagement of volunteers in sport governance. Last, but not the least, the outflow of volunteers was also connected with a transformation of the job market in the Czech Republic and higher migration rates, although still relatively low when compared to other European countries.

Fourth, Czech sport governance during transformation and post-transformation periods had to deal with the question of property. In particular, sport governance officials had to return expropriated property to the Sokol movement and other previously banned associations. Moreover, sport facilities often constructed with public subsidies during the era of communism were passed to independent sport clubs and associations, and this sometimes provoked conflicts among competing groups within sport clubs who claimed their rights to the property. In some cases the disputes were even accompanied with police intervention and court decisions. Last, but not least, sport facilities constructed in the era of communism were sometimes built on land which had been expropriated from private entrepreneurs who reclaimed ownership.

The Czech sport governance crisis: towards a new transformation

The experience of spontaneous and unregulated developments of Czech sport governance in the 1990s and after the turn of the millennium provided the main impetus for contemporary developments. Czech sport governance is currently facing a period of deep crisis as its representatives are confronted with unintended and detrimental consequences of the transformation period in the 1990s and post-transformation era. The crisis of Czech sport governance culminated in the spring of 2011 with the bankruptcy of Sazka, the biggest lottery company in the Czech Republic. Sazka represented a significant resource of revenue (more than 10 per cent) for the Czech sport movement. The ČSTV, as the key umbrella sport association, was the main shareholder of Sazka with around 68 per cent of shares (Novotný, 2011). The ČSTV's role, as the major stakeholder, was to maintain control over the company's management, but it failed as its representatives approved decisions that pushed the lottery company into insolvency. Even before the crisis entered mainstream public discussion, for more than five years Sazka's poor financial position had been pointed out by former ČSTV board opponents, without gaining a sufficient response in the sport movement.

The first wave of substantial criticism occurred in relation to the construction of the multi-functional arena built for the 2004 Ice Hockey World Championship. The cost of construction significantly increased from initial estimates and the lottery company Sazka, as the main investor, was not able to cover the financing of the arena without distributing less money to the Czech sport movement. A new board of the ČSTV was elected following Sazka's bankruptcy, and a new executive committee elected in January 2012, promoting internal structural changes for the ČSTV. It broke with the previous style of governance, calling for higher transparency and responsibility for decision-making processes.

In addition to legal action against the former Sazka management, and a rational approach towards resource management, the changes in governance are primarily characterised by a weakening of the position of the ČSTV and a reinforcement of the Czech Olympic Committee's position. The ČOV should progressively take responsibility for governance and decision-making processes in Czech sport and the ČSTV should continue to act as a service organisation, providing administrative support for sport clubs, ensuring lobbying at the public authority level.

The bankruptcy of the Sazka lottery company represents the most significant milestone for Czech sport governance in the last 20 years. In a sense, it provides a testimony as to the vulnerable and weak pillars of the system of Czech sport governance that were not able to take advantage of the chance for autonomous and independent governance. An enthusiastically driven process of separation of sport governance from the state after the Velvet Revolution resulted in a complex system of governance involving not only enormous chances for active civic engagement, but also for too many blind spots leading to mismanagement. The system of sport governance in theory invited everyone to take part in decision-making processes to promote rational discussion and collaborative civic engagement. However, in reality it remained highly exclusionary and depended upon power networks. The opportunity for volunteers to decide on autonomy and the fate of Czech sport was missed, and only recently has the system of Czech sport governance become an object of reform.

So as not to provide a biased image, which would be exclusively based on the description of crisis and mismanagement, this picture of Czech sport governance must be completed with some trends to the contrary, and an increasingly frequent use of sport as a tool to achieve social development objectives. Sport associations are increasingly involved in initiatives that promote the social benefits of sport and acknowledge its potential to act as a tool for crime prevention, social inclusion or educational objectives. These initiatives silently but steadily have transformed the nature of contemporary Czech sport governance and its engagement with corporate social responsibility. To provide examples, the initiative Sport without Prejudice (www.sportbezpredsudku.cz) is a partnership between public, private and non-governmental sectors. It is managed primarily by the Czech Rugby Union and is a typical example of one of these initiatives. The initiative has been in action for nine years. By enhancing grassroots sport, the initiative attempts to prevent crime and to promote a healthy lifestyle for youth. Last, but not least, contemporary Czech society, in particular the political arena, currently is in a period of strong anti-corruption and anti-mismanagement campaigns. It is unlikely that the sphere of sport will remain immune to these initiatives.

Summary

Czech sport governance has lived a long and rich history, balancing between civic engagement and autonomy on the one hand, and dependence on the state and political ideologies on the other hand. The democratic roots of Czech sport governance connected with the Sokol movement and the ideas of civic engagement that were enhanced during the period of the First Republic (1918–1938) were destroyed during the eras of Nazism and communism.

The space for democratic and autonomous sport development was reopened during the Velvet Revolution in 1989. Sport governing bodies were liberated from central planning with the sphere of sport becoming more pluralised and fragmented. Hand-in-hand with increasing complexity, Czech sport governance became more fragile vis-à-vis political and business interests. It was this fragility that mainly contributed to the contemporary period of crisis.

To conclude, Czech sport governance represents a vivid and dynamically evolving social sphere. It is most likely that a new wave of seismic change is about to happen in the world of sport. Considering these Czech sport governance dynamics, their intensity and the scope of changes, this chapter risks becoming a mere historical testimony rather than a timely portrait of existing conditions. Czech sport governance is probably waiting for a period of new transformation and for a new reform and redefinition. Further developments will suggest whether these transformations will only be related to the formal structure of sport governance or also to its sociocultural assets, such as mentalities, attitudes, norms and values.

Review questions

1   How would you characterise the main aspects of contemporary Czech governance taking into consideration the importance of governmental and non-governmental pillars?
2   Define the main aspects of sport governance in the communist era in the former Czechoslovakia.
3   Which were the the main causes of the contemporary crisis of Czech sport governance?

Further reading

Flemr, L., Bunc, V., Dohnal, T., Hobza, V., Kopřiva, M., Kovář, K., & Numerato, D. (2009). *Prostorové podmínky pro podporu aktivního životního stylu současné populace.* Prague: Karolinum.
Nolte, C. E. (2002). *The Sokol in the Czech lands to 1914: Training for the nation.* New York: Palgrave Macmillan.
Riordan, J. (ed.) (1978). *Sport under communism: The U.S.S.R., Czechoslovakia, the G.D.R., China, Cuba.* London: C. Hurst & Company.
Slepičková, I. (2007). *Sportovní organizace: Teoretická východiska a situace v ČR po roce 1990.* Prague: Karolinum.

Websites

Czech Olympic Committee: http://www.olympic.cz/en/
Situation in the motorcycle sport in the Czech Republic: http://www.czechmotosport.com/index_en.html
Sport bez předsudků: http://www.sportbezpredsudku.cz/

References

Černek, M. (2008). Sokolství a Olympismus. *Tělesná kultura*, 31(1), 48–56.
Chaker, A. N. (2004). *Good governance in sport: A European survey.* Strasbourg: Council of Europe Publishing. Dovalil, J. (2004). Olympijské hnutí. In J. Dovalil, K. Bauer, T. Doležal, A. Hogenová, M. Chalupecká, M. Choutka, N. Knorre, F. Kolář, A. Rychtecký, & B. Svoboda (eds). *Olympismus.* (pp.44–61). Prague: Olympia
ČSTV (2012). *Ročenka ČSTV 2011.* Prague: Olympia.
Dovalil, J. (2004). *Olympismus* [Olympism], 1st edn. Prague: Olympia.

Duke, V. (1990). Perestroika in progress?: The case of spectator sports in Czechoslovakia. *British Journal of Sociology*, 41(2), 145–56.

Duke, V. (2011). From Bohemian rhapsody to a new world: The organisation of football in the Czech Republic. In H. Gammelsæter & B. Senaux (eds). *The organisation and governance of top football across Europe: An institutional perspective,* (pp.238–52). London: Routledge.

European Union (2007). *White paper on sport*. Brussels: European Union.

Fasting, K., & Knorre, N. (2005). *Women in sport in the Czech Republic: The experiences of female athletes*. Prague: Norwegian School of Sport Sciences and Czech Olympic Committee.

Flemr, L. (2009). Závěry. In L. Flemr, V. Bunc, T. Dohnal, V. Hobza, M. Kopřiva, K. Kovář, & D. Numerato (eds). *Prostorové podmínky pro podporu aktivního životní stylu současné populace,* (pp.182–89). Prague: Karolinum.

Kolář, F. & Kössl, J. (1994). Origin and development of the Czech and Czechoslovakian Olympic Committee. *Journal of Olympic History*, 2(3), 11–26.

Kostka,V. (1978).Czechoslovakia. In J. Riordan (ed.). *Sport under Communism* (pp. 54–66). London: C. Hurst & Company.

KPMG (2012). *Koncepce financování sportu v České republice*. Prague: KPMG.

MŠMT (2011). Letter of the MŠMT to Fédération Internationale de Motocyclisme. 7 October 2011.

MŠMT (2012). Letter of the MŠMT to Autoklub ČR. 15 June 2012.

Nolte, C. E. (2002). *The Sokol in the Czech lands to 1914: Training for the nation*. New York: Palgrave Macmillan.

Novotný, J. (2011). Czech Republic. In Eurostrategies (ed.). *Study on the funding of grassroots sports in the EU – Final reports Volume II* (pp.46–59). Available online at http://ec.europa.eu/internal_market/top_layer/docs/FinalReportVol2_en.pdf.

Numerato, D. (2009). The institutionalisation of regional public sport policy in the Czech Republic. *International Journal of Sport Policy and Politics*, 1(1), 13–30.

Numerato, D. (2010a). Czech sport governance cultures and a plurality of social capitals: Politicking zone, movement and community. In M. Groeneveld, B. Houlihan, & F. Ohl (eds). *Social capital and sport governance in Europe* (pp.41–62). London: Routledge.

Numerato, D. (2010b). Between small everyday gestures and big symbolic acts: Ways of resistance in sport against the Communist regime in Czechoslovakia. *Sport in Society*, 13(1), 107–20.

Slepičková, I. (2007a). *Sportovní organizace: Teoretická východiska a situace v ČR po roce 1990*. Prague: Karolinum.

Slepičková, I. (2007b). From centralized to democratic sport governance and organization. *Transitions*, 1(5), 95–106.

Thorne, V. (2011). Těla v pohybu: Masová gymnastika jako kolektivní sociální představení. *Sociální studia*, 8(1), 97–116.

Uhlíř, J., & Waic, M. (2001). *Sokol proti totalitě 1938–1952*. Prague: FTVS UK.

Ústavní soud (Constitutional Court) (2012). Usnesení Ústavního soudu ÚS 3494/11. 16 April 2012.

Valjent, Z., & Flemr, L. (2010). Počátky vysokoškolského sportu na českých vysokých školách (1907-1914). *Česká kinantropologie*, 14(2), 37-45.

Waic, M. (1997). *Sokol v české společnosti 1862-1938*. Praha: FTVS UK.

Legislation

Government resolutions

Usnesení vlády č. 2/1999. koncepce státní politiky v tělovýchově a sportu v České republice.

Usnesení vlády č. 673/2003. ke Směrům státní politiky ve sportu na léta 2004 až 2006.

Usnesení vlády č. 167/2011. o Koncepci státní podpory sportu v České republice.

Legislative acts

Zákon č. 115/2001 Sb., o podpoře sportu, ve znění novely zákona č. 219/2005 Sb. Sbírka zákonů České republiky, 2001.

Zákon č. 187/1949 Sb., o státní péči o tělesnou výchovu a sport.

Zákon č. 68/1956 Sb., o organisaci tělesné výchovy.

Zákon č. 71/1952 Sb., o organisaci tělesné výchovy a sportu.

16 New Zealand

Lesley Ferkins, Uma Jogulu and
Trevor Meiklejohn

Topics

- Introduction to the New Zealand sport governance landscape
- Historical influences on sport governance in New Zealand
- Gender diversity in New Zealand sport governance
- Evolving governance design in New Zealand sport organisations.

Objectives

- To introduce the current sport governance landscape in New Zealand including a discussion of the sport system as it relates to sport governance
- To identify and discuss historical influences on sport governance in New Zealand with a focus on government involvement in sport
- To analyse the issue of gender diversity in relation to national sport organisation boards in New Zealand
- To analyse the interrelated and systemic nature of sport governance in New Zealand and discuss evolving design issues in the governance of national sport organisations.

Key terms

Board gender diversity   Refers to a mix of men and women on the board.
Organisational governance   Refers to governance *of an* organisation.
Systemic governance   Refers to governance *between* organisations.
Governance design/structure   In this context refers to how organisations choose to design/structure the interrelationships between organisations.

Overview

This chapter begins by introducing the sport governance landscape in New Zealand, establishing context for the ensuing discussion of national sport organisation (NSO) governance. Key historical influences on the way that sport is governed in New Zealand are identified, with an emphasis on the influence of sustained government involvement in sport. Following this, the issue of gender diversity in relation to NSO boards in New Zealand is discussed. Additionally, a feature of the sport governance landscape in New Zealand is the interrelationship between sport organisations and how it impacts on the ability of NSOs to perform their governing role. The evolving nature of NSO governance design and structures (these terms are used interchangeably) is analysed as an increasingly important sport governance issue in New Zealand. This issue is further explored in the case of the New Zealand Rugby Union (NZRU), presented in the second half of the chapter.

Introduction to the New Zealand sport governance landscape

The New Zealand sport governance landscape is a curious combination of public (central and local government), non-profit, and commercial organisations charged with delivering sport or providing services and products to sport organisations. Despite the global trend toward the commercialisation of sport (i.e., payment of athletes and private ownership of sport), the New Zealand sport governance landscape is still dominated by public and non-profit organisations (Hoye & Doherty, 2011). Drawn from a population of over 4,400,000 people with a rich sporting tradition (Leberman, Collins & Trenberth, 2012), there are 90 registered non-profit NSOs, each affiliated to multiple regional associations (Sport New Zealand, 2012). There is also over 14,500 independent legally constituted clubs across all sporting codes, affiliated with their respective regional association or, in some instances, directly with the NSO (McConnell, 2001). In most instances, these clubs, which are also non-profit entities, are governed and administered by volunteers.

Sport New Zealand, the crown agency for sport, is joined by 78 local government bodies that contribute public-sector funds to the sport sector (Sport New Zealand, 2012). In 2010/2011, Sport New Zealand's revenue totalled over $NZ 110 million ($US 88 million), while local government expenditure on sport is estimated to be over $NZ 450 million ($US 359 million) (McConnell, 2001; SPARC, 2011). Local government bodies, known as territorial authorities, play an important role in the provision of sport facilities, events, and programmes, while the central government agency has a more direct funding relationship with sport bodies, particularly NSOs. In addition, 17 regional sports trusts, legally constituted as charitable organisations, provide services and support to the sport sector, essentially, on behalf of Sport New Zealand, but also as agents of the regional community within which they are situated. Schools and tertiary institutions also play an important role in the delivery of sporting activities, sport education, and research.

In accordance with global trends there is a growing commercial and professional sector within New Zealand sport that has impacted governance practice (Ferkins, Shilbury & McDonald, 2005). In terms of sporting codes, the New Zealand Rugby Union leads the way in 'professionalism' with five New Zealand rugby franchises (although ownership structures are non-profit) that play in an international Super Rugby competition. Significantly for women's sport, Netball New Zealand too has five semi-professional (non-profit) franchises that compete with five Australian teams in a Trans-Tasman competition. In conjunction with the semi-professional aspect, netball is the largest participation sport in New Zealand secondary schools, and the largest women's participation and media sport (Netball New Zealand, 2011). While netball and rugby are sports that involve player payments and are professionally run commercial organisations, neither supports full private ownership of the semi-professional/professional aspects of their sports.

There are just a handful of sports in New Zealand that have embraced a fully commercial, private franchise model, namely: basketball (SKYCITY Breakers), rugby league (Vodafone Warriors), and football/soccer (Wellington Phoenix). These privately owned teams operate independently from their respective NSOs, yet it is the NSO which has responsibility for elite athlete pathways and national selection. With the NSOs remaining non-profit organisations, a curious interface is created between 'private commercial', and 'non-profit membership' based organisations, and their respective governance models. The case study presented later in this chapter explores the governance design of rugby union. It details how the NSO has dealt with the growing professional element to its game, while also retaining a focus on participation and the tenets of non-profit community sport.

While the professional and semi-professional competitions can dominate the headlines (e.g., rugby and netball are among the leading media sports), as noted above, the majority of sport organisations are non-profit incorporated societies or charitable trusts. Other influential non-profit sport bodies include the New Zealand Olympic Committee, Drug Free Sport New Zealand, and High Performance Sport New Zealand (a subsidiary of Sport New Zealand). Figure 16.1 indicates relationships between major public sector and non-profit sport organisations in New Zealand, highlighting geographic levels and major categories of organisations. This interesting blend of public, non-profit, and commercial entities has important implications for the governance of NSOs in New Zealand, the focus of this chapter.

NSOs are part of a federated network of organisations that govern their respective sporting codes (Leberman *et al.*, 2012). As NSOs in New Zealand seek to compete on the world stage in the high-performance domain, as well as fulfil their role in fostering community level participation activities, many have embarked on a series of reforms in a search to improve governance designs (as discussed later). Other important issues to have emerged in the governance of these peak bodies in New Zealand include the way the boards of NSOs have embraced their strategic function (Ferkins & Shilbury, 2012), the balance of power and leadership between the board and CEO (Ferkins, Shilbury & McDonald, 2009), and the challenge to understand and define the board's governing role in light of dynamic environmental changes in the professionalisation of sport (e.g., paid staff, player payments, business-like approaches etc., see Hoye & Cuskelly, 2007). Concern has also been expressed at apparent gaps in board gender diversity in these important decision-making bodies (Cockburn, Gray & Thompson, 2007). For the purposes of this chapter, the focus is on issues of board gender diversity, and governance design within NSOs. The next section outlines historical influences in sport governance in New Zealand, which sets the foundation for a more indepth discussion of these issues.

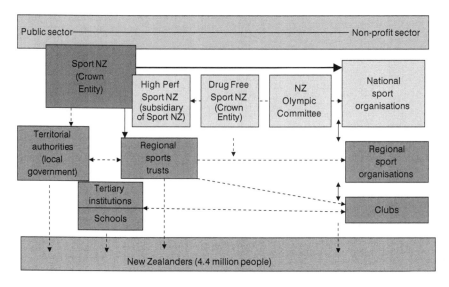

Figure 16.1 New Zealand sport system: major public and non-profit entities

Historical influences on NSO governance in New Zealand

Unsurprisingly, the way NSOs are governed in New Zealand has been influenced by a myriad of social, governmental, and commercial agendas. As the writer of a major report for the Ministerial Taskforce on Sport, Fitness and Leisure (2001), McConnell, insightfully noted (p. 22):

> Sport has become a major consideration in the social and economic life of New Zealand. It has, arguably, become justified less on grounds of social and moral values than as the domain of fitness, commercial imperatives and branding. In 2000 AD recreation and sport may be viewed significantly through the lens of the media, vested commercial interests, the 'amateur–professional' debate, or bound up with international competition, politics, funding, national prestige, or the subtle forces of symbolism.

This statement is reflective of the development of sport in New Zealand society, and how it has evolved from a physical pastime, and set of rituals and training (equated activities since pre-European settlement), to an important social, political, and economic mechanism through which, arguably, New Zealand's nationhood is often defined (Thomson & Sim, 2007). As with other Commonwealth countries (e.g., Australia, Canada, UK), New Zealand governments have involved themselves in the funding of sport in order to leverage the social, political, and economic benefits for its citizens. New Zealand is one of the first Commonwealth countries to legislate for government involvement in sport, beginning with the Physical Welfare and Recreation Act 1937, passed by the then Labour Government, concerned with low fitness levels of New Zealand youth and the implications of this for defence (McConnell, 2001). According to McConnell (2001, p.20), the act and resulting initiatives (see Table 16.1) were set against a backdrop of 'Parliamentary rhetoric [that] revealed bipartisan beliefs in the moral and social values of sport for the individual and society'.

Such were the foundations of successive governments' involvement in sport, largely achieved through the establishment of a Crown agency, designed to operate at 'arm's length' from government. As a consequence, public-sector involvement in sport has been influential for NSOs in New Zealand as set out in Table 16.1. Also detailed in Table 16.1 are the major pieces of legislation that have affected NSOs in New Zealand and provided for the establishment of crown entities in sport.

Interestingly, McConnell (2001) noted, 'Arguably, these structures have assumed de facto roles of social organisation and control of recreation and sport through their powers of financial disbursement and economic patronage' (p.20).

Officially, these crown agencies have sought to encourage, promote, and support physical recreation and sport in New Zealand by activities of leadership and facilitation, capability development, and investment (via funding) within the sport system. NSOs have always been a focus of these efforts. In recognition of the growing influence of governance, in 1999 the then Hillary Commission released its first of a number of resources targeting the governing function of sport organisations. This series of resources, which became increasingly specific to the governance of NSOs, was also supported by workshops and training initiatives for CEOs and board members (Hillary Commission, 2001; Sport and Recreation New Zealand, 2006).

Many NSOs in New Zealand are over 100 years old and, in terms of organisational governance, have evolved from large volunteer councils and representative committees to modern boards of directors. Today, NSO boards in New Zealand are mainly comprised of seven to nine directors (usually voluntary), with positions on the board allocated to regionally elected members as well as independent directors. As Ferkins and Shilbury (2012, p.72) observe, 'Board composition of this nature is considered to be a "hybrid" which allows for the democratic ideals of an election process to remain, supplemented by individuals chosen for their professional expertise, as well as "outsider" perspectives'.

In many instances, the way NSO boards are comprised and the way they have gone about their governing processes and decision-making, has been influenced by what Sport New Zealand and its predecessors have determined as good governance practice. While the crown agency has never dictated NSO governance practice, collective thinking, often disseminated via this peak agency, has influenced governance designs, processes and practice, as NSOs have sought to understand and enact their governing role. The next section, in focussing on organisational governance, discusses board composition as it relates to the issue of gender diversity in New Zealand NSO boards.

Table 16.1 Selected New Zealand sport legislation affecting NSOs

Act of parliament	Primary purpose of the act	Implications for NSOs
The Physical Welfare and Recreation Act 1937	Provided for central government funding to local government for sports facilities.	Facility provision. Stimulated the establishment of a National Council for Sport to support sport bodies.
The Recreation and Sport Act 1973	Established the Council for Recreation and Sport, and created the Office of Minister of Recreation and Sport.	Paved the way for funding and support of NSOs.
The Recreation and Sport Act 1987	Established the crown entity, Hillary Commission for Recreation and Sport	The Hillary Commission funded registered NSOs on an annual basis.
The Sport, Fitness and Leisure Act 1992	Renamed the crown entity, the Hillary Commission for Sport, Fitness and Leisure.	NSOs became a key 'investment' partner of the Hillary Commission with funding subject to multi-year criteria based 'investment'.
The New Zealand Sports Drug Agency Act 1994	Established the crown entity, the New Zealand Sports Drug Agency, to provide for testing for the use of drugs in sport, and to encourage drug free sport.	Compliance and educational role for NSO high performance programmes.
Sports Anti-Doping Act 2006	Reconfirmed purpose of agency, renamed Drug Free Sport New Zealand and to comply with World Anti-Doping Code.	Compliance and educational role for NSO high performance programmes
Sport and Recreation New Zealand Act 2002	Established the crown agency called Sport and Recreation New Zealand (referred to as SPARC and renamed Sport New Zealand in 2012).	Dissolution of the NZ Sports Foundation (a non-government agency established in 1978 to fund and support elite athletes/high performance sport). SPARC (later Sport New Zealand) established the NZ Academy of Sport (which later became High Performance NZ) which provides services and funding for NSOs (effectively replacing the work of the NZ Sports Foundation).

The issue of gender diversity in NSO governance in New Zealand

In general, gender diversity on boards has become increasingly important for governance. Diversity can create a competitive advantage and enhance organisation performance (Carter, Simkins & Simpson, 2003). In short, good organisational governance values diversity and capitalises on the benefits that difference can bring (Cunningham, 2008). Therefore, when NSO boards limit the inclusion of women, the question of whether NSOs are maximising their talent pool for critical decision-making roles comes to the fore.

It is known that sport governance practice is not necessarily reflective of gender diversity (Cunningham & Fink, 2006) across the globe, with New Zealand no exception. The resistance to appoint women into NSO board positions can hinder the level of success and performance of distinct board tasks. Curiously, some research suggests that women, when holding board memberships, are more likely to generate ideas about strategic input and often show interest and involvement with issues of a strategic nature (Nielsen & Huse, 2010). They are also likely to invest in developing formal board structures through introduction of diverse members, a significant characteristic that is known to enhance group productivity (Gist, Locke & Taylor, 1987). In addition, women at board level are more likely to introduce social initiatives including flexible work conditions and work life balance policies to provide an inclusive and balanced work environment (Francoeur, Labelle & Sinclair-Desgagne, 2008).

Despite the advantages of having diversity as part of governance, there is considerable evidence that suggests women represent a minority group of people in sport organisations (Cunningham, 2008). In New Zealand, research conducted by Cockburn, Gray and Thompson (2007) surveyed 47 NSOs on behalf of the New Zealand Olympic Committee. They found that women held approximately 27 per cent of NSO board positions. They also found that over half of the organisations surveyed did not meet the International Olympic Committee guidelines of a 20 per cent minimum of NSO female board membership. Additionally, only 19 per cent of the NSO boards surveyed reflected the gender composition of the sport's participants. There were also 10 boards (21 per cent) with no women. In linking board gender composition with organisational policies, Cockburn *et al.* (2007) found that few NSOs had national development programmes for women (6 per cent), and only 9 per cent of the NSOs surveyed had sub-committees or special groups that focused on women's policies for their respective sports.

So, why is this low level of involvement by women occurring at NSO board level? The tradition of seeing sport as a masculine domain with women perceived to not possess the biological skills or interest in physically challenging activities has perpetuated in the sport industry since sport was created (Messner & Solomon, 2007). This view may also explain why women are given less opportunity to develop governance skills. Indeed, board membership appears to be where gender segregation is most pronounced (Cunningham & Fink, 2006).

Positioning this argument within the feminist research suggests that the differences between the sexes emerged because women have been universally responsible for early childcare (Chodorow, 1978). How men and women are placed socially in society determines sex-differentiated perceptions held about their organisational capabilities. This further leads to the formation of gender roles 'by which people of each sex are expected to have psychological characteristics that equip them for the tasks that their sex typically performs' (Chodorow, 1978, p.701). Nevertheless, research continues to question the reasons for women's low representation at board level in sport organisations to gain further insight into potential ways of including women so that they can contribute in this role. Developing a better understanding about women's contributions will, potentially, help challenge some of the perspectives around gender and board membership in New Zealand NSOs.

The issue of governance design in New Zealand NSOs

In terms of governance structure or design, most New Zealand sports consist of a complex 'network' of organisations that, essentially, make up the sport (i.e., a federation). At the heart of this network is the club (explained earlier as a separate legal entity and usually voluntarily run). Most traditional New Zealand sports with their roots in Britain have adopted the club as the fundamental provider or caretaker for the sport at the local level (Leberman *et al.*, 2012). Football (soccer), for instance, New Zealand's largest youth participation sport with over 105,000 players (female and male), consists of 325 football clubs across the country (New Zealand Football, 2011).

Centuries on from the establishment of the first clubs in Britain when decisions were made as how to structure the interrelationships between these organisations (Szymanski & Ross, 2007), in many respects New Zealand NSOs are still facing the same challenge today. How should the sport structure itself to coordinate its members, manage its competitions at various levels, develop the game, provide pathways for players, coaches and officials, and market and promote the sport? Furthermore, if the sport has a professional arm, how should this resource-demanding aspect of the sport be incorporated (or not) into the sport's network? These questions, while addressed in part by administrative and management orientated structures, are also critical to the design of NSO governance structures.

Indeed, the above notions are integral to the concept of systemic governance (governance between organisations) as opposed to organisational governance (focused on single organisation boards) (Henry & Lee, 2004). Within a sport context, governance becomes somewhat more intriguing due to the simultaneous cooperative and competitive actions of member organisations within a sport code (Dickson, Arnold & Chalip, 2005). At the basic level, clubs exist as both single autonomous entities as well as a collection of clubs as part of the local, regional or national governance structure of a sport. On the one hand, a club may be competing on the field with other clubs, and competing for players and commercial revenue off the field. Yet, on the other hand, a club will be cooperating with other clubs regarding rules and regulations and joint initiatives aimed at the betterment of the sport. Such a unique dynamic requires careful consideration of the governance structure(s) adopted by the national governing body providing a framework for national delivery and direction of the sport. The parallels are evident when observing the governance of networks within a broader 'inter-organisational relationship' context, and are highlighted by Powell, White, Koput and Owen-Smith (2005, p.1133) who referred to 'illuminating the structure of collective action'.

With the club in mind, many New Zealand NSOs adopted a 'bottom-up' system consistent with their British origins. In this system, local clubs formed associations based on cities or geographic regions which, in turn, create a national structure and the establishment of a national governing body (Houlihan, 1997). Traditionally, netball in New Zealand has reflected this structure, consisting of 1000 clubs, 92 centres aligned to 12 regions, and the national body, Netball New Zealand (NNZ). Like other NSOs in New Zealand, however, NNZ has addressed systemic governance issues with the advent of professionalism (Freeman, 2007). After major consultation, NNZ members voted in 2012 for changes that will see the 12 regional entities abolished and replaced with five zones that directly reflect the Trans-Tasman competition franchise zones. NNZ's (2012) articulated rationale for these proposed changes emphasises greater efficiencies and synergies, with each zone responsible for all areas of netball in the zone (i.e., grass roots to high performance, including the Trans-Tasman franchise team).

It is apparent that the role of the netball centres will remain unchanged; however, they will fall within one of five zones as opposed to one of 12 regional entities (NNZ, 2012). This is a bold and innovative move by NNZ in response to both professionalism (player payments) and professionalisation (a more business-like approach, increasing paid staff, etc.). In particular, it demonstrates a willingness to adapt historical and traditional governance entities for a governance design that meets with existing and future challenges.

In addition to those addressing the professional component of their sport, many other NSOs in New Zealand are looking to reduce the number of regional associations in search of a more streamlined approach to governance. This, in turn, has created uncertainties for affected members and stakeholders (Freeman, 2007). Examples of this type of adaptation include Football New Zealand's formation of seven 'federations' in 2000, Tennis New Zealand's move from 24 associations to six regional bodies in 2007, and Athletics New Zealand, which, in a ground-breaking step in 2010, entirely removed the regional layer of governance that had been in place since 1902 (Athletics New Zealand, 2010). In this governance design, often referred to as a 'unitary model' (Shilbury & Kellett, 2006), athletics clubs rather than centres (i.e., regional associations) became members of the national body and, thus, the equivalent of 'shareholders'. As such, the clubs now have the opportunity to vote on matters of national governance, including the board composition of the NSO. Rugby has also undergone changes to its governance designs as is now illustrated in detail in the case study section below.

Case study: New Zealand Rugby's evolving governance design

This case study explores the systemic governance design of New Zealand's leading NSO, the New Zealand Rugby Union (NZRU). It details how the NSO is adapting the growing professional element to its game, while also retaining a focus on sport participation in changes made to governance design. Hoye and Cuskelly (2007) suggested that governance structures may be conceptualised and analysed from three different perspectives: organisational theory, governance models, and inter-organisational relationships. This case study takes an inter-organisational relationship approach to examining the wider systemic governance design of rugby union. In this way, the notion of 'network governance' (Provan & Kenis, 2008) is also used.

As highlighted in the body of this chapter, most sporting codes in New Zealand exist as a network. Each entity within this network operates autonomously and as a collection of organisations. This is underpinned by the competition/cooperation dynamic which, as debated by Smith and Stewart (2010), is considered a 'special feature' of the sport sector. Provan and Kenis (2008) asserted that network governance involves structures to coordinate and control joint action across the network. This has indeed proved to be an ongoing challenge for the NZRU, particularly as historic and institutionalised governance structures are confronted with professionalism and globalisation (Ferkins *et al.*, 2005). For example, when the All Blacks (New Zealand's national rugby team) won the 2011 Rugby World Cup, the global audience was estimated to be four billion people (IRB, 2012). By comparison, the All Black's first World Cup win in 1987 was beamed out to just 300 million people globally (IRB, 2012). In addition, in term of global presence, the All Blacks has the best winning record of any national team in the world (IRB, 2012). So, how have such successes and rapid advances in the sport impacted governance design of NSOs in New Zealand?

Background to the New Zealand Rugby Union

The NZRU is a non-profit incorporated society formed in 1892 and charged with fostering, developing, administering, promoting, and representing the game of rugby in New Zealand. More specifically, this involves community and provincial rugby, national competitions, Super Rugby in New Zealand, international Test matches in New Zealand, and resourcing national teams such as the All Blacks (NZRU, 2012). In this way, the NZRU is clearly mandated to govern both elite and now professional elements as well as local level participation in the sport, often involving volunteer officials. As New Zealand's largest NSO, the NZRU employs 80 full time staff, headed by a CEO, and split amongst six functional teams which represent the integration of community rugby and professional rugby (NZRU, 2012).

The NZRU board is comprised of nine members: two representatives from each of three designated zones within New Zealand (i.e., North, Central and South), one Maori (indigenous people of New Zealand), and two independently appointed

Table 16.2 Provincial entities within New Zealand rugby

Super Rugby Franchise (Base Union)	Blues (Auckland)	Chiefs (Waikato)	Hurricanes (Wellington)	Crusaders (Canterbury)	Highlanders (Otago)
Associated Unions (NZRU primary members 'owners')	Northland, North Harbour	Counties Manukau, Bay of Plenty, King Country, Thames Valley	Manawatu, Hawkes Bay, Taranaki, East Coast, Poverty Bay, Wanganui, Horowhenua, Kapiti, Wairarapa Bush	Tasman, Buller, West Coast, Mid Canterbury, South Canterbury	Southland, North Otago

directors (New Zealand Rugby Union, 2011). This board composition reflects the federated nature of the NSO's governing structure which, as noted earlier, is also viewed as a network of inter-organisational relationships. Unusually, the NZRU has retained many aspects of a representative model, ensuring each member organisation has a mechanism for input at board level. In the commercial world, the board governs on behalf of its owners (i.e., shareholders). Translated into the non-profit sport domain, and as is the case with the NZRU, the 'owners' or 'shareholders' are referred to as 'members'. As stipulated in the NZRU constitution, the members of the NZRU are its 26 provincial unions (see Table 16.2), the associate members, the life members, and the New Zealand Maori Rugby Board Inc. Considered this way, the NZRU is both 'owned' by its members (the majority of which are its 26 unions) and reliant upon its unions as a crucial part of its governance network.

In 2011, the NZRU reported 145,689 players registered to 600 clubs and a network of secondary schools across New Zealand which, in turn, are members of the provincial unions (New Zealand Rugby Union, 2011). Each of the 26 provincial unions is also a non-profit incorporated society. These provinces have a governing role in overseeing (directing, controlling, coordinating) administrative, developmental and promotional aspects of rugby, including local community competitions, as well as the management and resourcing of representative teams at a provincial level (NZRU, 2012). Therefore, while the entire New Zealand rugby network may be viewed as a federation with the NZRU as its prime governing body, there are also 26 'sub-networks', or provinces, with a federated structure within them (i.e., the provincial unions comprising affiliated clubs and schools). In this way, governance of rugby in New Zealand is clearly affected by the inter-organisational relationships between members of the network. Next, we consider the forces of professionalism on governance design and how the NZRU, in particular, has responded.

Professionalism and governance designs in rugby union

Many sport codes have been confronted with the introduction of professionalism, or at least semi-professionalism. Such changes have challenged existing governance structures and/or prompted change. In some sports, the professional arm has split from the amateur bodies allowing private investors to develop commercial organisations and devise rules that are suited to their interests as owners (Szymanski & Ross, 2007). This model is reflective of professional leagues in the USA (e.g., NFL, NBL, MLB etc.). In New Zealand rugby, both sides of the game have remained united and controlled within a federated network.

Under the threat of 'shamateurism' (illegal payment of players), on 26 August 1995, the International Rugby Board declared rugby union an 'open' game and removed restrictions on payments and benefits to those involved with the game. Another major threat to amateur rugby union came from Super League (a short-lived commercial governing body for rugby league football) which threatened to draw players to rugby league by offering large salaries. Thus, in many respects, the IRB was forced into allowing rugby union to become professional to avoid what it considered to be the hypocrisy of widespread player payments. In doing so, it also sought to keep control (a key pillar of governance) of rugby union (Fitzsimons, 1996).

O'Brien and Slack (2004) observed the change in professionalism within English rugby, and highlighted the growing pains that occurred in this traditional federated network with the sudden influx of private investors to clubs, and the lack of coordination, advice or strategic guidelines from the governing body as to how to proceed with professionalism. They asserted that changes were ad hoc and somewhat frantic in response to professionalism. They also noted that it took some time for the game to develop a coordinated approach and a 'new professional logic' to be established with associated governance structures in place.

In contrast to the above English Rugby example, the transition to professionalism in New Zealand rugby was very much managed and orchestrated by the NZRU. As soon as rugby became professional in 1995, and to counter the Super League threat, the NZRU joined with the South African and Australian Rugby Unions to legally form SANZAR. SANZAR proposed a provincial based competition with teams from all three countries. Denoting the number of teams, this competition became the Super 12, then Super 14, before assuming its current identity as Super Rugby (SANZAR Rugby, 2012).

In terms of governing models, New Zealand was allocated five franchises in this professional competition, which the NZRU owned 100 per cent. Clearly, numerous governance structures were available to the NZRU regarding the configuration of these franchises. Highlighting the NZRU's desire to maintain ownership of the professional arm of the game and, thus the right to govern, the NZRU centrally contracted all Super Rugby players. In order to engage member unions and continue to foster participation and grassroots opportunities in the sport, the NZRU also opted for regional franchises. In this process, each of the 27 provincial unions (later reduced to 26) was allocated to a franchise zone in which it resided (refer to Table 16.2).

Under this governance framework, one provincial union (i.e., the Base Union) within each of the five franchises was then given the responsibility to manage the franchise on behalf of the NZRU. This occurred via a franchise agreement between the NZRU and the provincial union or, more specifically, a management company 100 per cent owned by the provincial union (NZRU, 2008). Each franchise, therefore, reflects a small regional network or cluster of provincial unions with one existing member managing its activities (Meiklejohn, 2010). Provan and Kenis (2008) referred to this type of network governance structure as 'lead organisation governance', where one existing member of a network takes a leadership responsibility. This role may naturally emerge or be mandated by a governing body, as was the case with the NZRU. In this case, the CEO of the provincial union is also the CEO of the Super Rugby franchise (see Table 16.2).

Since the introduction of Super 12 Rugby, numerous discussions and reviews have occurred around independent governance of, and private investment in, New Zealand Super Rugby franchises. At this time two franchises, (the Chiefs and the Highlanders), are demonstrating independence from their base union with separate CEOs. The NZRU has also gone to the market for licences to manage four of the five franchises. The NZRU would, however, retain ownership and thus the right to governance (or governance involvement) of the franchises (Super Rugby, 2012). This new scenario poses interesting potential developments from a systemic governance perspective for the sport of rugby in New Zealand.

Case Study conclusion

The details presented above highlight the intricacies of systemic governance. Cornforth (2011), an influential scholar who writes about governance in the non-profit domain, has criticised the over-emphasis on organisational governance (i.e., the work of the board). He states that research efforts have not kept pace with the:

> changing context in which many non-profit organizations operate or the complexity of governance arrangements ... this has led to an overly narrow conceptualization of non-profit governance that largely ignores the influence of the wider governance system.
>
> (Cornforth, 2011, pp.2-3)

In essence, Cornforth is urging that notice is taken of the inter-organisational relations between organisations in the consideration of the notion of governance. This case study, while not research-based, nonetheless illustrates the complexity of such relationships, and framed in a governance sense, shows the notion of systemic or network governance in play.

The case study also reveals the challenges and responsibilities faced by the NZRU. Together with its primary members ('owners'), the 26 rugby unions, the NZRU has embarked on important governance reforms to accommodate the professional elements of its sport. The choices it is making in systemic governance design, which often contrast other countries, demonstrate how professional sport might coalesce with sport participation. It remains to be seen whether this sport can remain committed to governance frameworks that accommodate both elements, and how it might respond to increasing commercial pressures in future systemic governance reforms. In following Cornforth's (2011) urging, research effort also needs to reflect the importance of this view of sport governance.

Summary

This chapter first introduced the New Zealand sport system before providing background on key historical influences on the way sport is governed in New Zealand. The influence of sustained government involvement in New Zealand sport was emphasised and discussed in relation to the way NSO boards are comprised and the way they have gone about their governing processes and decision-making. The challenge and importance of gender diversity was also raised as a concern for NSO boards in New Zealand. The evolving nature of NSO systemic governance design was emphasised as an increasingly important sport governance issue in New Zealand, and was illustrated by the case of New Zealand Rugby Union. Governance is considered by many to be a lynchpin of any organisation (Pye, 2004) and in the sport domain, the added complexity of systemic governance brings fascinating challenges as the dynamic landscape of sport in New Zealand illuminates.

Dedication

This chapter is dedicated to the late Ron Garland, the best academic colleague one could hope for. We miss you terribly Ron.

Acknowledgement:

Thank you to Fraser Croad for his background support work with this chapter.

Review questions

1   Debate how sustained government involvement in New Zealand sport might have impacted the governance of NSOs.
2   Why might there be concern about a lack of female board members on NSO boards in New Zealand, and what might contribute to this?
3   Explain the notion of 'systemic governance' and provide examples from the New Zealand sport governance context.

Further reading

Cornforth, C. (ed.) (2003). *The governance of public and non-profit organisations: What do boards do?* London: Routledge.
Henry, I., & Lee, P. C. (2004). Governance and ethics in sport. In J. Beech & S. Chadwick (eds), *The business of sport management* (pp.25-41). Harlow: Pearson Education.

Hoye, R., & Cuskelly, G. (2007). *Sport governance.* Sydney: Elsevier.

Leberman, S., Collins, C., & Trenberth, C. (eds) (2012). *Sport business management in New Zealand and Australia.* 3rd edn. Melbourne: Cengage Learning Australia.

Websites

Netball New Zealand: http://www.mynetball.co.nz/
New Zealand Rugby: http://www.nzrugby.co.nz/
Sport New Zealand: http://sportnz.org.nz/

References

Athletics New Zealand (2010). *An enhanced Athletics New Zealand.* Wellington: Athletics New Zealand.

Carter, D. A., Simkins, B. J., & Simpson, W. G. (2003). Corporate governance, board diversity and firm value, *Financial Review*, 38, 33–53.

Chodorow, N. (1978). *The reproduction of mothering.* Berkeley, CA: University of California Press.

Cockburn, R., Gray, K., & Thompson, R. (2007). *Gender balance in New Zealand Olympic sports: Report to the New Zealand Olympic Committee.* New Zealand: NZOC.

Cornforth, C. (2011). Non-profit governance research: Limitations of the focus on boards and suggestions for new directions. *Nonprofit and Voluntary Sector Quarterly,* 41(6): 1118–36.

Cunningham, G. B. (2008). Creating and sustaining gender diversity in sports organizations. *Sex Roles*, 58, 136-145.

Cunningham, G. B., & Fink, J. S. (2006). Diversity issues in sport and leisure: Introduction to a special issue. *Journal of Sport Management*, 20, 455-65.

Dickson, G., Arnold, T., & Chalip, L. (2005). League expansion and inter-organisational power. *Sport Management Review*, 8, 145–65.

Ferkins, L., & Shilbury, D. (2012). Good boards are strategic: What does that mean for sport governance? *Journal of Sport Management*, 26, 67–80.

Ferkins, L., Shilbury, D., & McDonald, G. (2005). The role of the board in building strategic capability: Towards an integrated model of sport governance research. *Sport Management Review*, 8, 195–225.

Ferkins, L., Shilbury, D., & McDonald, G. (2009). Board involvement in strategy: Advancing the governance of sport organizations. *Journal of Sport Management*, 23, 245–77.

Fitzsimons, P. (1996). *The rugby war.* Sydney: Harper Collins.

Francoeur, C., Labelle, R., & Sinclair-Desgagne, B. (2008). Gender diversity in corporate governance and top management. *Journal of Business Ethics*, 81, 83–95.

Freeman, F. (2007). Regional sport study: Report commissioned by Bowls New Zealand. Auckland: Bowls New Zealand.

Gist, M. E., Locke, E. A., & Taylor, M. S. (1987). Organizational behaviour: Group structure, process, and effectiveness. *Journal of Management*, 13, 237–57.

Henry, I., & Lee, P.C. (2004). Governance and ethics in sport. In J. Beech & S. Chadwick (eds), *The business of sport management* (pp.25-41). Harlow: Pearson Education.

Hillary Commission for Sport, Fitness and Leisure. (2001). *Legal obligations of boards.* Wellington: Hillary Commission

Houlihan, B. (1997). *Sport, policy and politics: A comparative analysis.* New York: Routledge.

Hoye, R., & Cuskelly, G. (2007). *Sport governance.* Sydney: Elsevier.

Hoye, R., & Doherty, A. (2011). Nonprofit sport board performance: A review and directions for future research. *Journal of Sport Management,* 25, 272–85.

IRB (2012). Taking RWC 2011 to an audience of 4 billion. Available online at http://www.rwc2011.irb.com/destinationnewzealand/news/newsid=2036054.html

Leberman, S., Collins, C., & Trenberth, C. (eds). (2012). *Sport business management in New Zealand and Australia.* 3rd edn Melbourne: Cengage Learning Australia.

McConnell, R. (2001). *Report of the Sport, Fitness and Leisure Ministerial Taskforce: Getting set for an active nation.* Wellington: Ministerial Taskforce.

Meiklejohn, T. (2010). The formation, processes and impacts of inter-organisational cliques: A study of New Zealand provincial rugby. Unpublished Masters thesis, School of Sport and Recreation, AUT University, Auckland, New Zealand.

Messner, M., & Solomon, N. (2007). Social justice and men's interest: The case of title IX. *Journal of Sport and Social Issues,* 31, 162-78.

New Zealand Football (2011). *Annual report.* Auckland: New Zealand Football.

NNZ (2012) Netball New Zealand. Available online at http://www.mynetball.co.nz/netball-new-zealand.html.

Netball New Zealand (2011). *Annual report.* Auckland: Netball New Zealand

New Zealand Rugby Union (2011). *Annual report.* Wellington: New Zealand Rugby Union

Nielsen, S., & Huse, M. (2010). The contribution of women on boards of directors: Going beyond the surface. *Corporate Governance: An International Review,* 18(2), 136-148.

NZRU (2008). NZRU discussion document. Franchise structure review. July 2008. Available online at http://nzru.co.nz/publications/strategicdocuments/tabid/1303/default.aspx.

NZRU (2012). What we do. Available online at http://www.nzru.co.nz/what_we_do

O'Brien, D., & Slack, T. (2004). The emergence of a professional logic in English Rugby Union: The role of isomorphic and diffusion processes. *Journal of Sport Management,* 18, 13–39.

Powell, W., White, D., Koput, K., & Owen-Smith, J. (2005). Network dynamics and field evolution: The growth of inter-organisational collaboration in the life sciences. *Journal of Sociology,* 110, 1132–205.

Provan, K.G., & Kenis, P. (2008). Modes of network governance: Structure, management and effectiveness. *Journal of Public Administration Research and Theory,* 18(2), 229–52.

Pye, A. (2004). The importance of context and time for understanding board behaviour: Some lessons from social capital research. *International Studies of Management and Organisation,* 34(2), 63–89.

SANZAR Rugby (2012). About Sanzar. Available online at http://www.sanzarrugby.com/about-.

Shilbury, D., & Kellett, P. (2006). Reviewing organisational structure and governance: The Australian Touch Association. *Sport Management Review,* 9, 271–317.

Smith, A., & Stewart, B. (2010). The special features of sport: A critical revisit. *Sport Management Review,* 13, 1–13.

SPARC (2011). Annual Report for the year ended 30 June 2011. Wellington: SPARC.

Sport and Recreation New Zealand. (2006). *Nine steps to effective governance: Building high performance organisations* (2nd edn). Wellington: Sport and Recreation New Zealand.

Sport New Zealand (2012). Welcome to Sport New Zealand. Available online at http://sportnz.org.nz/.

Super Rugby (2012). Invitation to submit an expression of interest in a license to manage a Super Rugby Team. Available on line at http://www.superrugby.co.nz/franchise_eoi/ InvitationToSubmitAnExpressionOfInterest.pdf

Szymanski, S., & Ross, S. (2007). Governance and vertical integration in team sports. *Contemporary Economic Policy*, 24(4), 616–26.

Thomson, R., & Sim, J. (2007). Sport and culture: Passion and paradox. In C. Collins & S. Jackson (eds). *Sport in Aotearoa/New Zealand Society* (2nd edn, pp.113–29). South Melbourne: Thomson.

17 Global sport organisations

John Forster

Topics

- The evolution of modern sport and its governance
- The global governance of sport and national governance bodies
- Specialist governance organisations
- WADA and ICAS/CAS: doping and disputes
- Corruption in global sport governance organisations.

Objectives

- To outline and explain the complexity of the relationships existing between sport governance organisations at the global, national and sub-national levels
- To outline parts of the relationships between global sport governing organisations and individual athletes
- To describe and analyse the role of global sport organisations with specialist functions, and the governance problems they face
- To outline the complex network of governing sport organisations at both global and national levels
- To outline some of the forces operating on sport governing organisations.

Key terms

Global sport organisations The supreme governing bodies at the global level of either specific sports, sport events, or a specialist sporting function.

Global sport governance hierarchy The order of precedence between the various governing bodies within a given sport or sporting function.

Doping The illegal and/or legal use of pharmacological, chemical and other substances by athletes to gain a competitive advantage.

Sport arbitration Quasi-legal decision-making about the rules and principles governing sport competition, and their application to individual athletes and their relationships to sport organisations.

Autonomy The ability of a governance organisation to make its own rules without any constraints being placed upon that ability by other governance organisations or institutions.

Overview

The role of global sport organisations (GSOs) in sport governance is analysed partly in terms of the relationships to national sport federations and partly in terms of specialist governance organisations operating across sports, notably in doping and dispute arbitration.

The context is the evolution of sport from the eighteenth century into the present 'open' era. GSOs appeared in the late nineteenth century, created by national sport federations wanting standardised international competition. As the GSOs formalised globally common rules, the national federations lost much of their autonomy. In turn, the GSOs lost autonomy, notably to the International Olympic Committee (IOC). This was partly due to the desire for common rules governing athletes across sports, especially for multi-sport events.

Standing apart from the governance hierarchies of specific sports are specialist governance organisations such as the World Anti-Doping Agency (WADA), the International Council of Arbitration for Sport (ICAS), and the Court of Arbitration for Sport (CAS). Autonomy is again further reduced. Challenges now face all of these organisations as society, technology and commerce change.

The evolution of sport organisations and governance

Global commercial forces shape sport governance – just as governance structures help shape sport competition. To understand the structures and processes of contemporary sport one doesn't have to go back very far in history. Sport leagues, for example, are a recent innovation. The first league, baseball in the USA, was founded as recently as 1871 (Sullivan, 1997). The globally commercial English Football League began later in 1888 with just 12 professional clubs. These were from the north of England, e.g. Manchester United and Burnley, and the Midlands, notably Wolverhampton Wanderers – 'The Wolves'. The Wolves were the first to score a penalty goal in 1891. Penalties were designed to solve a governance problem and were a means of sanctioning a team breaking the rules of play, and which could be imposed while the game was still on. A parallel occurs in the case study presented later in the chapter. The International Court of Arbitration for Sport adjudicates 'ad hoc' in just 24 hours during Olympic Games, so as not to impede competition. Local and global governing bodies evolved during the same period.

The first Global Sport Organisation was the International Gymnastics Federation (FIG) founded in 1881. More specifically, FIG was the first international sport federation (IF) governing a specific sport. The term GSO is a more general term, which includes not only the IFs but other global sport governance bodies. One such body is the International Olympic Committee founded in 1894. Other early GSOs included the Fédération Internationale de l'Automobile (FIA) governing motor sports now including Formula One and the Fédération Internationale de Football Association (FIFA), both founded in 1904. The International Rugby Board (IRB) came about in 1886. Notice how close these dates are, suggesting common factors in the global development of all sport. The International Amateur Athletics Federation (IAAF) was founded by 17 national athletics associations in 1912. These associations 'saw the need for a governing authority, for an athletic programme, for standardised technical equipment and world records' (IAAF, 1999). The IAAF's global governance autonomy was short-lived due to a need for common rules relating to athletes for multi-sport events, particularly the Olympics. Since then global special interest groups such as the General Association of International Sports Federations (GAISF), renamed SportAccord in 2009, Association of IOC Recognised International Sports Federations (ARISF), Association of Summer Olympics International Federations (ASOIF), and Association of International Olympic Winter Sports Federations (AIOWF) have come into being, but all recognise the hegemony of the IOC, thereby putting limits on their own governance autonomy. It is from these non-profit and mostly amateur organisations, as well as underlying market forces, through which sport, its organisations, codes and governance has evolved into the 'open' era.

Codification and governance

With few exceptions, sport before the late eighteenth century was mostly informal and local. Then codification, and with governance, began. Rules governing cricket were written in 1727 and Broughton's rules for boxing in 1743. Why then and not before? Codification followed the rise of per capita incomes, the growth of leisure time, urbanisation, and often overlooked, the beginning of universal literacy. Why literacy? Because you only write down rules when enough people can read them. It was also in this period that sport newspapers began creating 'sport news' that massively promoted commercialisation.

So codification began in eighteenth-century Britain. Why? Because the conditions needed were more intense than anywhere else; with commercial sport appearing, viewing sport became a saleable product. Often paying spectators were watching sport played by amateurs or a mix of amateurs and professionals. Thus, commercial sport and professional sport are not the same. Professional sport is when players are paid. Some individuals and clubs were not interested in profit, but were interested in sporting success. Consequently they employed professionals, creating the amateur/professional distinction. This was the major governance issue of the late nineteenth to mid-twentieth century. Governing bodies were more concerned to maintain the amateur status of a sport, its events, and athletes, more than they were concerned with doping and other forms of cheating. This amateur–professional distinction was exemplified in cricket by the annual Gentlemen v Players (i.e. amateurs v professionals game) in England, which played until 1962. The International Amateur Athletics Federation only changed its name to the International Association of Athletics Federations in 2001 (www.iaaf.org/aboutiaaf/history/index.html) providing overdue recognition that athletes were being paid.

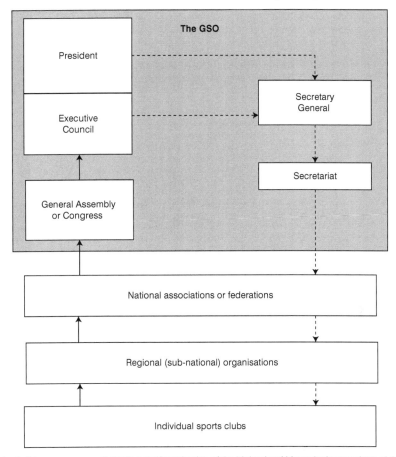

Note: Solid arrows represent election and/or selection of the higher level hierarchy by members of the lower level. Dashed arrows represent directives from the higher-level hierarchy to members of the lower-level hierarchy.

Figure 17.1 A global sport governance hierarchy: the GSO and the national federations

Global sport governance hierarchies and governance autonomy

Each sport was originally self-governing through its national and then global governing bodies. By creating their own global organisations, national governing bodies lost much of their governance autonomy to a global governance hierarchy (see Figure 17.1). (For governance hierarchies see Croci and Forster, 2004; Forster and Pope, 2004; and Forster, 2006). The concept of sport organisation autonomy is dealt with in Chappelet, Bousigue and Cohen (2008), although their primary concern is sport and European governments. In this chapter the focus is the loss of autonomy within the global governance mechanism.

An example of a sport with such a governance hierarchy is (target) archery. Its ruling GSO is the International Archery Federation (FITA), at least as far as Olympic representation is concerned. It was founded in 1931 and is now also called the World Archery Federation. This is important as there are several versions of recreational, professional and sport archery. Figure 17.1 shows the relationship between national federations and their global bodies. Target archery organisations fit well with this general structure. FITA promotes archery, and creates and interprets its own rules. It conducts international competitions including the FITA World Championships. FITA's congress (Figure 17.1) is its highest governing body. This congress has 149 national target archery federations as its membership of which Archery Australia, the national governing body in Australia, is one. Between its biennial congresses, FITA is overseen by the FITA Council (council/executive council in Figure 17.1) to which the president, vice presidents and council members are elected for four year terms. As well as its administration (the right hand side of Figure 17.1), there are permanent committees and ad hoc committees to deal with specific issues. Having little commercial clout, the recognition of archery as an Olympic sport is of utmost importance to FITA. Thus, Hollis's (1995) point is vital. 'The IOC delegates to individual IFs (International Federations) the technical control of all aspects of the sport they supervise, as well as authority for suspending or disciplining individual athletes who violate the IF's rules or code of conduct' (p.185). The use of the term 'delegates' suggests that the balance of power in archery is with the IOC, not FITA.

Nevertheless, FITA performs governance functions, some of a highly technical nature. In the Olympics for example, only recurve bows obeying standard FITA rules are allowed. Figure 17.2 shows a 'recurve' bow of the type used in target archery in the Olympics. Even the diameter of arrows is subject to regulation. In non-Olympic FITA competitions there are also 'compound' bows. Compound bows were invented in the 1960s, and more complex sights are allowed but with 'barebows' and 'longbows' no sights are allowed. Similarly, there are different competitions including target, match play, field, and clout. As Figure 17.2 indicates, these bows can be immensely complex and technologically advanced. The riser, the central section of the bow, its limbs, and the arrows are of high tech materials including carbon fibre. This bow was photographed during competition at the Mount Petrie Bowmen (MPB) Club in Australia. It is remote from FITA's headquarters in Europe, but FITA regulations ensure this bow is allowed for competition around the world. To ensure this, and for fair competition, this bow and all the other bows are inspected by judges prior to competition, ensuring adherence to FITA's global rules. In each sport technicalities can often determine the outcome of a sporting contest, so these technicalities are themselves often contested within governance bodies. This is seen even more dramatically in the case study.

Also in the governance hierarchy are international regional bodies. In target archery these include the Asian Archery Federation, Federation of African Archery, Oceania Archery Confederation, World Archery Americas, and World Archery Europe. An excerpt of the governance regulations of the Oceania Archery Confederation to which Archery Australia belongs, reads:

OCEANIA CHAMPIONSHIPS REGULATIONS (as adopted at the 7th Congress of the Confederation held at Papeete, Tahiti on 30 October 2008).

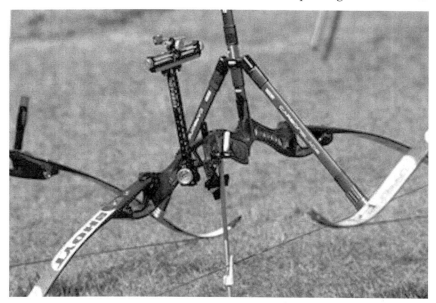

Figure 17.2 A modern recurve bow consistent with FITA rules shown in its strung state for shooting (photograph courtesy of Grahame Amy)

These Regulations are made under the authority of the CONSTITUTION, and the Definition and Interpretation provisions thereof (Sections 2 and 3) apply equally to these Regulations:

> 1. GENERAL: (1) Every second year, the Confederation shall hold tournaments to be known as the "Oceania Outdoor Target Archery Championships" and "Oceania Youth Outdoor Target Archery Championships". In Olympic years these Championships may incorporate the "Oceania Olympic Qualifying Tournament"…" (www.sportingpulse.com).

So, by conducting tournaments and selection procedures under FITA rules, Archery Australia sends either teams and/or selected members to the Olympics and FITA international competitions.

The mutual interests of the various national governing bodies of archery in Australia led to a joint body called Archery Alliance Australia (AAA). AAA was created in December 2010 by a memorandum of understanding (MoU) between Archery Australia (AA), The Australian Bowhunters Association (ABA), and the 3D Archery Association of Australia (3DAAA). Archery equipment is complex, but its organisation and governance is even more so. To add even more complexity, each Australian state and territory has its own governing body, all under Archery Australia. Yet, there are historical anomalies. So, in Queensland there is no state-wide organisation. However, there is a South Queensland Archery Society (SQAS), the governing body in its eponymous area. Moving down the governance hierarchy (Figure 17.1), below the SQAS are individual clubs such as MPB in

Brisbane. MPB represents the most elemental organisational unit in sport, the 'club'. Its membership comprises individual archers, male and female, junior and senior, competitive and recreational. So, being in the FITA hierarchy, MPB can run FITA-recognised competitions. Thus, MPB can and has hosted the Australian national titles competition at both junior and senior levels governed by FITA and Archery Australia rules. As a member club, MPB adheres to these rules so that the results are recognised both nationally and internationally. So when SQAS and MPB, and other SQAS member clubs make decisions about eligibility of archers and of equipment, such as the recurve bow in the photograph, these are largely mandated by FITA rules. It has little autonomy in this respect.

This section described the hierarchy of organisations within archery in Australia, but the governance hierarchy is similar among sports, each one modified by history. A major role of each organisation and level in the hierarchy is the governance of the sport, its athletes and the governance of the organisations themselves. But, in the informality of a purely MPB club competition, a longbow archer can stand next to a compound bow archer while shooting. Conversely, the following case study considers extremely formal elements of governance.

Case study: Specialist global sport governance organisations – The World Anti-Doping Authority (WADA) and The Court of Arbitration for Sport (CAS) and its governing body The International Council for the Arbitration of Sport (ICAS)

Two specialist GSOs are analysed. These are WADA (sport doping) and ICAS/CAS (adjudication and quasi-legal issues). Both are recent governance innovations. Both have rapidly gained prominence in global sport governance. Their existence further reduces the governance autonomy of all other GSOs. Complexity abounds. Often WADA and ICAS/CAS interact. Certainly ICAS/CAS has reduced the governance autonomy of WADA in doping cases by overturning some WADA decisions in cases it has adjudicated, but it has upheld and strengthened WADA in others. With the major exception of corruption within GSOs, ICAS/CAS may have become the final arbiter of global sport governance. Yet, ICAS/CAS has no powers to deal with corruption, one of the most pressing problems in sport governance, because it is within the governing bodies themselves.

A dispute between WADA and the British Olympic Committee (BOC), and brought to CAS by WADA, introduces this case study. The dispute revolved around BOC's governance autonomy and was resolved in WADA's favour. The establishment and function of WADA is then described followed by that of ICAS/CAS, including the dispute that led to a major change in the governance of CAS itself. A standard doping dispute is then described. The case study then looks at some of the situations being dealt with by CAS. Two examples in particular are cited, neither yet completely resolved, nor will be until definitive cases come before CAS. The first considers Oscar Pistorius and the second Caster Semenya, both of whom wished to compete at the London Olympics. Finally, albeit briefly, the limitations of ICAS/CAS in relation to corruption in sport and its implications are examined.

The introductory example involves both ICAS/CAS and WADA (CAS 2011/A/2658 *British Olympic Association (BOA) v. World Anti-Doping Agency (WADA)*). WADA had challenged a by-law of the BOA that related to doping and team selection by informing BOA that its by-law (7.4) broke the WADA World Doping Code. This code, to which BOA is a signatory, is intended to apply uniformly across all athletes, sports, and associations. The BOA by-law departed from the WADA Code by imposing an extra sanction (CAS 2011/A/2658 *British Olympic Association (BOA) v. World Anti-Doping Agency (WADA)*, p.2) on British athletes, when compared to other athletes around the world. WADA made this determination based on an ICAS/CAS case decided in 2011 (ICAS/CAS, *U.S. Olympic Committee v. International Olympic Committee*, CAS 2011/O/2422). The BOC appealed to CAS that its by-law was valid, but the case was decided in WADA's favour. It is important that in CAS's case award summary, the term 'autonomy' appears several times. One important part of the award illustrates this.

> As the BOA argued, NOCs [national Olympic committees] have great autonomy to develop their selection of representatives to a national Olympic team. The WADA Code does not and is not intended to intrude upon the autonomy of an NOC (such as the BOA) in developing these policies. In the normal course of events, the WADA Code and an NOC's selection policy rarely intersect each other.
>
> However, NOCs like BOA have agreed to limit their autonomy by accepting the WADA Code. In particular, Article 23.2.2 WADA Code, requires that its Signatories, including NOCs, do not make any additional provisions in their rules which would change the substantive effect to any enumerated provisions of the WADA Code, including its sanctions for doping.
> (CAS 2011/A/2658 *British Olympic Association (BOA) v. World Anti-Doping Agency (WADA)*, p.26)

The outcome is that the governance autonomy of the BOA is diminished and that of WADA is strengthened.

Fairness in competition can be claimed to be at the heart of both WADA and ICAS/CAS. The two interact because many ICAS/CAS cases involve doping, as when an individual athlete appeals against a WADA finding and penalty (such as being banned from competition for a period of time). These two GSOs are clearly different from those governing individual sports such as FITA. WADA and ICAS cover all sports and all athletes. Their creation is based on the perceived need for a unified approach to global sport governance. To better understand this a little history is worthwhile.

WADA was established in 1999 as an international independent agency composed and funded equally by the sport movement and governments of the world. Its key activities include scientific research, education, development of anti-doping capacities, and monitoring of the World Anti-Doping Code – the document harmonising anti-doping policies in all sports and all countries.

WADA is a Swiss private law foundation. Its seat is in Lausanne, Switzerland, and its headquarters are in Montreal, Canada (http://wada-ama.org).

There are significant but contested ethical, moral, and medical arguments against doping being used, either for enhanced performance in competition or for greater training efficiency. One is that doping gives an unfair advantage to users. Financial imperatives for individual athletes, teams, managers, and administrators make it easier to overcome these objections. A related GSO established in 1928, the International Federation of Sports Medicine (FIMS), is made up of sport medicine associations, multinational groups, and individual practitioners of sport medicine. It has expertise in this area, including drugs. But despite this, it has no governance role except to offer advice. It is suggested that this expertise will become increasingly necessary. Furthermore, if the international stance on drugs changes, this could impact sport governance of drugs. Decriminalisation can undermine the efforts of WADA. At the moment WADA may be succeeding but the evidence is partial. One piece of evidence that it is succeeding is that Tour de France speeds are believed to have decreased from being relatively drug-free (Stephenson, 2012). WADA had bitter arguments with the Union Cycliste International (UCI) before becoming established in cycling (Stephenson, 2012).

CAS was established by the IOC in 1984, possibly as an attempt by the then IOC President, Juan Antonio Samaranch, to increase the IOC's hegemony. Not surprisingly then, CAS's impartiality was questioned. In 1994 a case adjudicated by CAS was appealed by Elmar Gundel, a jockey, in dispute with the International Equestrian Federation (FEI). The case arose because Gundel had earlier 'lodged an appeal for arbitration with the CAS, based on the arbitration clause in the FEI statutes in which he challenged a decision given by the federation' (Blackshaw, 2003, p.64). CAS rejected Gundel's appeal against FEI. Gundel then appealed against CAS's decision to the Federal Supreme Court of Switzerland as CAS comes under Swiss federal law. The Swiss court decided in CAS's favour, but noted the dependency of CAS on the IOC, including financial dependence. This was a governance issue for a governance body. So the International Council of Arbitration for Sport was founded to govern, administer, and finance CAS, reducing the IOC's role in CAS.

The resulting statutes describe ICAS and CAS as:

> S1 In order to settle sports-related disputes through arbitration and mediation, two bodies are hereby created:
> - the International Council of Arbitration for Sport (the 'ICAS')
> - the Court of Arbitration for Sport (the 'CAS').

> S2 The task of the ICAS is to facilitate the settlement of sports-related disputes through arbitration or mediation and to safeguard the independence of the CAS and the rights of the parties. To this end, it looks after the administration and financing of the CAS.

> S3 ....the CAS...provides for the resolution of sports-related disputes through mediation

(TAS/CAS n.d.)

Nevertheless, ICAS retains links to the IOC, as the ICAS website indicates.

Most ICAS/CAS cases are either soccer transfer market or doping related. The key interaction between WADA and ICAS is through the World Anti-Doping Code of 2009. Crucially, if GSOs wish to be recognised by the IOC, they have to explicitly recognise the authority and jurisdiction of ICAS/CAS for all sport code violations including doping disputes. This decreases their autonomy, often in ways they do not like. CAS recently reported:

> CAS imposes a two-year suspension on Zoltan Kövago (Hungary).
>
> **Lausanne, 26 July 2012** – The Court of Arbitration for Sport (CAS) has rendered its decision in the urgent appeal filed by the International Athletics Association (IAAF) against the decision of the Doping Committee of the Hungarian National Anti-Doping Organisation dated 6 June 2012 exonerating the Hungarian discus thrower Zoltan Kövago from any sanction. The CAS Panel was comfortably satisfied that the athlete refused or failed without compelling justification to submit to sample collection after notification or otherwise evaded sample collection on 11 August 2011.
>
> The case was referred by the IAAF to the Hungarian Athletics Association and the Doping Committee of the Hungarian National Anti-Doping Organisation found the athlete not guilty and did not sanction him. On 6 July 2012, the IAAF filed an appeal at the CAS in Lausanne.
>
> The CAS Panel in charge of this case found that Zoltan Kövago was guilty of an anti-doping rule violation and sanctioned him with a two-year period of ineligibility.
>
> The full award with the grounds will be notified to the parties in a few weeks.
>
> (Rahim, 2012)

The quotation is at length because it suggests that Hungarian sport authorities were unwilling to sanction one of their own athletes. Consequently, supporting WADA, the IAAF and its own prerogatives, IAAF appealed to ICAS/CAS. The high stakes are clear as Hungary lost this athlete for the 2012 Olympics. So, clearly sport governance is not by any single organisation but an interlocking of organisations. And clubs, such as MPB in archery, are also ultimately committed to WADA and ICAS/CAS for governance. This is not uncontested by clubs that are powerful, rich, and willing to use other legal avenues (Chaudhary & Fifield, 2003; Feess & Muhleuber, 2002; Scott, 2003). But it means that individual athletes can use these links in path-breaking ways. This was the case for Bosman, a soccer goalkeeper, whose 1995 case to the European Court of Justice fundamentally changed the global soccer transfer market (McCardle, 2000). It is unlikely that Bosman would have achieved the same result through CAS. The ICAS/CAS decision might have been different, but it now has to follow the Bosman ruling.

Nevertheless, what is happening is the creation of an extra-territorial global sport law, a '*lex sportiva*' (Casini, 2010). If so, when judicial bodies, as opposed to the ICAS/CAS, try cases involving sport, they can potentially use *lex sportiva*.

Both ICAS and CAS are domiciled in Switzerland and have to both obey and be consistent with Swiss cantonal and federal laws. On occasion appeals have been made to the Swiss justice system against CAS rulings, e.g. the Gundel case. In one case, the Swiss courts system determined that an appeal against a CAS ruling should be successful, as the CAS ruling and its method of determination was inconsistent with Swiss law. This places the Swiss legal system in a special place in sport governance, especially as WADA also follows Swiss law, despite its headquarters being in Canada.

WADA's jurisdictional situation is also different as many of its cases deal with what may be criminal behaviour as opposed to purely civil cases. Many of the drugs prohibited by WADA are also illegal in many criminal codes. Due to this, few governments are willing to completely delegate sports anti-doping to WADA. The International Intergovernmental Consultative Group on Anti-Doping in Sport (IICGADS) is an outcome of this reluctance. It is a means by which governments can 'govern' WADA. Around 200 national governments have ratified UNESCO's 2007 International Convention against Doping in Sport. This, coupled with IICGADS, gives WADA the governmental mandate it requires.

The use of performance-enhancing drugs in sport has a long history and until the 1960s/1970s was largely unregulated. Despite the successes of WADA, there are some who regard the drug battle as lost and/or fundamentally misdirected. Those who believe defeat is inevitable argue for giving way, in much the same way that the amateur ethos had to give way to professionalism and 'open sport'. The preservation of amateurism that was long the central concern of sport governance has now disappeared. In this argument drugs are 'aids to performance' in the same way as any other device. It is then a question of where sport governance draws the line, and how far athletes and their sport medical teams wish to go. Perhaps not as far as Harold Abrahams suggested in his statement, 'Perhaps one day we shall be transplanting hearts and lungs for athletic purposes – to produce a three minute miler. God forbid – but one never knows!!' (Abrahams, 1968, p.168).

Ironically, there is now a World Transplant Games Federation but its purpose is very different to that envisaged by Abrahams. Abrahams' statement is noteworthy as he was an Olympic gold medal winner at the 1924 Paris Olympics. His exploits were a major focus of the 1983 Oscar Best Picture winner, *Chariots of Fire*. Another is that Abrahams was an influential sports writer. That the statement was made in 1968, when amateur athletics was still a dominant sport ideology, reinforces the view. A final irony is that this view was in a memorial lecture to his older brother, a sport medicine pioneer for the British Association for Sports Medicine (Abrahams, 1968).

The problem posed by Abrahams is now pressing for ICAS/CAS and sport in general. Consider the double leg amputee, Oscar Pistorius, who competes on J-shaped limbs (Cheetah Flex-Foot blades). He has been picked by the South African Athletics Federation for their London Olympics and Paralympics teams. Previously he had been banned from competing against able-bodied athletes by the IAAF. According to ICAS/CAS this was due to IAAF Rule 144.2(e) which states that:

For the purposes of this Rule, the following shall be considered assistance, and are therefore not allowed: [...] (e) Use of any technical device that incorporates springs, wheels, or any other element that provides the user with an advantage over another athlete not using such a device. Where there is no sufficient evidence of any metabolic advantage in favour of a disabled athlete – a double-amputee using a prosthesis – due to the fact that the disabled athlete uses the same oxygen amounts as able-bodied runners at a sub-maximal running speed and no evidence that the biomechanical effects of using this particular prosthetic device gives the athlete an advantage over other athletes not using the device, the disabled athlete cannot be banned to compete in international IAAF-sanctioned events alongside able-bodied athlete.

(CAS, 2008)

The CAS resolution states crisply and clearly that the IAAF biased the tests against Pistorius so he would be found to have an unfair advantage by being a double amputee runner on flex-blades. Also, the CAS found that the IAAF's voting procedures to decide on Pistorius were what 'can only be described as less than perfect' (CAS, 2008). The voting procedure was that IAAF Council members were only given from Friday 11 January 2008 to Monday morning 14 January 2008 to decide and vote. Any abstentions were to be counted as votes against Pistorius's eligibility. Furthermore, this was then used to state the vote against Pistorius was unanimous (CAS, 2008, Points 18 and 19). You are strongly urged to read this CAS report! As a consequence, ICAS/CAS upheld Pistorius's appeal against the IAAF findings on both procedural and substantive grounds. However, ICAS/CAS explicitly limited its findings to Pistorius alone, and for him to only use the type and model of Cheetah Flex-Foot blades he then used. This opens a huge area of governance uncertainty in sport, but ICAS/CAS cannot be blamed for this. It is logically possible that improved prosthetics can provide greater performance than for any unaided, able-bodied athlete. It is quite proper, therefore, that the CAS summary in effect leaves open the question of potential use of prosthetics conferring an unfair advantage.

Another challenge for sport governance also comes from South Africa. It has yet to come to ICAS/CAS but this is a distinct possibility. Caster Semenya is a female athlete who has female hyperandrogenism. This means that she has very high levels of naturally occurring androgens (male hormones). This may or may not have aided her performance, but it has certainly caused her challenges in her eligibility to compete in (female) athletics almost her entire career. Part of the reason is that performance of female and male athletes may partly differ due to males producing greater levels of hormones that enhance both strength and speed. The artificial use of such hormones and the artificial boosting of the body's own production of these hormones are forbidden in WADA's Anti-Doping Code. But in Semenya's case, it is natural.

Initially her gender was questioned, but no longer. Foekje Dillema was just one athlete whose career was destroyed by her gender being questioned (Ballantyne,

Kayser & Grootegoed, 2011). After Semenya's problems with the IAAF and South African athletics authorities were overcome by battles outside ICAS/CAS, it seemed she would run in the London Olympics. However, the IOC issued regulations concerning hyperandrogenism, which stated:

> If, in the opinion of the Expert Panel, the investigated athlete has female hyperandrogenism that confers a competitive advantage (because it is functional and the androgen level is in the male range), the investigated athlete may be declared ineligible to compete in the 2012 OG Competitions.
>
> (IOC, 2012)

Apart from its content, which has been heavily criticised and commented upon (for examples see Karkazis, Jordan-Young, Davis, & Camporesi, 2012; Jordan-Young & Karkazis, 2012), this document's timing is remarkable, being dated 22 June 2012. It does not name Semenya but was clearly aimed at her. The IOC has not banned her, which would create enormous image problems for the IOC, but this document created an opportunity for an appeal against any athletic victory that she might have. Presumably in response to this, the South African Olympic Committee (SAOC) appointed Semenya as the flag bearer for the South African Olympic team for the London Olympics opening ceremony. Why? The reason may perhaps be because Semenya had an extraordinarily good chance of winning a medal, including gold. It might also be that she had won hearts and minds in South Africa. The ramifications of the IOC document go beyond Semenya and even beyond all female athletes with female hyperandrogenism. Notice how these two individual cases have set the IOC and SAOC, both Olympic organisations, on different sides of the governance fence.

Note that these two cases are not used because they are rare and difficult. Rather they demonstrate that increased scientific knowledge and increased emphasis on human rights are making sport governance increasingly uncertain. The case study shows that sport governance is, via a complex network, under increasing internal and external tensions.

The IAAF's actions in the Pistorius case can only be considered as morally indefensible. The same is true of the sport organisations in the Semenya case. They are a form of corruption and are not isolated. An important point in both cases is that neither individuals nor organisations suffer sanctions for their behaviour. That ICAS/CAS has no power to order sanctions, as opposed to WADA, is clear. But the fact that ICAS/CAS cannot sanction is often a strength. Parties to a dispute can suffer sanctions, except the costs of the action, making it easier for CAS to be accepted. CAS relies on the organisations involved in cases facing sanctions for non-compliance from other bodies such as the IOC.

But it remains a weakness that for both political and financial corruption internal to sport organisations, ICAS/CAS has no powers at all.

Corruption in global sport governance organisations

Several sport organisations have demonstrated to be corrupt in both political and financial terms, the two usually going hand in hand. The IAAF has been accused of corruption (AGGIS, 2011). Although not proven, the accusations are persistent. Accusations also affect FIFA and the IOC. Before the London Olympics it was announced that João Havelange, a previous FIFA President, had accepted enormous bribes (Rubenfeld, 2012). FIFA has admitted it was aware of this at the time but did nothing. It is also suggested Havelange was politically corrupt in the manner he gained and kept the FIFA presidency (Darby, 2003). Darby indicates that he fostered further corruption in soccer federations, especially in Africa. The method was to grant development funds from FIFA that were then not made properly accountable (Darby, 2003). Similar accusations have been made by Jennings (2000). FIFA has problems with accusations of governance into the current presidency. Michel Zen-Ruffinen, then FIFA's secretary general, alleged financial mismanagement under FIFA's current president, Sepp Blatter. Swiss authorities cleared Blatter of any impropriety (Ledsom, 2002). The same is true for the IOC, and again these accusations have been made by Jennings (2000). Such is Swiss law that after a 1992 television documentary Jennings was sentenced to a five-day suspended jail term in the Lausanne District Court for criminal libel against the IOC. Again the Swiss legal system is deeply embedded in the global governance of sport, not always to the good. Foibles of this specific legal system, such as allowing extreme confidentiality, have become endemic to global sport governance.

Not surprisingly, the organisations seem incapable of reforming. Brewer (2001) pointed out that these organisations, FIFA and the IOC, do not publish financial accounts. There have been promises made that this will occur but they remain only promises, with perfunctory financial statements published. Forster (2004) made the same point. Being non-profit governance organisations means there are no 'owners' interested in where their money went. Yet it is precisely these organisations that are to uphold sporting ideals! They hold athletes to these ideals, while adhering to no morally defensible stance themselves. Unfortunately, having enormous power, protected by secrecy and anti-whistleblower laws, and enormous finances, these organisations offer great rewards to corruption. The only limits to their power are the national federations that make up their elected councils (Figure 17.1). These ineffective councils seem a critical weakness in global sports governance.

Summary

There is governance, decision-making, and an administrative hierarchy in each sport that begins with clubs, and then moves up to the sport's global organisations. In each sport there are variations to this model. Archery was an example used demonstrating this within a specific sport. The national federations and the GSOs of individual sports are all to a degree subordinate to global multisport events such as the Olympics.

The role of specialist GSOs was discussed. These organisations stand outside individual sports, but are central to sport governance. Probably the most important are WADA and ICAS/CAS. The commercialisation of sport and the immense rewards to winning are responsible for their significance. However, the social and technological parameters of sport are shifting, including the largely unrecognised acknowledgement of the human rights of athletes. The previously unchallenged decision making prerogatives of sport governance regimes are being questioned. This is not only by individual athletes but by sport organisations at all levels, by governments, legal systems, and the general public. Behind all these lies a spectre of corruption at the highest levels. The resulting governance battles will not be conducted in the sporting manner that the governance bodies insist upon for their athletes.

Review Questions

1   Explain the interactions between WADA and ICAS/CAS, and what role commercial aspects of sport play in determining these interactions.
2   Why have specialist governance organisations grown in importance over the past 60 years?
3   How and why have the national governing bodies of sport lost much of their governance autonomy since the end of the nineteenth century?

Further reading

Forster, J. & Pope, N. (2004). *The political economy of global sporting organisations.* London: Routledge.

Websites

FITA: http://www.worldarchery.org
Tribunal Arbitral du Sport-Court of Arbitration of Sport: http://www.tas-cas.org
World Anti-Doping Agency: http://wada-ama.org

References

Abrahams, H. (1968). The changing face of international sport: The Sir Adolphe Abrahams Memorial Lecture, *Bulletin of the British Association of Sport Medicine,* 3(4) 164–8.
AGGIS, (2011). *IOC investigates the President of International Athletics for corruption.* Action for Good Governance in International Sports Organisations (AGGIS). Available online at http://www.playthegame.org/knowledge-bank/theme-pages/action-for-good-governance-in-international-sports-organisations.html.
Ballantyne, K., Kayser, M. & Grootegoed, J. (2011). Sex and gender issues in competitive sports: Investigation of a historical case leads to a new viewpoint. *British Journal of Sports Medicine*, Available online at http://bjsm.bmj.com/content/early/2011/05/03/bjsm.2010.082552.full.pdf+html
Blackshaw, I. (2003). The Court of Arbitration for Sport: An international forum for settling disputes effectively 'within the family of sport', *Entertainment Law*, 2 (2) 61–83.

Brewer, J. (2001). This sporting life. *Corporate Governance International*, 4 (3) 2–3.

CAS (Court of Arbitration for Sport) (2008). Arbitration CAS 2008/A/1480 *Pistorius v. IAAF*, award of 16 May 2008. Available online at http://arbitrationlaw.com/files/free_pdfs/CAS%202008-A-1480%20P%20v%20IAAF%20Award.pdf.

CAS (Court of Arbitration for Sport) (2002). Final award in the arbitration between Troy Billington and Federation Internationale de Bobsleigh et de Tobogganing. CAS Arbitration No. CAS OG 02/005, 18 February, Salt Lake City, UT. Available online at http://jurisprudence.tas-cas.org/sites/CaseLaw/Shared%20Documents/OG%2002-005.pdf

Casini, L. (2010). The making of a Lex Sportiva: The Court of Arbitration for Sport 'The Provider', IILJ Working paper 2010/5, Global Administrative Law Series. Available online at http://www.iilj.org/publications/2010-5.Casini.asp

Chappelet, J-L., Bousigue, A. & Cohen, B. (2008). *The autonomy of sport in Europe.* Strasbourg: EPAS, Council of Europe.

Chaudhary, V. & Fifield, D. (2003). G14 ready to block friendly call-ups. *The Guardian,* 5 February. Available online at http://www.guardian.co.uk/football/2003/feb/05/newsstory.sport?INTCMP=SRCH

Croci, O. & Forster, J. (2004). Webs of authority: Hierarchies, networks, legitimacy and economic power in global sport organisations. In G. Papanikos, (ed.). *The economics and management of mega athletic events: Olympic Games, professional sports and other essays*, (pp1–11) Athens: ATINER.

Darby, P. (2003). Africa, the FIFA presidency, and the governance of world football: 1974, 1998 and 2002. *Africa Today*, 50(1) 3–24.

Feess, E. & Muhleuber, G. (2002). Economic consequences of transfer fee regulations in European Football. *European Journal of Law and Economics*, 13(3) 221–37.

Forster, J. (2004). The finance, accountability and governance of global sports governing bodies. *Symposium of* Accountability, Governance and Performance in Transition. Available online at http://www.griffith.edu.au/school/gbs/afe/symposium/proceedings.html.

Forster, J. (2006). Global sports organisations and their governance: Corporate governance. *An International Journal of Business in Society,* 6(1) 72–83.

Forster, J. & Pope, N. (2004). *The political economy of global sporting organisations.* London: Routledge.

Hollis, E. (1995). The United States Olympic Committee and the suspension of athletes: Reforming grievance procedures under the Amateur Sports Act of 1978. *Indiana Law Journal,* 71(1) 183–200.

IAAF (1999) History. Available online at http://www.iaaf.org/aboutiaaf/history/

International Olympics Committee (2012). IOC regulations on female hyper-androgenism: Games of the XXX Olympiad in London, 2012. Available online at http://www.olympic.org/Documents/Commissions_PDFfiles/Medical_commission/2012-06-22-IOC-Regulations-on-Female-Hyperandrgonism-eng.pdf.

Jennings, A. (2000). *The great Olympic scandal: When the world wanted its Games back.* London: Simon and Schuster.

Jordan-Young, R. & Karkazis, K. (2012). Abandon this false start. *New Scientist,* 215, July, 2874.

Karkazis, K., Jordan-Young, R., Davis, G. & Camporesi, S. (2012). Out of bounds? A critique of the new policies on hyperandrogenism in elite female athletes. *The American Journal of Bioethics,* 12(7) 3–16.

Ledsom, M. (2002). Blatter cleared of corruption. 4 December Available online at http://www.swissinfo.ch/eng/archive/Blatter_cleared_of_corruption.html?cid=3058302

McCardle, D. (2000). *From boot money to Bosman: Football, society and the law.* London: Cavendish Publishing.

Rahim, A. (2012). The Court of Arbitration for Sport (CAS) imposes a two year suspension on Zoltan Kovago. Available online at http://theolympicssports.com/other-sports/the-court-arbitration-sport-cas-imposes-two-year-suspension-zoltan-kovago.html.

Rubenfeld, S. (2012). ISL Docs allege FIFA's Havelange, Teixiera took millions in bribes. Available online at http://muckrack.com/link/8k6W/isl-docs-allege-fifas-havelange-teixiera-took-millions-in-bribes

Scott, M. (2003). FIFA facing legal threat from G14: Top clubs demand voice. Available online at http://www.guardian.co.uk/football/2003/dec/04/newsstory.sport4?INTCMP=SRCH

Stephenson, W. (2012). Tour de France: Are drug-free cyclists slower? Retrieved from: www.bbc.co.uk/news/magazine-18921784.

Sullivan, D. (Ed.). (1997). *Early innings: A documentary history of baseball, 1825–1908.* Lincoln, NB: University of Nebraska Press.

TAS/CAS (n.d.) Statutes of ICAS and CAS. Available online at http://www.tas-cas.org/statutes

18 The future

Trends and challenges in sport governance

Trish Bradbury and Ian O'Boyle

Topics

- Why the dominant discourse and approach to sport today is a business one
- Developments in sport governance throughout the world
- Emerging trends that will impact sport governance in the future
- Present and future challenges for those involved in the governance of sport.

Objectives

- To appreciate the role of sport as a business and governance practices to maintain sustainable sport organisations
- To compare and contrast the developments in sport governance throughout the world
- To recognise and understand the emerging trends impacting sport governance
- To discuss the calibre of the board within sport organisations
- To identify the present and future challenges facing stakeholders involved in the governance of sport.

Key terms

The business of sport   The application of traditional business management principles and practices within the sport industry.

Trends   The general direction in which something tends to move or a pattern of gradual change in an output or situation

Challenges   Something that requires skill, energy, and determination to deal with or achieve, especially if it is something never done before

Unitary boards   One-tiered board governance structure

Overview

This chapter concludes this book, *Sport governance: International case studies*, by describing why the dominant discourse and approach to sport today is a business one. It briefly summarises, compares and contrasts developments in sport governance throughout the world. The governance structure of New Zealand Cricket is used as a final case study to portray what is largely being acknowledged as best practice within the field of contemporary sport governance. Finally, the emerging trends, and present and future challenges facing sport practitioners, managers and those involved in the governance of sport, are discussed.

A new context for sport

Chappelet and Bayle (2005) suggest that sport is playing an increasingly important role in a rapidly changing economic, political, cultural and social world. A new context for all levels of sport is developing around the globe, providing an extraordinary opportunity to discover and develop new areas of sport management in amateur and professional contexts. Many commentators (Mahony & Howard, 2001; Miller, 1997) who discuss sport as a business suggest that the managers and governors involved in the sport industry are limited by their ability to transfer knowledge of conceptual business practices to the sport business environment. However, Chelladurai (2005) insists that sport organisations are in desperate need of managers from within their own ranks who have the capabilities of managing the performance of their organisation and developing their strategic goals. Regardless of where they are sourced, one of the greatest challenges for sport organisations is to ensure that their current and future managers have the necessary skills to lead in the twenty-first century sport industry.

It is clear that the contemporary sport organisation's administrative and daily operations require increasingly specific industrial knowledge. To sustain the development of sport, managers and governors must be equipped with the necessary skills to lead these organisations into the future and a more professional approach must be adopted particularly at executive and board levels. These individuals must ensure they are proficient within the various management techniques required to perform well within the modern sporting environment, which often requires adaptation of existing techniques applied in traditional businesses practices.

Sport has evolved to encompass a role in education, healthcare, economic development, the labour market and various social issues. The way in which these organisations are governed, is therefore required to differ from traditional corporate governance. The principles, methods and conditions that exist within a sport organisation must be analysed before the board can decide on the best style and form of governance that suits their organisation. These organisations are being confronted with an operating environment that has seen substantial change relating to competitiveness and professionalisation. As a result, there is a need for these organisations to progress from simply performing administrative functions to being held accountable through a responsible corporate governance approach.

Sport today is big business

Westerbeek and Smith (2003, p.1) open their book *Sport business in the global marketplace* with the question 'When did sport become a business?' This is a question they did not clearly answer but did conclude that 'Sport has always been a business and always will be' (p.2). To get to this conclusion they travelled through the years suggesting that the beginnings of sport as a business came when a renowned baseball owner in 1956 grumbled 'Baseball is too much of sport to be a business and too much of a business to be a sport' (p1.). Or maybe sport became a business when the 1984 Los Angeles Olympic Games were the first to secure sponsorship, something that the Olympics nor sport in general, could now do without. They even trace sport as a business back as far as 78BC when money, infrastructure and spectatorship were spoken of in regards to cities' expenditures on sporting contests. Many people today would now agree that sport *is* a business.

Leberman, Collins and Trenberth's 2012 book focuses on the *business* of sport management and supports the discourse of sport as a business one as do several other academic and practical sport management books (Smith & Westerbeek, 2004; Trenberth & Hassan, 2012). Sport managers today do not only need sport specific knowledge but also business nous. Some academics and practitioners believe business expertise is required more so than sport specific knowledge while others support the view that sport managers must understand the sport product and environment. Whichever the case, the global understanding of sport and its governance, structure, and organisation is a requirement as are other traditional business skills of financial and strategic management, communication and media relations, and marketing and sponsorship ability.

Sport is not only a big business due to the number of participants worldwide in the spectator, participatory, elite and professional spheres but also economically as the global spend on sport is phenomenal. Milner (2006), cited in Li, MacIntosh and Bravo (2012), estimated that over US$85 billion was spent on sport events in 2005 and Korkki (2008), also cited in Li *et al.* (2012), determined that spending on sport goods such as footwear, apparel and equipment reached US$278.4 billion in 2007. Research completed by PricewaterhouseCoopers in 2010 indicated that worldwide spending on sport would increase from £97 billion in 2009, even with the economic downturn then experienced, to £113 billion by 2013 (Lynes, 2010). And, sport suppliers like Nike, the world's leading supplier of footwear and apparel, earned in excess of US$24.1 billion in the 2012 fiscal year and employed more than 44,000 people worldwide. These figures indicate that a substantial amount of money is spent on sport and if financial prosperity means business, then sport is a business.

Worldwide sport governance: a summation

This book covered many 'degrees' and 'stages' of sport governance throughout the chapters and countries presented. Some governance structures or advancements relate to the historical context of the country such as Russia, China, and Brazil while others relate to their economic prosperity like Greece. Some governance configurations were in their infancy while others had reached their teenage years extending into adulthood and yet others were reaching a mid-life crisis. Whatever growth spurt they are experiencing, it is prudent and essential that sport organisations continue to search for best practice governance activity.

Thoma and Chalip's 1996 book, *Sport governance in the global community*, was the first to be written on global sport governance. In the preface the then president of the International Olympic Committee, Juan Antonio Samaranch, stated that to complete a global analysis of the structural governance of sport was 'a truly difficult task, because of its widespread, complex, and interdisciplinary nature' (p.xi). Sport's structural governance today and the task of compiling this book, *Sport governance: International case studies* is no different.

Many governance structures exist and are utilised worldwide. As noted, some countries' sport systems are quite advanced, while others are still in their infancy, and this affects the type of governance structure or governance models they might apply. Various governance structures were presented in the preceding chapters some of which are listed below.

- Systemic or network governance: refers to governance *between* organisations such as was discussed in the case study on the New Zealand Rugby Union in Chapter 16.
- Federated system: also seen as a network of inter-organisational relationships whereby an NGB is the prime governing body with provincial or state bodies comprising clubs, associations or schools working together as discussed in Chapter 3, Australia.
- Lead organisation governance: where one existing member of a network takes a leadership role in managing all the network's activities.
- Delegate system: representatives from a provincial or state sport club or association who are nominated/elected to represent the club/association's views at the NGB level.
- Board of directors: elected or appointed individuals who are responsible for the strategic vision and long term future of the organisation. In an NSO case, they generally come from a state or provincial sport club, association or body.
- Independent board of directors: have the same functions as a board of directors except independent directors do not have any previous relationship or affiliation to a sport club, association, or organisation and thus do not represent a specific alliance.
- Hybrid model: a melange of the delegate system and the independent board structure whereby members are both appointed and elected, also discussed in Chapter 3.

The calibre of the board

The calibre of the board within sport organisations is becoming an increasingly important focus point for many entities as the performance of sport organisations begins to be scrutinised in a manner that has of yet been unseen within the industry. The calls for greater transparency, accountability, and professionalism within the sport sector and its governance have resulted in the need to adopt a board who have the necessary skill set to satisfy these internal and external demands. The traditional delegate system that has been, and is still, in place within many NGBs and other sport bodies is slowly becoming redundant and we are now seeing greater involvement of independent board membership within the governance structures of these entities than ever before.

The delegate model may have been appropriate in the past when sport had yet to evolve into the professional business that it is today, as described earlier in this chapter. The individuals elected through this model are often members of regional bodies within the NGBs structure which in the past has resulted in cases of blatant parochialism and a board that was not acting in the best interest of the sport body as a whole. Furthermore, the skill set of an elected board within the delegate model can vary from year to year depending on who has been chosen to lead the sport organisation, including managing the overall performance of the entity. There is no guarantee within this system that individuals with the appropriate skill set will be elected and therefore the delegate system puts the organisations at risk of having a board that do not possess the necessary competencies to fulfil their various governance functions, as described within the opening chapter of this book. In addition, these individuals will often serve terms of up to three years within the entity and have the possibility of being re-elected for three consecutive terms in some instances. Therefore, it is perfectly feasible to suggest that a board within a sport organisation may consist of individuals who are charged with leading and managing the performance of an entity for up to nine years and may not have the necessary skill set or relevant competencies to carry out that function – an alarming thought. As noted in the Cyprus chapter, perhaps one way to overcome board members being elected to a board for exceedingly long terms would be to put a limitation on the number of years that a board member could serve in consecutive terms.

This situation has been well noted within previous research and indeed within practice of some forward thinking, proactive NGBs. New Zealand Cricket (NZC) was one of the first major NGBs within world sport to abolish the traditional delegate system in favour of a wholly independent board of directors. The following section documents this 'new' system of governance which has been widely regarded as representing best practice within the industry.

Case study: New Zealand Cricket – the independent board

The structure of governance within NZC is unique within world cricket and New Zealand sport in that they are the first NGB to adopt the implementation of a completely independent board of directors. In contrast to the traditional delegate system, the six major associations of NZC nominate directors, but they are then interviewed by a panel including the board chairman to assess their suitability of joining the NZC board. This approach was adopted following the Hood Report (1995) which recommended that NZC implement an independent board to remove issues of parochialism, nepotism, and self-interest, and appoint individuals who could lead the organisation in challenging times ahead for sporting entities.

Following the Hood Report (1995) the size of the board in NZC was also reduced from 13 to eight. The change to independent boards has also been adopted by all provincial (major) associations within cricket in New Zealand. In total, eight directors sit on the board for four-year terms and can also be reappointed to their positions following the end of those terms. The verification of the need for the adoption of the new board became apparent as revenue within the organisation doubled within three to four years following the implementation of an independent board and a CEO with traditional business experience.

Papadimitriou and Taylor (2000) and Papadimitriou's (2007) claim of the need for high-calibre board members is also apparent within the independent board in NZC. The new board structure within NZC seeks individuals with a corporate knowledge; it has moved on from just people who have a love and passion for the game to demanding high-calibre individuals with traditional business acumen – the skill set that is required to govern a contemporary NGB such as NZC. The skill set of the board may be centred on traditional business acumen; however, there is still sufficient knowledge of how cricket and sport in general operates within the board make up. The board consists of business people and leaders, and there are currently two ex-internationals on the board who are also involved within the traditional business sector. This aspect of the board is important as it is imperative to understand the culture and ethos of these unique entities combined with professional business expertise.

As stated above, it has been suggested that NZC is one of a select group of NGBs leading the sporting world in terms of sport governance and that other sport bodies, including the International Cricket Council (ICC), are also seeking advice on the implementation of an independent board. However, this new style of governance is by no means a perfect model without limitations and stakeholder management in particular appears to be a major issue with the implementation of an independent board. The traditional delegate system makes it easier to connect with stakeholders through regional representation on the board – something that is absent within the adoption of an independent board. Stakeholder management and communication are key issues for the organisations who adopt this governance approach and they must ensure all relevant entities are communicated with proactively in the absence of regional representatives.

A further limitation of this governance structure and within NZC in particular, lies with the appointment process of the board. The organisation is dependent on major associations nominating suitable candidates and putting forward high-calibre people, which may not always happen. In order to combat this issue, applications for board membership should be a completely open process by advertising for positions in the general media. It can be argued that nominations from the major associations put a filter into the process that is not required. This would be the necessary move to facilitate the implementation of a 'truly' independent board. A final issue with the composition of the board is the fact that the CEO is considered a board member within NZC. As described in the opening chapter of this book, this is not regarded as being best practice within elite-level sport governance, and this policy should arguably be reviewed to ensure the capability of the board is not undermined in terms of assessing management performance and forming strategic direction.

Emerging sport governance trends

The trends in sport governance are apparent but yet evolving as sport organisations expand and progress, and the external business environment meets volatile and turbulent times. Thoma and Chalip (1996) speculated and summarised their views of the future of sport governance basing them on Naisbitt and Aburdene's (1990) projected 10 trends (see Naisbitt & Aburdene, 1990), which were claimed to shape the world in the twenty-first century. A look at some of these claims sets the scene for this understanding these current trends in sport governance.

One of Naisbitt and Aburdene's claims was 'the development of "free market socialism"' (Thoma & Chalip, 1996, p.189) also supported by Amara, Henry, Liang and Uchiumi (2005) who used the term 'state-sponsored restricted capitalism' (p.194). Many of the then Eastern Bloc countries (Czechoslovakia and the Soviet Union and now the Czech Republic and Russia respectively) and other nations such as Brazil, China and Greece all felt the effects of a market-based economy. This in turn affected athlete funding from government coffers, the ability of athletes to more freely compete in Western countries, the increase of athletes turning professional and vying for contracts in the global sport market, and the diminishing volunteer base due to the advent of capitalism and economic-inclined working trends to name a few. Review of the chapters on Brazil, China, the Czech Republic, Greece and Russia will make this point clearer to the reader.

Another significant trend that Naisbitt and Aburdene (1990) foresaw was the increase in the number of women in leadership positions and management. Although this increase has been proven globally in all factions of employment, it has not been so pronounced in the world of sport. The IOC began considering the involvement of women at the leadership level in 1981 (International Olympic Committee, 2012) but still fewer than 10 per cent of IOC members were women in the 1990s (Thoma & Chalip, 1996). The IOC then set a target of 20 per cent representation of women on governing boards to be achieved by 2005 (International Olympic Committee, 2012) but unfortunately, still in 2012, this is not the case. Statistics of women on boards of sporting organisations are similar, or not that farther advanced today, even though the goal of gender equality is enshrined in the Olympic Charter (Olympic Charter, 2011). The chapters on Cyprus, New Zealand, Scandinavia and global sport organisations all recognised that the numbers of women in leadership, i.e. board positions, was below expectations.

Forster, in the chapter on global sport organisations, discussed trends in respect to specialist governance organisations who try to defend sport from the detrimental consequences of the advances of science and technology that are developed to improve sport performances by illegal, unethical or damaging means. Naisbitt and Aburdene referred to these trends as the increased application of biological sciences. The specialist organisations responsible are the World Anti-Doping Agency (WADA), the International Council of Arbitration for Sport (ICAS), and the Court of Arbitration for Sport (CAS), whose roles include eliminating/minimising sport doping, and adjudication and management of quasi-legal issues respectively.

The final trend that has relevance to global sport governance is sport for participation versus sport as spectator entertainment. This trend as a whole is not specifically related to discussions in this book but the 'sport for participation' aspect, also referred to as 'sport for all' or mass participation sport, was presented in the chapters on Brazil, Cyprus, Greece, Russia and Scandinavia. It is generally considered that sport for all or mass participation provides a base of athletes who could graduate to the elite pool of national team potentials. Unfortunately most of these countries are experiencing money being drained from sport for all programmes to elite programmes. One would hope that those in governance roles would realise the need for sport for all experiences for the masses and the potential on flow or impact for high performance sport.

Other trends are also evident. Shilbury in Chapter 3 endorsed the use of an independent board structure over the delegate or federated systems but suggested to minimise the backlash from current board members that a hybrid model of governance be initially introduced followed by the complete independent board structure. This was described above in the discussions relating to the calibre of board members within contemporary sport organisations and the NZC case study.

A unitary board, that is when an organisation has a single governing body, was also discussed, and as Tricker (2012) supported, the down-side of unitary boards is that they evaluate their own outputs which is not ideal, as was presented in Chapter 1. In the corporate world two-tier board structures help overcome this by having an executive board responsible for performance and a supervisory board for operations and compliance. Also to help with this dilemma the view that independent board members should be sought to sit on a board, something that some sport organisations in Australia, Brazil and New Zealand are already doing, was put forth. Sport has recently seen the implementation of the independent board member structure but has not yet trialled the two-tier board. This is something that sport organisations, like the research on Cyprus sport organisations in Chapter 14 showed as needed, may embark on to overcome some of the governance challenges experienced. This type of board governance will be a trend in the coming years.

Finally, the adoption of corporate social responsibility (CSR) and sustainability policies, and the reporting of their subsequent outputs, as seen in the chapters on Cyprus and Scandinavia in particular, is another emerging trend. The IOC, IFs and NGBs must be conscious of the effects had on the physical environment when they hold mega events like the Olympics, the FIFA World Cup, or the Volvo Around the World Yacht Race. Attention to CSR and sustainability are now compulsory in event bidding documents. Global sport organisations will have to be more open to the acceptance and integration of these concepts in their governance policies.

Present and future challenges

There are common challenges that sport organisations will face worldwide. The degree to which these organisations are challenged will depend, again, on their stage of development and the environment within which they exist.

One continuous and much discussed challenge is board gender diversity. Much has been written in the academic literature (Inglis, 1997) about board gender diversity as women maintain a low presence on boards of NGBs, IFs and global sport organisations (Sydney Scoreboard, n.d.). A challenge that the governance of sport faces is not only considering gender diversity but diversity in the wider context to include ethnic cultural diversity, race diversity, age diversity and even 'thinking' or 'judgement' diversity, for example. By valuing diversity sport organisations open the opportunity to embrace innovative avenues for new markets, participants and spectators; creative ideas; and responses to challenges in the dynamic and competitive environment they live and operate in. By ignoring diversity Tricker (2012) suggested organisations could suffer from the loss of potential talent, absence of experience and insight, and the lack of fairness; all objects that sport should not ignore.

An organisation's external environment consists of volatile conditions including economic, sociocultural, political-legal and technological ones (Schermerhorn, Davidson, Poole, Simon, Woods, & Chau, 2011). These are challenges that organisations worldwide, sport focused or not, must face. A diverse board, with experience in the global marketplace, can help strategise and plan for forward movement when these conditions present challenges. Diversity can help to understand these conditions and also others such as social trends, emerging risks, and the design of strategies, to meet these challenges head on. As noted in Chapter 16, good organisational governance values diversity and capitalises on the gains that divergence can bring (Cunningham, 2008). This is something that sport organisations need to take note of.

A brief summary of other challenges that sport organisations could potentially face, that students and practitioners alike should consider, include:

- For increased numbers of NSOs globally to move from the federated board model to the independent board model. To do this, sport organisations must shift their mind set. For example, a state or provincial sport body must forego furthering their own interests and think of the greater good of the NSO.
- For direction to come from the top down in regards to governance diversity. Some ask where it is best placed to come from. Sound leadership from the top provides opportunities for growth and acceptance from the bottom up.
- For board of directors to focus on their core responsibilities of strategic vision, governance and accountability and not get involved with operational issues they are passionate about like high-performance issues, for example.
- Many sport organisations are being 'over'-governed with too many levels of governance. Some do not understand what 'good' governance is or what best practice preaches. The challenge is for boards to up skill and professionalise themselves to comprehend the notion of good governance and its application to their particular organisation and situation.
- This also goes for the staff employed by sport organisations. They must also be given opportunity for professional development so they can continue to grow and improve in their roles so they can carry out governance directives operationally.

- Perhaps, controversially, for people in charge of sport organisations, the chief executive officer or general manager, to be deemed responsible for tackling board (gender) diversity head on with the requirement to report on the progress in diversity accomplishment, and even be remunerated or given a performance bonus for achieving targets.
- Volunteers are essential to the health and welfare of sport. Many are there due to their passion for the sport. They do not want to have their leisure time or hobby taken over by a business-like activity such as governance.

Summary

In a 2009 study completed by Harvard Business School researchers, six areas were identified to improve a board's performance. The six areas are:

- clarifying the role of the board;
- acquiring better information and understanding of the organisation;
- maintaining good relationships with the organisation's management;
- controlling and overseeing the organisation's strategy;
- sustaining management and succession planning;
- enriching risk-management processes.

(Tricker, 2012)

These are governance areas, some of which have already been mentioned in this book, that sport organisations must heed to ensure their continued growth and survival in a constantly changing world.

This chapter began by discussing how a new context for sport is emerging and how the governance structures within sport organisations must adapt to this rapidly changing environment. This was followed by an analysis of how sport is no longer viewed as just a recreational past time and that it has evolved into a significant business industry. A summation of worldwide sport governance preceded a discussion relating to the calibre of the board within sport organisations and emerging trends within the field. Finally, present and future challenges were addressed that are currently or will impact upon the governance of sport organisations as the industry continues to evolve over the coming years.

This book as a whole provided a global snapshot of governance practices in various nations and continents. One thing to be sure of is that the governance of sport bodies will continue to evolve with some moving faster than others and others trying to catch up.

Review questions

1   Identify the main sport governance models implemented worldwide and explain their differences.
2   Discuss the emerging trends of sport governance with a classmate and identify the impacts of a sport you are involved in.

3   What are some of the governance challenges that sport managers today will face at the domestic, national and international levels of sport?

Further reading

Groeneveld, M., Houlihan, B. & Ohl, F. (2011). *Social capital and sport governance in Europe*. New York: Routledge.

Hums, M. & Maclean, J. (2008). *Governance and policy in sport organisations*. Scottsdale, AZ.: Holcomb Hathaway Publishers.

Li, M., MacIntosh, E. W., & Bravo, G. A. (eds). (2012*). International sport management*. Champaign, IL: Human Kinetics.

Websites

New Zealand Cricket: http://www.blackcaps.co.nz/nz-cricket/

Sport Business: http://www.sportbusiness.com/

Sydney Scorecard: http://www.sydneyscoreboard.com

The Rules of the Game: http://www.fia.com/public/fia_structure/resources/governance_sport.pdf

References

Amara, M., Henry, I., Liang, J. & Uchiumi, K. (2005). The governance of professional soccer: Five case studies – Algeria, China, England, France and Japan. *European Journal of Sport Science*, 5(4), 189–206.

Chappelet, J. & Bayle, E. (2005). *Strategic and performance management of Olympic sport organisations*. Champaign, IL.: Human Kinetics.

Chelladurai, P. (2005). *Managing organizations for sport and physical activity: A systems perspective* (2nd edn). Scottsdale, AZ: Holcomb Hathaway.

Cunningham, G. B. (2008). Creating and sustaining gender diversity in sports organizations. *Sex Roles*, 58, 136–45.

Hood, J. (2005). *The Hood report: A path to superior performance*. Christchurch: New Zealand Cricket.

Inglis, S. (1997). Roles of the board in amateur sport organizations. *Journal of Sport Management*, 11, 160–76.

International Olympic Committee (2012). Women and Sport Commission. Available online at http://www.olympic.org/women-sport-commission.

Leberman, S., Trenberth, L. & Collins, C. (2012). *Sport business management in Aotearoa/ New Zealand*. Southbank: Thomson.

Li, M., MacIntosh, E. W., & Bravo, G. A. (eds). (2012*). International sport management*. Champaign, IL: Human Kinetics.

Lynes, J. (2010). Global sports spending 'to continue its rise'. *Accountancy News*, 26 May. Available online at http://www.ashdowngroup.com/news/global-sports-spending-to-continue-its-rise--news-19801624.

Mahony, D. & Howard, D. (2001). Sport business in the next decade: A general overview of expected trends. *Journal of Sport Management*, 15, 275–96.

Miller, K. L. (1997). *Sport business management*. Gaithersburg, MD: Aspen Publishers.

Naisbitt, J. & Aburdene, P. (1990). *Megatrends 2000*. New York: William Morrow.

Olympic Charter (2011). Lausanne: International Olympic Committee. Available online at http://www.olympic.org/Documents/olympic_charter_en.pdf.

Papadimitriou, D. (2007). Conceptualizing effectiveness in a non-profit organizational environment: An exploratory study. *International Journal of Public Sector Management*, 20, 572–587.

Papadimitriou, D. & Taylor, P. (2000). Organisational effectiveness of Hellenic national sports organisations: A multiple constituency approach. *Sport Management Review*, 3, 23–46.

Schermerhorn, J. R., Davidson, P., Poole, D., Simon, A., Woods, P. & Chau, S.L. (2011). *Management* (4th Asia-Pacific edn). Milton, Queensland: John Wiley and Sons.

Smith, A. & Westerbeek. H. (2004). *The sport business future*. NewYork: Palgrave Macmillan.

Sydney Scoreboard (n.d.). Legacy of the 5th IWG World Conference on Women in Sport. Available online at http://www.sydneyscoreboard.com/global-scoreboard/

Thoma, J. E. & Chalip, L. (1996). *Sport governance in the global community*. Morgantown, WV: Fitness Information Technology.

Trenberth, L. & Hassan, D. (Eds.). (2012). *Managing sport business: An introduction*. London: Routledge.

Tricker, B. (2012). *Corporate governance: Principles, policies, and practices*. London: Oxford University Press.

Westerbeek, H. & Smith, A. (2003). *Sport business in the global marketplace*. New York: Palgrave Macmillan.

Index

220, **221**, 282; gender (in)equality
170, 249–50, 283, 285; independence
of 13–14, 38, 281–2, 284; length of
membership 220, 281; modernisation
in the UK, impact of 119–20;
motivation of 216; National Collegiate
Athletics Association (NCAA) 29;
New Zealand Cricket 281–2; New
Zealand Rugby Union (NZRU) 252–3;
performance measurement 222;
political affiliations of members in
Greece 187; roles and responsibilities
10–11, 14–16, 221–2; Russian Modern
Pentathlon Federation (RMPF)
85–6; Scandinavia 170; selection of
members 13, 282; size of 11–13, 219;
skills and knowledge of 219–20, 281,
282; strategy, board involvement in
113–20; unitary 284
Bowers, M.T. 25
Bowls Australia (BA) 44
Bravo, G.A. 279
Brazil: Agnelo-Piva Law 147; Athlete
Subsidy Law 147; clubs, sports 144–5;
constitutional status of sport 145–6;
football 145, 146–7; funding priorities
148; government intervention 145;
growth of sports industry 144; high-
performance sports 148; legislation
145, 146–8; Olympic Committee 148;
private sponsorship 149, 151–2; safety
standards of events 147–8; status and
leadership of 143–4; success in sports
144; Volleyball Confederation 149–52
Brewer, J. 273
*British Olympic Association (BOA) v.
World Anti-Doping Agency (WADA)*
267
Bueno, L. 145
business, sport as 278–9

Canada: Canada Games 55; Canadian
Sport Policy 57, 61–4; capacity
of the system 64; coordination
between organisations 63; current
system 57, 60–1; direction, lack of
56–7; divisionalised organisation
57, 60–1, 70; elite sport, focus on
55–7, 64; Fitness and Amateur Sport
Act (C-131) 55; formal affiliation,
lack of 64; history of sports system
55–7, *58–9*; ice arenas, multiple user
strategy for 61; Mills Report 56; 'Own
the Podium' programme 57, 62–3;

participation sport 63; policies 57;
policy 57, 61–4; professional sport
64–5; ringette: authority for rule-
making 68–9; in Canadian system
67, 69; coaching 66; funding of 68;
leagues and championships 67; local
associations 65–6; national level
67–8; officiating 66; origin of 65;
ownership of national associations
68–9; teams for 65–6; stakeholder
theory 63–4
Carter, C. 47–50
Chaganti, R.S. 11
Chalip, L. 25, 280, 283
challenges, present and future 284–6
Chappelet, J. 278
Chatzigianni, E. 187
Chelladurai, P. 278
chief executive officers 13
China: All-China Sports Federation
(ACSF) 126–7; basketball: Chinese
Basketball Association 133–4;
Chinese Basketball Association
Professional League (CBAPL)
135–6, **138**, *139*; Chinese Basketball
Association Professional League
Committee (CBAPLC) 136, *139*;
Chinese Basketball Management
Centre (CBMC) 133–4, **134**, *139*;
clubs 137, *139*; players 137–9,
139; training and selection system
137–9, **138**; centralised system
126–9; commercialisation 131–2,
132; communist sport 124; Cultural
Revolution 128–9; elite sports 128–9,
129–30; General Administration
of Sport of China (GASC) 132;
ju-guo-ti-zhi 125; Olympic strategy
125, 130–1; reform and opening-up
policy 124–5, 129–31; State Physical
Culture and Sports Commission
(SPCSC) 127–9, 130, 132; structure
of governance **132**
coaching: ringette in Canada 66; Russia
81–2
Cockburn, R. 249
codification, development of 262
collaborative governance theory 38, 44–5
college football in the US 29–30
college systems 24
Collins, C. 279
commercialism: Australia 41–3; China
131–2, **132**; New Zealand 245;
public, non-profit bodies 245, **246**